SOUTH-WESTERN SERIES IN
HUMAN **R**ESOURCES **M**ANAGEMENT

STRATEGY AND
HUMAN
RESOURCES
MANAGEMENT

John E. Butler, Ph.D.
Assistant Professor of Management and
    Organization
University of Washington

Gerald R. Ferris, Ph.D.
Professor of Labor and Industrial Relations
    and of Business Administration
University of Illinois at Urbana-Champaign

Nancy K. Napier, Ph.D.
Associate Professor of Management
Boise State University

GJ60AA
PUBLISHED BY
SOUTH-WESTERN PUBLISHING CO.
CINCINNATI, OH   WEST CHICAGO, IL   DALLAS, TX   LIVERMORE, CA

Publisher: Roger L. Ross
Production Associate Editor: Thomas E. Shaffer
Production House: Bookmark Book Production Services
Cover and Interior Designer: Barbara Libby
Marketing Manager: David L. Shaut

Copyright © 1991
by South-Western Publishing Co.
Cincinnati, Ohio

1 2 3 4 5 6 7 M 5 4 3 2 1 0

Printed in the United States of America

Library of Congress Cataloging-in-Publication Data

Butler, John E.,
    Strategy and human resources management / John E. Butler, Gerald
R. Ferris, Nancy K. Napier.
        p.   cm. — (South-Western series in human resources
management)
    Includes bibliographical references.
    ISBN 0-538-80123-9
    1. Personnel management.   2. Strategic planning.   3. International
business enterprises—Personnel management.   I. Ferris, Gerald R.
II. Napier, Nancy K.   III. Title.   IV. Series.
HF5549.B927 1991   89-48498
    658.3'01—dc20   CIP

EDITORS' INTRODUCTION TO THE HUMAN RESOURCES MANAGEMENT SERIES

The effective management of human resources has been of interest to organizational scientists and administrators for quite some time. But, perhaps due to productivity concerns and the contemporary quality of work life focus, human resources management issues have never been more prominent. As a result of this renewed interest, there is a greater need and demand for educating people about human resources management in organizations, which has manifested itself as expanded curriculum in this area in business schools and labor institutes, as well as in management education and development programs.

The South-Western Series in Human Resources Management is designed to provide substantive knowledge and information on important topics in the field to researchers, students, and practicing professionals who wish to more fully understand the implications of theory and research for the management of human resources. The topics for books in this series are carefully selected with a concern for traditionally important issues, new topics in the field, and new, innovative treatments of traditional topics. Thus, the series is open-ended with regard to both content and size, with no constraints on the number of volumes that will be included. The volumes in the series are all written by notable scholars, recognized throughout the field of human resources management.

Gerald R. Ferris
Kendrith M. Rowland
Series Consulting Editors

PREFACE

In writing this text we sought to create a volume that would recognize the separate and combined contributions of both human resources management and strategic management. This resulted in a volume that is theoretically demanding, but designed to fall into the interest area of both graduate students and academics. In many respects this work is much like a handbook because it includes literature reviews, theory development, and application chapters. Unlike traditional textbooks, but like many handbook chapters, original material has been included.

The volume has been written to be comprehensive. Referencing is extensive, and a special appendix has been included that provides a strategic human resources management bibliography by subject area. Chapters have been written so that they can stand alone, for those interested in narrow areas. The volume can also be used as a supplemental reading or as the principal text for a graduate course in strategic human resources management. The comprehensive nature of this volume will also make it a useful first source for academics interested in this area.

Hopefully, the student and academic will find this text worthy of a permanent space in their management library. It is designed, together with the subsequent volumes in the South-Western Series in Human Resources Management, to provide a comprehensive and scholarly treatment of an important subject area.

We have benefited from the comments and assistance of many during this project. We would like to thank Douglas T. Hall and Lloyd D. Baird of Boston University for reading several preliminary chapters. We are especially appreciative and indebted to Randall S. Schuller of New York University who was generous with his time and charitable with his comments. The research assistance and intellectual insights of K. Michele Kachmar, Texas A & M University, are highly valued; they enhanced the finished volume. The administrative and editorial support of Norma Taylor at Texas A & M University and Kathleen Anderson at Boise State University is deeply appreciated. The support of the faculty, staff, and administration at Boise State University, Texas A & M University, the University of Illinois, and the University of Washington is deeply appreciated. Any errors of commission or omission rest with the authors.

CONTENTS

INTRODUCTION

Fata sua habent libelli (Thomas Mann, 1933).[1]

In the past twenty years senior executives have become more strategic in their thinking. They have also become more aware that human-related considerations can be critically important to their firm's success. As competition became more global, and the pace of technological development accelerated, more sophisticated frameworks for managing this complexity were developed. The strategic management paradigm, which stressed longer-term planning through the examination of a set of environmental, public policy, industry-structure and organization factors, was one such framework. Sophisticated techniques for the staffing, training and development, performance and reward systems, and industrial relations functions were also introduced. Thus, while planning and strategy became "buzz words," analytic techniques for human resources management (HRM) also increased in popularity. Inspired by these events, academic research responded with sophisticated products that served the narrow needs of either strategy or HRM, but seldom both.

As managers and firms increasingly began to use these evolving paradigms, it became apparent that "carburetor adjustments" type approaches could only carry the firm so far and did not fully satisfy the requirements of a business environment that was becoming increasingly complex. To deal with this complexity, an integration was called for, but planning departments tended to be more comfortable operating in an isolated fashion. HRM departments were also happy with the amount of autonomy they were given, and preferred to operate in their own realm. Strategic plans often failed to account for important factors, either from a content or implementation perspective, that were related to HRM. This was also true of other areas, such as manufacturing, which eventually was able to force its way back into the front line of corporate-strategy formulation. However, it was at the implementation stage where it first became apparent that HRM was a critical factor.

This movement toward inclusion, popularly labeled strategic human resources management (SHRM), involved linking HRM to firm-level outcomes with financial and strategic importance. Thus, it became necessary to understand HRM in terms of a broader set of conditions. The evolution, from record

---

[1] (Translation—Books have their own fate.)

keeper to full strategic participant, reveals an increased appreciation of how HRM policies can be used to bring both profit and an enhanced competitive position to the firm. This time-trace also reveals that academics in the HRM area have begun developing a more macro perspective. This expansion of perspective has not diminished research in the main content areas of staffing, training and development, performance and reward systems, and industrial relations. However, it has intensified research efforts examining how decisions in these content areas affect the performance and competitive position of the entire organization.

Strategic management evolved in a similar fashion. Beginning as an isolated planning function, with a restricted set of responsibilities, it gradually expanded. Again, research developed showing how strategic conduct was linked to firm performance. The focus of interest gradually moved beyond formulation issues, to also include factors affecting the implementation of strategy. Prescriptions were offered suggesting human resources management and planning as ways of ensuring successful implementation. Gradually, academic research came to recognize that strategic human resources management and strategic human resources planning (SHRP) should be fully incorporated into the strategic planning process of the firm. In this way, issues related to HRM and strategy could be approached in an integrated fashion.

EVOLVING RELATIONSHIP OF HRM AND STRATEGY

This book takes the position that when deciding on the conduct of the firm both HRM and strategy, and their interrelationship, must be considered. The book unfolds much like a four-part card, with each fold representing the gradual development of these fields. (See Figure 1-1.) The first fold, depicted in Figure 1-2, represents the fields of HRM and strategy in their developmental stages. Each operates in isolation and attempts to make an independent and separate contribution to the firm.

As the HRM and planning groups began to develop ties, the relationship became one better described by the second fold, which is depicted in Figure 1-3. Direct links between the HRM and planning groups were developed. The HRM group began to provide important information, and the planning group became the actual formulator of strategy, rather than simply a provider of planning reports. It was during this phase that the value of HRM to successful implementation began to be noticed.

The third fold depicts the fullness of the HRM-strategy relationship. (See Figure 1-4.) It shows the HRM group providing direct input for both the formulation and implementation efforts, although implementation links are more likely to be established first. Areas of HRM responsibility are actively managed to maximize the HRM contribution during strategy formulation and to ensure successful implementation. At this point the firm can be accurately described as having a functioning SHRM process.

DEVELOPMENT PHASE	INITIAL LINK PHASE	DEVELOPED LINK PHASE	MAXIMIZATION PHASE
Strategy and HRM operate and develop in isolation. Each attempts to make its own separate contributions, in order to gain status within the firm.	The HRM group begins to provide important information, and the planning group actually begins to formulate the strategy of the firm.	SHRM moves toward independent strategy formulation and implementation. The ability to respond to nonprogrammed change through emergent action, by the HRM group, allows the firm to expand its portfolio of strategy options.	HRM begins to provide direct input for both formulation and implementation. A SHRM process emerges, with both planning and HRM groups recognizing its importance.

FIGURE 1-1. Evolution of Strategic Human Resources Management.

The maximization of the benefits possible from establishing this linkage between HRM and strategy requires one further stage of development. This fourth fold is depicted in Figure 1-5. What it shows is how the development of

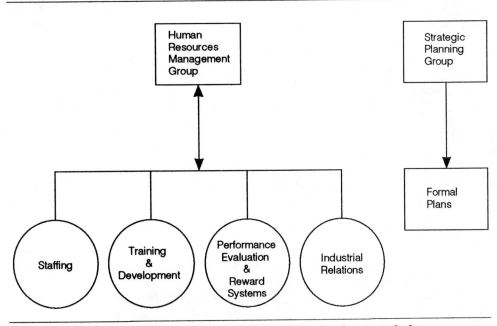

FIGURE 1-2. HRM and planning during their developmental phases.

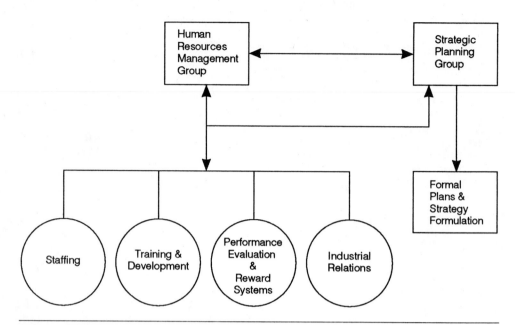

FIGURE 1-3. Direct links develop between HRM group and the corporate-level planning group.

a SHRM posture facilitates the ability of the firm to cope with organizational and environmental contingencies. Three contemporary contingencies, related to mergers and acquisitions, international operations, and corporate entrepreneurial behavior are used to highlight behavior in this maximization phase. However, these are not meant to be an exhaustive list, but rather major illustrations relating to areas of current importance. The full development of a SHRM capability is designed to develop organizational capabilities that ensure the firm is capable of responding to future, unidentified contingencies. As unplanned-for events occur, this ability to respond in a nonprogrammed manner is important and produces behavior that actually becomes part of the strategy of the firm.

While these major themes, or folds, represent the broad general developments between these fields, the single, and most important, underlying premise is that HRM is important and that it relates directly to the success of the firm. Existing theoretical and normative literature is used to support this point, but original-theory extension and development are also attempted in some areas. The role of HRM is depicted in dynamic terms, and SHRM is viewed as a natural outcome of this dynamism. The strategy-HRM impact is presented as one that extends beyond formalizing and implementing strategy, to the culture that underlies behavior within the firm. The existing state of knowledge is accepted and provides the basic foundation, while the focus of the book is on continuing the theoretical development of these fields.

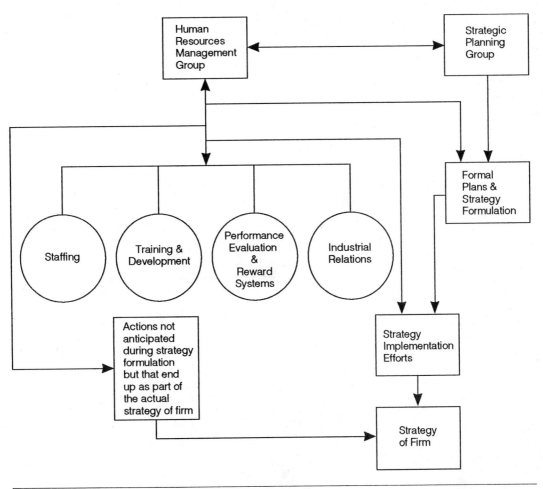

FIGURE 1-4. Completed linkages required for an effective SHRM process.

OUTLINE OF THE TEXT

Chapter Two examines the evolution of HRM from record keeping to SHRM and argues for a more macro perspective. A model, detailing the requirements related to an effective SHRM function, is presented. Each of the model's components is briefly reviewed with respect to the strategic contributions possible from HRM functions related to staffing, training and development, performance and reward systems, and industrial relations.

Chapter Three attempts to expand the notion of strategy beyond its classical definitions and adopts the concept of strategy including both planned and unplanned actions. A general discussion of the strategic planning process, especially as it relates to exploiting environmental changes, is used to develop an expanded strategic model, which is later used as groundwork for the logic

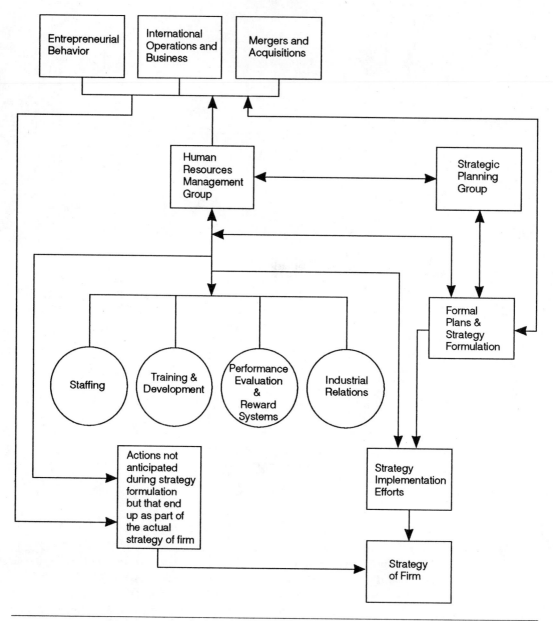

FIGURE 1-5. Synergistic benefits incorporated into a fully operationalized SHRM process.

behind the inclusion of HRM as a "mainstream" component in the strategy-making process of the firm.

Chapter Four presents a profit-generation theory of HRM and strategy. The attempt is made to extend HRM beyond its traditional bounds and relate it, theoretically, to strategy. The manner by which this relationship brings profit to the firm is discussed, using concepts from economics that are related to market imperfections. It is the constancy of these imperfections, or opportunities, that allows firms to exploit markets and gain above-normal returns on an ongoing basis. Ways for HRM to assist in this exploitation, as a tool for both formulation and implementation, are introduced. In this way HRM can support the constant need for strategic initiatives as well as the ongoing, and more formal, planning needs of the firm.

Chapter Five looks at the anatomy of strategic planning to show where and how HRM fits into the process. The ways that planning can be used to achieve strategic advantage, enhance environmental-coping capabilities, and extract profit through entrepreneurial behavior are discussed. SHRP, as a process, is tied to the corporate planning process using a multistage model that includes phases related to justification, objective setting, program development and implementation. The SHRP process is then related to the environmental, organizational and industry market-structure analysis, which is necessary for a comprehensive planning effort. This is followed by a discussion of ways to develop and maintain a SHRP effort.

Chapter Six is the first of the four content chapters which relate to the traditional activities of the HRM group. This chapter discusses strategic staffing. The increased importance of staffing is related to the changing nature of competition. The role of staffing in strategy formulation and implementation is outlined and related to both its deliberate and emergent components. The strategic implications associated with various staffing options are discussed.

Chapter Seven reviews performance evaluation as it relates to strategy formulation and implementation. The chapter examines reasons for making performance evaluation part of the strategic management process, and explores how the "mechanics" of evaluation, such as who to evaluate, criteria for evaluation and impacts on management performance can contribute to strategy.

Chapter Eight examines the nature of the link between performance and reward systems and strategy. After providing a brief review of some basic compensation concepts, this chapter examines ways in which policies related to performance and reward systems can be directed toward supporting the strategic posture of the firm. A model that develops the links between the firm's performance and reward systems and strategy is presented. Examples of how firms have affected this linkage are presented.

Chapter Nine incorporates training and development into the strategic time frame of the firm. This is accomplished by depicting development efforts as moving along a time line that includes activities related to training, the use of assessment centers, targeted development, mentoring and career planning. This time line is viewed as running parallel to one defining the firm with respect to its organizational life cycle. This allows for a contingency-type relationship to be deduced, which suggests certain development efforts as appropriate during different stages of the life cycle.

Chapter Ten reviews research and proposes ways the industrial relations process can be incorporated into strategic management. The chapter considers issues that may inhibit union involvement in strategy formulation or evaluation, as well as factors that encourage its inclusion. Finally, the chapter briefly examines how unions have begun using strategic planning.

Chapter Eleven examines the first of the three contemporary contingencies. This relates to corporate entrepreneurship and the impact that HRM has on the ability of the firm to maintain its entrepreneurial posture. A brief examination of how entrepreneurial behavior occurs is related to the natural tendencies of firms to become more bureaucratic as they grow in size and age. HRM is posited as having the appropriate tools to re-create, or maintain, an entrepreneurial posture. The impact that HRM policies can have on the culture of the organization is one way this is manifested.

Chapter Twelve examines HRM as it relates to the increased globalization of business. The chapter reviews research in the personnel area as well as more recent efforts to uncover how the link between international business and HRM affects the firm's strategy, and ultimately its performance.

Chapter Thirteen looks at the role of HRM in the mergers-and-acquisition process. An extensive review of the literature is used to outline ways in which the HRM group can help plan for and facilitate implementation of a successful merger or acquisition. Conceptual frameworks are offered as guides, which relate human resources practices to merger or acquisition outcomes. Reasons for considering HRM options, as early in the merger or acquisition process as possible, are outlined.

Chapter Fourteen summarizes and points toward the future by outlining future research needs in the field.

Finally, an appendix containing a detailed bibliography of the literature relating to SHRM is included. This is prompted by the desire to extend the value of the volume beyond what is written on its pages. While there seem to be many sources for identifying the literature of strategy, a reasonably comprehensive, and topic-orientated source of SHRM material is lacking. This bibliography is designed to facilitate course construction, reading lists, and/or research efforts. The hope is that it will inspire work in this area, and accelerate the rate of theoretical development.

HUMAN RESOURCES MANAGEMENT: MOVING TOWARDS A PARADIGM AND OBTAINING ADVANTAGE

We found that we needed to get human resources considerations introduced into the planning process at an earlier stage because if we waited until the plans were formalized and then stepped back, the human resources decisions were already made and a lot of them were necessarily accommodating, since they were treated as a derivative rather than a primary function (Fombrun, 1984c, p. 429).[1]

The evolution of the modern industrial system from a craft to a technologically sophisticated one has, in part, accounted for the corresponding emergence and development of the HRM function (Lawrence, 1985a). As organizations evolved, additional content areas were assigned to HRM. Rather than forging links and using HRM's content expertise, responsibility was exclusively delegated and this may be one of the reasons why HRM has remained so narrowly focused for such a long period of time. Human-planning systems have to be appropriately adapted to take on new responsibilities in response to environmental changes or new research findings. This readaptation process accounts for the degree to which HRM is perceived to be more or less relevant to firm performance. Thus, while HRM is often divided into separate components for examination purposes, its value comes from its ability to be dynamic.

The strategic imperative associated with the HRM function, while formally raised late in the historical scheme (i.e., early 1980s), also resulted from the dynamic nature of industrial evolution. The increased globalization of markets, the dynamics associated with currency fluctuations, the increased pace of technological development, and the changing expectations of the public and employees resulted in a much more turbulent environment. It was this increased turbulence that forced firms to be more long-range in their strategy development and increased the importance of strategy formulation as

---

[1] Comments from an interview with Frank Doyle, Senior Vice-President of Corporate Relations at General Electric.

a corporate function. It was then only natural that academics would begin to consider the strategy-HRM interface (Devanna, Fombrun, & Tichy, 1981; Nkomo, 1980; Odiorne, 1981), and that business executives would come to consider the role that HRM could play in this strategic process (Lawrence, 1985b).

This chapter has two central themes. First, the historical evolution of HRM is examined. This historical perspective provides a context from which to view the evolution of HRM from a narrow to a more macro perspective. Second, an attempt is made to point out the manner by which HRM policies can be causally significant to the success of the firm's strategies, to the same degree as are other functional and planning activities.

THE HISTORICAL EVOLUTION OF HRM: MOVING TOWARDS A PARADIGM

Currently, HRM has been experiencing a transition. Changing views and perspectives on the field are perhaps more obvious with respect to the practice of HRM, where arguments have been made on behalf of its increased importance to the overall effectiveness of the firm. What may be less apparent are the challenges that the field faces with respect to theory and research. Historically, scientific inquiry in HRM has been decidedly micro-oriented, tending to adopt a psychological perspective and proceeding at the individual level of analysis. While suggestions have been made that adopting an organizational-level perspective might help to advance theory and research in HRM, there has been no attempt to date to provide a critical evaluation and integration of such work. Because this book tends to take a macro perspective and argue this is necessary if strategic linkages are to be established and maintained, a historical overview of HRM is helpful in positioning this as a natural theoretical extension of the field.

The field of HRM has undergone tremendous changes and growth over the past 200 years. Although greatly simplifying the evolution, four major shifts can be identified to summarize the changes. The first shift occurred when workers left their homes and went to work in factories. This allowed organizations to increase production through machinery and work techniques. Soon, it became obvious that the myopic concentration on production left workers unhappy and rebellious. In order to deal with these problems attention was turned to the workers. More recently, in an effort to remain competitive, it became apparent that a more balanced approach between production requirements and employees' needs was required. Finally, steps have been taken to treat the separate HRM functions as a whole.

Pre-1900's

While the majority of historical reviews of the field of HRM begin with the early 1900s, it can be traced as far back as the 1600s. Lawrence (1985a) suggested that the "craft" system of human resource management dominated industrial life in the United States for approximately 200 years. Under the craft system, the production of goods and services was performed by workers in small workshops. The work was scheduled on a customized basis and carried out by single teams composed of a master craftsman, journeymen, and apprentices.

The master craftsman usually ran the shop with the help of a few journeymen and apprentices. The roles each held were well understood and legitimized by both law and tradition (Lawrence, 1985a). Apprentices who joined a shop would expect to remain in that trade for life. Their career path flowed from apprentice to journeyman to master craftsman.

The craft system, because it was protected by traditions, proved successful and harmonious for many years (Lawrence, 1985a). With respect to wages and hours, both apprentices and journeymen were treated fairly. Because of this, turnover was low, layoffs and strikes were infrequent, and power was relatively balanced between employers and employees.

A second system of organized labor that flourished during this time period was the result of the industrial revolution (Rowland & Ferris, 1982). During the industrial revolution, production became less of a craft and more mechanized. As machines and factory methods increased production, work settings became more structurally organized by division of labor and hierarchy of authority, resulting in longer hours and lower pay (Dalzell, 1987). The work itself became routine and less challenging, but production increased.

During this time period, no formal HRM departments existed. The day-to-day relations with employees were left to the foreman (Eilbirt, 1959). To handle the clerical aspects associated with calculating hours worked and pay, a factory clerk or timekeeper might be hired, but normally only in larger organizations.

Early 1900s

While only limited agreement concerning the field of HRM exists prior to 1900, there is considerable agreement about influences on the field in the early 1900s. Two innovations that had a substantial influence on the field of HRM during this time frame were scientific management and welfare practices (Baron, Dobbin, & Jennings, 1986; Eilbirt, 1959; French, 1986; Mahoney & Deckop, 1986; Rowland & Ferris, 1982).

The essential premise of scientific management was that waste represented costs. The costs included out-of-pocket expenses as well as hidden costs such as poor methods of management (Eilbirt, 1959). To control these costs, time and motion studies and job analysis were performed. Attention was also given to codifying job requirements, introducing job descriptions, and formalizing job training (Baron et al., 1986).

The forces behind these changes have often been identified as Frederick Taylor and Frank and Lillian Gilbreth (French, 1986). By extending techniques used by scientists in the laboratory, these pioneers felt that efficiency in the workplace could be increased (Gilbreth, 1914; Taylor, 1911). Because Taylor's accounts of his experiments with Schmidt showed applications of how job design, selection, training, and performance and reward systems can be used on human resources, the HRM function has often been attributed to the influence of scientific management (Mahoney & Deckop, 1986).

While scientific management compensated workers mainly for following orders and working hard, welfare practices emphasized increasing employees' overall quality of life. Welfare practices may be considered early versions of modern benefits packages. However, during the early 1900s they were considered philanthropic endeavors (Baron et al., 1986).

The opportunities made available through welfare practices varied. Some organizations offered facilities such as libraries and recreational areas while others offered financial assistance for education, home purchases, and home improvements. Some emphasis was also placed on increased hygienic measures as well, such as providing medical care (Albro, 1922; Eilbirt, 1959). To oversee all of these benefits, firms began to employ staff members called welfare secretaries (French, 1986). These positions evolved into the modern personnel administrator (Eilbirt, 1959).

Lawrence (1985a) suggested that the events in the early 1900s occurred because of the improvements in transportation and communication facilities, and that this caused the evolution of the field from a craft system to a market system. A market system consisted of large factories that employed both skilled and unskilled workers who used powerful machines in jobs that required few skills. Workers were rewarded based upon the market value of the work performed. Because of the ample supply of labor, employers were in control of the organizations. To strengthen their positions, workers banded together or unionized. Intense conflicts between labor and management, as well as strikes, were pervasive.

Another turn of events in the early 1900s has been called the industrial-psychology era (Rowland & Ferris, 1982). The focus moved toward the individual and became less concerned with the job. Personnel practices that fostered long-term employment were adopted (Baron et al., 1986). One of the best examples of using this type of practice was the work done by Hugo Munsterberg (1913) for selecting streetcar operators and telephone operators.

Other personnel policies such as centralizing hiring, promotions, and firing, interviewing exiting employees, keeping systematic turnover records, and introducing job ladders and salary classifications were also established. Furthermore, training began to be viewed as a remedy for correcting an improper job-person match (Rowland & Ferris, 1982). It became possible to change employees to better fit their jobs, rather than designing jobs around particular employees.

Even with this increase in personnel functions in the early 1900s, the emphasis remained on technical efficiency. According to Lawrence (1985a), after World War I, the HRM system evolved from a market system to a technical system. The actual technical HRM system began in Henry Ford's car plant at Dearborn, Michigan. At this plant, Ford combined division of labor, automated assembly lines, and high wages. This combination of factors dropped turnover and costs and increased volume and profits.

The two major parts of the technical system, division of labor and automation, influenced all aspects of the organization (Lawrence, 1985a). Because of the automated assembly line, the work pace was preset, which allowed pay to be based on an hourly rate rather than a piece-rate system. This decreased conflicts over and increased the level of wages. The division of labor allowed workers to become virtually interchangeable with little training time, which allowed workers to be dismissed with little impact on the company's production.

Mid 1900s

Although all of the changes in the early 1900s lead to a substantial increase in production, the workers' needs were still virtually ignored. In an effort to emphasize workers' needs, the human-relations era emerged (French, 1986; Rowland & Ferris, 1982). This movement has been a major influence on modern HRM (French, 1986).

The human-relations movement emphasized improving social relationships between supervisors and employees in work groups (Rowland & Ferris, 1982). Specifically, how group behaviors and workers' feeling related to productivity and morale was central to this movement. The most important experiments that took place during this movement were performed by Elton Mayo (1933) and Fritz Roethlisberger (Roethlisberger, Dickson, & Wright, 1939) at Western Electric's Hawthorne plant. Although these researchers examined the influence a change in lighting had on productivity, they concluded that human interaction, not the lighting, influenced production changes (Greenwood & Wrege, 1987). These results highlighted the importance of social factors in organizations.

Late 1900s

Further concern about the influence organizations had on their workers led to another phase of HRM, quality of work life (QWL). This movement, in part, was legitimized by the passing of federal laws concerning equal employment opportunity (Civil Rights Act, Title VII), safety and health (Occupational Safety and Health Act), and the protection of retirement income (Employee Retirement Income Security Act) (Rowland & Ferris, 1982). Although organizations continued to be concerned about productivity and efficiency, this concern was no longer at the expense of employees.

Eight criteria for analyzing the QWL in organizations have been summarized by Walton (1975). They are: (1) fair and adequate compensation, (2) safe and healthy working conditions, (3) an opportunity for employees to use and develop their human capabilities, (4) an opportunity for employees to grow and to have reasonable job security, (5) social integration of employees into the work organization, which also adds to the quality of their work life, (6) the organization's adherence to the concepts of due process and rights to privacy, (7) a balance between work- and non-work activities for all employees and, (8) the organization's providing of socially beneficial and responsible work for its employees.

A more current system influencing HRM's attempt to combine the emphasis on production without sacrificing the employee emphasis of the QWL era, has been referred to as the "career system" (Lawrence, 1985a) or the "behavioral systems theory" (French, 1986). The major issue under either of these systems is to understand how a change in one HRM function, such as selection, will influence other HRM functions, such as performance appraisal and evaluation or reward systems.

The career system, as described by Lawrence (1985a), is based on human resources flow policies. Prior to recruiting employees, the specific duties, responsibilities, and potential mobility associated with the position are documented. This benefits both the potential employee and the organization. It allows the organization to offer new employees a long-term career while the organization can benefit from knowing where the employee will begin as well as to where they will progress. Replacement charts can easily be created and maintained to aid in long-term human resources planning.

Similarly, the behavioral-systems-theory perspective emphasizes the relationships of the parts of HRM to the total HRM system (French, 1986). This allows personnel managers to consider the repercussions that a single change in any HRM function may have on the other functions. In essence, this perspective allows HRM to be viewed in a more macro perspective than had previously been the case.

TOWARDS A MACRO PERSPECTIVE

The importance of and reasons for a more macro perspective of HRM have only recently been examined. One of the most obvious reasons is the phenomenal growth in the field of HRM (Hoyt & Lewis, 1980; Van Cleve, 1982). Thus, as the number of researchers in this area increases, it is able to exert demand side pressure. Within the firm, this may translate to a more meaningful, or broader, role.

A second reason for a more macro perspective is that the HRM function has gained importance and status within the organization. Several reasons for this can be delineated. Legal constraints on organizations have increased, and timely and correct information is needed to abide by and deal with these constraints. HRM functions, which have the knowledge necessary to deal with the legal constraints, become important and influential because information is often exploited to enhance one's power position (Pfeffer, 1978). In essence, HRM has become a boundary-spanning function, controlling and interpreting the information coming from the external environment to the organization (Russ & Bettenhuasen, 1988).

The increasing degree to which HRM is being linked to strategic planning has enhanced its status within the organization (Mahoney & Deckop, 1986). Firms are becoming more inclined to include HRM in the strategic planning process because personnel costs are more often seen as a critical factor when evaluating strategic alternatives. HRM has also come to be seen as a provider of valuable inputs with respect to the firm's inventory of human resource capabilities, which may be relevant to the selection of the appropriate strategy.

A final reason HRM should be viewed in a more macro perspective is the need to advance the degree to which the field has a strong theoretical base that can be scientifically validated (Dyer, 1980). The field of HRM has long been criticized for being atheoretical in nature. Treating each function of HRM as a separate entity may have perpetuated this problem. Forcing scholars to examine all of the "partial models of HRM" together should increase the probability that a common theoretical framework will emerge (Dyer, 1980). This may show that certain concepts that have been historically measured by using different scales, may be quite similar (Dyer & Schwab, 1982). Further, the concentrated efforts may lead to a generally accepted taxonomy, which is one of the initial phases of theory building (Landy & Vasey, 1984).

It is not a new development for organization scientists to question the nature and progress of sub-disciplines or areas. Some have argued about domain issues relative to differences between HRM and organizational behavior (OB) (Cummings, 1978; Rowland & Ferris, 1982; Strauss, 1970), others that fragmentation of the discipline might be resulting (Zammuto & Connolly, 1984a; 1984b), and still others have attempted to reconcile the nature of reality reflected in the body of knowledge in the organizational sciences (Astley, 1985; Astley & Van de Ven, 1983). Particularly the efforts made to delimit rigid boundaries between HRM and other areas of the organizational sciences seem less fruitful for advancing the field in a scholarly sense. One might argue that an effective means of promoting the integration of knowledge and information, and a concomitant advancement of the science of organizations, is to begin to take an "issues" focus. Such an approach would permit a convergence and integration of theory and research from different perspectives and different levels of analysis focusing on a particular issue in the organizational sciences such as management selection/succession.

The various literatures examining this issue often tend not to be acknowledged or be aware of each other. Perhaps this is at least partially due to the fact that HRM research has been predominantly micro-analytic, operating at a single level of analysis. Perhaps, this suggests a need to consider the potential benefits of pursuing more organizational-level research in HRM. Two issues that merit consideration are: (1) what exactly is the domain of HRM? and (2) what should be the level of the analysis?

The Domain of HRM

Traditionally, HRM has been considered an applied, practitioner-oriented field of inquiry (Rowland & Ferris, 1982). Research and theory-development efforts have been confined to individual HRM components, which generally include the recruitment, allocation, and utilization of human resources (Mahoney & Deckop, 1986). However, by focusing on each of the subcomponents, at the expense of the total picture, research processes may be impeded (Wallace, 1983).

Research progress may also have been impeded by the way in which the field of HRM has evolved, as a source of solutions for the problems of managers (Mahoney & Deckop, 1986). This overemphasis on "fire-fighting" can be seen by reviewing the historical shifts in the field of HRM, outlined earlier in this chapter. One of the first problems faced by the field of HRM was how to efficiently use labor. As an answer to this problem, scientific management was introduced. However, the scientific-management approach had the problem of ignoring the workers, so a more human-relations approach evolved. Concentrating on just the workers also led to problems, suggesting that a reasonable solution might be a more macro perspective that integrated the needs of the workers with the needs of the organizations.

Various ways to delineate the domain of HRM have been suggested. Heneman (1980) believed that the dependent variables studied by a field of inquiry could be used to distinguish it from other fields. Rowland and Ferris (1982) suggested that the assumptions made about the phenomena being studied, especially as they relate to the dominant paradigm and philosophy-of-science issues, are a useful way to categorize fields. Finally, boundary lines can be drawn so that the distinctive competences of HRM are highlighted and its areas of overlap with other disciplines are identified (Rowland & Ferris, 1982; Strauss, 1970).

Domain issues are usually normative in nature. Thus, these types of discussions could continue indefinitely, without an acceptable resolution. The importance of maintaining distinctions among the fields in the organizational sciences pales in comparison to the need to integrate the fragmented theories surrounding the field of HRM. A more macro perspective, integrating what is known, should allow advancement of the field more readily than a clear understanding of what is and what is not considered a HRM issue.

Level of Analysis

A second issue, which has also hindered progress, is the level of analysis used in most HRM research. Many aspects of traditional HRM view the employee only at the individual level. Therefore, the conceptual analysis of these topics has been generally limited to utilizing models of individual behavior (Mahoney & Deckop, 1986). This traditional level of analysis, although necessary in some cases, limits integration efforts. However, aggregation of data across organizational levels may be inappropriate and certainly challenging.

One solution to this problem, suggested by Heneman (1969), was a system of linkages among classes of variables, referred to as vertical synthesis. This type of synthesis recognizes that behaviors at one level of analysis affect behaviors at other levels. Thus, scholars must include this interactive nature when developing models to test phenomena that cut across such classes. A well defined macro perspective of HRM may well fit the category of vertical synthesis.

Even though this section alludes to the fact that a macro perspective of HRM has rarely been taken, research along these lines does exist. For instance, organizational career and internal labor market research, and the integration of HRM activities with corporate strategy have the potential to integrate the HRM research efforts (Mahoney & Deckop, 1986). These ideas and others are specifically addressed in the following sections.

ORGANIZATIONAL-LEVEL PERSPECTIVE OF HRM

Several organizational scholars have argued for theory and research that places HRM in a broader context (Dyer, 1980, 1984, 1985; Kochan, Mitchell, & Dyer, 1982; Milkovich, 1988; Wallace, 1983; Zedeck & Cascio, 1984;). The empirical work to date that has examined HRM issues in a broader perspective, and perhaps higher level of analysis, has tended to manifest itself in essentially two ways. One is through the advancement of SHRM, which is a direction suggested by several as an effective means of placing HRM in a broader context (Mahoney & Deckop, 1986; Kochan et al., 1982). The other is through research that has simply raised the level of analysis to the organizational level, and investigated HRM issues from that perspective.

SHRM is a concept that has gained considerable momentum in the late 1980s. Generally, this concept refers to a simultaneous long-term and integrative perspective to planning for and management of an organization's human resources. Conceptual developments have focused on further refining relevant issues and concepts in a general sense (Baird & Meshoulam, 1988; Butler, Ferris, & Smith, 1988; Napier, 1988; Schuler, 1988), as well as in specific contexts, such as declining environments (Ferris, Schellenberg, & Zammuto, 1984). Whereas most of the work in this area has been conceptual in nature, empirical research is beginning to appear in the literature. Two studies, for instance, have distinguished between productive and nonproductive organizations' attempts at managing their human resources practices strategically (Cook & Ferris, 1986; Misa & Stein, 1983).

It is unduly optimistic to suggest that the concept of SHRM has been met with no skepticism and has enjoyed widespread acceptance. However, this book and others (Fombrun, Tichy, & Devanna, 1984; Walton & Lawrence, 1985) argue that a definitive determination of the merits of these theoretical advancements is premature at this point. SHRM and other macro perspectives are at a preliminary point in their evolution, with the need for much development, but also the opportunity and potential for contribution.

Perhaps a more profitable line of inquiry might be that the SHRM perspective expands more traditional views of HRM issues by broadening the context, and level of analysis, within which such issues are viewed, and in the process raises awareness that macro-organizational concerns represent an important part of scholarly inquiry in the field of HRM (Dyer, 1985; Milkovich, 1988). Such an argument suggests that the streams of research on SHRM and on general organizational-level perspectives of HRM issues, while they have pursued rather independent courses, are not independent at all. In fact, it might be argued that there is a desperate need to integrate the two streams in order to effectively assess the current state of knowledge. Furthermore, it appears that substantially more is to be gained toward advancing the field of HRM by an integration than by maintaining independence.

APPROACHES TO THE STRATEGY-HRM INTERFACE

As mentioned above, HRM is usually described through its activities: (1) staffing, (2) training and development, (3) performance evaluation and reward systems, and (4) industrial relations (e.g., Alpander, 1982; Fombrun, Tichy & Devanna, 1984). However, the inadequacy of this list approach becomes apparent as researchers attempt to come to grips with the full impact of the SHRM process. Figure 2-1 depicts the nature of the communication linkages involved in each of these relationships.

Each of these linkages, depicted in Figure 2-1, represents an increase in the munificence of the relationship between the corporate planning and HRM

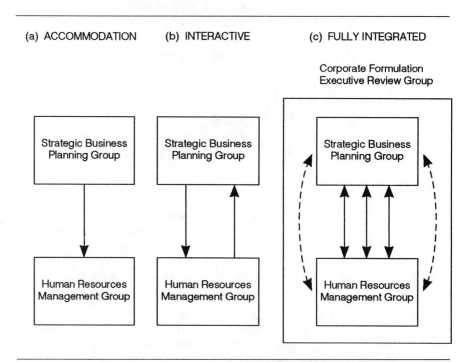

FIGURE 2-1. Comprehensive strategic human resources planning system. (adapted from Butler, J., Ferris, G., and Cook, D., 'Exploring some critical dimensions of strategic human resource management', In R. Schuler, S. Youngblood and V. Huber (Eds.) *Readings in Personnel and Human Resource Management* (p. 4). Copyright (1988.) Reprinted by permission of West Publishing Co.).

groups. The realization that HRM policies can affect the eventual success of a chosen strategy initiates the reassessment of the strategy-HRM relationship. Normally, this leads a firm to initially pursue an accommodation approach, where HRM is only concerned with facilitating the implementation of the chosen strategy. External events, especially those related to environmental change, are most likely to provide this initial impetus. Thus, in an examination of mature industries in their decline stage, HRM was often an afterthought, which played an accommodation role with respect to the implementation of a chosen strategy (Cook & Ferris, 1986; Ferris, Schellenberg, & Zammuto, 1984). In this mode, HRM policies are seen as a response tool. The unidirectional arrow in Figure 2-1(a) depicts the condition where the HRM group is simply expected to accommodate and facilitate the strategy formulated by the planning group.

The problem with the accommodation relationship is that it minimizes the potential for an HRM contribution. It is inconsistent to attempt to exclude HRM from the strategy-formulation process and expect an optimal implementation-supporting contribution. The full and energetic employment of HRM tools will not be sufficient to overcome obstacles that could have been identified if HRM personnel had been part of the strategy-formulation process.

A two-way communication process between the HRM and planning groups is depicted in Figure 2-1(b), as the second mode of approaching the strategy-HRM interface. This is a natural second step in the evolution and with this approach HRM begins to assume a more proactive role and becomes much more central to organizational effectiveness (Tichy, Fombrun, & Devanna, 1982). The impact associated with this approach extends beyond formulation to its direct influence on the management philosophy of the firm in general. The linkage between the two groups and processes is much more fully developed in firms capable of this approach, which has become increasingly common (Golden & Ramanujam, 1985).

The interactive approach increases the benefits available from the strategy-HRM interface, but the relationship between the two groups is managed in a fairly mechanical fashion. Alpander (1982) provided a good analogy by equating this process to horizontal and vertical integration. Successfully completing the process of horizontal integration involved linking all of the areas or activities directly associated with HRM. Having completed this task, the process of vertical integration could begin, which involved developing the links to the strategic planning group and to those involved in this process.

The evolution of the strategic planning-HRM relationship to a fully integrated approach has been rare, but if achieved "provides a dynamic, multifaceted linkage that is based on an interactive instead of a reciprocal relationship" (Golden & Ramanujam, 1985, p. 436). The extent and directionality of communication, using this approach, is depicted in Figure 2-1(c). The interactions are depicted as numerous and mutually interactive. Dotted lines indicate that the communication process extends beyond the formal requirements needed for organizational effectiveness to informal communication, which can have a more direct impact on the strategy of the firm

(Mintzberg, 1978). Under this fully integrated system, HRM managers are more likely to be included in the top-level executive team that formulates the firm's strategy, which accounts for the common grouping of the planning and HRM function in Figure 2-1(c).

Once the firm is willing to make the initial movement toward SHRM, it seems appropriate to move toward the fully integrated approach. The reasons for this will become more apparent in Chapter Three and Chapter Four. However, the way the organization views and benefits from the HRM function depends on the current stage of accommodation as well as the manner in which each of the HRM task areas is exploited to achieve strategic benefits.

OBTAINING ADVANTAGE FROM HRM FUNCTIONS

While the theoretical view espoused earlier in this chapter was that HRM's value to strategy is maximized using a fully integrated approach, value also flows from the specific HRM functions. Although the separate HRM content areas are important, and are discussed in Chapters Six through Ten, a broad general consideration, provided in this chapter, is also relevant. Because these HRM activities are often performed in an isolated fashion, especially in larger firms, it is important to understand how they fit together from a strategic perspective.

Strategic Human Resources Planning

A recent study by Mills (1985) of firms with sales in excess of $50 million, found that 15% of these firms did no planning. If such things as company picnics and short-term head-counting are excluded, almost 60% of the firms could be eliminated from having a strategy-HRM linkage. Thus, the existence of a competent strategic planning group provides the initial constraint to having such a linkage, but its presence does not ensure the existence of a mutual-accommodation type relationship (See Figure 2-1(a)). A second condition for the existence of SHRP relates to competence. The ability to effectively incorporate HRM into the strategic planning process relates to the ability to be competent at the planning process itself (Mills, 1985).

Assuming the firm has developed a competent business planning unit, there are few well-established rules as to how to proceed toward the fully integrated strategy-HRM interface depicted in Figure 2-1(c). For a large multi-business firm, this means that the corporate, business, and functional areas must have a corresponding HRM counterpart. For a highly centralized, single business firm, where planning is done exclusively at the corporate level, this would require a similarly focused HRM unit. The situational requirements require the development of a theoretical justification that transcends organizational-design characteristics.

Thus, the concentration here is more on the form of HRM planning as it relates to the strategic process, although special-case applications are considered later. This is consistent with earlier theoretical prescriptions (Dyer,

1985; Mills, 1985). Figure 2-2 depicts diagrammatically what might occur in a comprehensive human resources planning system. This is a general case and

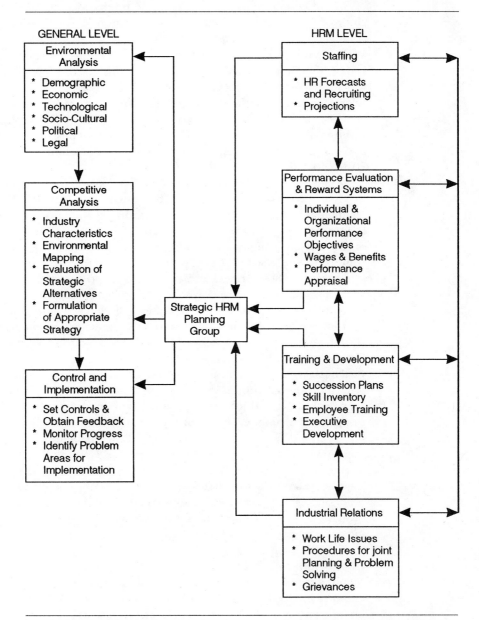

FIGURE 2-2. Approaches to strategic human resources management. (Adapted from Butler, J., Ferris, G. and Cook, D., 'Exploring some critical dimensions of strategic human resource management', In R. Schuler, S. Youngblood and V. Huber (Eds.) *Readings in Personnel and Human Resource Management* (p. 6). Copyright (1988). Reprinted by permission of West Publishing Co.)

many more communication links, both formal and informal, would exist between the strategic planning and HRM groups.

The comprehensive strategic-HRM model, depicted in Figure 2-2, includes three general-level activities that are more normally associated with the strategic planning function: (1) environmental scanning, (2) competitive analysis, and (3) implementation and control. In this book, the position taken is that the impact of HRM is important at this general level. The manner by which that impact is theoretically manifested is discussed later, but the content of that impact is briefly discussed here. For instance, at the environmental-analysis, or scanning, level there should be a joint HRM/planning group involvement. The HRM group can bring a different perspective, which should make it increasingly likely that threats and opportunities, based on existing HRM capabilities, will be identified.

Each of the relevant content areas, listed as an HRM Level consideration in Figure 2-2, is relevant because the extent to which the HRM group is competent in these functional areas determines the value of its input during the environmental analysis. In addition, the range of elements considered during the environmental-scanning effort is affected by the functional level competence of the HRM group (Aquilar, 1967). This is because the HRM group can provide a richer impact when it appreciates the tasks involved in each of the functional areas. Just as a competent planning group is necessary for consistency in strategy formulation, high-level functional HRM competence is required to obtain value from the strategy-HRM interface.

A competitive analysis normally follows the environmental-scanning effort. Simplistically, this process involves the mapping of a firm's strengths and weaknesses onto environmental threats and opportunities (Learned, Christensen, Andrews, & Guth, 1965). An HRM input is critical at this stage, because specific HRM activities must be identified to determine the appropriate response needed for each alternative. If a particular strategic alternative would be supported or hindered by existing HRM capabilities, this is the time to recognize that fact so that the area can be strengthened or the strategy adjusted. It may be too late to make this adjustment at the implementation stage because of the time lags associated with taking corrective action.

During this stage HRM's capability and knowledge should also be brought to bear on the strategy-formulation process. For instance, the forecasting activity associated with the strategy process is also conducted with respect to the HRM capability. The firm's senior management must determine the extent to which HRM capabilities can contribute to competitive success. This requires measuring HRM in terms that are more normally associated with organizational effectiveness, such as the present - value impact, revenue-growth impact, and market-share implications for various HRM alternatives. These impacts, especially where they are different with respect to competing strategies, can have a direct impact on the strategy formulated or alternatives selected.

Once a strategy has been formulated, the HRM group has the same responsibility as other functional areas. Control and implementation issues should have been considered in advance, but new discrepancies will surface during the implementation stage. As this occurs, local HRM content areas should begin to take the steps necessary to ensure that sufficient human talent is available and motivated to facilitate strategy implementation. Controls, information systems, and feedback procedures must be established to ensure that the relationship between the HRM and planning groups is sustained throughout this process.

The model depicted in Figure 2-2 makes it clear that a comprehensive set of decision rules cannot be constructed in advance. However, it does suggest that the organization must be capable of engaging in those activities that are needed to sustain this process. A competent HRM group and strategic planning group must be linked during all stages of the strategic process. An HRM perspective must be brought to each stage of the process to ensure that relevant HRM considerations are presented. Finally, the HRM group must ensure that its inputs support the strategic thrust of the firm. Each of the functional specialties listed as HRM-level considerations in Figure 2-2 is considered separately below.

Strategic Staffing

From a SHRM perspective, staffing is more than equal employment opportunity compliance, interviews and test validation, or providing realistic job previews (See Chapter Six). Different types of staffing modes have to be measured in terms of their strategic relevance. For instance, a strategy requiring a highly decentralized organizational design may put unique demands on managers, which requires them to behave more entrepreneurially. On one level this may drastically alter the selection profile, while on another level it may make many of the bureaucratically required administrative tasks, which entrepreneurial type managers are inclined to ignore, more difficult.

Aside from separating the staffing needs by employee type, it is also important to determine the extent to which the existing culture of the organization is important. In some firms, the culture is moving toward one of mutual commitment, which may result in the frequent movement of employees to different positions in response to fluctuations in demand. Selecting employees who will support the culture can be extremely important to strategy implementation, especially in competitive situations requiring high levels of organizational flexibility. This development of "importing controls," relating employee characteristics to firm needs, is designed to help ensure that employee selection will have a synergistic effect on corporate strategy. The ability to supply employees who are likely to support the existing culture is more important during periods of rapid growth because neither time nor development resources will be sufficient to engage in a wholesale employee transformation effort.

When the firm has selected a strategy that requires a different culture, the staffing problem is far more complex. New employees tend to be socialized into the existing culture. Thus, staffing should be combined with employee-development efforts designed to change the attitudes of existing managers and employees. This is the reason for the feedback loops depicted between various HRM content areas in Figure 2-2. The match between culture and HRM policies determines how things get done and "successful companies guide and shape their company's culture to fit their strategy" (Phillips & Kennedy, 1980, p. 218).

At the managerial level, new notions about appropriate managerial behavior, such as Theory Z (Ouchi, 1981) or "management by walking around" (Peters & Austin, 1985a), call for managerial behavior that cannot be easily measured, especially at the entry level. To the extent that firms also expect strategies to emerge or be revealed incrementally (e.g., Mintzberg, 1978; Quinn, 1980), new notions about how to staff firms with managers capable of resisting bureaucratic socialization need to be developed.

Another important concern related to managerial staffing is the issue of succession. As the diversification trend continues, major corporations are increasingly managing their portfolio of businesses much as investors manage their portfolios of stock. Funds are channeled from business units producing more profits than needed to sustain their competitive position, to those units in fast-growing industries that need an influx of cash just to maintain their market position. Managerial demands are drastically different, depending on the type of unit managed. At the corporate level, managerial demands do not necessarily correspond to those at the business level, when the corporation is following a portfolio approach to strategy. Under this type of corporate strategy, staffing forecasts based on the different types of business units, as well as on the managerial needs at the corporate level, must be maintained. Managerial success at the business unit level does not necessarily indicate that a manager will succeed at the corporate level. It also means that managers must be found who are competent to manage business units that provide cash and who are willing to develop expertise at, and be willing to continue, managing these less glamorous types of business units.

Strategic Performance Evaluation and Reward Systems

Much of the focus and interest in performance evaluation has centered around the mechanics of measurement rather than on examining the impact and role of performance evaluation practices on overall organizational effectiveness (Lawler, Mohrman, & Resnick, 1984). (See Chapters Seven and Eight.) One of the key findings of the Lawler et al. (1984) study, which was conducted at General Electric, was that where the SHRM process was an important part of the organizational culture, performance evaluation served as a key link. The need to expand the scope of appraisal activities, so that job design and managerial behavior provide clear signals concerning the type of behavior superiors wish to encourage, is just one aspect of this task. Within the HRM area, more attention needs to be paid to consequences (Napier & Latham, 1986), especially as related to their links to the performance evaluation and reward systems. Incongruity between these systems, as well as between development efforts, will negate the positive impact this area can have on corporate-level strategy.

Complicating the administration of evaluation and reward systems is the fact that strategy is formulated at three levels: the corporate, the business, and the functional. Performance evaluation and compensation play different roles at each of these levels. Consideration must also be given to the nature of the business, because start-up firms will have very different needs than firms competing in mature and declining industries.

At the functional level, it may be important to train individuals to assess subordinates, while at the corporate level, attention has to be given to the type of criteria needed to measure the long-term potential of managerial talent. With respect to reward systems, movement from wage and salary administration to long-range compensation programs designed to support corporate values is desirable.

In developing performance evaluation and reward systems that support the desired management philosophy and also act as controls, their compatibility with the strategy of the firm should also be considered (Kerr, 1982; Leontiades, 1982). Because firms go through life cycles, it is important to use compensation as a tool to support strategic objectives. For instance, offering a large equity position may be one way of attracting competent managers during the business start-up phase, while a bonus linked to growth might be more appropriate once the firm has survived this initial period. Later, if the firm itself is in an industry that is experiencing permanent long-term decline in demand, a bonus or appraisal scheme linked to managerial cost cutting might be more appropriate. The portfolio approach used by many large firms complicates the administration of reward systems to an even greater degree because the corporation is looking to have business units in all of the various industry life-cycle stages.

The portfolio approach suggests that cash should flow to those business units most likely to experience growth. While this may be a practical way to manage the distribution of limited resources, it also means that resistance and subterfuge may appear if compensation schemes developed for top executives are not designed to produce behavior supporting corporate objectives. Managers assigned to a favored business unit are likely to be perceived as high performers if traditional revenue and profit indicators of performance are used for evaluation purposes. Managers assigned to business units designated as cash providers will suffer in performance evaluations and are unlikely to willingly cooperate. New models of evaluation and compensation have to be developed, which are related to the management of a diversified portfolio of business units, if managers of less glamorous business units are to be expected to support corporate portfolio strategies.

Strategic Human Resources Development

Hall (1984, p. 159) pointed out that "the strategic development of human resources is virtually nonexistent." Thus, Chapter Nine, which deals with this issue more fully, concentrates on telling firms how they should behave rather than describing how they behave. As depicted in Figure 2-2, human resources development provides important inputs to the other HRM functions as well as directly to the SHRM planning group.

In the past, development efforts have been seen in rather static terms. Training was directed toward maximizing managerial effectiveness in terms of contributing to some presently perceived functional need. As firms became more long-term and strategic in their outlook, it became increasingly necessary to match the managerial training efforts of today to the strategic needs of tomorrow. If managers with development expertise are not included in the SHRP process and allowed to provide input into the overall corporate planning effort, this is unlikely to occur.

Ultimately, the exclusion of human resources development may lead to a crisis mode of operations, as HRM professionals seek to find managers capable of functioning in a more complex environment, which could have probably been predicted. Outsiders may have to be recruited to fill important managerial positions because talented individuals inside the firm were not appropriately developed to cope with the demands of a new strategy. Other important areas related to the inventory of needed skills and issues of managerial succession may be glossed over by those less inclined to focus on these types of issues.

Strategic Industrial Relations

Although there is some debate about whether labor, or industrial relations can be strategic (Lewin, 1987), the perspective taken in this book is to view industrial relations as necessary to the SHRP process (See Chapter Ten). One could take a narrow historical view, with industrial relations involving no more than competent negotiating on the part of the corporate legal and personnel staff. However, there is some historical evidence that suggests that a strategic perspective may be appropriate.

One instance of firms, governments, and unions attempting to alter their basic relationship with each other occurred during the labor shortages of World War I. Corportists' views of industrial relations, based on the belief that collective bargaining could be based on harmony, were adopted by most business firms in the United States (Gerber, 1988). At the same time, unions were advancing a more pluralist model, based on equality in negotiations flowing from conflict and compromise. The government attempted to achieve mutual assent, but the labor surplus after the war and the depression that followed ensured the corportists' views of business prevailed. However, from a strategic sense, one wonders if slight movement toward the position of labor at this time, might have been more supportive of the long-term strategies of these firms.

Additionally, the central thesis of *The Transformation of American Industrial Relations* (Kochan, Katz, & McKerzie, 1986) is that industrial relations involves long-term strategic decisions related to both corporate investment and union organizing options. Because they include government, unions, and corporations, the links between industrial relations and other strategic components seem more obvious.

Another recent study by Mishel (1986) examined the impact of structural determinants on the ability of unions to extract concessions. In a manner, this represents the flip side of Porter's (1980, 1985) argument that firms' strategies should recognize the importance of market structure characteristics. Thus, while strategic planners are attempting to exploit market structure, union bargaining power may also benefit. Interestingly, as unions begin to base bargaining on the same factors that firms should be considering when formulating strategy, the link between industrial relations and strategy should become even stronger.

SUMMARY AND CONCLUSIONS

The ongoing evolution of HRM from its record-keeping origins to a condition of strategic participation has been a natural progression. As HRM evolved through craft technology, to scientific management techniques, to the complex environmental contingencies of the contemporary industrial environment, it gradually began to acquire a more macro perspective. This macro perspective explains some of the movement from an isolated emphasis on content areas to a movement toward SHRP.

Central to this achievement of an effective SHRP function is the acceptance of HRM's participation in the strategic management process. Thus, firms should seek to move to first accommodate HRM and then fully integrate it into the strategic management process. In this way, the full benefits available from HRM can be captured.

Having arrived at a willingness to include HRM in the strategic process, the final step involves ensuring that a comprehensive SHRM planning function is in place. At the corporate level, this involves environmental analysis, competitive analysis, and procedures for control and implementation. At the HRM level, it involves making decisions and providing information about staffing, performance evaluation and reward systems, employee development, and industrial relations from a content as well as a strategic perspective. It is this rather inclusive notion of SHRP that forms the substance of the chapters that follow.

EXPANDING THE
STRATEGY-MAKING CONCEPT

A moral lesson this might teach,
Were I ordained and called to preach;
For men are prone to go it blind
Along the calf-paths of the mind,
And work away from sun to sun
And do what other men have done.
They follow in the beaten track,
And out and in, and forth and back,
And still their devious course pursue,
To keep the path that others do.
(Foss, 1918, p. 1896–1897).[1]

The classical notion of strategy centered around the winning of wars (e.g., Clausewitz, 1832) and the use of military power for nationalistic purposes (e.g., Mahan, 1890). Strategy was seen as providing broad general direction, while tactics were left to battlefield commanders. Clausewitz, in detailing his model of the role of strategy in the conduct of war, described a process that could easily be transferred to the contemporary business firm.

> Strategy is the use of the engagement for the purpose of the war. The strategist must therefore define an aim for the entire operational side of the war that will be in accordance with its purpose. In other words, he will draft the plan of the war, and the aim will determine the series of actions intended to achieve it: he will, in fact, shape the individual campaigns and, within these, decide on the individual engagements. Since most of these matters have to be based on assumptions that may not prove correct, while other, more detailed orders cannot be determined in advance at all, it follows that the strategist must go on campaign himself. Detailed orders can then be given on the spot, allowing the general plan to be adjusted to the modifications that are continuously required. The strategist, in short, must maintain control throughout (Clausewitz, 1976, p. 177).

Mahan (1890) took a much less "hands on" view of the role of the strategist by positioning strategy as a process that was independent of the technological

---

[1] Original inspiration from Schendel and Hofer (1979).

developments that were increasing the effectiveness of the weapons of war. This military aspect has often been picked up "as business policy's battlefield analogy" (Astley, 1984, p. 526).

Recently, coordination in addition to competitiveness has been viewed as essential when dealing with strategic problems. As environmental complexity increased, additional functional and staff areas became valued as sources of inputs that were relevant to solving strategic problems. The inclusion of HRM in the strategic process reflected top-management's recognition that including HRM in the strategy equation leads to better performance. Thus, in a generalized way, it makes sense that the desire to more effectively coordinate and compete would lead to the eventual consideration of all relevant staff areas.

EMERGING STRATEGY RESEARCH

The recognition that performance improvements could be generated from either coordination or competition occurred in practice long before it was noticed in the academic research literature or in professional schools of business. This probably resulted from the fact that it is difficult to recognize firms' actions as having a cohesive pattern and because many firms act incrementally and inconsistently. It also has to be recognized that there is no premium associated with revealing one's strategy or its link to a positive performance outcome (e.g., Quinn, 1980). Chandler (1962, 1977), using a historical methodology, established the importance of having an optimal match between the strategy and structure of the firm. He also noticed that as the complexity of commerce increased, businesses began to internalize specialized functions. The need to provide direction to operating managers was an outcome of the growth process. In this way the independent operating style of individual managers could be guided by the coordinating thrust of a single strategy. Strategy, as a coordinator, helped ensure that all the managers were pulling in the same direction. The coordinating- thrust aspect of strategy helps explains why much of the early research in strategy centered on "business policy" as a way of meshing the various functional groups within the firm into a coherent whole (e.g., Schendel & Hofer, 1979). This probably explains why synergy was seen as a desired strategic outcome, which would eventually lead to enhanced firm performance.

Chandler (1962) and others (e.g., Ansoff, 1965; Learned, Christensen, Andrews & Guth, 1965) expanded "policy" beyond the integration of functional areas. Chandler (1962, p. 13) developed his concept of strategy by relating it to " . . . the basic long-term goals and objectives of an enterprise, and the adoption of courses of action and the allocation of resources necessary to carry out goals." While Chandler was primarily concerned with structural responses to strategy, Learned and his colleagues (Learned et al., 1965) provided a framework that suggested firms map their strengths and weaknesses on environmental threats and opportunities. This expanded the scope of strategy to include " . . . the pattern of objectives, purposes, or goals and major policies and plans for achieving these goals, stated in such a way as to define what business the company is in or is to be in and the kind of company it is or is to be" (Learned et al., 1965, p. 15). At a more basic level, this "scope" translated into defining strategy in terms of which products to sell and which markets to serve. Product market choices added complexity to the extent that they represented a change in position that required a " . . . redistribution of a firm's resources—a pattern of divestments and investments in company acquisitions, product development, marketing outlets, advertising. . . . " (Ansoff, 1965, p. 12).

While these initial research efforts built a case for the importance of strategy, they also highlighted its complexity in ways that suggested firms give it more than *ad hoc* treatment. They envisioned the evolution of strategy beyond being just a tool for coordination to one where it would serve as a vehicle for competitive advantage. Beyond the normal process-type benefits, these early researchers suggested that the formulation and implementation of a strategy which was at least incrementally superior to competitors' helped to explain the relative positions of firms within an industry. Two competing firms might reflect high internal consistency, with respect to their strategic direction. However, different strategic choices would eventually be reflected in different levels of profit and competitive position. Thus, choosing the correct strategic path became just as important as having the entire firm pulling or pushing the firm in the same direction.

ELABORATION OF THE PROCESS MODEL

As with many emerging fields, the research on strategy began to reflect its increasing complexity through an elaboration of the process model and an extension of the number of content areas considered relevant. With respect to process, strategy models evolved to a generally accepted sequential ordering of activities, which generally include most of the following: (1) goal formulation, (2) identification of existing strategies (3) macroenvironmental scanning, (4) assessment of internal resources, (5) alternative evaluation and strategy formulation, (6) development of mission statements and action plans, (7) control process and other issues related to implementation, and (8) information systems to provide feedback for gap analysis. On the content side, this development is reflected through an expanded agenda that now includes issues related to diversification, innovation, internal corporate entrepreneurship, manufacturing, market structure, international market, takeover and acquisition, and human resources considerations. Thus, in terms of the emergence of SHRM, the need is not new. However, the strategy process, within firms, had to develop sufficiently so that it could benefit from the incorporation of it. An important side benefit from the elongation of the process model and the expansion of the content bases of strategy, was that the theoretical underpinnings of strategy were also expanded and now include organizational theory, sociology, psychology, marketing, finance, and industrial-organization and institutional economics. Process, content, and theoretical contributions are all possible, and the broadest contribution to the strategy paradigm occurs when new knowledge can be brought to bear on all three fronts. This research effort seeks to fully exploit the contributions of HRM on all three dimensions. The extent of the content contribution of HRM and its relationship to the various components of the strategic management process were outlined in Chapter Two and are more fully developed in later chapters. This chapter attempts to detail a view of strategy that allows HRM to be incorporated as a working component in the strategy-formulation process. The theoretical justification for both process and content linkages enhances the strategic paradigm by extending the role of HRM to both that of a coordinating agent and a competitive force. By showing how strategy has evolved, and adopting a view of strategy as partially emergent (Mintzberg, 1978), it is possible to present strategy as an ongoing process rather than as some discrete output of a planning department. In this chapter the concept of an "emergent strategy" component will be presented, and it will be incorporated into the strategy-HRM model that is presented in Chapter Four.

THE STRATEGY PROCESS

Before moving to a discussion of "emergent" strategy, a brief review of the strategic process and evolutionary development of the field is warranted. A flow diagram of a generalized version of the strategic management process is depicted in Figure 3-1. Essentially, a sequential process is presented that moves from the identification of the existing strategy to the implementation of a new strategy. The environment, internal resources of the firm, and the values and preferences of stakeholders are factors that are relevant to the evaluation of the current strategy. The generation and evaluation of a new set of alternatives repeats this process, although there is a little less certainty about the outcomes. Implementation is concerned with identifying and removing roadblocks to the selected strategy, although major concerns with respect to implementation may also eliminate an alternative.

The ongoing nature of the strategic process was a prime factor in the decisions by many firms to dedicate some personnel exclusively to strategic planning, which accounts for the emergence of formal planning departments. The generation and evaluation of alternatives and the subsequent selection of a new strategy are usually discussed as a discrete event, which appears to be developed much as an R & D department would develop and introduce a new product. The feedback loop, between outcomes and goals, depicted with a dashed line in Figure 3-1, serves as the basis for gap analysis. When the discrepancies between outcomes and goals reach some critical point, they signal a new round in the strategy process. Scanning, which is related to informational inputs, serves as the basis for subsequent rounds of strategy

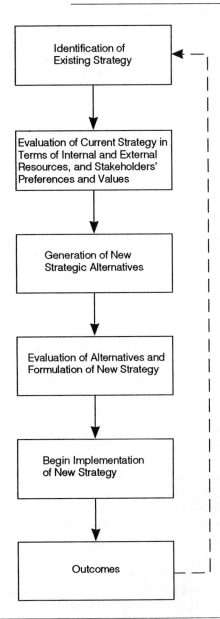

FIGURE 3-1. A flow diagram of a generalized version of the strategic management process, using an intended decision model of strategy.

formulation or as the basis for fine-tuning the existing strategy. Before discussing the relationship between the intended model of strategy and HRM, a brief introduction to those components is presented for those unfamiliar with the field of strategic management.

Evaluation of Current Strategy

The first stage in the strategy process usually involves identifying the current strategy of the firm. While the firm may have some written statement of its strategy, it is often expressed in vague terms. This conscious act of determining the existing strategy is necessary if those responsible for formulating a new strategy are to have a true sense of the *status quo*. This deduction may involve a careful assessment of prevailing goals, current product market choices, and the determination of how the firm is positioned relative to competitors. In this way, not only is a picture of the current strategy drawn but the firm's goals and product market choices provide some standards that are helpful in identifying reasons for the gap between desired and actual performance. The ability of the firm to sustain the current strategy with its existing resources, during prevailing environmental conditions, and given the values and beliefs of important stakeholders is the central issue in the evaluation of the current strategy.

Generation of a Future Strategy

In addition to certain mechanical process requirements, a certain amount of creativity is desired during the effort to generate alternatives. There are no absolute scientific rules or prescriptions for how this process can be programmed and it requires the "mental perspiration" associated with inventive activity. The evaluation of alternatives occurs along much the same lines as did the evaluation of the existing strategy. SWOT (strengths, weaknesses, opportunities, threats) analysis is often used to provide a framework for the generation and evaluation phase (Learned et al., 1965). The strengths and weaknesses of the firm are mapped onto environmental threats and opportunities. In this way the fit between the firm and its strategy can be assessed. Stakeholder considerations that might modify the choice can then be factored into the equation (Freeman, 1984). More recently, market structure analysis, using the industrial organization economics framework, has become very popular (Porter, 1980).

There is some debate as to whether implementation occurs independently of formulation, but it is recognized that there is an identifiable set of issues related to implementation (Hrebiniak & Joyce, 1984). In some cases an option that would appear to be a viable strategic alternative to an outside observer will be eliminated because the firm lacks the ability to implement it. In other cases implementation issues will be identified in advance, and this process will occur concurrently with the selection of the new strategy. There is also an ongoing aspect to implementation that relates to dealing with problems that emerge and affect the success of the new strategy. As can be seen from the discussion in Chapter Two, HRM has often been seen in terms related to facilitating implementation of a strategy.

Feedback

Feedback helps determine when a new strategy should be formulated, because it provides the information for gap analysis (Fry & Killings, 1986). With the development of management information systems the sorting and interpreting of feedback has become an analytical exercise of considerable scope. Planning departments are kept busy on a full-time basis analyzing the wealth of information that is collected. With an intended model of strategy, feedback, in addition to providing the information for gap analysis and for the analysis of strategic alternatives, also serves as a vehicle for control. These controls may be stated or implied, but it is likely that operating managers will be aware of the nature of the information flowing to the planning department. At times the control function may inhibit the formulation of new strategies if it provides information that signals a deterioration in performance. Planners may be reluctant to attribute a deterioration in performance to the exiting strategy because they participated in its formulation. Like most groups, the use of influence is likely to be accepted by planners, but they are less comfortable with transferring the power to make the final decision to others (e.g., Gamson, 1968; Tannenbaum, 1968).

Evolution of the Model

Initial debate centered less around the value of the strategic process than it did around the value of instituting a formal planning group at all. Given this resistance, it was only natural that these newly established planning groups wanted their output to reflect careful consideration so that it could stand up to the scrutiny of other staff and functional groups. Empirical investigations by academics did little to clarify the value of formal planning because the time lags and system-like relationships associated with this function are not easily interpreted using summary statistics based on cross-sectional comparisons. For large firms, the initial resistance has gradually dissipated, and almost all large firms now have a formal planning group responsible for activities such as scanning, evaluation, formulation, and the monitoring of feedback (e.g., Ramanujam & Venkatraman, 1987). However, organizationally these larger firms reflect the effects of growth and aging that generally lead to increased bureaucratization as controls are introduced to ensure standardization. Like many functional and staff areas, planning departments also seek to institute controls designed to ensure that they maintain sole ownership of the firm's strategy.

Interestingly, this evolution toward a formal planning function and institutionalized environmental scanning has not occurred on as large a scale in smaller firms (e.g., Diffenbach, 1983; Robinson & Pearce, 1984), but there is no indication that smaller firms formulate strategy using a less deliberate process. They are just more *ad hoc* in carrying it out. Thus, while smaller firms do not have institutionalized controls to the same degree as do larger firms, their mode of strategy making appears to be equally formal. For firms with formal planning, it appears that institutional controls may hamper further evolution of the strategy process, but they at least have evolved to a point where the full range of functional and staff contributions is sought. For firms without formal planning, there may be fewer institutional roadblocks with respect to the strategic process, but they are more likely to be completely ignoring the contributions of an area that is seen as tangential, such as HRM.

For firms without a formal planning function, the existing literature seems to suggest that the internalization of the strategy-formulation function is related to an increase in the number of factors with strategic relevance. During periods of environmental turbulence it becomes more difficult to determine which factors should be monitored (Ansoff, 1979). Rapid change also makes it difficult to monitor the environment on an *ad hoc* basis, and a logical institutional response is the internalization of the planning function. In rare cases, such as when deteriorating U.S.-Cuban relations eliminated the American-Cuban Sugar Corp., environmental obstacles may be insurmountable. However, the general view is that an effective scanning function, internalized through a planning department that uses a formal strategy-making process can better deal with high levels of environmental turbulence and this should enhance organizational performance (e.g., Bourgeois, 1978; Hedberg, Nystrom & Starbuck, 1976). Ansoff (1979) suggested that competitive advantage will also rest with firms that engage in formal planning, if relevant competitors have no planning effort.

The purpose here is not to downgrade the value of formal planning or the use of intended decisions in strategy formulation. Rather, this is seen as only one side of the process, although it may be a necessary initial phase in the movement toward a more comprehensive mode of strategy making. Research may eventually show that the establishment of formal planning departments, designed to produce strategies, is essential in developing the knowledge base across managers and supporting corporate culture needed for a meaningful emergent component.

HRM IN THE INTENDED STRATEGY MODEL

One of the problems with strategy research is that it requires a focus on past action although its thrust is toward the future. For instance, Hambrick's (1983, p. 5) definition of strategy as "a pattern in a stream of decisions (past or intended) that (a) guides the organization's ongoing alignment with its environment and (b) shapes internal policies and procedures" reflects the historical perspective often required of strategy researchers. This definition is adapted from Mintzberg (1978), who makes a distinction between the intended strategy and what was realized. His view that strategy is partially unintended (emergent) is gaining increasing support (e.g., Mintzberg, 1978; Mintzberg & Waters, 1982, 1984, 1985; Mintzberg & McHugh, 1985; Quinn, 1980; Wheelwright, 1984) and is useful in supporting the linkage being established between HRM and strategy formulation, which is a pivotal theme in this book. By viewing strategy as both intended and emergent decisions, the role of allied contributors can be viewed differently. Intended components are more like full strides, developed from a formal planning effort, while the emergent components are more like a series of child-size steps. The traditional HRM impact has been seen in terms of its ability to keep the large strides on track, but HRM systems can also formulate strategy by taking emergent steps. The consideration here will relate to the more traditional role for HRM systems, while the emergent role of HRM will be discussed in Chapter Four.

When strategy is considered in intended terms, HRM's contribution tends to be rather mechanically framed within one of the existing components. The strategic process is seen as a distinct set of activities, each with a discrete output, and the nature of the HRM contribution is seen in similar terms. The initial contributions of HRM to strategy were set in terms of this intended-decision model because the framing of their contribution in a manner that corresponded to that used by the planning group was required to gain entry. This is because staff and functional areas, wishing to make their initial strategic contribution, had to present it in a manner that related to the existing model used by those charged with formal planning. Initial strategic HRM research attempted to match its value to discrete events in the strategic process (e.g., Devanna, Fombrun, & Tichy, 1981). For instance, while there is now less debate about the value of a HRM contribution, some research suggests that HRM has to be fit into the internal or external scanning apparatus to be seen as having value during this stage of the strategic process (e.g., Aguilar, 1967; Venkatraman & Camillus, 1984; Hitt, Ireland, & Palia, 1982). At the implementation stage HRM's contribution was seen as an obvious tool for dealing with resistance. Resistance has often been encountered by many planning departments when they were first established and HRM was seen as having a role in ensuring that new strategies were not adversely affected by deep-seated organizational resistance (e.g., Lenz & Lyles, 1981; Lyles & Lenz, 1982). These were areas where HRM could make a contribution and, more importantly, that contribution was recognized and accepted by those responsible for strategic planning.

During the initial stages of the strategy process, which are primarily evaluative, HRM could be related to internal resources capabilities. New strategies might require new skills and HRM professionals are capable of highlighting this fact. This can be especially relevant during the assessment of alternatives. The argument to include HRM managers in strategic planning met with less resistance because it was easy to highlight cases where past participation could have produced more satisfactory results. Identifying human resources hurdles that might affect the optimal strategic choice requires a sufficient time horizon to ensure that needed HRM components are in place. Because strategic choice was seen in discrete terms, needed HRM complementary contributions were also seen in these terms. In addition to this limitation in scope, this tended to limit the impact of HRM to those times when choices about new strategic directions are being made.

Current practice suggests that HRM managers may be part of the formulation and evaluation process, but the focus of their contribution tends to be seen as related to implementation. Once a strategy is selected, the implementation role of HRM is even more direct. Under ideal conditions, the HRM group should begin work on those problem areas that had been previously identified as inhibiting the desired strategic outcomes. Beyond this preplanned facilitation, HRM can also provide *ad hoc* assistance to the strategy implementation process by dealing with unanticipated problems as they emerge. A certain amount of HRM flexibility is needed because the extent and nature of organizational resistance and the exact human-planning needs for a particular strategy cannot be perfectly precalculated. Under an ideal system, HRM managers would be able to engage in independent action designed to facilitate implementation. Ongoing communication between the various functional and staff groups is required so that there is an appreciation of the forces being brought to bear to expedite the chosen strategy. For this reason it is suggested that HRM managers have access to both formal and informal avenues of communication, which prevents their contribution from having to fit into an agenda with a limited time frame where they can only provide formal input.

HRM managers use their expertise and information to influence the selection of the "best alternative." They tend to do this by mapping the full range of their content responsibilities, which were outlined in Chapter Two, on issues related to strategy implementation. While the foci of their contributions centered on implementation, once they became involved in the strategy-making process the HRM group gradually expanded the range of its inputs. Thus, the decision to include HRM managers more fully in the strategic planning process, both formally and informally, was based on improving the chances for optimal alternative-selection and facilitating implementation rather than broadening the formulation base. The intended-strategy model could not easily provide an action mechanism for the HRM group to actually make strategy. The addition of an emergent component to the strategy model permits the consideration of certain benefits available from HRM that could not be theoretically justified from the intended model.

STRATEGY AS AN EMERGENT CONCEPT

A series of studies by Mintzberg and his colleagues (Mintzberg, 1978, 1987; Mintzberg & McHugh, 1985; Mintzberg & Waters, 1982, 1984, 1985) were directed toward examining strategy as a process. By identifying and classifying decisions, they found that consistent patterns tended to emerge. It is these consistent patterns that actually identify the realized strategy of the firm. By investigating the origins of these strategies, they found that the realized strategy reflected both intended decisions made in a formal strategy process and emergent decisions that were more *ad hoc.* They concluded "there is no such thing as a purely deliberate [intended] or purely emergent strategy" because

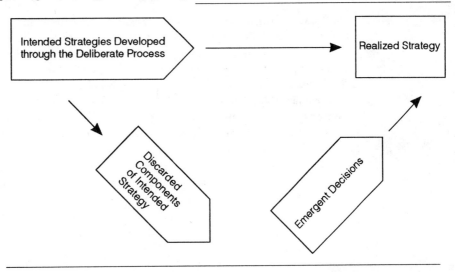

FIGURE 3-2. A model of the emergent strategic management process. (Adapted from Mintzberg, H. and Waters, J.A., 'Of strategies deliberate and emergent', _Strategic Management Journal_, Vol. 6, p. 258. Copyright 1985). Reprinted by permission of John Wiley and Sons.)

the realized strategy represented both components (Mintzberg, 1987, p. 69). The general form of this model is depicted in Figure 3-2.

The proportion of realized strategy that is intended or emergent bears some relationship to both organizational characteristics and the nature of the environmental impact. By tracking the strategic decisions of Steinberg, Inc. (Mintzberg & Waters, 1985), Canadian Lady (Mintzberg & Waters, 1982), and the Film Board of Canada (Mintzberg & McHugh, 1985), Mintzberg and his colleagues were able to provide systematic support for the existence of emergent components in the realized strategy. In the case of Steinberg, Inc., these decisions appeared to be both opportunistic and planned. In some cases planning seemed to deal more with publicizing the existing strategy than with formulating new strategies. By tracking the firm from its entrepreneurial stages to the present, they found that the culture at the top had a major impact on the strategic behaviors that emerged. They also found that the strategy-influencing behavior of managers, while affecting the organization, was also affected by it (Starbuck & Hedberg, 1977). The presence of an emergent component was confirmed in a follow-up study at Canadian Lady (Mintzberg & Waters, 1984). That firm, a manufacturer of women's undergarments, which was also started by an entrepreneur, parallels many of the patterns of strategy-making seen at Steinberg, Inc.

Having established that dual sources exist for strategy-type decisions and the importance of the interrelationship between managers and organization, Mintzberg and McHugh (1985) looked to determine the impact of the organization's design. In a study of the National Film Board of Canada, they found that an adhocracy form of management (Bennis & Stater, 1964; Toffler, 1970) was especially suitable for organizations with unique outputs, facing dynamic and complex environments. The role of managers in directly affecting strategy, through their behavior, was observed in the adhocracy configuration. Ideas for films emerged from the bottom of the organization and structure was adapted to satisfy production needs. Consistent strategies seemed to emerge because the organization wanted to take advantage of the knowledge and skills of employees as well as the current norms of the organization. External events, financing options, and some intended top-down plans also affected the strategy that emerged. In this case the adhocracy appears to be especially suited to take advantage of environmental opportunities as they emerged.

Mintzberg and McHugh (1985, pp. 194–195) used this study to provide support for a different classification of the formulation process. Allegorically, the emergent component of strategy was seen much like a weed. Some of the decisions in a realized strategy could be traced back to carefully cultivated intended decisions made during the deliberate strategy-formulation process. Other decisions were like weeds, and were part of the realized strategy because they had been gathered by some individual manager who had sufficient authority to act. In this respect the prevailing culture of the organization has a major impact, when the percentage of the realized strategy that is emergent is higher. The second aspect that was found relevant was the degree of consistency between emergent decisions. Since consistent patterns of behavior often were preceded by periods of divergence, it appears that across-organization communication may gradually lead to more consistent behavior. It would also appear that universal participation, by those capable of making strategic decisions, is important. Clearly, HRM managers would fall into this category since many of the decisions they have been delegated have the potential for long-term impacts on the competitive position of the firm.

The linkage between thought and action, first developed by Mises (1949), is necessary if learning and consistency are to be achieved across the various actors making decisions that could be classified as emergent. Patterns emerge and these can be classified as strengths when the linkage between ideas becomes sufficiently consistent. In firms the consistency through learning that results from a positively cast emergent strategy, becomes institutionalized. Mintzberg points out that this can be a very hands-on process.

> Managers who craft strategy do not spend much time in executive suites reading MIS reports or industry analysis. They are involved, responsive to their materials, learning about their organizations and industries through personal touch. They are also sensitive to experience, recognizing that while individual vision may be important, other factors must help determine strategy as well (Mintzberg, 1987, p. 73).

Thus, it appears that certain norms begin to develop with respect to decisions that affect the emergent-strategy component of a firm.

The use of a central vision, clearly communicated to all managers, is one way to ensure that emergent decisions are consistent with intended decisions. The establishment of shared beliefs, use of boundary constraints and process controls are all designed to ensure consistency but limit the extent of the emergent component. By removing constraints on where strategies can emerge, the organization is more likely to have a larger proportion of this component reflected in its strategy. This makes it more difficult to maintain consistency across emergent components and between emergent and intended components. Thus, the organization can choose to encourage and increase the component of strategy that is emergent by increasing the range of acceptable origins for this component.

THE CONTINUUM OF REALIZED STRATEGY

A final issue to be considered is the proportion of realized strategy that should represent emergent decisions. This relates back to a central issue in strategy formulation concerning the extent to which the environment is imposing solutions. For the organization it is important that there be a correspondence between the way intended and emergent decisions are relating to the environment. Although the environment will dictate certain patterns of response, and in a rare instance may completely dominate a firm's strategic decisions, this is not a sustainable long-term situation. Figure 3-3 represents the continuum between a totally planned (intended) and totally environmentally-imposed (emergent) decision (Mintzberg & Waters, 1985).

While each of the strategies depicted represents points along a continuum of varying degrees of environmental imposition, these categorizations are intended to depict typical proportions of emergent decision making for the strategy, not law-like statements. In all cases the environment is a contingency variable because it also affects the proportion of realized strategy that represents emergent decisions. Thus, the notion of strategy being both intended and emergent requires that the firm also relate the source of strategy to environmental conditions. This is necessary so that there is consistency between the source and type of strategy. For corporate components, such as HRM, this is especially important because their boundary-spanning role means that they are more likely to be aware of the need to make what is essentially an environmentally-imposed decision. To get a better appreciation of how these tradeoffs are played out, the discussion that follows looks at several cases where firms are forced to deal with the variation in forces as depicted in Figure 3-3.

Environmental Influences

Edward C. Acker, CEO of Pan American World Airways headed a firm that had historically been facing a placid environment where a totally intended mode of decision making was highly desirable. When the environment changed it began to impose certain decisions on Pan Am. Assets had to be sold, market share sacrificed, and operating profits disappeared (Bennett, 1987).

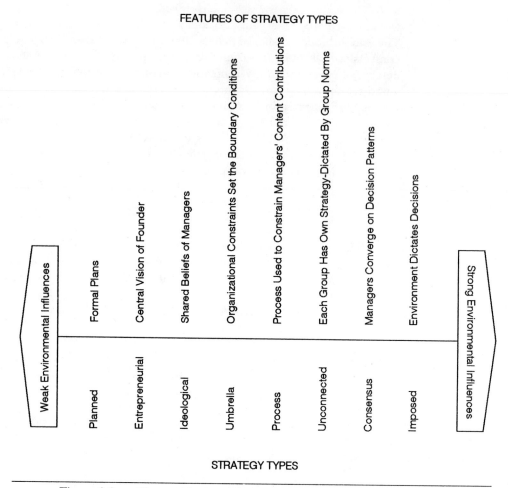

Figure 3-3.   **The continuum of strategy types and their associated features
the range of environmental influences.**

Banks were no longer willing to extend credit and even Pan Am's attempt to
sell junk bonds failed. When events in Europe, such as bombings of jets and
the devaluation of the dollar occurred, Pan Am appeared incapable of making
the type of emergent decisions that were needed.

Thus, while cost cutting and asset sales were imposed by the environment, it appears that these decisions only emerged because of strong environmental pressure, but this did not enhance the firm's capability of making
emergent decisions. When European demand dropped in 1986, Pan Am
should have made a series of decisions that would have reallocated planes from
European to North American routes. However, the environmentally-forced
nature of some of its emergent financial decisions appeared to leave it even
less capable of making emergent decisions in the operational area. It also

appeared that its planning department had lost much of its ability to competently formulate strategy in an intended manner. From an organizational perspective this may mean that it is unwise to reduce either the intended or emergent component beyond some point. There may actually be a "forgetting curve" operating that results in firms becoming less efficient at developing intended components of strategy.

A second interesting aspect of Pan Am intended strategy relates to the source of decisions that are not environmentally imposed. A stream of emergent decisions appeared to flow from Acker's macro-financial perspective of the firm's strategy. However, the views of most operating managers centered more on Pan Am as an operating airline. The shared beliefs of management, which should serve as a guide and constructive force in emergent decision-making, showed the CEO and the operating managers operating on two different sets of beliefs. Since this divergence is likely to be recognized by operating managers, it is unlikely that they will engage in much emergent decision-making although this is exactly what the firm may need. The firm ends up in a situation where there is no effective mechanism guiding its emergent decisions.

While the value of shared beliefs is important it does not relate to situations such as at Atlantic Stewardship Bank that pays "10% of its pretax profits to Christian Charities" (Moffett, 1985, p. 33). In this case the shared values do not seem to be reflected in strategic decisions. However at Odetics, a high-technology electronics firm, a strong belief in the value of having fun appears to be directed toward a strategic purpose (Apcar, 1985). Belly dancers, a company alligator, a swimming pool, and even a sock hop are designed to support a climate of creativity. The company has two flags that proclaim "Long Live Liberty" and "An Adventure in American Creativity." These seem to reflect a tone of shared values that is desired to encourage emergent decisions designed to provide the firm with a competitive edge when developing products for the space and defense industry.

Changing Patterns of Environmental Influence

Another interesting question relates to how firms cope with changing environmental influences. In the 1970s Gulf Oil was a firm that appeared to seldom let environmental factors interfere with its intended strategy. Gulf did not let U.S. Government objections interfere with its exploration activities in Angola. The way the organization controlled the environment may not have been exemplary and "Gulf had the Foreign Corrupt Practices Act created virtually in their honor" (Brinelow, 1981, p. 7).Gulf's diversification strategy was so planned that Brinelow (1981, p. 7) thought it would "try to take over Moscow Norondy Bank" if that contributed to its strategy. Money was dispensed to national and international figures and shareholders and outside board members were viewed with suspicion (Wyndham, 1976). The focus was on reducing environmental influences so that the intended strategy could proceed uninhibited.

By the 1980s conditions had changed dramatically in the oil industry. Environmental influences were unpredictable and oil firms' stock was trading at bargain prices. It was no longer possible to operate in a manner that constrained emergent decisions and ignored environmental imperatives. Eventually SOCAL acquired Gulf, and a *Business Week* (1984) cover story characterized Gulf's CEO as dallying and unaware of the threat from competitors. In fact the reaction to the takeover attempt among Gulf executives was incredulity, tinged with anger (Wells & Hymowitz, 1984). Interestingly, Gulf had begun to allow a great deal of emergent decisions just as it began to feel the effects of its past model of intended strategy-making. SOCAL had begun the adjustment much earlier although the evolution had been more gradual. While the causes of SOCAL's acquisition of Gulf are complex and relate to a host of issues, Gulf's inability to balance emergent and intended components of strategy with environmental change may have also been a contributing factor.

SUMMARY AND CONCLUSIONS

The theoretical justification for an elaboration of the strategy-making process was outlined in this chapter. The recognition that there is an emergent component in the firm's realized strategy makes the contribution of all staff and functional areas, outside of the planning department, more relevant. This is because the level of strategic contributions moves from persuasion to direct action. For the firm, this means that its relationship to the environment is more likely to produce appropriately induced decisions. Emergent decisions, likely to be affected by the environment, can be controlled through a variety of techniques that include entrepreneurial vision, shared beliefs, and concurrence.

From an outcome perspective, the notion of emergent strategy requires a respecification of the profit model guiding the firm. Because both the proportion of, and the means used to guide, emergent decisions relates at the individual level, the impact of HRM is more relevant. The general model seems to suggest that HRM should have a larger role to play in setting up the conditions that guide emergent decisions as well as playing a direct role in strategy-making. It is this expanded role for HRM that is discussed in the next chapter.

A PROFIT-GENERATION THEORY OF STRATEGIC HUMAN RESOURCES MANAGEMENT

If the activities of men were arranged in sequence according to the degree in which he shares them with other parts of the animal kingdom, theory making would surely rank amongst the most exclusively human (Shackle, 1967, p.1).

ANTECEDENTS OF A THEORY

The development of a theory, which relates to the profit-generating capability of HRM, requires the consideration of several important antecedents. Thus, the discussion of HRM in Chapter Two drew from the main theoretical streams that characterize much of the research in the strategy-HRM area (e.g., Dyer, 1985; Gould, 1984; Henn, 1985; Walker, 1980). In Chapter Two the emphasis was on the functional expertise provided by the HRM group and the value of exploiting that expertise during the organization's formal planning process. Using that functional HRM expertise to improve the probability for successful strategy implementation was a central issue in the discussion of the HRM process. The discussion of the HRM process, in turn, was used to show how specific HRM actions could facilitate both strategic objectives and bottom-line outcomes (Evans, 1986; Frohman, 1984; Misa & Stein, 1983). The early placement of that interrelated model, introduced in Chapter Two, was necessary because it comprises important antecedent streams of theory.

An additional antecedent stream was discussed in Chapter Three. There, strategic management was examined in terms of both its intended and unintended components. This dual-role theory of strategy provides a justification for increasing HRM's operating latitude, which is important to the theory of strategic human resources management (SHRM), which is developed in this chapter.

PROFIT AND THE STRATEGY-HRM RELATIONSHIP

The existing theoretical antecedents, extracted from the strategic management and HRM literature, are important but they fail to provide an explanation of how the ongoing strategy-HRM relationship produces profit, and tend to skirt the issue of autonomous strategic action. The development of a theory of SHRM suggests that it is important to justify the efforts, and associated investment, needed to effect this coupling and to show that positive performance outcomes are likely. While the concentration, in this book, is on profit-generation, this should not be interpreted as disparagement of research that has focused more narrowly on the value of it to successful strategy implementation. It does suggest the manner by which this linkage actually generates profits, such as are associated with investments relating to capital assets or new products. The question driving this research extends to the determination of how investments in the strategy-HRM linkage can produce behavior that reflects the same rate of return as other successful projects. Even more important is the conceptual analysis needed to move beyond a normatively constructed explanation of the theory of strategic human resources management.

Since profit is realized in the marketplace, the market mechanism seemed the logical place to look, to determine if its operation could provide the means to explain a profit-generating strategy-HRM interface. In economics most discussions of the market mechanism use a comparative statics approach. The intersection of the supply and demand curves, at a given point in time or under a particular set of conditions, represents the focus of the analysis. The intersection marks equilibrium, which serves as a comparison point with equilibrium points prevailing under different conditions. The efficient operation of markets is usually related to perfect and complete information requirements. The acceptable rate of return is incorporated into the equilibrium price-quantity position, and profits cannot exceed this rate because adjustments are viewed as instantaneous. Figure 4-1 represents such a model, with equilibrium points E_1 and E_2 marking two different price-quantity positions. With this form of analysis, considerations relate to the benefits associated with being at one equilibrium position vis-a-vis another. Thus, what becomes important is the determination if [(price)(quantity) -(costs)] at E_1 is larger than at E_2. If the equilibrium position is not optimal there will be an adjustment, but the exact firm-specific behavior involved in this adjustment is not normally considered. The type of behavior that occurs as the firm adjusts to equilibrium-point changes—in the example depicted in Figure 4-1 this might involve the movement from E_1 to E_2—provides an essential piece of theory in the model developed here.

A theoretical stream of research that relates to this movement, between what are perceived to be points of equilibrium, provides the final theoretical antecedents needed to construct the model. Imperfections, with respect to the dissemination of information, are used to move toward a dynamic analysis of the market. This concept of market dynamics is used to develop a theoretical basis for the above-normal profits that can result from SHRM action. The concept of a synergistic interface and its associated benefits are not being discarded, but additional types of SHRM behavior will be introduced that are often equated with entrepreneurial behavior (e.g. Dolan, 1976; Kirzner, 1973, 1979). SHRM behavior is possible because of the uncertainty and variety of

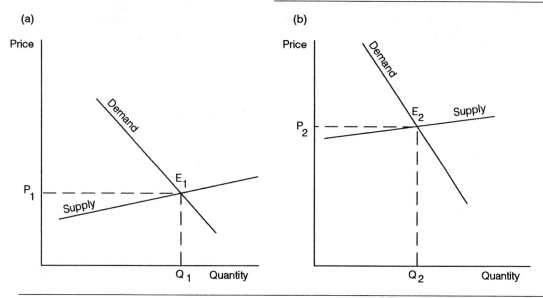

FIGURE 4-1. Price/quantity market equilibrium positions for two different time periods.

estimates that exist among competing firms with respect to the exact price-quantity relationships prevailing in the market at a particular time. Thus, the relationship between HRM action and concepts related to less-perfect market dynamics provides the logic behind this performance-enhancing link. It also helps us understand how HRM policies and action work to facilitate implementation and/or actually formulate strategy. Thus, in this chapter these antecedents related to opportunity-availability, market dynamics, and HRM entrepreneurial action are combined with earlier theoretical antecedents to complete the theory of how SHRM generates profit. A conceptual model of this process is then developed.

THE AVAILABILITY OF OPPORTUNITY

The availability of market opportunities provides the stimuli for SHRM actions. With respect to strategy implementation, HRM has face validity, but the constant availability of opportunities provides a reason for extending its role beyond facilitating. Thus, to a certain extent the suggestion will be made that the HRM function also move beyond the comparative statics of textbook economics, as depicted in Figure 4-1, toward a more dynamic conceptualization. Such a dynamic concept of the market, built on the availability of opportunities, has been long theorized by economists of the Austrian School (e.g., Bohm-Bawerk, 1884; Hayek, 1937, 1945; Kirzner, 1973, 1979; Mises, 1949). The dynamic view of the market-adjustment process, which relates to the movement between equilibrium and disequilibrium, will be used to illustrate how performance outcomes can be obtained through SHRM action. To provide the justification for above-average returns, action is equated to entrepreneurial behavior. These concepts combine to produce an HRM action-and-response capability, which makes it relevant to (1) a more comprehensive strategy-implementation role, (2) a direct role in developing organizational norms that are conducive for unintended strategic action, and (3) the display of entrepreneurial behavior. All three roles have the effect of enhancing strategic objectives and bottom-line profit.

Constraints of an Equilibrium Perspective

Interestingly, the justification for a theory of less perfect market dynamics flows from the nature of the constraints associated with using an equilibrium perspective, where all participants are knowledgeable about price and quantity positions (e.g. Clark, 1907; Keynes, 1936; Marshall, 1890; Walras, 1926). Neoclassical economic notions about markets being in equilibrium required perfect and complete information by all participants. The theory also seemed to imply that markets must be driven into disequilibrium if advantage is to be gained (e.g., Morgenstern, 1976; Richardson, 1960). Price-quantity positions were the focus of concentration and the movement from one equilibrium position to another was seen as instantaneous, or a given. Omitted were the time frame in which the adjustment occurs and questions relating to the potential of firms to gain advantage during this period of adjustment.

Schumpeter (1934, 1942) provided the reasoning as to how profit flowed to firms during the market-adjustment process. He attempted to fit his theory into prevailing concepts by using entrepreneurial behavior as the disequilibrium mechanism. He saw new products and technologies as the tools used to disrupt the market mechanism and believed these disruptions explained why the market moved from one price-quantity position to another. Firms introducing new products or manufacturing with new technologies were able to charge less for the same product or more for an enhanced product. Schumpeter envisioned this as their reward for entrepreneurial behavior. However, he did not view market distortions as the norm because competitors normally could copy the original innovation. The movement of the entire market to a new equilibrium position provided the explanation for real economic growth. His framework allowed individuals and firms to achieve entrepreneurial profits but placed some constraints on action. Second-mover firms were normally assumed to take action directed toward copying the original entrepreneur, although the potential to bypass through a new series of innovations was recognized.

Schumpeter's view of how disequilibrium occurs is consistent with the dominant perspectives of strategy research and the strengths-weaknesses-opportunities-threats (SWOT) analysis commonly used in teaching, which suggests that managers map the firm's strengths and weaknesses on environmental threats and opportunity (e.g., Alexander, O'Neill, Snyder, & Townsend, 1984; Learned et al., 1965). The belief that strategy helps create its own opportunities, in a proactive and intended way through the manipulation of factors within the control of management, can be equated to the entrepreneurial behavior that Schumpeter (1934) theorized produced market disequilibrium. The defensive side of strategy can be seen as part of the second-mover copying that restores market equilibrium and eliminates the competitive advantage of the entrepreneur. Unlike many economists, Schumpeter recognized that the lags between the initial disequilibrium-creating action and the return to equilibrium had a time dimension. However, his focus was on the creation of disequilibrium, and strategy played a role to the extent it facilitated the development of new products or technologies. In this framework HRM, like most functional areas, was left in an accommodating posture more suited toward strategy implementation.

Information Fragmentation

Leading theorists of the Austrian School of Economics have consistently attempted to explain firm and individual behavior in terms that recognize that markets are never in equilibrium because information is usually too fragmented among participants (e.g., Bohm-Bawerk, 1884; Kirzner, 1973, 1985; Mises, 1949). This position sacrifices the theoretical convenience of using equilibrium as a "point of tranquility" when considering price-quantity relationships. Between-firm comparisons are much more complicated, but our knowledge about decision making and strategy formulation suggests that a diverse range of perceptions actually exists about price-quantity positions and relationships (e.g., Quinn, 1980; Simon, 1976). This range of perceptions results from the imperfect nature of information search and information processing (Hayek, 1937). The nature and extent of these imperfections, associated with information collection and processing, is unique to each market participant. In total, the extreme perceptions, marking the high and low estimates of price-quantity positions, are what define the full impact of "information fragmentation." Thus, a market system is characterized by multiple beliefs about both prices charged and the quantities of products and services offered. This range of perceptions provides the reason markets are always in disequilibrium. Each firm assumes the market is in equilibrium, but each has a different perception about the location of the equilibrium point. The range of points defines the extent of disequilibrium. The extent of disequilibrium provides a measure of the population of opportunities.

Figure 4-2 is designed to help clarify how this divergence of perceptions leads to opportunity creation. The single set of supply and demand curves, popularized by Marshall (1890) and depicted in Figure 4-1, has been expanded to depict a market that is characterized by a wide range of perceptions about prices and quantity. The unique perceptions of each firm result in a series of demand and supply curves, each of which has some relevance. The curves that mark the extreme bounds of these perceptions are depicted in Figure 4-2. They combine to create an "area available for opportunity exploitation" and it is in this area where action can lead to enhanced performance outcomes. The "area available for opportunity exploitation," shaded in Figure 4-2, suggests the limits to profit-generation available from action at a given point in time and

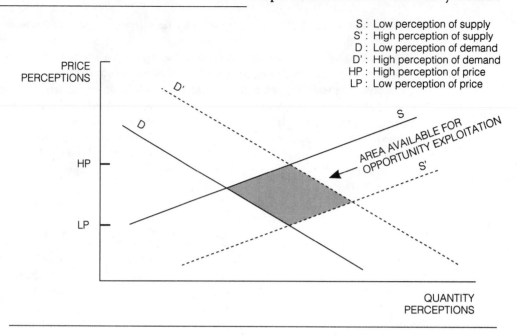

FIGURE 4-2. Perceptions of price/quantity market equilibrium positions across multiple observers in a single time period.

with respect to a specific market. The distance between D and D' represents the extreme range of perceptions about demand. Similarly, the distance between S and S' represents the range of perceptions about supply. A similar range of perceptions would also exist about the appropriate shape of the supply and demand curves. Obviously, the range of perceptions with respect to shape might also have major competitive implications with respect to price-quantity tradeoffs. The "area available for opportunity exploitation" captures the full extent of these distortions and indicates the magnitude of opportunity-identification possibilities with respect to any particular market. A similar area would exist with respect to any two firms, or sets of firms, within an industry. However, any firm might be able to exploit these differences in perceptions to its own advantage, especially in an industry that is segmented geographically. A firm might choose to compete in or avoid certain markets, based on the prevailing range of perceptions that characterized the existing competitors within a particular segment. This "area available for exploiting opportunity" is in constant flux because perceptions constantly change as a result of information collection and processing. Strategy defines the relevant market but the size of the "area available for opportunity exploitation" cannot be precisely forecast and constantly changes. This ever-changing population of opportunities provides the action arena for HRM by providing an explanation of how its action contributes to profit and/or creates conditions leading to competitive advantage.

The connection between information fragmentation and the level of opportunities is especially relevant to HRM because of the important role it should play in the collection, processing, and assessment of information. With respect to the acquisition, development, and maintenance of human resources, the HRM group is in the best position to gauge the degree of variance in firms' perceptions. To the degree that the labor component is significant in the production of a product or service, so will be the potential profit associated with the content expertise of the HRM group. This may be especially relevant in a labor-intensive industry because the total potential returns from exploiting information discrepancies in the labor market could be significant. Firms capable of using their HRM expertise for competitive advantage should welcome the uncertainty flowing from information fragmentation. The higher the level of uncertainty the greater the extent of market disequilibrium, which gives more strategic value to HRM than is possible if markets were really characterized by equilibrium and perfect information assumptions. Disequilibrium creates the "area available for opportunity exploitation" that makes it possible for HRM to impact directly on the firm's performance. Because uncertainty always exists and because profit opportunities flow from this uncertainty, profit opportunities are always available and unique efforts are not required to bring them into existence. More important to the firm is the generation of actions that convert these opportunities into what Kirzner (1973, 1979) would label entrepreneurial profit.

While information fragmentation provides the opportunity for an HRM contribution, it does not assume any firm-specific conversions. In fact, all competitors may be earning normal, and acceptable, rates of return. Little pressure may be on any functional area or staff group to engage in the entrepreneurial behavior needed to exploit these opportunities. The real incentive to develop an organization capable of this type of action has as much to do with strategic outcomes as with short-term entrepreneurial profits. HRM action introduces an unintended component into the emerged strategy and, through the feedback process, this eventually provides strong signals to those responsible for formal planning. As was pointed out in Chapter Three, successful strategies have both an intended and unintended component, and the role of "action" to the unintended component is discussed next.

THE USE OF ACTION

Opportunity becomes more than an object of theoretical interest when the action side of the equation is considered. Some measure of the potential return from action can be gauged by the distance between the lowest perception of price [LP] and the highest perception of price [HP]. Figure 4-2 can be used to illustrate how this process might occur. Assume Firm A believes that LP is the appropriate perception of price. Firm A believes market demand is low relative to supply and that the intersection of D (i.e., the lowest perception of the demand curve) and S' (i.e., the highest perception of the supply curve) indicate market equilibrium. Under these conditions Firm A would set its price at LP. Assume Firm B is a second competitor, believes demand is much higher, and that the intersection of D' (the highest perception of the demand curve) and S (the lowest perception of the supply curve) marks the appropriate equilibrium point. Firm B could be expected to set its price at HP. Now, from a practical standpoint one might conclude that Firm A would sell all of its output at LP while Firm B would only be left with residual demand at HP. However, if these competitors are operating in different segments or countries their perceptions might be based on actual market conditions, which means that individual firms' sales might not immediately reflect these distortions in perceptions.

Now the question might be asked, if neither firm's sales are affected, why do these distortions in perceptions matter? The reason is that any firm capable of noticing these discrepancies is capable of exploiting the situation. For instance, assume that another competitor, Firm C, is operating in the same industry. Firm C's perception is that the appropriate price falls somewhere between the perceptions of Firm A and Firm B. Such a position might be characterized by the intersection of D and S, which means Firm C has a low perception of both the demand and supply curves. If Firm C became aware of the divergence in the price perceptions of Firm A and Firm B, it could make a decision to expand output, enter Firm B's market, and sell at some price equal to or less than HP. In this way Firm C would increase revenue and we can assume it would earn an acceptable return on the assets needed to produce this additional output. Alternatively, Firm C could purchase the additional output from Firm A at LP and then market it in Firm B's segment at HP. In this case the return [(HP - LP)(quantity)-(additional transaction costs)] would be independent of an asset investment and the expectation of returns associated with expanding production capacity. Obviously, this example is somewhat contrived, but it emphasizes that opportunity noticing is important and that action can lead to profit. Firm C recognized that a gap between Firm A's and Firm B's price perceptions could be exploited. The fact that there are multiple inputs and markets to consider may complicate this process, but it also expanded the opportunities for action.

Thus, as appropriate action is taken on noticed opportunities, the distance between D and D' (the highest and lowest perceptions of demand) and S and S' (the highest and lowest perceptions of supply) decreases. This compression in the range of perceptions occurs because action facilitates information dissemination and processing, which reduces the fragmentation-of-information effect. This convergence may actually result in the market temporarily reaching an equilibrium position, where there will be no area available for the exploitation of opportunity. However, these periods of limited opportunity will be short-lived, because new applications, uses, and environmental changes will reactivate the information-fragmentation/perception-distortion process. In many cases, these external distortions will also provide the impetus for a reformulation of the intended components of strategy. They also provide the incentive for unintended action by facilitating opportunity identification for firms having this capability. HRM is relevant because it can play a role with respect to the formulation and implementation of new strategies.

Because of its boundary-spanning role, HRM is well positioned to notice market opportunities, and is capable of actions that contribute to the unintended strategic component through the exploitation of market opportunities.

HRM as Initiator, Facilitator, Enhancer

The dual strategic contribution possible from HRM, which is based on and represents an elaboration of the Mintzberg and Water's model (see Figure 3-1), is depicted in Figure 4-3. This model can be interpreted as depicting HRM as (1) an **initiator** of action, (2) a **facilitator** of action, and (3) an **enhancer** of strategy. To the extent that HRM uses policies and actions that lead to direct exploitation of available opportunities, it acts as an initiator by contributing to the component of strategy that is unintended. This type of strategic action can flow from any of HRM's content areas of expertise. To the extent that HRM policies influence the norms, culture, and behavior of the organization it acts as a facilitator for action by others. This action is also reflected in the unintended-strategy component. Finally, as an enhancer, HRM provides important human resources inputs during formal strategy formulation and then adapts human planning systems in ways that enhance the prospects for the successful implementation. A more detailed discussion of each HRM role follows.

The model of the strategy process depicted in Figure 4-3 is not intended to diminish the importance of HRM with respect to formal planning, strategy

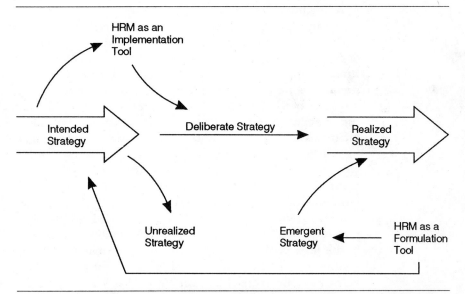

FIGURE 4-3. Model of the strategic process that includes the HRM input as both an intended and realized component (adapted from Mintzberg, H. and Waters, J. A., 'Of strategies deliberate and emergent,' *Strategic Management Journal*, Vol. 6, p. 258. Copyright, 1985). Reprinted by permission of John Wiley and Sons.

formulation, or implementation. It is designed to depict an enhanced HRM function. The proportion of emerged strategy that is intended should normally be high, and HRM policies are important with respect to its implementation. During the formal planning process, HRM professionals can provide valuable inputs that should be considered before selecting from the feasible strategy alternatives (Alpander & Botter, 1981; Baird, Meshoulam, & DeGive, 1983; Galosy, 1983; Mills, 1985). HRM considerations that are relevant can be presented during the formulation process so existing constraints will not be first surfaced after the fact. HRM also becomes important after the strategy has been formulated. Almost all formulated strategies can be presumed to require some HRM adjustments that are specifically related to enhancing the prospects for successful implementation. Synergy considerations are important and the content expertise of HRM can be brought to bear so that a productive strategy-HRM interface results. Thus, as an enhancer, HRM has both a pre- and post-formulation role.

As a facilitator, HRM is important because it can modify certain natural tendencies of the bureaucratic process. This role relates directly to the concept of organizational flexibility. As organizations grow (Child & Keiser, 1981; Kamien & Schwartz, 1976) and age (Starbuck, 1965), they become more bureaucratic. Peterson (1981) actually labeled this dysfunctional process "the iron law of ossification." This same process can occur within the HRM group as they "become more rigidly systematic in the way they define jobs, delineate objectives, and narrow task focus and responsibility" (Levinson, 1970, p.140). Avoiding the effects of ossification is important because it restricts the ability of the firm to act. This becomes critical during periods when organization-environment relations are undergoing rapid changes, such as are common during periods of environmental turbulence (e.g., Ansoff, 1979). This is why a strategic approach to HRM would suggest different HRM strategies (e.g., performance evaluation and reward systems, staffing) at different points in the evolution of the life cyle or age of the firm. HRM's facilitator role suggests its use to reduce the impact of age and growth on flexibility so that the firm maintains a competitive advantage with respect to action on opportunities, and in redefining its organization-environment relations during periods of environmental turbulence. In this role HRM policies are used to create conditions that facilitate entrepreneurial action that contributes to the unintended-strategy component.

While information fragmentation sets the limits for opportunity exploitation at the market level, organizational flexibility may further constrain action at the level of the firm. Organizational flexibility also defines the limits of contribution possible from HRM, with respect to unintended action. Firms lacking a sufficient level of flexibility are likely to foster and develop organizational capabilities directed toward insuring implementation of their intended strategy. Control mechanisms will be developed and monitored to reduce the portion of intended strategy that becomes unrealized. While this appears desirable, from an implementation perspective, these excess controls will limit the action-related contributions by those most capable of exploiting opportunity. Realized strategy will be much closer to intended strategy, but the situation will not be optimal in a competitive sense, especially in those industries characterized by a wide range of perceptions, with competitors having higher levels of flexibility.

To a certain extent, the ability of the HRM group to be an initiator of strategic action depends on its success as a facilitator. HRM is constrained by organizational norms that stress controls rather than encouraging action, just as are other groups and individuals in the organization. HRM's role as a strategy initiator has tended to be ignored in the literature and, because it relates to the unintended component of strategy, it has historically been viewed as a "maintenance function." Until the studies by Mintzberg and his colleagues (Mintzberg, 1978; Mintzberg & McHugh, 1985; Mintzberg & Waters, 1983, 1984, 1985), this aspect of strategy formulation received little attention. The impact of HRM on the underlying culture of the firm is widely accepted, but the ability of what has often been seen as a lower-status group (e.g. Schlesinger, 1983) to engage in action that could be characterized as entrepreneurial is novel. However, if one looks at the breadth and impact of HRM policies and actions, it seems pervasive, and its potential for generating profits is as likely as for other functional and staff areas. In addition, the HRM function tends to be in a continuous-action mode, which suggests HRM may be better positioned for ongoing action.

Consequences of Action

A final consideration relates to the consequences resulting from action. What happens to the firm and industry as a result of action on opportunity? In the case of the industry, action brings additional information to all market participants. This information is especially valuable to those firms with the most extreme perceptions, because the benefits from adjustment are greater. Thus, in our earlier example, Firm A would become aware that its perception about market price was too low, while Firm B would discover that its was too high. When the firms adjust their market prices, Firm A should be able to get a higher price for its output while Firm B should be able to recover lost demand by lowering its price. Eventually, Firm C should no longer be able to exploit the difference between them.

Now the benefits associated with the decision by Firm C to not invest in additional production facilities become more apparent. If they had invested in plant and machinery, as demand declined, they would have been forced to decide between capacity underutilization and price reductions. In either case, this would result in a return that was no longer acceptable. However, if Firm C had used entrepreneurial action to exploit this situation, it would not incur a performance-penalty after the price adjustments by Firm A and Firm B. Now, two different firms will have the extreme perceptions of price. If the gap between these firms' perceptions of price is sufficiently large, Firm C can repeat the process. Obviously, firms capable of this type of action on a continuous basis should have a long-term competitive advantage.

Although not theoretically formalized in exactly the same terms as above, much of the recent research on planning-systems development has advocated high levels of initiatives for all areas of the organization (e.g., Chakvarthy & Lorange, 1984). Notions about strategies being changed on some scheduled basis are being replaced by the recognition that strategic planning is a complex and continuous process and that the firm does not stop operating between formal planning sessions (e.g., Capon, Farley & Hulbert, 1980; Lorange & Vancil, 1977; Skinner, 1978). It is important that HRM recognize the importance of a timely response to environmental turbulence through independent action rather than assuming that information has the same value at some later point in time (e.g., Burack, 1985; Dyer, 1985; Gatewood & Gatewood, 1983).

Beyond the niceties associated with having an efficiently functioning formal planning system are the outcome implications associated with the inability to act. Because professional sports teams highlight, on a daily basis, many of the control-flexibility issues discussed previously, they illustrate the downside consequences in a more visible manner. The desire for bureaucratic controls by those in the front office often clashes with the spontaneity needed for athletic success. This conflict surfaced repeatedly during the period when the Columbia Broadcasting Company owned the New York Yankees professional baseball team. It also surfaced when Dave Debusschere was dismissed as the general manager of the New York Knicks professional basketball team. He attributed the firm's lack of success to insufficient organizational flexibility. Reflecting on how strategy should emerge in his organization, he stated:

> Upon reflection, no team has ever been successful when operated as part of a big business. This is true in all professional sports. The way it works inhibits and prohibits immediate action, quick decisions and the necessary decision-making that has to be done on one level and one level only (Vecsey, 1986:23).

In his own way DeBusschere was making the point that a basketball team owned by the Gulf and Western Corporation was resting too much on a totally intended strategy and was not able to benefit from the unintended-strategic component, as might a team owned by a sportsman-entrepreneur such as Connie Mack.

The link between the HRM decisions of the coach and the strategy of the organization are more visible with a sports team. If the coach is continually playing veterans while the front office is committed to younger players, for either cost or development reasons, this inconsistency may affect performance outcomes. Front office controls will impact on the norms and organizational culture of the team. In some cases this may result in players using their mobility to join other teams that they feel have more action flexibility at the playing level. HRM considerations can get lost if the attempt is made to develop a fully programmed strategy. More managerial flexibility, rather than increased controls, might be warranted. This involves developing a tolerance for an increased proportion of unintended strategy. Associated with developing a system that tolerates flexibility is an increase in the level of uncertainty, but the ability to cope with this additional uncertainty should lead to positive performance outcomes.

UNIFIED MODEL OF THE STRATEGIC-HRM PROCESS

The theoretical antecedents drawn from strategy-, HRM-, and disequilibrium- notions of market dynamics are reflected in the unified model of a profit-generating strategic-HRM process, which is depicted in Figure 4-4. By linking these antecedent theoretical streams, the impact of HRM can be traced in a more systematic manner. At the level of the economy, the ability to act on opportunities may relate to both national and firm advantage. This is one of the reasons that a distance dimension has been included in the model. In addition to dealing with certain international aspects of HRM, which are discussed more fully in Chapter Twelve, this dimension also relates to macroeconomic benefits that flow to an economy populated by firms capable of acting on opportunities. These macroeconomic considerations may pose a dilemma for the firm that must evaluate national concerns versus the problem associated with setting up operations in another country whose infrastructure may be more conducive to action.

Market operations and opportunities also serve as a basis for planned and intended strategies. HRM should be represented, in both a formal and informal way, on the formal planning group. In this way, HRM will know where guidelines need to be formulated or policies adjusted to support the implementation of the intended strategy. This role also relates to competitive advantage because it is designed to maximize the returns that are generated by the strategy formulated during the formal strategy process.

The impact of unintended action has implications for both the firm and industry. Action affects the population of available opportunities in a direct but not in a predictable manner. In addition, action transmits information, which means that competitors' responses will provide a series of adjustments that may produce a further ripple effect. This results in increased industry-level dynamics that make it difficult to gauge strategic-group or market-segment membership. For the individual firm, unintended action produces profit and is reflected in the firm's emerged strategy. Over time, this pattern of behavior has important implications with respect to the way organization-environment relations are defined. Actions that lead to greater profit are more likely to be institutionalized in the behavioral sets of the organization (Metcalfe, 1981).

As a system, the model suggests dynamics that are related to uncertainty, exploiting uncertainty, actions to reduce uncertainty, and a readjustment that combines with environmental changes to insure that the process is continuous. Uncertainty and change are the reasons that a time dimension has been included in the model. Growth and age have implications at the level of economy, industry, and firm. For the firm, this is usually discussed in terms of a life cycle. Periods of changing demand, with respect to either growth or

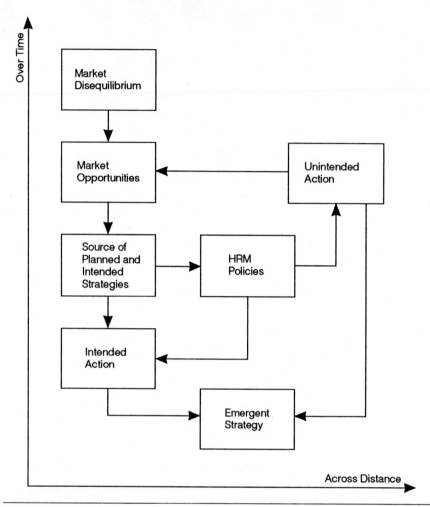

FIGURE 4-4. Unified model of the strategic-HRM process. (Adapted from Butler, J., 'Human resource management as a driving force in business strategy', *Journal of General Management*, Vol 13 (4), p. 97. Copyright (1988). Reprinted by permission of Braybrook Press Ltd.)

decline at the industry or firm level, require different sets of HRM considerations. Managing these considerations becomes more complex with the degree of diversification. Diversified firms tend to have business units distributed across the life cycle. Thus, the HRM action and facilitating posture may have to be customized to local conditions.

Thus, this unified model of the strategic-HRM impact provides a useful vehicle for examining both the process and content of HRM in relation to a firm's strategic response to market dynamics. These impacts vary, depending on the stages of products' and firms' life cycles. National boundaries become important to the extent that the infrastructure flexibility affects the level of uncertainty. Disequilibrium is important because it initializes the system, which creates the environmental uncertainties that become the basis for the planned-strategy component. These opportunities also serve as the fuel for unintended action. In this respect, market dynamics are a necessary but not sufficient condition, which enhances the extent and value of the HRM contribution because they impact directly on both components. Profit-generation is the theme that underlies the entire model.

SUMMARY AND CONCLUSIONS

The purpose of this chapter has been to make a theoretical contribution to HRM as profit-generator within a strategic context, without losing the implications for practicing managers in the process. The model is broad, combining notions from economics, strategy, and HRM, but the broadness is designed to provide theoretical justification for both HRM's strategic participation and incremental profit-generation. Extension of the strategic-HRM framework across boundaries, time, and all functional and staff areas recognizes ongoing reality and is part of the current problem-inventory of practicing human resources managers. HRM has been tied to the market mechanism because its contribution is just as pervasive. The implications are even more important although they have been downplayed slightly. HRM facilitates the efficient operation of markets, provides entrepreneurial returns to the firm and the economy, and plays an important role in real economic growth. The model does not suggest that the traditional view of HRM be discarded, but it does enhance its role by suggesting that HRM is a necessary rather than an optional ingredient.

The number of ways and various modes by which HRM actions enhance strategy and affect performance are covered in the chapter that follows, but the specific nature of opportunity and the form of entrepreneurial behaviors cannot be fully specified in advance. Opportunities are available, action requires alertness, and HRM has as pervasive an impact as other action vehicles available to the firm. The next six chapters discuss these HRM content areas and HRM's role in planning, in more detail.

HUMAN RESOURCES
AND THE ANATOMY
OF STRATEGIC PLANNING

> *To attempt to operate a plant without careful planning*
> *would be very much like the case of a general who masses*
> *his forces for an attack without knowing where the enemy*
> *is located, equips his soldiers with baseball bats to meet*
> *artillery fire, and then gives orders for each man to follow*
> *his own ideas as to the best way to win the battle.*
> *Every person, who has any responsibility in an industrial*
> *organization, should plan according to the weight which*
> *he carries. (Gardiner, 1925, pp.77–78)*

The omission of human resources, as a vital element in the "anatomy of corporate planning" (Gilmore & Brandenberg, 1962, p.61), is a by-product of the historical development of this area. In developing a list of 43 items that should be included in top management's planning framework, Gilmore and Brandenberg (1962) never explicitly mentioned human resources. Implicitly, HRM issues were placed under the umbrella of "immensely greater difficulties" that might be "encountered when the joint or synergistic effects associated with combinations are considered" (Gilmore & Brandenberg, 1962, p.69). The macro side of corporate planning became the focus of attention and HRM issues were not generally related to the central core of planning. More recently, this historical omission has been corrected, and strategic human resources planning has almost come to achieve "buzzword" status (e.g., Burack, 1988; Walker, 1980).

The underlying explanation for this change has both a process and content side. On the process side, we have developed an appreciation of strategy in both continuous and discrete terms as was outlined in Figure 4-3. This ongoing, process-type view of strategy fits in much better with the continuous and dynamic nature of HRM. Having developed an elaborated model of the strategy-making process, it then became equally important to identify the relevant "content" of the human resource input. Since this relationship between "content" and "process" is an iterative one, it also became important to specifically address the process by which the strategic human resources component of strategy is formulated.

ENVIRONMENTAL AND ORGANIZATIONAL TRENDS

While our intellectual development and appreciation of strategic management explains some of the enhanced awareness of SHRP, certain environmental and organizational trends are also relevant (e.g., Burack, 1988; Manzini, 1988). They include:

1. entrepreneurial advantage,
2. environmental coping, and
3. synergy.

Each has served to enhance the importance of SHRP, because managers have come to recognize that "human resource management affects competitive advantage in any firm" (Porter, 1985, p.43).

Entrepreneurial Advantage

The role of nonprogrammed, entrepreneurial-type behavior in enhancing organizational performance is receiving increased attention (e.g., Mintzberg, 1978). This nonprogrammed aspect relates directly to the emergent-strategy component, but it also relates to the desire to avoid organizational ossification that is associated with growth or age (e.g., Peterson, 1981; Starbuck, 1965). Many top executives see SHRP as a way to insure that policies are fashioned that support the strategic process, and do so in ways that allow the firm to better exploit the current population of environmental opportunities (Mills, 1985; Walker, 1988). It is this ability to exploit that allows the firm to achieve advantage with respect to its set of relevant competitors. Innovative, in the sense that they are strategy-driven, human resources policies are used to supplement the more familiar, functional personnel polices (Manzini, 1988). This supplementation both permits and encourages spontaneous, entrepreneurial-type behavior that enhances the effectiveness of the firm's strategy. This ability to extract additional value has prompted top management to take this second look at SHRP (e.g., Porter, 1985).

Environmental Coping

The pace of a deliberate planning process is more nearly matched to the success requirements associated with a placid environment. This is because the time delays associated with formal planning are more easily forgiven in a placid environment. To the extent that human resources considerations appeared to be relevant, after the fact, some content accommodation can usually be made to facilitate strategy implementation. However, as a turbulent environment became the norm (Ansoff, 1979), slow-paced accommodation was no longer adequate. The earlier planning frameworks, which had been copied from the military, tended to stress completeness of analysis rather than the speed of reaction. As high levels of turbulence came to characterize most firms' environments, managers began to recognize that SHRP was an effective coping mechanism (e.g., Wils, Labelle & LeLouarn, 1988). Firms failing to recognize this link, a priori, were more likely to see failure serve as a catalyst for instituting a SHRP function (Sibson, 1983).

Inflation, currency fluctuations, computer technology, and changing demographics appeared to be areas on which SHRP could provide an appropriate focus and enhance the quality of remedies (Fombrun, 1983). SHRP provides a way to identify the means to institutionalize the general form of the firm's response. This institutionalized-boundary condition can result in a managerial work force that is more capable of adjusting the strategic posture of the firm, within the time demands of an increasingly turbulent environment. In this sense, SHRP "involves the identification, analysis, and activity scheduling for events that impact the management of personnel in the business of the future" (Sibson, 1983, p.39). Within the context of strategic management, SHRP has moved from an output, or after-the-fact, activity to one that recognizes the interactive nature of the strategy-HRM relationship (e.g., Napier, 1988).

Synergy

The justification underlying early planning frameworks was that synergistic benefits were possible (e.g., Ansoff, 1979). The contemporary focus is more on the maximization of these benefits. The content areas, around which human resource decisions are made, explain part of the increased attention being afforded SHRP (Napier, 1988). Decisions relating to staffing, training and development, performance evaluation and reward systems, and labor relations are now seen in terms of how they relate to the overall strategy of the firm (e.g., Peters, 1988; Sheppeck & Rhodes, 1988; Stumpf, 1988). Making these decisions in a strategically logical manner can create synergistic benefits. These synergistic benefits also make it possible for a "win-win" situation to exist for both the employees and the firm.

Compensation policies have been one of the first areas to see this rationalization (Gomez-Mejia & Welbourne, 1988; Muczyk, 1988). Human resources planners are able to develop compensation systems that naturally support the strategy of the firm because they are structured to encourage behavior that is directed toward achieving strategic objectives (Napier, 1988). As the effects associated with using HRM policies to enhance strategy became more apparent this also encouraged top management to give increased attention to SHRP. Synergistic benefits are also possible when other HRM content decisions are considered as part of the overall organizational context. A recent example was the manpower decision-support system developed by the U.S. Army to ensure that recruitment and training, enlistment, separation, and other related factors are incorporated into top level planning decisions (Eiger, Jacobs, Chung & Selsor, 1988). A more detailed discussion of the nature of the HRM-strategy relationship, as it relates to functional HRM policies, is covered in the following five chapters.

STRATEGIC HUMAN RESOURCES PLANNING

Before proceeding with a discussion of a model designed to guide SHRP, some content discussion is warranted. Interestingly, the content discussions of SHRP abandon the "list approach," which characterized the early planning literature. The focus of top management on the firm's success, and competitiveness, were the common denominators that linked the reasons cited at the beginning of this chapter as accounting for the increased importance of SHRP. This common thread also can be found in many of the formal definitions of SHRP. This can be manifested either through the benefits associated with (1) supporting the firm's objectives or (2) developing managers capable of contributing to ongoing strategic analysis.

Baird, Meshoulam, and DeGive (1983) defined SHRP as the process of identifying the organization's strategic goals and the use of these goals as the basis for personnel practices and procedures. This definition seems to imply that the human resources group has both a proactive and supportive function. On one level, the organization is seen as gaining competitive advantage if human resources managers develop practices and procedures that will complement and reinforce the organization's strategic objectives (Gutteridge, 1988). On another level, the assumption is made that an independent interpretation is required, and that a certain amount of independence is desirable when human resources managers formulate their strategic response.

Having managers capable of directing and coordinating SHRP is seen as equally important to the success of the process. In suggesting that SHRP "involves the identification, analysis, and activity scheduling for events which will impact the management of personnel in the business in the future," Sibson (1983, p.39) took a more developmental approach. The importance of SHRP, according to Sibson, can be found by contrasting the performance of firms engaging in this activity with those who do not. He found firms performing SHRP were more adept at dealing with events that required unique managerial responses with respect to personnel issues. He also found that failures related to personnel issues often prompted the initiation of SHRP efforts.

Thus, whether the link is a direct one or effected through managerial personnel, the outcome defines the area as important. The specific content associated with SHRP is depicted in Figure 2-1, and Chapters Six through Ten discuss these content areas in more detail. For firms interested in initiating SHRP efforts, or for academics interested in the process, the fragmented nature of the existing literature suggest that a more detailed description of SHRP is needed.

THE SHRP PROCESS

Existing theoretical models of the SHRP process can generally be delineated by the degree to which they address any, or all, of four distinct phases. These phases are depicted in Figure 5-1 and include:

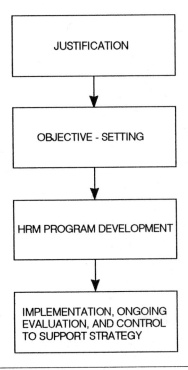

FIGURE 5-1. A macro view of the strategic human resources planning process.

1. a justification phase,
2. an objective setting phase,
3. a phase where personnel programs are developed, and
4. a phase that deals with ongoing evaluation and control.

The human resources planning system, depicted earlier in Figure 2-1, includes most of these stages, although the details of the process are sometimes more implicit than explicit. The purpose of this chapter is to detail the working elements associated with each phase and to relate the SHRP process to the SHRM process. Although SHRP and SHRM are often used interchangeably, it is important to remember that SHRP is a component of SHRM, which is a component in the strategic management of the firm.

The Justification Phase

The strategic human resources planning process calls on as many political as professional skills, and without it SHRP is unlikely to be much more than a mental exercise. In Chapter Two, the accommodation, interactive, and fully integrated categorization were presented as points along a continuum of participation. Omitted from the earlier discussion was a detailing of the effort needed to even reach a position where the accommodation mode is possible.

Several key steps are involved in this process (Hooper, Catalanello & Murray, 1987).

First, it is important to identify just how the human resources function can be used as a high-leverage variable to enhance performance. Pointing out how opportunities might have been lost or more effectively implemented if the SHRP group existed and was interfacing with those involved with strategic planning is one way to achieve this acceptance. External evidence, such as academic research of SHRP success, can also be used to supplement this initial effort. For instance, one might point out that SHRP can lead to increases in organizational commitment (Galosy, 1983).

Coalition building is also an important element in gaining acceptance. Key managers, from other functional/line and advisory/staff areas could be both formally and informally included in the HRM information loop (Hooper et al., 1987). Mills (1985) was even more specific and comprehensive in detailing the groups of managers who should be included. However, it may be more appropriate to concentrate on certain key managers during their initial stages of the justification process. As Mills (1985, p.99) points out, "Companies that engage in people planning do it because their top executives are convinced that it gives them a competitive edge in the market place." The "best approach" to achieve this "top executive" commitment will vary by firm and environmental contingencies. The HRM managerial group will have to determine if a direct attempt to convince top management, or the slower process of building a broad base of support among all operating and line managers, is more appropriate. Although the latter approach may appear more satisfactory in the long term, environmental contingencies may suggest that a direct line to top management is needed.

A third possibility for achieving justification should also be recognized. The human resources management group may be very comfortable operating as an isolated, and completely functional, unit. It may be top management, or managers in some other functional areas, who first recognize the value of SHRP and actually impose this new planning function on the more narrowly operating personnel group. In this case the same base of support must be built up within the HRM group. This special justification case is equally difficult, especially if new HRM managers are hired to help achieve the new mode of operation. In this case they must convince the personnel managers to widen their scope of operations. This may be quite difficult if the organization has stressed narrow bounds for many years.

The justification process, discussed above, is outlined in Figure 5-2. Both routes to acceptance are depicted, with Figure 5-2(a) showing the case where HRM initiates the process and Figure 5-2(b) showing HRM as a reluctant participant. The important point is that justification is not complete until all three managerial groups (top management, advisory staff and functional managers, and human resources managers) accept the fact that SHRP can, and should, make a strategic contribution. It may be possible, because of environmental or competitive emergencies, to begin installing SHRP before the

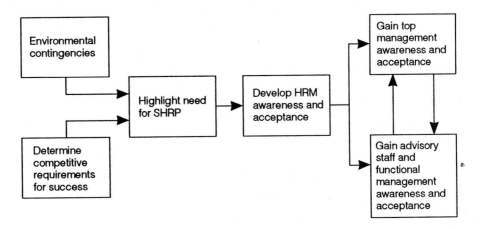

5-2 (a) Standard Case—HRM initiates process

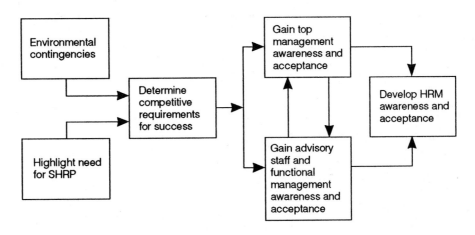

5-2 (b) HRM as last player in process

FIGURE 5-2. HRM justification phase activities.

justification process is completed, but its long-term viability suggests that full-acceptance be the goal.

Objective-Setting Phase

Strategic objective setting refers to the overall competitive objectives of the firm, not to more narrowly defined functional goals relating to efficiency. The process involved in setting these objectives requires some recognition of how the organization's structure will interact with the competitive features, or structure, that characterize the industry. Academically, this represents the intersection between industrial-organization economics and organization theory. A consideration of the boundary defined by this intersection helps define the feasible set of strategic objectives for any firm. Given the intersection, the firm must first develop, or identify, its underlying corporate philosophy. In strategy this is usually referred to as a mission statement. The mission statement provides an essential guide for the formulation of strategic objectives. The process by which the firm moves from mission statement to the development of objectives is depicted in Figure 5-3.

Mission of the Firm.   The setting of objectives is guided by the mission statement. However, the actual formulation of objectives depends on the ability of the firm to analyze (1) its environment, (2) the market structure of the industry, and (3) its firm-specific internal capabilities. This analytic process insures that "pie-in-the-sky" objectives are not set, and that objectives are consistent with the underlying philosophy of the firm.

In an ideal situation, HRM should provide some input into the verbalization of the organization's mission. This is desirable because the "essence" of the firm flows not from some definitional exercise but from the substantive

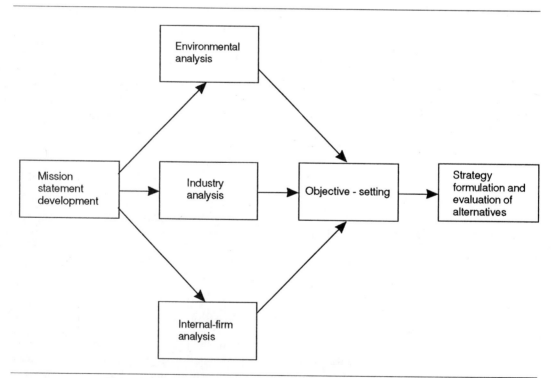

FIGURE 5-3. Overview of the role of SHRP in the strategy formulation process of the firm.

behavior of the firm. Since this behavior flows through the actions of employees, HRM managers are best situated to identify relevant considerations. With respect to achieving a consistent pattern of emergent-strategic action, this input is especially important.

While it is ideal that the development of the organization's mission be a joint effort, the SHRP group should address this task alone if necessary. The first step in this process is to identify the existing mission and strategy of the firm. The various planning groups must first identify the current posture of the firm. For those involved in SHRP, this usually means an inductive exercise, because written or verbalized mission or strategy statements may be inaccurate or not exist. Specific actions such as product/market choices and ways in which the firm competes may have to be used to infer the existing pattern of organizational objectives (e.g., Fry & Killings, 1986). The extent to which there is some consistency among these decisions over time will facilitate the identification of the existing strategy and its underlying mission (e.g, Hambrick, 1983a; Mintzberg, 1978). Absent consistency, the HRM planners will at least be aware of the fact that the firm lacks the uniformity of behavior, across functional departments or time, needed to sustain a strategy.

At the SHRP level, a good first question relates to the unique aspects of the firm (Walker, 1980). Asking basic questions about what makes this firm different from others, what purpose the firm serves, and what are the values and motives of employees and owners, provides some direction to this analysis. The SHRP group must ensure that the mission statement reflects these human values so that strategies will either build on them or be aware of implementation difficulties in advance.

The mission statement that emerges from SHRP should have some correspondence with those of other functional planning groups. The emphasis may be different for each group, but a lack of consistency indicates a lack of direction in the firm's past activities. When this occurs a situation results where top management, representing all groups, may have to use the disparate statements as bases for developing a common mission statement. Whether the mission statement can be induced from past actions or requires a proactive formulation, it must be accomplished before the planning process proceeds to additional analysis or strategy formulation. Once developed the mission statement helps focus the environmental, industry, and internal analysis that is necessary to complete the strategy-making process.

Internal Analysis of the Firm.   Defining the strengths and weaknesses of the firm is an essential step in the strategy-formulation process (e.g., Learned et al., 1965). HRM has not always been seen as central in this process, although it is generally given some mention. Because "the manager's position and responsibility in the organization are crucial influences on the way in which . . . the process of defining strengths and weaknesses" is carried out (Stevenson, 1976, p.64), it is important to have complete functional representation. Planning professionals, and managers from other functional areas, will not define the same set of organizational competence as would HRM professionals. Expanding the base of participation will also enhance the prospects for a complete internal assessment.

In his prescription on defining strengths and weaknesses, Stevenson (1976) suggested that HRM professionals should provide information about personal values and aspirations, employee attitudes, and union agreements. HRM professionals bring a different perspective because they analyze and relate to these data in different ways than would managers in other areas. For instance, HRM managers should be best positioned to evaluate (1) demographic trends, (2) employee appraisal results, (3) employees' and managers' interests, and (4) education- and experience-based capabilities (Gatewood & Gatewood, 1983; Walker, 1978). Since these factors may have a critical impact, with respect to strategy formulation and implementation, it is important that they be addressed a priori.

Retaining a narrow focus is important at the initial stage because the assessment of strengths and weaknesses should be complete and as objective as possible. Items should not be deleted because they seem to be without strategic importance. When strategies are modified or proposed, the impact of individual strengths or weaknesses, thought to be insignificant, may become more apparent.

The simplicity of the analysis should not be confused with the depth of effort. What is required by the SHRP group is a full-blown analysis of the performance evaluation and reward systems, training and development efforts at all levels, an inventory of employee and managerial capabilities, a review of staffing and labor-relations efforts, and a candid assessment of the HRM group based on current professional standards. This relates to the functional level capabilities outlined earlier in Figure 2-1.

After developing an initial list, prioritization can be achieved by asking "what factors may enhance/limit the choice of future courses of action" (Walker, 1980, p.79). In this way, strengths and weaknesses can be seen in terms of whether they enhance or limit the ability of the organization to act. For instance, Walker's (1980) research suggested over-specialization by key managers, or the lack of promotable talent at any level, might be factors that could limit strategic choice or delay implementation.

Developing an inventory of managerial talent is also an important part of the assessment. In this way employees' capabilities can be matched to the needs of the firm. A matrix framework, based on two continua: (1) type of job and (2) organizational level, was suggested by Hoffman, Wyatt, and Gordon (1986). As the increments are outlined along each continuum, they can be connected to form a series of cells, with each cell representing a position in the firm. Empty cells will highlight human resources weaknesses, while full boxes highlight human resources strengths.

A less traditional approach to assessing managerial talent was presented by Stybel (1982). He used Maccoby's (1976) framework, which was presented in his book *The Gamesman,* as the basis for categorizing managerial talent. The craftsman, jungle fighter, company man, and gamesman are managerial types that are needed, in varying proportions, at different points in the organization's life. Stybel(1982) suggested that managers be characterized according to this typology so that empty or over-populated cells can be identified. Strengths-and-weaknesses evaluation based along these lines can be extremely important when evaluating strategic alternatives.

Other functional areas, such as negotiating skills, an audit of key positions, and an examination of labor requirement tables and an inventory of skills, are important in a more basic way (Alpander, 1982). Job analysis and review of the compensation scheme are also important at this stage. While the specifics of all the ways this analysis can be done are beyond the scope of this chapter, the focus of the process should be clear. The evaluation should be as complete as possible so that the members of the SHRP group can maximize the contributions they can make when their efforts are synthesized with others at the firm level.

Environmental Analysis.   The end product of this type of analysis involves the identification of environmental threats and opportunities. Environmental scanning is the term used to define this activity and it was first popularized through the publication of Aquilar's (1967) dissertation, *Scanning the Environment*. This research effort identified the links in this process. What information to obtain, where and how to obtain it, and how to use the information in the strategy-making process were the principal themes explored.

In one sense, Aquilar (1967, p.1) took a broad approach by viewing the "scanning for information about events and relationships in a company's outside environment, the knowledge of which would assist top management in its task of charting the company's future course of action" as capturing the essence of this activity. The use of the word "external" may be critical, because Aquilar's model of scanning included information relating to human resources and the personal values of employees as part of the internal environment of the firm. Because he took this focus, his empirical investigation largely ignored the HRM role in external environmental analysis.

By casting issues in terms of external or internal environment, functional areas found themselves assessed in terms of the firm's strengths and weaknesses, while the assessment of the external environment was seen through the top management's or the planning group's lens. This may have resulted in an accurate assessment of HRM, but it fails to provide an HRM assessment of the external environment. Since opportunities and threats relate to the functional areas as well as to the entire organization, this was an important omission. As a result the linkage between an external event and internal conditions, which actually defines a threat or opportunity, was more easily missed. Aquilar (1967, p.190) saw "the exchange of information among the various decision-making centers" as essential to the effort, but tends to relate this to providing information on the sources of information and to the stages immediately before formulation. Because communication was likely to center around the external environment as defined, which included economic, technological, social and political factors, the realm of discussion was limited.

A central thesis in this research is the inclusion of HRM in the external scanning effort. HRM is seen as a content element in the external environmental factors as well as a vehicle for enhancing the scanning effort. The inclusion of additional functional lenses allows for a more complete assessment of external data. Each functional group is likely to collect and assess data differently and this leads to a more complete environmental analysis.

By expanding the notion of what constituted the external environmental sector, Hambrick (1982) provided a framework that is more receptive to the inclusion of HRM. By developing sectors that were related to the managerial activities, as identified by Miles and Snow (1978), he was able to capture some of the interrelationship between internal and external events. Thus, "Events or trends bearing on determination of roles and relationships in the organization were important" (Hambrick, 1982, p.161) and were seen as essential to environmental scanning. The recasting of the external environment into sectors related to entrepreneurial, engineering, administrative, and regulatory activities is more supportive of both emergent and deliberate notions of strategy. The impact of external events on these activities also suggests a more active role for HRM in the scanning process.

Walker (1980, 1988) was one of the first to suggest HRM take a more proactive role, but suggested that the external influences that were important were economic, social, technological, and political changes. Because he saw environmental change in traditional terms, it was difficult to theoretically justify why additional manpower should be directed toward the evaluation of the external environment. Nkomo (1987), probably because her study occurred after SHRP had received some legitimacy, assumed that there was some analysis of the external environment that was occurring from the HRM perspective. She found that firms saw SHRP in rather macro terms, but were often unable to identify specific steps or the contributions that might be expected to flow from those steps. This more recent finding seems to suggest that SHRP groups make specific efforts to identify the benefits flowing from each of the components that define their total planning activity.

At a mechanical level, Hooper et al., (1984) suggested examining the data collected concerning environmental conditions to formulate likely trends and issues that could impact the organization's human resources. These trends and issues could then be converted into "impact statements" that outlined the implications and possible action needed to cope with them. At a more general level the recent work of Walton and Lawrence (1985) was directed toward recognizing the long-term environmental trends and the challenges they pose for HRM.

From a value-creation perspective the inclusion of human resources managers in the scanning effort is important because of what they see and how they see it. In some cases environmental factors, related to the present and future people needs of the firm, are likely to be noticed only by this group. In other cases human resources managers will, along with other functional and staff managers, see the identical data but provide a unique interpretation. For example, a human resources manager noticing a change in attitudes among students with respect to corporate decision-making may see this as having a significant impact on the future administrative practices of the firm (Gutteridge, 1988). This same piece of data might be considered insignificant by managers in other functional groups.

Industry Analysis.   Industry analysis is important because of the relationship between certain structural characteristics of the industry and the appropriate conduct of the firm (e.g., Porter, 1981). Although this line of reasoning represents a well-established body of research in industrial-organization economics, the recent research of Michael Porter (1980,1981,1985) largely explains its recent popularity. Porter uses industry-structure characteristics to build a framework that serves as a guide during strategy formulation. This is accomplished by specifically including "industry opportunities and threats" within "the context in which competitive strategy is formulated" (Porter, 1980, p.xviii).

While human resources considerations have not been traditionally included within the industrial-organization economics framework, Porter's (1981, p.4) model of the forces driving industry competition included factors related to the HRM function. Specifically, he enumerated four factors, which include (1) the threat of new entrants, (2) the bargaining power of suppliers, (3) the bargaining power of buyers, and (4) the threat from substitute products or services. Although not specifically addressed by Porter, the HRM group could play an important role with respect to the collection of data about suppliers, buyers, and competitors. To the extent that the firm recognizes that the existing force of employees as well as applicants can provide useful competitive-type information, the HRM group may be best positioned to systematically collect this information, especially from those outside the formal planning loop.

In addition to serving a general role in the data-collection effort, the HRM group is well positioned to provide some analysis with respect to each of the important industry-level considerations. Shortages with respect to certain critical skills are relevant when developing strategic alternatives. To the extent that individuals with these skills areas comprise a major cost component, they can use their supplier power to demand higher wages. Since this could alter the relative position of competing strategic alternatives, this information should be highlighted early in the formulation process (Dahl, 1988). To the extent that the employee force is relatively fixed, because of contractual arrangements or the existing nature of plant and equipment, new technologies may be important. HRM personnel are better placed to recognize these human barriers to exit (e.g., Harrigan, 1985), which may be relevant to new strategies that incorporate new technologies.

On the buyer side of the equation, the HRM group is well positioned to recognize changes in buyer power. Since different approaches are required for a large number of different, as opposed to a smaller number of concentrated, buyers this may call for different interpersonal skills with respect to those individuals coming into contact with these external constituencies. The maintenance of personality profiles, or the selection of individuals who have a greater range of capabilities, may or may not be appropriate depending on the strategic direction being taken by the firm. Because the HRM group is more apt to relate the existing inventory of skills to dynamic changes in the buyer population, than would the marketing or planning group, their collection and analysis of this data could be significant.

While the threat of new entrants and substitutes does not seem to relate directly to HRM, this lack of direct impact does suggest some important reasons for inclusions. With respect to existing product/market choices, the HRM group is less likely to be wedded to status-quo notion of how the industry works. Those with a vested interest, whether financially or organizationally, may be reluctant to fully recognize the potential for new products or competitors to make incursions. In this respect the HRM group provides a means by which an internal and independent assessment can be made. With respect to the HRM group this does require that they have some members with broader functional competence if they are to fully participate in this aspect of industry level analysis in a meaningful way.

INCLUDING HRM IN THE STRATEGY PROCESS

Having made a case for the validity, or at least for the reasonableness of including HRM in the strategy process, a discussion of how that should be done seems warranted. Up to this point the discussion of HRM has been set in terms of how it relates to a larger organizational context. According to Dyer (1983), the first completely internal step in the SHRP process is the setting of specific HRM objectives. Dyer believed that these objectives should be set along two dimensions: (1) the determination of specific HRM needs, and (2) making sure employees are available to meet these needs. The first dimension, related to HRM needs, must be conducted along two fronts. One side of this equation includes the determination of future staffing needs by examining the strategic business plans developed by the corporate planning staff (Dyer, 1983). These business plans, which predict the organization's future in terms of its financial, technological, and production requirements, must be interpreted by HRM planners to determine the types and numbers of employees needed to fully support these plans.

The other side of this initial equation, as related to HRM objective setting, relates to setting objectives for strategies that have yet to be formulated. This requires HRM professionals to develop objectives based on a scenario of likely strategic postures, which may emerge at the end of the planning process. Both the generation of scenarios and the accuracy of the scenarios generated will depend on the interrelationship that the HRM group maintains with the corporate planning and other functional groups, as well as from the feedback process that operates throughout the various phases. However, the actual generation of these objectives is a largely internal HRM activity. An overview of this stage of SHRP is depicted in Figure 5-4.

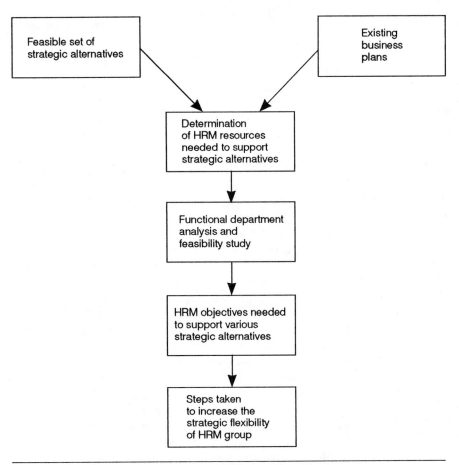

FIGURE 5-4. Flow diagram of the HRM objective-setting process.

Having generated a series of HRM objectives for both the existing and likely future strategic plans, the issue of variance must now be considered. In the unlikely event that the objectives associated with all the potential strategies are identical, from the HRM perspective, this step will be trivial. However, under normal conditions it is expected that there will be variance in both the number and nature of future HRM needs across the potential strategies. Thus, the SHRP group must give some consideration not only to how to achieve some single set of objectives but also to how to best remain poised so that it can achieve any set, which will be determined as corporate strategies are set or evolve.

Setting Objectives

Walker (1980) provided the HRM professionals with some specific guidelines for objective-setting, designed to accompany the more general process model of objective setting. These include the gathering of financial data, especially with respect to sales, profit, and return on investment. Some determinations should also be made about the time frame in which the firm expects to achieve these financial goals. The HRM group should then determine if the collective management style of the organization is likely to support or thwart the timely achievement of financial goals. In some cases the underlying structure of support may have to be altered if certain financial goals are to be achieved (e.g. Kerr & Bettis, 1987). The HRM group will have to develop an evolving set of HRM policies designed to insure that the financial objectives of the organization are in sync with its culture.

The job matrix discussed earlier, based on (1) type of job and (2) level of job, is a qualitative technique that may be useful at this stage (Hoffman et al., 1986). Each of the boxes that result when the two continua are appropriately divided can be examined to determine future needs. Boxes that are empty, or likely to become empty, can be evaluated in terms of their strategic impact. The addition or subtraction of positions is also more apparent using the matrix, because this results in the boxes becoming smaller or larger and allows the SHRP group to have a visual perception of what the addition, or subtraction, may mean. To the extent that the size of these boxes is related to responsibility, the SHRP group can assess whether it wishes to create jobs with increasing amounts of responsibility and duties.

In addition to these kinds of qualitative considerations, which are related to organizational culture or climate, quantitative goals also need to be given some consideration. Actual numbers need to be associated with future employee needs, and the specific nature of the jobs that will need to be filled must be identified. Statistical techniques should be used to help forecast both the size of the future employee demands and the likelihood that existing sources of supply will be adequate (Niehaus, 1988; Nkomo, 1987). The important thing at this stage of the analysis is to remember that it is the setting of HRM objectives that is important, not analysis for the sake of analysis.

All of the forecasts should be considered over a range of time frames (Walker, 1980). According to Walker, short-range manpower forecasts are developed by most companies. This is the most common way that managers determine their current human resources supply and needs. Intermediate-range forecasts are less precise, but managers can rely on assumptions to help fill in for missing data. Longer-range forecasts are projections of the HRM needs of the organization out into the future (Walker, 1980). To develop a forecast beyond ten years, the SHRP group must incorporate the technological and environmental analysis that it conducted as part of the organization's general planning effort. These longer-range forecasts require that HRM assumptions be combined with environmental assumptions to achieve reliability. Obviously, the difficulty of this task explains why few firms engage in longer-term forecasts (Walker, 1980).

Feasibility Testing.   Feasibility testing is the next logical step in this internal process (e.g., Hooper et al., 1987). Before any actions are taken it is important that a careful evaluation, of the functional departments involved, be conducted. This will ensure that these departments are fully aware of the nature of future HRM needs, and this will provide feedback to the HRM group with respect to their objective-setting. Additionally, the internal capabilities of the SHRP group should be given some consideration. This should consider not only staff, funds, and equipment issues but it should also carefully examine the managerial capabilities of the SHRP group. It is important to know if this group has the technical skills and managerial talent needed to successfully implement any of the likely strategic alternatives.

Legal Restrictions.   It is also important that legal restrictions, such as those associated with Executive Order 11246 and Title VII of the Civil Rights Act of 1964, and recent Supreme Court decisions affecting their interpretation, be considered. While these regulations prescribe monitoring criteria, it is likely that other functional and corporate planning groups will be familiar with these requirements (Alpander, 1982). While a strategy involving a more sophisticated and less labor-intensive technology might appear optimal, it might also alter the percentage of minority employees. In this case the SHRP group might have to begin planning on ways to move minorities into more technically advanced jobs or to place them in greater proportions in other types of positions as a first step in achieving a more uniform distribution.

Another way to achieve this aim is to redesign the jobs to suit the applicants the firm wants to attract. In homogeneous populations, such as Volvo had in Sweden (Gibson, 1973), this is easier, but it may be possible to make some skill adjustments in jobs to satisfy legal requirements. In any case, this is an issue that the SHRP group should consider.

It is important that these legal restrictions be considered, because government-imposed affirmative-actions plans may involve unanticipated costs, which would have made another strategic alternative preferable. This problem can also be important in fast-growing industries. Mills and Balbaky (1985) found that HRM recruitment and selection plans, with respect to under-represented groups, fell quickly apart during period of rapid growth. Thus, it appears that the SHRP group has legal considerations that are relevant in a variety of industry-growth and firm-strategy alternatives.

As depicted in Figure 5-4, objectives should be in place when a deliberate strategy emerges from the corporate-level planning group. The SHRP group must have the objectives in place before the strategy-alternative evaluation process is complete, because the HRM group must have sufficient time to plan and develop programs if they are to be positioned to support implementation.

Implementation, Ongoing Evaluation, and Control

This includes those activities that must begin with strategy selection and continue throughout the strategy process. This would include functional HRM items such as the selection, orientation and socialization of new employees, management succession issues, career development and outplacement, as well as monitoring the fulfillment of HRM goals in terms of the demands of the strategy selected.

Selection, orientation, and socialization of new employees are likely to be among the first steps associated with the strategic-implementation process. Whether the firm is embarking on a high-growth strategy, which will require large numbers of new employees, or a retrenchment strategy, which may involve only a few key replacements, this effort is likely to be central to the strategic-implementation effort. If the new strategic direction of the firm requires employees with more technical flexibility, long-term potential or formal education, the selection process may have to be altered to reflect this. Thus, the SHRP group must ensure that the HRM recruiting and selection efforts reflect the strategy-implementation concerns of the firm (Alpander, 1982).

In some cases a pool of potential employees may not be available who reflect these new needs. In these cases an orientation program and socialization process may be warranted so that new employees recognize that a more varied set of skills or additional education are now valued by the firm. Because most orientation programs and socialization processes are designed to help new employees define their behavior in terms of existing cultural norms, this process is much more difficult where the new strategy dictates new cultural norms (Hall & Goodale, 1986). While the new employees are undergoing a socialization process, which should involve (1) anticipatory socialization, (2) accommodation, and (3) role management (e.g., Berlew & Hall, 1966; Feldman, 1976; Wanous, 1979), a parallel effort may also be needed to change the socialization patterns of existing employees. The process is somewhat more complex for existing employees because they must be divorced from the long-prevailing, existing, culture.

Some attention also has to be given to managerial succession. The SHRP group should be constantly involved in identifying likely successors for key managers, as well as developing their sources for entry-level managers. Research indicates that most firms indicate they give some attention to managerial succession (e.g., Mills & Bulbaky, 1985), but a uniform consideration of the problem, over all levels of management, is rare and should be addressed by the SHRP group.

Training and development programs, for both managers and employees, are important to most implementation efforts. Since strategy is a response to the dynamic change in the environment, it is unlikely that a static set of employee skills and managerial talents will be sufficient (Sheppeck & Rhodes, 1988). Although the SHRP group will not be directing these efforts, they should be communicating with those involved in training and development to ensure that they have a good understanding of the changing strategic direction of the firm and how that impacts on the HRM needs of the firm.

For many strategies the issue of outplacement should also be addressed. Since many strategies involve a retrenchment, especially as the industry matures and the opportunities for growth become rare, employee reductions are necessary to cost-cutting strategies. By ensuring that outplacement programs are in place, the SHRP group may help increase the numbers of voluntary retirements as well as voluntary exits. The SHRP group may also want to ensure that employees deemed critical to future success become aware of their role in the future of the organization (Abelson, Ferris, & Urban, 1988).

Obviously, the list of examples that might be considered, with respect to facilitating implementation, is limitless. The SHRP group must ensure that their analysis is comprehensive and work closely with others in the HRM group to ensure that likely barriers to strategy implementation are identified early in the process. They must also encourage others in the HRM group to develop the necessary policies and programs, which will be needed to support the new or altered strategy.

Finally, the SHRP group must recognize that the strategy will now begin to be altered through emergent behavior. A mechanism for feedback must be developed so that the achievement of HRM objectives can be monitored. The SHRP group is also well positioned to evaluate emergent HRM behavior to determine if it is supporting and extending the existing deliberate strategy's direction, or if additional controls should be instituted to help focus this behavior.

SUMMARY AND CONCLUSIONS

It is because the importance of SHRP is so obvious and intuitive that we are likely to forget it. For this reason it is essential to remain in touch with the role SHRP plays in completing the planning skeleton. It is also important that the SHRP group have both an external and internal focus. That external focus relates to their relationship with the corporate planning group and other functional departments. In this capacity the SHRP group is a full participant in the industry market-structure, internal firm, and environmental analysis that is essential to strategy formulation.

The internal aspects of SHRP relate to their relationship with other managers and areas within the HRM group. Planning at this level is more narrowly, although not exclusively, directed toward issues of strategy implementation. While issues related to staffing, performance evaluation, reward systems, and training and development must be performed by other HRM professionals it is important that these functions are included in the planning framework of the SHRP group. The more specific details of how this process works is discussed in the next five chapters, but it is important that they are part of the SHRP process. The essential lesson of SHRP is one of inclusion. As SHRM is to corporate planning and strategy formulation, so will be the various HRM areas to the SHRP efforts.

STRATEGIC STAFFING

"Personnel selection is decisive. People are our most valuable asset." (Joseph Stalin).[1]

"The selection of employees at all ranks is one of the greatest cares of executive authority." (Fayol, 1916, p. 79).

Closely tied to the process of planning for human resources is strategic staffing. Its importance in the overall strategic-management process stems from trends both external and internal to business firms (Fombrun, Tichy, & Devanna, 1984). External trends encompass work force changes, technological advances, and industry restructuring through deregulation, mergers, and acquisitions. The post baby-boom birth dearth has forced firms to be more competitive in acquiring and retaining entry-level employees. Technological innovation has allowed firms to move into an era of the "smart machine" but has initiated almost unprecedented wrenching changes for existing employees (Zuboff, 1988). As a result, firms more frequently face staffing decisions of whether to replace current workers with already trained new hires or provide existing employees the opportunity to gain needed skills. As deregulated industries such as banking, transportation, and communications revamp the way they do business, managers are forced to select employees who can adapt to continuing, inevitable change. Finally, the merger-and-acquisition wave in the 1980s has generated new types of problems. An acquiring firm's managers encounter questions of which employees of that target firm to keep and which to let go; those strategic staffing decisions frequently are complicated by conditions of limited information and time. Likewise, acquired firm managers face situations where they must generate creative ways to retain key employees who could smooth a merger transition.

Other factors that magnify the role of staffing in strategic management stem from changing attitudes inside firms and on the part of researchers. By the mid-1980s, human resources managers began gaining greater business knowledge and familiarity with strategic planning. Those who think strategically are proactively developing an expanded role for human resources management activities in strategy implementation and formulation (Borucki & Lafley, 1984). Senior management attitudes are also changing dramatically (Bowman, 1986). CEOs and boards of directors have faced situations where strategic

---

[1] As cited by Taylor, W. "Who said that?" *Harvard Business Review* no. 66, (1988) 156.

staffing decisions can have major positive or negative consequences, such as the selection of a key leader or the unexpected death of a CEO. As a result, these managers more frequently seek HRM input in making strategic decisions. In addition, even traditional HRM researchers (e.g., Schmitt & Schneider, 1983) have argued that research on personnel selection/staffing should be moved to a higher level of analysis. This would include perspectives at both the organizational and strategic levels. They have suggested that the critical question for future investigation is the extent to which staffing practices affect overall organizational effectiveness.

STAFFING AND SHRP

Once human resources planning has occurred (see Chapter Five), staffing comes into play. While human resources planning provides the overall direction and framework in determining the types and numbers of employees an organization will need, staffing encompasses the implementation, namely, the tasks of getting the right people in the right jobs at the right time. The staffing function has traditionally involved those tasks associated with acquiring and allocating employees within an organization: (1) recruitment and selection, (2) orientation and socialization, and (3) employee movement within a firm related to promotions, transfers, and demotions. The strategically savvy human resources manager and staff increasingly use the design of staffing activities to implement firm strategy (Lundberg, 1986; Miller, 1984; Olian & Rynes, 1984).

With regard to formulating intended strategies, staffing's role is relatively unexplored and under-researched as a critical component, or even catalyst. For example, a firm seeking an intended strategy of diversification should consider staffing loads, skill inventories in the firm, and ability of existing employees to learn new business areas (Prahalad & Bettis, 1986) as it formulates plans for diversification. If the firm moves into areas unfamiliar to employees, for instance, management must consider trade-offs of hiring employees to manage the new business area versus retraining a work force that is perhaps more committed and certainly is more knowledgeable about the organization.

While research is limited with regard to staffing's role in formulating intended strategy, it is almost nonexistent on the issue of staffing's role in unintended strategy development. Nonetheless, this is an area of potentially major importance for the staffing function. For example, if a university department seeks a reputation in research on the human resources impacts of mergers and acquisitions, and it wants to build that reputation quickly, the department would implement that plan by hiring researchers with established records in the mergers-and-acquisitions area. Thus, staffing is used as a method to implement strategy.

An unintended future strategy may develop, however, as the cadre of mergers-and-acquisitions researchers change their interests and skills over time (e.g., Butler, Dutton, & Kabaliswaran, 1986). Because of market opportunities, such as the availability of new data bases, new issues raised by managers, opportunities for access to organizations, or new analytical techniques, the researchers may seek to investigate topics that are no longer directly related to mergers and acquisitions. Such new directions may include studies on managing other types of change, planning/carrying out divestitures, or understanding international joint ventures. As a result of the changing portfolio of faculty members' interests, the department's strategic emphasis may unintentionally change, from focusing on mergers and acquisitions to some other area(s).

Similarly, a heavily labor-intensive manufacturing firm or industry facing a dwindling work force may be unable to acquire workers with needed skills at a price the firm is able to pay. As a result, management may decide to pursue other manufacturing areas, to automate, or to use flexible manufacturing in conjunction with other firms. In both the university department and manufacturing firm, unintended strategic directions can emerge as a result of staffing-related issues, such as the changing interests of work force members, or the general availability of employees.

The focus of this chapter is on the role that staffing can play in the processes of implementing and formulating strategy. Implementation is discussed first because of the relatively greater amount of research that has been done in the area.

STAFFING AND STRATEGY IMPLEMENTATION

The literature addresses several ways in which staffing can or does play a role in implementing strategy. This section briefly discusses three strategy-implementation components—structure, systems, and culture—and their links to staffing (Figure 6-1), expanding on the idea developed in Chapter Four that staffing (as part of HRM) can be a tool for implementation. Briefly, structure can facilitate the implementation of strategy through decisions relating to "shaping" an organization. The "shaping" process can be affected by specific staffing decisions, such as choice of a leader, determining which jobs are critical for the organization, and identifying criteria needed by people who fill jobs. Each of these decisions typically requires judgments based upon staffing information, which comes from activities such as job analysis or the assessment of skills of employees.

A second component of strategy implementation concerns the design and use of various systems, information/computer systems, resource-allocation decision systems, control systems, and human resources systems. This book has emphasized the ways that various HRM systems (e.g., staffing, performance evaluation and reward, development) contribute to the implementation of a specific strategy. Staffing, in particular, is a crucial tool because it encompasses key steps for achieving strategic direction. These include: (1) the identification of talent through job analysis, skills inventories, and recruitment needed to enhance strategy; (2) the acquisition of that talent through recruitment and selection; (3) the processes of making employees part of an organization

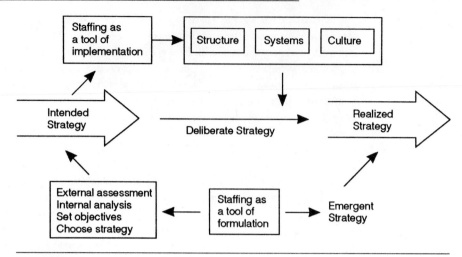

FIGURE 6-1. Staffing's role in implementing and formulating strategy.

through orientation and socialization; and (4) the movement of employees within an organization through promotion, transfer, and demotion.

A final contributing element to strategy implementation is organization or corporate culture. As the "glue" that holds an organization together, culture represents the unwritten rules of how a firm works. Again, staffing also plays a role in implementation through its contribution to the culture of an organization, by the selection and placement of human resources.

Staffing's role in each of the three main components (i.e., structure, systems, culture) is discussed below.

The Role of Staffing in Structure

The purpose of organization structure as a strategy-implementation method is to mold or shape an organization in a way that will make it more efficient and effective in achieving goals and objectives. Structure emerges from the decisions leaders make to determine how various organizational units relate to one another. Accordingly, structure includes such topics as managerial span of control, organization shape (e.g., lean, tall, flat), and the extent of centralization.

While research examining the relationship between strategy and structure or technology and structure is common, literature directly addressing structure and staffing is rare. A study by Miller, Kets de Vries, and Toulouse (1982) looked at executive personality, as measured by locus of control, and found it to be relevant in maximizing the match between strategy and structure. HRM professionals should attempt to exploit this kind of information when making staffing decisions. Since changes in structure are also a function of the emotional responses of employees, it may be possible to use staffing to control the interpretative schemes that result (Bartunek, 1984). Hiring new, or repositioning existing, employees in a manner that reduces this emotional response may enhance the prospects for strategic success. Notions related to control (Dunbar, 1981), the social psychological approach of Katz and Kahn (1978), and the sociological approaches of Perrow (1972) suggest staffing plays an important role in the realignment between strategy and structure.

While there is little literature directly relating structure and staffing (Miller et al., 1982), one area in which there is a long history of research is leader or manager succession, which has both structural and staffing implications (e.g., Carroll, 1984; Cowherd, 1986; Friedman, 1986; Gordon & Rosen, 1981; Grusky, 1960, 1961, 1963; Guest, 1962; Helmich, 1977; Perucci & Mannweiler, 1968). Clearly, organizational manager selection is the key to subsequent structure decisions, which in turn should enhance strategy (Friedman, 1986; Lundberg, 1986). Other staffing activities can also support decisions relating to structure. For example, the activities of acquiring and moving employees represent mechanisms through which desired organization-design issues, such as span of control, can be implemented. Further, desired degree of centralization may be enhanced through selection and socialization of employees comfortable with more control in the work environment.

The present discussion of staffing's relation to structure is based on the premise that management succession (i.e., selection) is a key staffing activity that can directly affect organization structure and, in turn, strategy implementation. As a result, the focus of the literature review is on factors influencing succession. Among the issues most relevant to staffing's relationship to succession are (1) the role of the board of directors, (2) organizational factors explaining succession, and (3) manager origin.

Board of Directors and Succession.   Through its influence on management selection, an organization's board of directors may affect strategy implementation. The impact of the board can emerge in at least three ways. First, the general makeup or composition of the board has been shown to relate to change in leaders. Helmich (1980) found that board membership composition was related to the frequency of president replacement in 54 firms over a 30-year time period: the more variation in board membership, in terms of replacement of members and general outlook of members, the more rapid the turnover of CEOs. There was also a difference between high- and low-performing firms, in terms of the variations in their boards. Successful firms tended to have less board member variation and more stable and formalized succession patterns. If turnover of CEOs creates internal instability, as Beatty and Zajac (1987) have suggested, strategy-implementation programs may be jeopardized or, at a minimum, fraught with inconsistency if each manager uses different approaches.

A second way the board of directors may influence manager succession is through its use of knowledge regarding types of criteria that are important in a given firm (Hambrick & Mason, 1982, 1984). The issue of linking strategy to leader characteristics is discussed more later, but it is important to recognize here that there do appear to be patterns of key manager characteristics in high-performing organizations (Allen, Panian, & Lotz, 1979; Friedman, 1986).

Norburn and Birley (1987), for example, recently found that high-performing companies tended to have CEOs who had liberal arts educational backgrounds and who had extensive experience in the output functions of the firm. Thus, such knowledge by board of director members regarding the type of leader a firm may require could indirectly affect structure and strategy implementation.

Board members should also be cognizant of the potential effects a change in leadership can have for an organization. The relationship between manager succession and organization performance has long been a puzzling topic (Allen et al., 1979; Brady, Fulmer, & Helmich, 1982; Brown, 1982; Channon, 1979; Friedman, 1986; Guest, 1962; Lieberson & O'Connor, 1972), because of the frequently inconsistent findings. Some of the more recent studies have examined the relationship of leader succession to organizational financial performance and market reactions (Beatty & Zajac, 1987; Chung, Lubatkin, Rogers, & Owers, 1987; Salancik & Pfeffer, 1980; Weiner & Mahoney, 1981). The findings have varied, but an overall conclusion has been that change in a top manager frequently has negative repercussions on financial measures such as stock price and can cause major internal turmoil. As gatekeeper for staffing of top management positions, therefore, the board should try to anticipate the implications of such staffing decisions on structure and strategy implementation.

Organizational-Level Factors and Succession. Several organizational-level variables appear to influence leader succession. Those factors include, for example, firm ownership, size and geographic dispersion, stage of maturity, strategy, internal turbulence, and hierarchical level (Carroll, 1984; Chaganti & Sambharya, 1987; Grusky, 1961; Helmich, 1978; Kriesberg, 1962; Perrucci & Mannweiler, 1968; Pfeffer & Salancik, 1977; Salancik & Pfeffer, 1980; Salancik, Staw, & Pondy, 1980; Scheibar, 1986; Weber & K'obonyo, 1987). Salancik and Pfeffer (1980) found that source of control, whether owner or managers acting for stockholders, was related to CEO tenure and firm performance. Profit margins and stock market returns were better when major control was held by groups other than founder/owners. Other literature has suggested that succession was more frequent in small, fast-growing firms and in large bureaucratic institutions (Grusky, 1961; Perrucci & Mannweiler, 1968). Helmich (1978) found that firms that were more spatially dispersed and had higher net stockholder equity tended to replace the CEO more frequently than firms which were more geographically concentrated. In addition, an early study by Kriesberg (1962) suggested that succession was more common at a higher hierarchical level in public health institutions: heads of state-level departments tended to have shorter tenures than heads of local-level departments.

Management Origin. A final management succession issue, which could affect approach to structure and implementation, is where a leader comes from (Beatty & Zajac, 1987; Brady et al., 1982; Dalton & Kesner, 1983; Daum, 1975). Chung et al. (1987) concluded that, under certain conditions, leader origin (inside or outside of a firm) has little effect on long-term profit, but does affect stock price. Stock prices rose when high-performing firms hired outside CEOs but fell when poor performers hired outside CEOs. Their explanation was that an outside CEO brought additional "energy" to a high-performing firm but added more confusion and turmoil to a poor-performing one. Clearly, succession is a strategic decision demanding the attention and understanding of major constituencies inside and outside a firm.

Staffing as a System Supporting Strategy Implementation

A second means for implementing strategy is to design appropriate systems that encourage organizational members to carry out strategy through those systems. In the current discussion, this implies that an organization should have staffing systems that enhance and facilitate a given strategy.

As mentioned, staffing includes three clusters of activities: (1) the acquisition of employees, (2) the orientation and socialization of employees, and (3) the movement of employees to appropriate positions within the organization. The existing literature has been negligent regarding staffing's role in strategy implementation (Borucki & Lafley, 1984; Gupta, 1986; Metz, 1984; Miller, 1984; Olian & Rynes, 1984). Much research in the area has concentrated on the "mechanics" of staffing activities. Indeed, Schmitt and Schneider (1983) concluded their extensive review of selection research literature with concern that the focus on psychological and individual-level issues such as job analysis techniques and reliability/validity of selection instruments had dominated research, to the exclusion of generating knowledge about the impact of selection activities on organizational effectiveness. Their concern was that, while research could give insights on the strengths and weaknesses of numerous selection or job analysis methods, it offered no conclusions about which methods are more effective or do a better job in helping an organization achieve its goals. Thus, the traditional literature said little about staffing's link to strategy, and it is only since the early 1980s that HRM researchers, and some strategic-management researchers, have taken a look at the broader picture.

This section discusses the three staffing-system activities in terms of their value for strategy implementation. The focus is on links between staffing and strategy, as well as on how staffing can contribute to organization performance.

Acquisition of Employees.   Researchers interested in staffing's role in strategy implementation have argued that having the right people in key positions is one of the most fundamental aspects of a successful strategy (Gupta & Govindarajan, 1984; Leontiades, 1982; Lundberg, 1986; Stybel, 1982). Both HRM and strategic-management researchers have proposed that once firms establish a strategic direction, they should acquire, or move into place through transfer or promotion, managers with the skill mix and characteristics appropriate for the strategy (Borucki & Lafley, 1984; *Business Week*, 1981; Gerstein & Reisman, 1983; Gupta, 1986).

Some literature has focused on matching stage of firm development or stage in the product life cycle with manager characteristics (*Business Week*, 1981; Herbert & Deresky, 1987; Lundberg, 1986). For instance, Lundberg (1986) made the case that in a firm's early stage of development, it is important to staff it with managers who will squelch intrafirm political struggles and focus on identifying major directions and issues for the embryonic firm's immediate survival. He then argued that mature-stage firms would be more likely to require managers possessing the ability to promote innovation, so the firm avoids stagnation or decline. Other researchers have used various strategy classifications, degree of diversification (Rumelt, 1974), prospector/analyzer/defender (Miles & Snow, 1978) and generic strategies (Porter, 1980), but their argument is essentially the same. Corporate and/or strategic business unit strategies should suggest both the key managerial characteristics needed for a firm and the staffing activities for acquiring those managers (Galbraith & Nathanson, 1978; Leontiades, 1982; Olian & Rynes, 1984; Schuler & Jackson, 1987; Szalagyi & Schweiger, 1984). Schuler and Jackson (1987), for instance, described how HRM activities, including staffing, could be designed to enhance any of three generic strategies by increasing quality, reducing costs, or increasing innovation. In their model, companies pursuing a strategy to increase quality would likely develop very explicit job descriptions and encourage continuous training and development for employees. Cost-reduction-oriented companies would employ clear, specific job descriptions and narrow career paths. Finally, firms seeking to increase their level of innovation would encourage less detailed job descriptions, and in fact actively pursue coordination among jobs and broad career paths. In each example, Schuler and Jackson (1987) argued that appropriate approaches to staffing activities could be used to implement strategy.

There are several limitations to the existing research linking staffing with stage of development or strategy. The principal drawback is the primarily conceptual nature of the research. As Lewin (1987) has noted with regard to industrial relations as a "strategic choice variable," the research in that area, as well as that linking strategy and staffing, has yet to show empirical evidence that one approach is better than another for strategy implementation.

Furthermore, Kerr (1982) faulted research that argues for matching manager characteristics to product life cycle, in particular. He claimed that other HRM activities such as reward systems, may be more effective implementation tools, because of their greater likely impact on managerial behavior. In addition, what appear to be intuitive "matches" may not be. While at first blush it may make sense to match a manager at the "caretaker" level of his or her career with a product at the end of its life cycle, it may in fact be more advantageous to put an "innovator" type manager in that job who might bring life to the declining product.

A final stream of literature linking the acquisition staffing-system activity to strategy implementation deals specifically with acquiring managers. Managers can be moved into place from within an organization (discussed in the section on movement of employees), or hired from outside. Research has suggested that firms pursuing certain types of strategies, operating in highly uncertain environments, or desiring specific characteristics in leaders may tend to hire from outside. In a longitudinal investigation of tobacco-industry firms, for instance, Chaganti and Sambharya (1987) found that prospector firms (Miles & Snow, 1978) tended to hire more outsiders with marketing orientation than did analyzer firms in the same industry, while defender firms were more likely to promote insiders with finance orientations. Helmich (1977) suggested that externally recruited CEOs were more task-oriented than internally promoted leaders, but had more trouble satisfying job-oriented needs. Finally, Salancik et al. (1980) found higher turnover among university department heads in departments with a history of internal turbulence, and in fields with less developed and accepted paradigms.

Few researchers have discussed job analysis specifically as a staffing activity that can enhance strategy. Olian and Rynes (1984) hypothesized how firms might design a selection process, including job analysis, to fit Miles and Snow's (1978) strategies, but have not tested their hypotheses. Job analysis provides managers with clear descriptions of jobs and may provide data to determine which jobs are most critical for a given strategy. Once the jobs and criteria are clear, other staffing activities (e.g., selection, socializing, movement) may come into play. For example, a firm pursuing a strategy to decrease costs might use job analysis to determine which jobs to keep, eliminate, or combine.

Recruiting, another step in acquiring employees, may also enter into strategy implementation. The process of recruiting, which may involve interviewing candidates without hiring any, can affect existing employees in several ways (Sutton & Louis, 1987). First, the recruitment process can increase employees' commitment to the firm and perhaps ultimately contribute to strategic implementation. As employees describe their firm to outsiders, they often desire to present a favorable image. Such a phenomenon is similar to the situation many Americans find themselves in when traveling. Even those who are critical of the U.S. find that, when traveling abroad, they end up defending many of the policies and practices they dislike.

A second benefit of recruitment to the strategic-implementation process is that the qualifications of newcomers or interviewees can alert existing employees to the types of skills their firm is seeking from outsiders. The recruitment process, then, acts as a signal as to the way the firm plans to meet its strategic goals, assuming the recruitment process is indeed tied to strategy. This could encourage employees to develop their own skills to a greater extent.

Making Employees Part of the Organization. Much research has examined the processes organizations use to socialize employees (e.g., Feldman, 1984), but as with other HRM areas, there is little discussion of the critical role socialization can play in strategy implementation. The processes of socialization and orientation give organization members the chance to clarify strategic goals and set early expectations with newcomers. Sutton and Louis (1987) suggested that firms could use the socialization process to increase commitment and possibly performance of existing employees, especially those with marginal performance. When such employees are placed in the role of socializers or, in a sense, "role models," this may rekindle commitment, reaffirm their reasons for joining and staying with the organization, and may increase their performance.

Movement of Employees.   A third aspect of the staffing system is movement of employees in an organization through promotion, transfers, or demotion. By far, the bulk of research in this regard has been on promotion, in particular on leader and management succession. Two fairly recent literature reviews on succession summarized major findings of the 30 years of research (Friedman, 1986; Gordon & Rosen, 1981). As suggested earlier, much research concentrated on causes or antecedents of succession. These include organizational characteristics such as strategy, firm size, geographic dispersion, internal turbulence, and hierarchical levels (Chaganti & Sambharya, 1987; Dalton & Kesner, 1983; Salancik et al., 1980; Weber & K'obonyo, 1987). Other literature on succession and movement of managers investigated the consequences of succession, or the degree to which improvements in organization performance resulted. A classic series of studies has investigated manager succession in sports teams (Allen et al., 1979; Brown, 1982; Eitzen & Yetman, 1972; Gamson & Scotch, 1964; Grusky, 1963, 1964). Perhaps partly to explain some of the lack of consensus from much of the research on succession, Beatty and Zajac (1987) proposed dividing the concept of succession into two complementary elements: manager effects, "a good leader does make a difference," and succession effects, "the manager doesn't matter; just the act of changing is what matters." An overall conclusion from studies on succession is that change in leaders is typically more positive when it is a promotion rather than an external acquisition.

Transfer of employees has also received attention as a staffing activity that enhances strategy objectives, in the context of acquiring employees or moving managers to "fit" corporate or strategic business units, discussed earlier (Herbert & Deresky, 1987; Olian & Rynes, 1984). In the international HRM literature (discussed in Chapter Twelve), Ondrack (1985) argued that acquisition, development, and transfer of managers was coordinated by the headquarters operations of multinational firms and treated as a strategic function similar to managing finance or operational areas.

Recent literature on the lack of international transfers by U.S.-based firms suggested that such decisions may have serious negative repercussions (Kobrin, 1988), perhaps ultimately hindering efficient strategic implementation. Firms seeking to expand markets through a strategy incorporating international operations are currently faced with increasing costs of transfer and anxiety over the safety of moving Americans overseas. Consequently, many firms are hiring more local and third-country nationals. Kobrin (1988) has argued that such a policy may conflict with an intended strategy of becoming more international because U.S. managers will not have had the opportunities to broaden their experience outside the U.S. Their thinking, as a result, may be "less global." Thus, lack of an international-transfer policy for home-country nationals could be a strategic deficiency.

A final type of employee movement within organizations is demotion. Defined as a relative loss in status, responsibility, or remuneration, it is rarely discussed or researched in HRM or strategic-management fields (Napier & Sullivan, 1983). Many organizations and individuals only reluctantly acknowledge that demotion occurs; some managers refuse to accept it even when faced with a demotion (Veiga, 1981). Demotion, as a staffing activity related to implementation of strategy is likely to become more evident, however, especially with the increase of mergers and acquisitions and the "restructuring" of organizations.

There does exist research in the career-management literature, however, that may shed light on how demotion or "downward movement" might be a positive means to implement strategy. Although they do not use the term "demotion," Dalton, Thompson, and Price's (1977) research on how professionals can move up and down through various stages of their careers may provide insight into a role for demotion. Briefly, they have argued that professionals *may* (do not always) move through four career stages, ranging from acting as an apprentice, an independent contributor to organization goals, a mentor, and a "shaper" of the organization and possibly the broader (e.g., industry) context. As individuals move into new learning areas, they may move from a more advanced stage to an earlier one. For example they may have to move from acting as mentors to becoming apprentices in a new area.

The following example illustrates how such a concept as "downward movement" could be applied to a situation where a new strategy needs to be implemented. A firm diversifying into new business lines may move individuals who have been in Stage III (mentor positions) into Stage I roles (where they act as apprentices, learning the new business). In Dalton et al.'s (1977) model, there is no stigma attached to such a move. Individuals are simply in a new career stage for the period during which they acquire new skills. In such a situation, people are clearly moved from positions of greater responsibility into ones where they are gaining new knowledge and expertise to facilitate a different strategic direction. It may be also a matter of effectively managing the communication, language, and symbols used to convey the proper image. While objectively the argument could be made that these people were "demoted," in this context, the movement could also be viewed as a positive contribution to strategy implementation.

Staffing's Role in Culture

A third means for implementing strategy is designing an organization's culture to enhance strategic objectives. This topic has received much attention from the academic (e.g., Fombrun, 1984a; Posner, Kouzes, & Schmidt, 1985; Schwartz & Davis, 1981; Ulrich, 1984) and popular press (Deal & Kennedy,

1982; Peters & Waterman, 1982). Its role in implementing strategy is closely linked with both design of structure and human resources systems.

Fombrun (1984a), for instance, has presented an overview framework for understanding and managing culture. He started with the argument that culture in a firm must be consistent with several other "cultures," at different levels. Specifically corporate culture must mesh with both society-level and industry-level cultures. Society culture emerges from political and social values that determine the relationship among business, labor, and government institutions. Likewise, a business firm must acknowledge and, if possible, "use" its industry culture as it designs its internal corporate culture. The industry culture is derived from the nature of the product, industry stage of development, technology and structure. Finally, firms face organizational culture, which can be designed to carry out strategy. Indeed, firms such as Hewlett–Packard may select employees who expressly fit or are consistent with the organization culture.

Other researchers and practitioners have used case discussions to illustrate culture's role in strategy implementation (e.g., Harris, 1984; Peterson & Waterman, 1982). Harris (1984), for instance, described how Hewlett-Packard has traditionally used the relationships between human resources systems (e.g., selection, evaluation, reward) and culture to implement strategy.

From a somewhat different perspective, Sutton and Louis's (1987) work on the impact of socializing newcomers provided impetus for the idea that such socialization may help reinforce, or perhaps formulate organization culture. In socializing newcomers, existing employees perform a bit of "self-socializing." Being put in a position of "explaining" culture to an outsider or newly joined organization member, an employee develops or reiterates his or her own perceptions and understanding of the way the organization works. In a sense, the employee may instill culture in the newcomers as well as himself or herself.

Selection and staffing can also act as a means of control. If selectors choose new employees who "think like they do," this could enhance internal power bases. Further, Gilmore and Ferris (1989) and Beer, Spector, Lawrence, Mills, and Walton (1984) have suggested that managers might become actively involved in the personnel-selection process to exercise control over what "types" of people are brought into the organization, with respect to skills, ideas, values, ways of thinking, and so forth. Such efforts, it seems, are ways for individual managers to increase their own power or base of influence by internal coalition building. It is clear that such efforts could be useful or detrimental to the extent to which these "personal political strategies" are consistent or inconsistent with organizational staffing strategies. As Ferris, Fedor, Chachere, and Pondy (1989) have suggested, myths (e.g., "only certain types of people 'fit' in this firm") and politics can reinforce an unwillingness to change. If, for example, top managers seek to implement a new strategy that demands a different kind of talent, existing employees may use myths and politics to resist such change and hinder achievement of strategy.

STAFFING AND STRATEGY FORMULATION

In practice and in the literature, the discussion of staffing as a human resources activity that may provide input to strategy formulation is essentially untapped and unexplored. Typically, human resources staff members have not been perceived to have the credibility to make valuable contributions to strategic planning and formulation. This is changing, however, as human resources staff members gain business expertise and top managers increasingly see benefits of early HRM input in the planning process (Fombrun, 1984c; Miller, 1984; Tichy, 1984).

As discussed in previous chapters, strategy formulation typically leads to intended strategy. As strategy making is more fully explored, however, it becomes clear that some strategies emerge unintentionally and informally, from outside the normal strategy-formulation process (Mintzberg, 1987). Strategy making thus comprises the formal formulation or planning process and the informal "bubbling up" process of letting strategies emerge. The more formal process, as discussed in Chapter Five, usually incorporates four broad strategic planning steps: (1) assessing the external environment for opportunities and threats to a firm, (2) evaluating a firm's internal strengths and weaknesses, (3) establishing goals and objectives, and (4) identifying and choosing among strategy options.

It is clear that staffing's role in strategy formulation can be present in these four steps. For example, a firm that recognizes trends toward a shrinking labor force as an external threat may likely consider alternative future directions through intended strategies, partly as a result of its recognition of this staffing issue. If the firm cannot hire workers to fill existing jobs, and it continues to see market opportunities in its current business area, it still has at least two strategy options: it could retrain workers doing other tasks, or consider moving into a different, but still favorable, line of business. The same firm, in assessing its internal strengths and weaknesses, including those related to staffing, may decide it does have potential, through existing human resources staff and available training programs, to train and move some current employees into the needed areas, allowing the firm to remain in the same business. Conversely, the firm may discover, through "skunk works" (Burgleman & Sayles, 1986; Peters & Waterman, 1982) projects by employees, unintended business directions and strategies. "Skunk works" projects are those done "unofficially," which employees pursue on their own time or surreptitiously on company time. Based upon those assessments, the firm may develop new goals/objectives and consider various strategic options. In these steps as well, staffing information is critical: a firm may ultimately choose, for example, to avoid certain business areas because of potentially tight long-term competition for a specific type of labor.

Staffing's role in each of the four strategy-formulation steps is discussed in more detail on pages 94–96: assessing the external environment, evaluating internal strengths and weaknesses, establishing goals and objectives, and choosing a strategy. Figure 6-1 illustrates staffing's role in formulating strategy.

External Assessment

A first step in strategy formulation is a scan of economic, social, governmental, and technical conditions external to an organization. The objective of the scan is to determine whether the environment presents any opportunities or threats to the firm.

As has been suggested through earlier examples, one way staffing can support the strategy-formulation process is through generating information regarding social and work force trends and their likely impact on a firm (Fombrun, 1984b). There are many examples of firms whose strategy formulation has or could be influenced by human resources information. Avon, for example, was traditionally a door-to-door cosmetics sales firm (*Business Week*, 1984). It found itself in a position of having fewer traditional customers as more women worked outside the home. This trend forced a major change in the way Avon did business: rather than relying on selling to women in the home, the firm began selling through catalogues and through working women who acted as Avon representatives in their firms. Such know-how on HRM issues clearly affected the firm's ability to operate and formulate future directions.

General Electric faced a similar realization in the late 1970s (Fombrun, 1984c). The company found that rapid external environmental changes, (e.g., the perception of the role of corporations in society, market opportunity in the U.S. and abroad) forced it to consider HRM issues earlier in its planning process. Recognition that the firm's business directions were implying different kinds of future human resources needs, the company began to "make investments in a campus presence" that would reflect skills needed 10 years down the road, rather than in the next 1-3 years.

Knowledge about links between staffing and the environment can be useful in strategy formulation in other ways. Once again, research on management and leader succession provides some information about environmental and industry characteristics as they relate to succession. Research has shown that variables such as industry structure and characteristics (e.g., growth rate), level of environmental uncertainty, and industry dynamism affect management succession (Lieberson & O'Connor, 1972; Pfeffer & Leblebici, 1973; Pfeffer & Salancik, 1977; Weber & K'obonyo, 1987). Overall findings have suggested that a leader is more likely to be changed under conditions of unstable environment unless the leader was particularly adept at coping with and managing that uncertainty (Pfeffer & Salancik, 1977).

Finally, Sutton and Louis (1987) suggested that recruiting and interviewing job applicants can be a valuable form of environmental scanning. From applicants, interviewers may gain useful information regarding competitors. If an interviewing firm learns, for instance, that a competitor is hiring large numbers of people with certain technical skills, this may be a clue that the competitor is planning a shift in product/service strategy. Regardless of whether the interviewing firm reevaluates its own strategic direction as a result of this information, it could nonetheless incorporate that knowledge into its external environmental data base.

Internal Assessment

A second step in strategy formulation is assessing internal firm strengths and weaknesses. Staffing can come into play in this step in the process of evaluating internal talent pools, especially of likely CEO successors. Firms such as Hewlett-Packard, GE, Weyerhaueser, and Honeywell, have long recognized the need to assess current talents to be able to plan for future management needs (Tichy, 1984). Empirical research also has suggested that firms may want to scan internally for managers who exhibit certain characteristics, before promoting or transferring them (Hambrick & Mason, 1984; Norburn & Birley, 1987). If a firm finds it lacks specific needed talents, based upon knowledge gained through its assessment of internal strengths and weaknesses, it could use staffing to implement a new strategy through the acquisition, development or movement of employees, or by developing a new strategy to match existing internal talent.

Staffing may also contribute to strategy formulation through the recruitment and selection processes used to acquire employees. Cohen and Pfeffer (1986) examined 254 San Francisco Bay area firms on the determinants of their selectivity in hiring practices (e.g., use of education credentials, use of written and unwritten tests, other screen approaches). The findings suggested that hiring standards reflected an organization's skill requirements and preferences for standards as well as its ability to enforce those standards. Such a situation may have potential implications for how a firm could generate intended strategy. If the hiring standards changed, either became much more or much less stringent, this could lead to hiring of a very different group of employees. For example if, over time, the standards were loosened, the quality and skill level may decline, possibly leading to a situation where a firm is unable to achieve its strategic objectives in an effective manner. Once this becomes evident, a firm may revise its strategic objectives to be less ambitious, very likely an unintended strategy. The acquisition process, then, acts as a channel through which human resources enter a firm. In its control of that channel, the staffing function may affect the strategy options available to a firm, in some situations leading it to pursue unintended strategies.

Finally, Sutton and Louis (1987) again offered insights from their study of newcomers' effects on insiders. Interviewing newcomers acts as a way for managers and employees to assess their own talents and skills, compared to what the firm views as "ideal." Recognizing a lack of certain skills may lead to upgrading or even strategy change.

Setting Objectives and Choosing Strategies

The last two steps typically used in strategy formulation are establishing goals and choosing a direction. The previous steps—assessing external and internal conditions—directly lead to choices regarding future strategic direction. Once again, a recognition of the usefulness of staffing information and activities can help a firm choose an appropriate strategy.

A recent survey of *Harvard Business Review* (1987) readers placed the primary responsibility for the loss of United States firms' competitiveness on the shoulders of management. This complements the thought behind the cartoon in which one spouse says to the other, "I want you to have a good breakfast dear. You might want to wrest control of something from somebody" (Cullum, 1988, p. 90). Clearly, the message is that staffing provides the breakfast for the organization. Unless the managers and employees recruited are capable of setting and achieving appropriate objectives and strategies, other areas of advantage may be useless. A study by Goold and Campbell (1988) found that different management styles were associated with different strategies. For HRM professionals, the staffing challenge is to insure that management style of executives selected, especially for senior positions, is compatible with the current and likely future strategies of the firm.

As illustrated earlier in the example of a firm that loosens selection standards, goal setting may be influenced by such changes in who is attracted to the firm. Another firm may use very different staffing practices, yielding another type of HR pool. For example, a firm willing and able to be very selective in its hiring practices, with development programs designed to provide continual upgrading of existing employee skill may find itself able to set very challenging strategic objectives (McCarthy, Spital, & Lauenstein, 1987). In such a situation, a firm may have the option to choose a strategy of increasing innovation or of providing unsurpassed service and be able to achieve such a strategy. Thus, the human resources staffing function could act as a monitor of the flow of certain types of people into and within an organization.

SUMMARY AND CONCLUSIONS

This chapter examined the role of staffing in the strategic-implementation and formulation processes. The two processes were broadly defined and then discussed in more detail in terms of existing research linking them to staffing.

Although staffing has only recently been acknowledged as a contributor to strategic management, its importance is clear. To be competitive, firms must incorporate staffing activities into their strategic implementation and, increasingly into planning and formulation. Further, staffing's role in generating unintended strategies needs to be recognized and explored.

STRATEGY AND THE PERFORMANCE-EVALUATION PROCESS

" . . . the organization [is] derived from evidence on interrelationships that arise when the different types of individuals function together . . . this is a smoothly working pattern, no important part of which can be produced by one type of individual apart from the others. These are interdependent individuals, therefore, whose collective accomplishments cannot be fathomed except by analyzing the types of interrelationships that unite them."
Schneira (1971, p. 264) on army ants.

"We should examine things deliberately, and candidly consider their real usefulness, before we place our esteem on them . . . otherwise, we may happen to admire those accomplishments which are of no real use, and often prove prejudicial to us, while we despise those things on which our safety may depend."
Aesop's Fables (1973, p. 29).

A goal of this book has been to view human resources management as an integral part of an organization's strategy and operation. Similar to the illustration above of ants in a colony, individual employees and the performance-evaluation process should clearly contribute to the broader picture. The present chapter discusses these ideas in more depth.

Chapter Six discussed the strategic importance of other human resources management practices related to staffing, including planning for, acquiring, and allocating employees. Simultaneously, an organization must also develop practices to yield desired behaviors and results from employees; a process accomplished through two key practices, performance evaluation (Chapter Seven) and reward systems (see Chapter Eight).

Performance-evaluation (PE) systems typically have three broad goals: (1) to inform employees about which behaviors and results they should continue or achieve, (2) to identify areas for future employee development, and (3) to generate data for making administrative decisions, such as promotions, pay increases, or transfers. Reward systems contribute to organizations by encouraging employees to join and stay with a firm, and act in ways beneficial to organizational outcomes. These two areas, discussed in Chapters Seven and

Eight, represent what some call the fundamental HRM practices, because they deal with behaviors and outcomes of employees on the job (Latham, 1984). Consequently, their roles in the strategic-management process are critical.

PERFORMANCE EVALUATION'S IMPORTANCE TO THE STRATEGIC PROCESS

Performance evaluation has gained increasing importance as a HRM practice for reasons similar to those that affect other human resources activities. Increased demand for innovation, competition for particular types of talent, changes in the work force, and technological impacts on the traditional nature of jobs have forced firms to consider more carefully what and how performance-evaluation systems should function (Spratt & Steele, 1985; Zuboff, 1988).

Several reasons exist for integrating performance evaluation into the strategy-implementation-and-formulation processes. First, PE can be crucial in implementing strategy because it embodies the descriptions of actions and results that employees must exhibit to make a strategy come alive. In principle, for a prospector strategy, in which growth is a key focus for the firm, performance evaluation would likely incorporate specific sales goals for employees, and call for behaviors that focus on developing a broader customer base, or identify and open new markets. For example, National Car Rental initiated behavior-based performance standards for car-rental agents to implement a new strategic direction (Beatty, 1989).

Furthermore, performance evaluation can contribute to other relevant administrative actions and decisions that enhance and facilitate strategy. One of the key purposes of PE can be to generate "strategic data" (Devanna, 1984), such as an inventory of existing and needed future skills within a firm. This may be especially true in a situation where a firm is shifting its strategic direction from a position of growth through internal development to one of growth through acquisition. With this type of a strategic transformation the need for a different portfolio of employee skills may emerge. As a firm makes such a strategic shift, skills that were previously more important, such as building internal networks of support for developing programs, could be superseded by different skills, such as the ability to assess potential acquisition candidates and integrate very different cultures of the merging firms. As was discussed in Chapter Six, a firm may develop these skills in existing employees or acquire people (i.e., hire from outside) with the needed skills in hand. In either case, the new strategy can be more smoothly implemented with input from a performance-evaluation system that indicates clearly the types of skills that will be needed, and the level of proficiency of such skills held by current employees.

Finally, PE is important for its potential in identifying and formulating new strategies. A recent educational emphasis on making students "computer literate" has opened the possibility of new technological directions for many firms. Firms may choose to investigate previously unintended innovation strategies, in part because of the growing availability of human resources capable of new directions.

Failure of Performance-Evaluation Systems

Despite its potential importance in the strategic-management process, many researchers have noted that traditional performance-evaluation systems are perceived to have serious weaknesses (Beatty & Schneier, 1988; Latham & Wexley, 1981; Odiorne, 1984). First, managers rarely see any payoff to conducting performance evaluations (Napier & Latham, 1986). In terms of his or her own evaluation or reward, it simply does not matter whether a manager does a good job with appraisals of employees. The process typically includes much paperwork, sometimes unpleasant confrontations with employees, especially poor performers, and often generates little return in terms of changed behavior (Meyer, 1983). In addition, it is often logistically difficult to evaluate employee performance. When employees are geographically separated and highly mobile, managers must use indirect, often sketchy and limited information on which to make assessments (Odiorne, 1984). Finally, Beatty and Schneier (1988) suggested other causes, such as managers' lack of proper training in performance management, inaccuracy of ratings, and the disagreement of whether PE falls under the domain of HR staff or line departments.

Such frustrations with performance-evaluation systems frequently lead organizations to modify or change completely their current systems. There can be a danger in such rapid turnover of performance-evaluation systems. Replacement systems may more likely address a symptom (e.g., dissatisfaction with the format, too little time to conduct an interview), rather than a deeper problem (e.g., managers are uncomfortable with the act of evaluation, the system is not linked to firm strategy or objectives). The goal of this chapter, then, is to assess how performance evaluation can be part of the strategic-management process, which should enhance its usefulness in organizations.

The chapter first examines research on performance-evaluation systems in general and then on the "mechanics" of conducting performance evaluation. These latter issues include who to evaluate, criteria for appraising employees, and identifying what affects management performance. Throughout, the discussion makes suggestions on how performance evaluation can contribute to strategy implementation and formulation.

AN OVERVIEW OF RESEARCH
LINKING PE SYSTEMS AND STRATEGY

Research on performance-evaluation systems has included conceptual frameworks linking strategy and PE as well as empirical work primarily investigating PE's role in strategy implementation. To date, research has not explicitly addressed performance-evaluation's role in formulation of a new strategy, although some studies provide insights on how this could occur.

PE and Strategy Implementation

Several researchers have suggested that performance evaluation be couched in a broader, strategic context (Beatty & Schneier, 1988; Devanna, 1984; Fombrun & Laud, 1983; Kerr & Snow, 1982; Lawler, 1984; Migliore, 1982; Salter, 1973), often as it relates to rewards. A limitation of much of the work on performance evaluation, similar to the other strategic HRM practices, is its presentation of conceptual models, with little testing of those models. Nonetheless, the section reviews three frameworks that have appeared in recent years to illustrate the general thinking in the area.

Cummings (1984) offered a comprehensive framework, focusing primarily on compensation, that brought performance evaluation into the process as a cornerstone for developing reward packages. He argued for "balancing" three clusters of variables as a firm determines the nature of its compensation system. Specifically, a firm should seek to match its "growth stage," and its internal HRM context, comprising key functions (e.g., promotion system, training and developing programs, evaluation system, and decision-making approach) with its compensation components. The compensation components include salary, benefits, perquisites, and short- and long-term incentives. A firm in an early stage of growth might have the following types of HRM components in its internal context: practices to promote people able to achieve rapid revenue growth and make relatively accurate and quick decisions, employee development opportunities that focus on adapting to new technology or fast growth, and a performance-evaluation system that calls for criteria encouraging these types of actions. Compensation components would then "match" growth stage and HRM context. Balkin and Gomez-Mejia (1987), for example, found that firms in a growth stage used incentive pay to a greater extent than firms in a mature stage. While Cummings' (1984) model emphasized key inputs to the design of compensation systems, PE clearly plays an important role in the broader context: strategy, compensation, and other HRM activities must be compatible to allow a firm to achieve its strategic goals.

In another framework, Stonich (1984) suggested that strategy influences management behavior and, ultimately, organizational success by its impact on four key variables: structure, HRM activities, management processes (e.g., decision making), and culture. His model reflected much of the literature linking other areas of HRM with strategy; a role of HRM (and, in this framework, especially performance evaluation) is to implement strategy by affecting managerial behavior in desired ways. The performance-evaluation function contributes by clarifying objectives and behaviors that should be compatible with organization structure, decision making, and culture. For example, in a highly decentralized structure, where managers are expected to exhibit decision-making autonomy and show independent contributions of their units, performance-evaluation criteria would be less likely to include requirements for "team work."

Finally, Von Glinow (1985) emphasized culture as a driving force behind performance-evaluation development. She proposed a two-dimensional matrix, using the axes of concern for people (high or low) and performance expectations (strong and weak), to generate four culture types: apathetic, caring, exacting, and integrative. The cultures, according to Von Glinow (1985), form a basis for developing performance-evaluation criteria and ultimately, reward systems. Using the matrix, an apathetic culture would evaluate employees not on performance, but rather on their political networking capabilities and willingness to conform and "play by the rules." The ideas associated with the role that politics plays in performance evaluation are gaining increasing attention (Ferris, Fedor, Chachere, & Pondy, 1989; Longenecker, Sims, & Gioia, 1987). In a caring culture, appraisal would be based on non-performance criteria, such as job type, tenure, and seniority. An exacting culture would use peer appraisals and multiple measures to assess output performance, whereas an integrative culture (high on both matrix dimensions) would encourage innovation and more willingly accept failure as part of expected performance.

The empirical research examining potential links between strategy and performance evaluation has focused principally on PE's role in the implementation of strategy (Bills, 1987; Fombrun & Laud, 1983; Gupta & Govindarjan, 1982; Kerr, 1985), rather than on its input to strategy formulation, although some research provides potentially useful insights in that regard (Ferris, Buckley, Yee, & West, 1988; Frohman, 1984).

The research linking strategy and performance evaluation has revealed mixed findings. Some studies have shown a weak relationship between strategy and performance evaluation, or certain aspects of the PE system (e.g., Fisher & Shaw, 1987; Napier & Smith, 1987). Other work has identified a link (e.g., Kerr, 1985). Fisher and Shaw (1987) used mail survey data from 174 Singaporean firms to test several hypotheses proposed by Olian and Rynes (1984), examining links between strategy groups and various HRM practices. Finding little relationship between strategy and performance-appraisal systems, they offered possible explanations: government and social pressure, including mimicry of firms for one another, to pursue certain HRM practices, regardless of "fit" with strategy, reluctance of firms to change practices once instituted, tight labor-market conditions, and limitations in their sample. Fombrun and Laud (1983) and Laud (1984) found that few firms in a sample from the *Fortune 1300* tended to use performance-evaluation information in strategic decisions, such as identifying high-potential employees or career-pathing decisions. Finally, Napier and Smith (1987) found firms at opposite ends of the diversification continuum, either very low or very high diversifiers, were more similar to each other in their criteria than were the related firms that were medium diversifiers. They speculated that a reason for the finding might be that high diversifier conglomerates and unrelated firms are in a sense a "collection" of low diversifiers, and thus use performance criteria that are similar to those of single-business or vertically integrated firms.

Other empirical research uncovered links between strategy and PE. For instance, Kerr (1985) examined 20 industrial firms to assess the relationship between diversification and reward systems, which appeared to reflect approaches toward performance evaluation. Through interviews with 89 compensation experts, business planners, and line managers, Kerr (1985) identified three clusters of compensation systems, based on hierarchical structures, performance, or a mixture of both systems. Hierarchy-based systems, common in firms with a steady-state strategic posture, used performance-evaluation criteria that rewarded employees' tenure with the organization and ability to help the firm maintain its current strong position. Firms with performance-based systems typically pursued evolutionary growth, evaluating and rewarding people for performance results and achievement of firm growth goals. Finally, other firms used "mixed" approaches, employing both hierarchy and performance-based systems to manage very diverse sets of activities and behaviors.

In a study bearing indirectly on links between strategy and performance evaluation, Bills (1987) found relationships among environmental conditions, strategies pursued by three different types of organizations, and their respective approaches to internal labor markets. While he did not explicitly examine human resources systems, his results have implications for HRM, especially for staffing and performance-evaluation systems.

Specifically, Bills (1987) found that in a hospital the need and desire to control and predict operations by knowing nursing levels in advance lead to a decision-making approach that was very much top-down regarding the types and quantity of nursing skills needed. Thus, the intended strategy (i.e., desire to have predictability in controlling operations) suggested a clear role for staffing and performance evaluation. The hospital needed to communicate clearly what tasks had to be done and the types of people required to do the work. This would suggest a need for sophisticated planning of staff loads and a performance-evaluation system with explicit criteria and expectations, perhaps including some provision for attendance. In contrast, Bills (1987) examined a consulting firm, which had a strategic posture of seeking flexibility; in this case, the organization required an ability to react quickly to marketplace demands. Such a firm's performance-evaluation system would be expected to concentrate on identifying needed skills in employees and encouraging them to stay current in high-demand technical areas. Finally, Bills (1987) examined a manufacturing firm pursuing a "fixed" wage structure, with a clear-cut "hard-liner" philosophy regarding employee relations. The philosophy was well known, both inside and outside the firm. The staffing system, then, could be somewhat self-reinforcing; many employees might tend to avoid (or seek) a firm with such a reputation. As a result, recruiting and selection might be more efficient. A performance-evaluation system in this type of firm might be expected to include specific and perhaps fairly narrow performance-output criteria, for example.

A final perspective on links between PE and strategy implementation embraces the notion that organizational-control systems can and should relate to performance. Essentially, the argument makes two points: (1) PE can be part of an overall control context (Baysinger, 1985) or (2) PE, as part of HRM, can be a control system in itself (Snell, 1988). Baysinger (1985) has argued that many factors influence organizational control (including strategy, structure, technology, and individual performance). The effectiveness of a control system will be influenced by the extent to which it "fits" the expectations of employees regarding the work situation and the severity of "road blocks" in the way employees approach their jobs (e.g., politics, time perspectives, and rational self-interested behavior).

Snell (1988) has suggested that HRM controls will vary and can be designed based on factors such as the type and level of administrative uncertainty perceived by managers. In particular, Snell (1988) argued that HRM controls can be used to influence performance: (1) *input controls* (e.g., staffing, training, socializing) affect individual performance before it takes place; (2) *behavior controls* (e.g., behavioral PE criteria, change in behavior, feedback) influence the job actions of employees; and (3) *output controls* (e.g., achievement of targets) tie rewards to employee performance for meeting goals. Various factors can affect these types of control, such as managers' ability to understand the controls and managers' perception of organizational administrative uncertainty.

PE and Strategy Formulation

Although research has not directly addressed the role of performance evaluation in strategy formulation, some studies may provide insights on the role PE could play in this area. Two studies reviewed here, one on the PE system in an R&D lab, the other on a firm that underwent a major culture shift, have implications for the possible role PE could play in strategy formulation.

In an R&D lab, perhaps more than in other settings, the PE system might be expected to play a role in formulating strategy, particularly unintended strategy. In such settings, one would expect professionals to be encouraged to exhibit innovation to develop products that are eventually marketable. Through such a process, a firm may well identify market opportunities and unintended strategies. An example of this is the 3M Company's unintended strategic shift into Post-It note pads.

Ferris et al. (1988) conducted an investigation to describe performance-evaluation systems for research and development professionals in high-technology firms. Although, they were not looking specifically for evidence of PE's role in strategy formulation, the research results revealed little evidence that might even hint at such a role. Most firms they examined had formal evaluation systems, using some form of management by objectives or goal setting. The systems typically used criteria that were both quantifiable (e.g., work accomplished), and more subjective (e.g., quality of work). Finally, the R&D professionals reported many of the same dissatisfactions with their PE systems that are found in other situations. Common complaints were that their managers did not implement and use the systems objectively, or weighted too heavily such non-performance-based criteria as effort and personality traits.

One might expect an R&D lab, perhaps more than other work settings, to use performance evaluation as a way to help generate ideas and marketable products, leading to unintended strategies. Granted, the Ferris et al. (1988) study did not directly address the role of performance-evaluation systems in strategy implementation or formulation, but their findings are nonetheless somewhat discouraging.

Another study provided a glimmer of a potential role for performance evaluation in the strategy-formulation process. In the early 1980s, Frohman (1984) assisted a high-technology firm that sought to increase its efficiency, partly through developing a more team-oriented culture. To achieve the goal, top management realized the need to increase the role of the HRM function and involve it in formulating its new direction. The desired culture, which would encourage teamwork, required a major revamping of management roles, and demanded performance expectations that would clarify behaviors and results needed for the new "mind set." While Frohman (1984) did not explicitly discuss performance evaluation's role in the change, his broad focus on HRM's importance in affecting the bottom line supported the general premise that HRM, when tied to strategy, can make a difference. In this case, PE's involvement early in the planning stage could play a critical role in the firm's ultimate success. A firm seeking to "change the mind set" of employees must assess whether employee behaviors can and will change, what new results are desired, and whether they are feasible for employees. Before deciding to pursue a new direction or culture, a firm should assess the feasibility of the change with regard to how performance evaluation and other HRM areas could enhance or hinder achieving the change. This experience illustrated how performance evaluation can be effectively brought into play in the formulation of the new direction, rather than strictly in the implementation phase.

PERFORMANCE-EVALUATION COMPONENTS AND THEIR RELATIONSHIP TO STRATEGIC MANAGEMENT

While the previous section reviewed performance-evaluation systems in general, this next discussion examines selected "mechanics" or components of performance evaluation. These components encompass the elements that can be manipulated in designing a performance-evaluation system.

Many components of performance evaluation have been exhaustively examined by scholars in the organizational-behavior (OB) and HRM areas (Bernardin & Beatty, 1984; Carroll & Schneier, 1982). Most of the emphasis has been on such topics as job analysis, legal aspects, formats for instruments, the effectiveness of appraisal information (i.e., its reliability, validity), and the process of conducting evaluation (e.g., rater training, motivation, the interview). The focus has clearly been on the performance-evaluation system itself, not on its role in the organization at large. This is similar to research on other human resources management practices, such as selection (Schmitt & Schneier, 1983), where until recently there was little recognition of performance-evaluation's role in a broader strategic context (Fombrun, Tichy, & Devanna, 1984; Napier, 1983).

This section discusses performance-evaluation components that can be key elements in strategy implementation and formulation: (1) who should be evaluated, (2) what criteria are appropriate for evaluation, and (3) what organizational factors affect performance (Figure 7-1).

Who to Evaluate

The question of who to evaluate is rarely addressed in performance-evaluation research. More often, the question is who should do the evaluating (e.g., superiors, subordinates, peers) (Bernardin & Buckley, 1981).

The issue of who to evaluate in PE systems that are tied to strategy is important for at least two reasons. First, research on evaluation of top managers versus other employees has been done by very different types of scholars, yielding few overlapping conclusions, since their interests and concerns have varied so much. Most of the extensive research on performance-evaluation systems and components has been done by psychologists and researchers in organizational behavior and HRM. (Carroll & Schneier, 1982; Latham & Wexley, 1981). This work has focused on PE systems as applied to

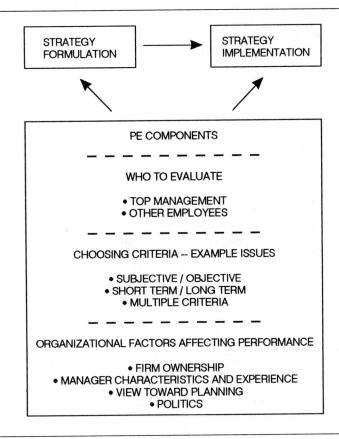

FIGURE 7-1. Performance evaluation components affecting strategy formulation and implementation.

employees below the top-management level, with little attention to top-management evaluation.

Executive evaluation has been discussed by strategic-management researchers or those who straddle the HRM and strategic-management fields (Devanna, 1984; Kerr, 1985; Napier & Smith, 1987; Pitts, 1974; Salter, 1973). This research stream has emphasized such factors as the success or failure of various criteria and reward packages in generating performance results from executives. Compared to exhaustive discussion in the HRM research area on rater biases, instruments, or accuracy, this latter research has been less specific regarding particular methods—other than reward and bonus packages—to encourage behaviors from managers. Thus, one stream of research (primarily from HRM) has examined PE components for a majority of organization employees (those below top management), while another research stream (mainly from strategic management) has focused mainly on how to evaluate a smaller, but very critical employee group. Because executives are considered more involved in strategic aspects of running an organization, the research from strategic management has tended to be more closely linked to strategy. To make performance evaluation "strategic" throughout an organization, it is necessary to consider aspects of PE systems and components for both groups of employees, those at senior-management levels and those below.

A second reason that the issue of who to evaluate is important relates to the first. Firms need to assess the advantages and disadvantages of involving all levels of employees in strategy implementation. If only certain levels of employees, such as top managers, are viewed as critical to strategy implementation and formulation, then one could argue that performance evaluation need only be made "strategic" for those managers. Linking strategy to performance evaluation for top managers might include, for example, developing goals that support the strategy, or using objectives and reward packages that encourage a long-run perspective. A major disadvantage of involving lower-level employees in a strategic performance-evaluation program is the additional time and effort required on the part of senior managers to clarify the strategy and perhaps the formulation process, and provide more detail of how each employee plays a role in its implementation. If, on the other hand, there is a perceived benefit to encouraging an organization-wide understanding of and involvement in strategy implementation, then the design of performance-evaluation and other HRM practices would be expected to include expectations for employees at all levels that relate directly to achieving strategic goals.

The contention of this and other books on strategic human resources management (Beer, Spector, Lawrence, Mills, & Walton, 1984; Fombrun et al., 1984; Odiorne, 1984; Walton & Lawrence, 1985) is that HRM activities can enhance and facilitate the processes of implementing and formulating strategy. An assumption underlying this argument is that HRM activities permeate an organization, from top to bottom. Thus, a PE system linked to strategy implementation, if not also formulation, should have meaning for and involvement of employees at all levels.

The link between implementation and performance evaluation for multiple levels of employees can be achieved several ways; one way is through specific performance criteria. While the issue of determining criteria will be discussed in more detail later, a brief example illustrates how "strategic criteria" could be used at various employee levels. As deregulation forces banks to become aggressively competitive, many have reacted by incorporating previously unimagined performance expectations into jobs at all levels. For example, banks pursuing market-growth strategies may build into their PE systems the expectation that all employees will work to attract new customers. Before deregulation, banks waited for business to arrive. Now, bank employees from tellers, to loan officers, to trust clerks are encouraged to use sales techniques to find new customers or sell additional services to existing consumers. To facilitate such behavior in employees, banks use incentive programs and performance goals (e.g., certain number of new customers per month).

Performance-Evaluation Criteria

A critical second component in a performance-evaluation system is identifying and communicating the criteria used in appraising employees. As suggested earlier, research linking strategy and criteria has most often applied to top-level managers. This chapter argues, however, that strategy-related criteria can and should be applied to lower-level employees.

Research on executive-level performance evaluation and reward systems has suggested that criteria are both objective and subjective (Crystal & Hurwich, 1986; Sethi & Namiki, 1987; Spratt & Steele, 1985). Frequently examined objective criteria include those that focus on corporate or unit financial goals, returns to the shareholder, and interrelationships of units within a firm (e.g., corporate-division, across divisions) (Kerr & Bettis, 1987; Salter, 1973; Schuler et al., 1985; Stata & Maidique, 1980). Subjective criteria are often implicit and include those such as a willingness to take risks (Salter, 1973; Hoskinson, Hitt, & Hill, 1987), organizational loyalty (Bower, 1983), and interpersonal competence (Beer et al., 1984; Schuler et al., 1985).

Much of the research on criteria for managers has been coupled with discussions of reward packages (Balkin & Gomez-Mejia, 1987; Migliore, 1982; Murthy & Salter, 1985). While some research has revealed links between executive reward and strategy (e.g., returns to shareholders) (Lewellen & Huntsman, 1970; Murphy, 1986), other work has not (Kerr & Bettis, 1987; Murthy & Salter, 1975). Part of the reason for lack of relationships may stem from organization and environmental change. Salscheider (1981) and Sethi and Namiki (1987) have suggested that factors such as increasing structural centralization, growth in unrelated mergers, and recognition of the effect of global markets, has increased the difficulty in designing and implementing reward systems.

There have been many suggestions about ways to design performance-evaluation and reward systems (Crystal & Hurwich, 1986; Salter, 1985;

Salscheider, 1981; Sethi & Namiki, 1987; Spratt & Steele, 1985). A repeated suggestion has been to develop approaches that encourage managers to focus more attention on attaining long-term objectives. This suggestion continually rankles scholars and practitioners who recognize the difficulty of instilling a sense of the imperative to achieve long-run goals, when managers perceive greater payoffs for delivering immediate, short-run results. Nevertheless, as illustrated later, some firms have tried to achieve such a balance between long-term and short-term goals.

A second suggestion from the literature has been to use multiple criteria in evaluation. This design element builds on the previous one, incorporating both long- and short-run goals into expected performance, and is commonly discussed regarding PE systems for non-management employees as well.

Multiple criteria are beneficial for at least two reasons. First, more performance measures can provide a fuller picture of employee performance. As mentioned earlier, there are situations, (e.g., geographically dispersed employees), which prohibit a manager or executive from closely observing a subordinate. Multiple criteria offer several forms and sources of information on which to evaluate. A second reason for using several criteria derives from the restructuring currently occurring in businesses. As organizations "downsize," some employees are doing more tasks in their jobs and thus additional criteria may be critical to capture the range of activities a job entails.

Another issue raised in the literature, as a result of executive-compensation trends in the last five years, is the importance of keeping reward levels in line with what is "reasonable" in the firm and the industry (Murthy & Salter, 1985). Executives who receive annual reward packages of several million dollars increasingly face repercussions of lower-employee morale or criticism from union spokesmen and stockholders.

Finally, the literature has reiterated the need for performance criteria and reward packages to be tied closely to a firm's business plan, which encompasses developing criteria that are appropriate for employees at several levels, while maintaining a sense of continuity and consistency across the criteria. Other than Latham (1984), who suggested that firms can apply selected general behavioral expectations for all levels of employees, the literature has not addressed this issue in any depth. The idea of using like criteria across levels should be considered very carefully. There is some research that would suggest criteria typically differ even across adjacent top-management levels (Pitts, 1974; Napier & Smith, 1987).

There exist some examples of firms that have tried to incorporate these critical components in developing performance-evaluation criteria and reward systems. One instance of a firm that had success was Analog Devices. In the early 1980s, Analog Devices sought to achieve both long- and short-run goals (increased sales while maintaining a high return on assets) in its executive-performance and executive-compensation systems. A major objective for the program was that it had clear performance measures and payoffs (Stata & Maidique, 1980). Using multidimensional criteria (sales growth to assess long-term results and ROA to assess short-term results) and comparisons to similar firms in its industry, Analog Devices designed a "bonus matrix." Executives in the program (senior executives and those 2-3 levels below general managers) had to achieve both types of goals, which were clearly exhibited.

A last example of a proposed approach to dealing with performance criteria was suggested by Odiorne (1984). He proposed that firms view their human resources in a portfolio perspective. Specifically, Odiorne (1984) offered a matrix to classify employees based on assessment of their actual performance and potential for the firm. The resulting "portfolio" of employee types includes workhorses (high-performance, low potential), stars (high-performance, high-potential), problem employees (low-performance, high-potential), and dead wood (low-performance, low-potential). According to Odiorne (1984), grouping employees this way allows an employee and manager to set different types of objectives: those to help the employee (and firm) become more innovative, those to solve specific problems, and those considered "regular" performance objectives. A firm could presumably use the "portfolio" of employees to make staffing and reward decisions. For example, drawing upon research discussed in Chapter Six, a firm could match employees to strategic business units.

Factors that Help or Hinder
Strategic-Management Performance

A well-designed, well-implemented performance-evaluation and reward system may be affected by several factors that work for or against effective performance. Researchers have suggested that factors such as firm ownership (Gomez-Mejia et al., 1987), manager characteristics and experience (McEnrue, 1988), inappropriate measures of performance (Kerr & Bettis, 1987), and firm view toward planning in general (Ramanujam & Vendatraman, 1987) may influence successful manager performance.

Another key factor that may influence successful PE programs is politics (Ferris et al., 1988; Longenecker et al., 1987). Ferris et al., (1989) suggested that politics and myths can be used to thwart changes in PE systems; indeed, they concluded from case study examples that when an organization faces a fundamental change, the employees are very likely to use myths and politics to resist the change. Finally, Longenecker et al., (1987) stressed the major role that politics can play when executives conduct appraisals. Indeed, the researchers concluded that managers may purposefully distort appraisal ratings (inflate *or* deflate) to encourage and motivate employees.

SUMMARY AND CONCLUSIONS

This chapter reviewed literature that addresses general PE systems and selected components that may affect the "strategic" nature of PE. As with the other HRM areas, research relating PE and strategy is in a developmental stage, with few firm conclusions. Even so, it appears that it is possible and beneficial to tie PE systems to strategy implementation and, where possible, to formulation.

STRATEGIC REWARD SYSTEMS

. . . wine maketh merry: but money answereth all things (Ecclesiates).[1]

The full extent to which reward systems can influence an organization are not clearly known at this time. Research efforts have suggested that reward systems can influence: (1) who is attracted to an organization as well as who remains in an organization (Mobley, 1982), (2) the level of employee motivation (Lawler, 1973; Vroom, 1964), (3) the overall culture or climate of the organization (Kerr & Slocum, 1988; Lawler, 1984), (4) the organization's overall structure (Lawler, 1981a, 1984), and (5) the level of operating costs (Lawler, 1984). More recent research has suggested that an organization's ability to fulfill its strategic plan may also be influenced by its reward system (Gomez-Mejia & Welbourne, 1988; Kerr, 1985, 1988).

A major reason for determining the influence the reward system may have on organizational functions is to increase the effectiveness of the organization (Spratt & Steele, 1985; Stonich, 1981; Tomasko, 1982). Many of the current reward systems tend to encourage behavior directed toward short-term gains. Reward systems of this type reinforce a short-term orientation, which may be at variance with the needs of the organization (Stonich, 1981). If changes can be made in current reward systems that encourage long-term achievements, more emphasis may be placed on strategic planning, which may lead to healthier and more prosperous organizations.

The main focus of this chapter is to examine possible ways that reward systems can be linked to the organization's business strategy (See Figure 2-2). This type of linkage will reinforce the organization's strategy by rewarding behavior that supports the business strategy.

Toward this end, several aspects that can be generalized to most reward systems must be reviewed. While outlining the format of the chapter, Figure 8-1 also highlights the areas where the strategic-management and reward-system processes have potential linkages that can be exploited.

As can be seen in Figure 8-1, four components of reward systems are discussed at length: (1) definition and domain, (2) objectives, (3) forms, and (4) special problems. On the strategic management side, four separate areas are examined. First, reasons why it is important to link the organization's reward systems and strategic business plans are delineated. Second, the stories of several companies that have successfully linked their business strategies to

---

[1] Chapter 10, verse 18 (King James Version).

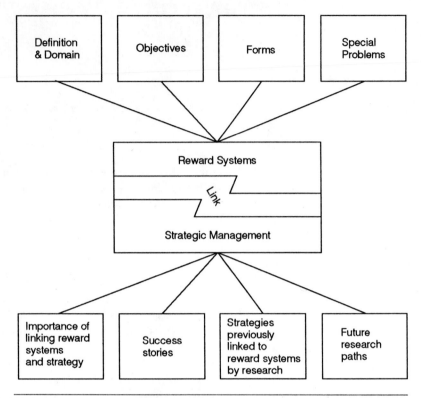

FIGURE 8-1. Format of the reward system-strategic management link.

their reward systems are related. Next, studies that have focused specifically on a business strategy and attempted to design reward systems to further the business strategy are presented. Finally, future research directions that indicate how else reward systems may be linked to an organization's business strategy are proposed.

DEFINITION AND DOMAIN

While compensation and reward systems are terms that are often used interchangeably, the position taken here is that monetary compensation is only one component of the firm's reward system. A basic definition of monetary compensation suggests that it is the money and benefits that organizations give employees in exchange for their labor (Hall & Goodale, 1986). When attempting to create a complete list of what could be considered a benefit, the problems associated with this simplistic definition come to light. Milkovich (1988) recently argued for a broader definition of compensation that recognizes its multidimensionality.

The multidimensionality of compensation was also clearly outlined by Hall and Goodale (1986). These authors suggested that compensation, one of the most complex functions for human resources executives, includes strategic, managerial, and operational issues of job worth, social and legal issues of equitable and fair treatment of all employees, motivational issues concerning the rewarding of outstanding performance, and external competition in the labor market. Further extending the boundaries of compensation, Walker (1980) suggested that compensation should also be linked to performance appraisals, job analysis, career-path design, and career management.

The working definition of compensation, used in the present chapter in an effort to take into consideration its multidimensionality, is a pattern of rewards, both monetary and nonmonetary, provided by the organization to elicit behaviors consistent with the goals of the organization.

OBJECTIVES

Various lists of common objectives of an effective reward system have been delineated (Alpander, 1982; Hall & Goodale, 1986; Lawler, 1984; Newman, 1988; Spratt & Steele, 1985). The most frequently occurring objective on the lists was equity. Three different types of equity have been examined: internal, external, and individual (Newman, 1988). Internal equity concerns the relationship between jobs within the company, and is normally determined by the organization. Organizations that highly value internal equity go to great lengths to ensure that employees performing similar jobs are paid the same even when the employees are located in various geographical locations or in different businesses (Lawler, 1984).

In order to determine which jobs are similar enough to warrant comparable compensation, a thorough understanding of what the jobs entail is needed. This can be accomplished through a job evaluation (Hall & Goodale, 1986). Although there are various methods of job evaluation in practice such as the ranking, classification, and point methods, the end result, determining the worth of jobs and ranking them in order of their worth, is normally the same. Once jobs have been evaluated and ranked, salaries can be assigned. This step results in a salary structure, which when graphed, represents the compensation policies of the organization (Hall & Goodale, 1986). Setting the actual pay ranges and determining the spread between the minimum and maximum pay for a given salary structure involves strategic-managerial decisions (Alpander, 1982). Before these decisions can be made, management must consider both internal and external factors.

The advantages of internal equity are numerous. First, internal equity can produce a homogeneous work environment stemming from feelings of fair and equitable treatment of employees. Also, internal equity can reduce the tendency of employees wanting to transfer to higher paying divisions or locations (Lawler, 1984). Finally, discontent over inequitable pay leading to increased turnover will not result (Alpander, 1982).

However, there are also disadvantages associated with internal equity in an organization's reward system. Salschneider (1981) reported that pay rates across the entire corporation may get set at the rate of the division located in the market with the highest inflation rate. Under these conditions the pay policies would force the organization into a situation where it cannot be competitive (Lawler, 1984). For a firm pursuing a low-cost strategy, this could lead to failure because other competitors may have avoided this dilemma.

The second type of equity, external, allows compensation to be determined by the market and economic conditions. If compensation for a job in one organization is at the same level for the same job in another organization, the compensation can be considered externally equitable (Hall & Goodale, 1986). Organizations normally determine if a job has externally equitable pay.

To determine external equity, organizations can conduct their own compensation survey or rely on a number of salary surveys conducted annually, such as the annual Bureau of Labor Statistics survey of professional, administrative, and clerical salaries (Alpander, 1982). Information collected concerning the market value of jobs can be used alone or in conjunction with internal-equity information in order to determine or verify salary structures (Newman, 1988).

Problems can arise when salaries dictated by internal and external equity conflict. For example, a salary structure created through a job-evaluation technique devised to eliminate internal inequity may not be competitive in the labor market, causing external inequity. When salary structures are not competitive in the marketplace, the organization will encounter difficulties in attracting and retaining employees. However, if steps are taken to adjust the salary structure to eliminate the external inequity, internal inequity is inevitable. From a strategic perspective, this means the firm will always be making adjustments in its reward system to help facilitate the current strategy of the firm.

The final type of equity discussed in the literature is individual equity. While an organization usually determines both internal and external equity, individual equity is determined by the employee (Newman, 1988). Individual equity is concerned with the extent to which an employee's monetary compensation is reflective of that employee's contributions (Hall & Goodale, 1986).

Contributions of an employee entail various forms. Tenure and seniority in an organization can be considered contributions as can performance as measured by a performance-appraisal rating (Hall & Goodale, 1986). If an employee feels his or her contributions are inadequately rewarded, feelings of inequity arise that may lead to dissatisfaction.

Another frequently mentioned objective suggests that the reward system should be an incentive for employees to perform well (Hall & Goodale, 1986; Lawler, 1984; Spratt & Steele, 1985). A well-designed reward system can motivate individuals and teams to develop new technologies, methods, or products, or to more carefully produce current products so that corporate performance increases.

One reason a reward system has the capacity to increase organization performance and effectiveness was offered by Vroom (1964). Employees behave in ways that they perceive will lead to valued rewards. Thus, if an organization can structure its reward systems to encourage employee behaviors directed toward improving corporate performance, employees should behave in a manner consistent with the needs of the organization. The notion of using compensation to support the strategy of the firm is relatively new, but is a variation of older schemes that were directly tied to financial performance.

A final objective of an effective reward system, which was mentioned by more than one author, is retention of employees (Lawler, 1984; Spratt & Steele, 1985). Research has indicated that key contributors, who are critical to the current and future needs of the organization, can be retained through a well-designed reward system (Spratt & Steele, 1985).

Lawler (1984) suggested that organizations who rewarded the most tended to attract and retain the best employees. He further suggested that high performers need to be rewarded more highly than poorer performers in order to be retained. Organizations aware of these results will be in a better position to retain valuable employees.

How rewards are administered may also influence who is attracted to and retained by an organization (Lawler, 1984; Mobley, 1982). An example that illustrates this point concerns high-performing individuals. Merit-based pay systems, designed to reward individuals for their accomplishments, tend to attract and retain high performers over low performers. Rewards available in a merit-based system are attractive to high performers and therefore may increase their retention rate.

Other objectives of an effective reward system, mentioned by only one author, included: (1) recognition of achievements that go beyond the normal highest level of expected performance (Spratt & Steele, 1985), (2) reinforcement and definition of the organization's structure (Lawler, 1984), and (3) linkage to the strategic business objectives of the organization (Hall & Goodale, 1986).

Even though the list of objectives varied from one author to the next, one common suggestion continued to surface. This suggestion was that no one reward system will work for every organization. Each company must tailor a system to meet its needs, strategies, and objectives (Spratt & Steele, 1985). Further, the reward system should not be static. As the organization evolves and grows, or responds to environmental turbulence with new strategies, certain components of the reward system may need modifications to continue serving the needs of the organization.

FORMS

Because no one reward system can fulfill every organization's needs, various forms of reward have been presented. Figure 8-2 lists and categorizes the major types of rewards. It is important for specialists in this area to be aware

Monetary Compensation	Benefits	Status Rewards	Social Rewards
Salary or wages	Stock options	Formal awards	Praise
Commission	Training	Plaques	Smile
Pay raise	Insurance coverage	Office decorations	Evaluative feedback
Performance bonuses	Company vehicle	Location of office	Compliments
Christmas bonuses	Product discounts	Size of office	Informal recognition
Deferred compensa-tion	Tickets to local events	Jewelry	Friendly greetings
	Recreation facilities	Perquisites	Nonverbal signals
Vacation pay	Club dues and	Public recognition	Pat on the back
Pensions or retirement	memberships		Dinner invitations
Profit sharing	Moving expenses paid		Social gatherings
Unemployment compensation	Employee assistance plans		
Worker's compensa-tion	Day care facilities		
Holiday pay	Parking		
Paid sick leave	Meals		
	Trips		

FIGURE 8-2. Forms of rewards.

of the full array of rewards if they are going to balance some of the internal- and external-equity trade-offs discussed earlier (Podsakoff, Greene, & Mc-Fillen, 1988).

Each of the rewards listed in Figure 8-2 can be used to reward individuals or groups, but they are used in different situations. For example, social rewards, which are generally given out in an informal manner, can reinforce appropriate behavior immediately, unlike a monetary bonus that must be normally approved through appropriate channels. However, the lasting effect of a social reward may not be as strong as a monetary bonus. Each category of rewards mentioned in Figure 8-2 is examined below.

Monetary Compensation

The most frequently administered form of reward is monetary compensation, specifically wages or salaries. Employees who do not draw a salary or earn an hourly wage normally work on commission. However, direct take-home pay typically is not the only form of monetary compensation an employee earns.

Another frequent form of monetary compensation is time off with pay. At lower levels in the organization, employees are allowed sick days, holidays, and vacation days with pay. Salaried employees may also have the luxury of "comp time" designed to compensate salaried employees who have worked more than 40 hours in a week.

Because paid time away from work will decrease a company's productivity, some organizations have developed incentives to encourage employees not to use all of the paid time away from work (Hale & Goodale, 1986). The incentives, usually monetary, would be less than the actual cost of the employee's daily pay. However, both the employee and the company gain financially if the employee takes the monetary compensation over the time away from work.

Performance bonuses are another type of monetary compensation, and they are normally reserved for salaried managers (Kerr, 1985). Some empirical research has been performed on the effect of bonuses on performance. Pitts (1974) examined how wide the bonus payoff range between high- and low-performing executives was. Personal interviews were conducted with top corporate personnel executives in 11 companies. The companies were categorized according to their growth strategies, either internal-growth or growth-through-acquisition. Results indicated that bonuses reached as high as 100 percent in organizations following an internal-growth strategy, while organizations following an acquisition-growth strategy reported bonuses no higher than 40 percent.

Different bonus-percentage ranges were reported by Kerr (1985), when the categorization of organizations differed. Data gathered from interviews with 89 compensation specialists, strategic planners, and line managers indicated three different designs of reward systems: (1) hierarchy-based, (2) performance-based, and (3) mixed. Hierarchy-based reward systems determined potential bonus awards by corporate performance and position in the hierarchy. The amount of the bonus was determined through both objective and subjective measures and was limited to 20 to 30 percent of an individual's salary.

Performance-based reward systems determined the amount of the bonus through formulae that were rarely modified. Receiving a bonus rested almost entirely upon performance of a manager's unit. The stated range of bonuses issued under the performance-based plan ranged from 40 percent to "no limit."

Bonuses issued through the mixed-reward system were both objectively and subjectively determined. However, the reasoning for the bonus was primarily based on the performance of a manager's subunit. The range of bonuses reported for organizations utilizing a mixed-reward system were from 20 to 75 percent of an individual's salary.

Migliore (1982) also examined bonuses, albeit not empirically. In an effort to link compensation practices to strategic practices, the author presented a reward system based on management by objectives (MBO). Managers who achieved their previously agreed-upon objectives would receive a bonus. The amount of the bonus would be determined by a criterion developed by the company. The criterion would be simple, straightforward, and well publicized. By carefully developing the objectives managers sought to achieve, the organization's strategy could be more effectively implemented.

A final issue discussed under monetary compensation is pay raises. Two basic types of pay raises have been discussed in the literature: (1) cost-of-living adjustments (COLA) and (2) merit-pay increases. COLA were common in the high-inflationary times of the late 1970s and early 1980s. During inflationary times, workers feel they deserve COLAs to compensate for their reduced buying power (Podsakoff et al., 1988). While organizations may feel compelled to award COLAs to their employees, this practice frequently leads to reduced merit-pay. This reduces the differential between high and low performers (Walker, 1980) and may result in employees not viewing the COLA as a pay raise.

The issue of merit-pay or pay-for-performance has been the focus of researchers' attention of late. Kiefer (1983) indicated that 77 percent of 305 major compensation plans examined were increasing their use of pay for performance, while 66 percent indicated that across-the-board increases were declining in use. Although evidence indicates an increase in the use of merit-pay systems and rewarding outstanding performances through increased pay, exactly how merit systems are implemented is still unclear.

In order for a merit-pay system to be effective, several conditions are necessary. First, the compensation rewards must be high enough to encourage effort. Second, rewards must be allocated differentially, based on performance. Performance must be clearly, validly, and inclusively measured. Information concerning how rewards will be allocated must be communicated to employees. Further, trust in management so that the communication of the reward system is accepted and the performance measures are believed is crucial. Finally, employees must accept the performance-based pay plan (Lawler, 1981b). Obviously, not all of these conditions are easily established, thus causing some difficulties establishing a link between pay and performance.

One major issue that must be dealt with when developing the conditions needed for a successful merit-pay system is to specify what is good performance (Podsakoff et al., 1988). A well designed performance- appraisal system may be able to satisfy this condition (see Chapter Seven).

A second issue that arises when developing the conditions necessary for a successful merit-pay system is timing (Podsakoff et al., 1988; Walker, 1980). Generally speaking, rewards are more likely to reinforce the behaviors required to perform effectively if they are given as quickly as possible after the performance has been evaluated. Further, inappropriate behavior that occurs between the performance evaluation and the receipt of the reward may be reinforced (Podsakoff et al., 1988).

Finally, problems can occur when developing the necessary conditions for an effective merit-pay system if employees refuse to accept the system. Much of the opposition of workers can be traced to lack of trust regarding management's regard for their well-being (Podsakoff et al., 1988). Unions frequently oppose merit-pay systems because they allow differences in pay levels. Also, groups of employees may restrict productivity in an effort to lower performance standards so that normal production will result in higher pay.

Benefits

Non-monetary benefits are a critical element in a reward system. Benefits have been defined as a wide range of supplementary forms of rewards provided to make employment more attractive (Hall & Goodale, 1986).

Walker (1980) reported results from a survey performed by the Chamber of Commerce of the United States concerning employer benefits. The types of benefits offered and the costs paid by employers varied across the 748 companies that participated. The bottom-line costs involved in employee benefits were calculated at 36.7 percent of the total payroll. For firms facing foreign competitors, the total cost of benefits can be a critical element in making a determination to pursue either a low-cost or differentiation strategy.

A more recent survey illustrates this fact. Mercer (1984) reported results from a survey of 305 chief executive officers. 83 percent of the respondents reported the rising costs of benefits, especially health-care costs, were the greatest single obstacle in designing reward systems. Many changes have occurred in health-care programs, in an effort to help organizations cope with their increasing costs. First, deductions paid by employees, which were previously covered by the organization, have increased (Hall & Goodale, 1986). Health maintenance organizations (HMOs) have evolved as a means of limiting an organization's health-care expenditures. Finally, some organizations have decided to provide their own health-care coverage. The money earmarked for health-care expenditures was instead invested and the proceeds used to cover health-care needs of employees.

Another recent change in the area of employee benefits intended to decrease overall costs was the introduction of flexible or cafeteria-style benefit programs (Lawler, 1984). This type of program allows the individual employees the ability to create their own benefit package tailored to their needs. The decreased costs arise because organizations pay only for benefits employees need and will use rather than over- or under-insuring the majority of the work force. This type of program may also increase employee satisfaction by offering them a voice in the total compensation package (Lawler, 1984).

Various other alternative benefits have been introduced recently. These benefits usually have a high value to the employee, yet are low in cost to the employer (Hall & Goodale, 1986). These benefits may also help to reduce organizations' total costs. Examples of these types of benefits might include financial and investment assistance, child-care services or assistance in obtaining it, and legal services. More creative benefits are sure to be introduced in the future as organizations continue to struggle with increased compensation costs.

Status Rewards

Status rewards are much less expensive but can be just as important to employees. The most frequently mentioned form of status rewards are perquisites (Walker, 1980). Perquisites represent important status or recognition symbols and may be linked to the perceived management hierarchy. Walker also noted that perquisites in the international environment, such as entertainment allowances and housing assistance, are becoming more and more popular.

Status rewards, other than perquisites, are also available. For example, clear nonverbal messages used by corporations to differentiate levels will be perceived as a reward by some employees and managers (Balkin, 1988; Balkin

& Gomez-Mejia, 1988). Other examples of status rewards include an office with a window, level in the building on which the office is located (i.e., the higher, the more status), the size of the desk, the number of pictures on the walls, or the number of secretaries "guarding" the entrance to the office.

Status rewards are more frequently used in mature corporations with a distinct hierarchy, thus allowing an indication of power, influence, and status, than in entrepreneurial organizations (Balkin & Gomez-Mejia, 1988). Entrepreneurial organizations generally have a flat structure and a strong need for teamwork. Rewarding individuals with status rewards would not reinforce the type of behaviors employees in an entrepreneurial organization should exhibit. Therefore, when this type of benefit is offered in an entrepreneurial organization, it is done so in a way that all employees can utilize (i.e., a dining room for all employees, not just executives).

Another distinction in the use of status rewards was offered by Lawler (1984) when examining the congruence of reward systems and organizational philosophy. He suggested that traditional organizations, using a Theory X type of management, would frequently utilize status rewards and that these rewards would be directly related to the position of the individual receiving the reward. Management would carefully allocate these rewards in an effort to achieve the appropriate response. Participative companies, using a Theory Y style of management, would rely less on status rewards. Because the goal of a participative organization is to include as many levels as possible in the decision-making process, distinguishing between organizational levels by rewarding workers with status rewards would be counterproductive.

Social Rewards

The final category in Figure 8-2 is social rewards, which are generally awarded on an informal basis. The degree to which social rewards are utilized by managers may depend on the type of management philosophy of the company as well as the climate and culture of the organization (Kerr & Slocum, 1988).

Social rewards are aimed at satisfying employees' need for affiliation and rewarding them in an informal, but immediate, way for exhibiting behaviors conducive to the goals of the organization. Although social rewards are less tangible than the other three types, they are not any less effective provided they are used in a timely and appropriate manner. Because rewards are most effective when they are matched to an individual's needs and to the purpose of the reward, a variety of compensation possibilities are needed. Social rewards are merely one type of compensation technique available.

New Forms of Reward

Besides the traditional techniques listed in Figure 8-2, several new forms of reward have been presented recently. Some of these techniques include an all-salaried work force, "paying the person," and lump-sum salary increases (Hall & Goodale, 1986).

The idea of an all-salaried work force has been introduced in many traditional manufacturing firms where two "classes" of employees existed: hourly and salaried. Hourly workers, who were previously required to punch a clock, lost pay if they punched in late, were given prescribed times for breaks, and were awarded little or no personal time, are now treated as typical salaried employees. This type of move occurred mainly in organizations that are trying to introduce a more participative style of management (Hall & Goodale, 1986). Union support for such plans has been lacking. The main rationale for the lack of support is the increased employee identification with management.

"Paying the person" or skill-based pay systems are based on payment for skills an individual possesses, not for the position that the person holds. As an individual acquires a new skill, his or her pay base would also increase. Organizations that have undertaken a job-redesign emphasis, have begun to use this type of reward system (Hall & Goodale, 1986). Although training costs incurred by such a system may be high, the related costs may decrease. Lawler (1981b) reported that skill-based plans have increased satisfaction with pay and quality of work life, while decreasing absenteeism and turnover.

Inflationary times have also produced another innovation in the form of rewards, specifically, lump-sum salary increases. Regular salary increases that are divided over 12 months and then are exposed to tax and other deductions may seem trivial. However, if the pay raise is given in one lump sum, the purchasing power of the raise increases. Lawler (1981b) indicated that companies such as B. F. Goodrich, Timex, and Westinghouse have begun offering employees an option of a lump-sum salary increase or having the raise distributed over the year. Contingency plans for handling employees who do not complete the year for which the raise was given have also been developed. Normally, the unearned portion of the raise is treated as a loan and repaid in this manner.

PROBLEMS

As with any functioning system in an organization, problems can occur when administering a complex array of rewards. The various types of problems that will be discussed in this section include: (1) wage compression, (2) external factors and economic conditions, (3) providing the wrong form of rewards, and (4) legal ramifications.

Wage Compression

In order for an organization to attract qualified candidates for entry-level positions, starting salaries have to be competitive. Further, high inflation in recent years has added increased upward pressure to starting salaries. Meanwhile, cost-of-living adjustments and merit pay raises for current employees have failed to keep a significant gap between entry-level and upper-level salaries.

In the past, a person beginning a job would be paid one-fourth of what his or her manager made, perhaps $15,000 to $60,000. The current ratio is closer to 1 to 2, perhaps $35,000 to $70,000. In universities, the ratio between beginning and tenured faculty has also decreased in a similar manner. In the late 1960s, the ratio of 4 to 1 ($40,000 to $10,000) was common. However, today the ratio averages 2 to 1 ($50,000 to $25,000) (Hall & Goodale, 1986). In some cases, especially in schools of business and engineering, incoming assistant professors have salaries that are higher than full professors with many years of service.

A question of distortion of the salary structure arises when wage compression is discussed. For example, young engineers currently command starting salaries in the $30,000 range. Managers, who began at a salary of $8,000 20 years ago, may have increased their salary to the $45,000 range. When the experienced manager learns that an entry-level engineer earns a salary similar to his or her own, feelings of inequity are sure to arise (Walker, 1980).

In an effort to combat wage compression, companies have been inventing ways of keeping entry-level salaries down as well as ways to deal with the internal inequity that arises when starting salaries equal or exceed current employees' salaries. One approach used by a chemical firm to control entry-level salaries included cutting the entry-level salary of chemical engineers by $4,000, but increasing the emphasis placed on the quality of the career environment of the company when recruiting. The quality of the recruits did not decline (Hall & Goodale, 1986).

Another approach to reducing starting salaries is to offer lower base salaries offset by company-sponsored perquisites. Among the perquisites included were company cars, club memberships, relocation allowances, or signing bonuses. Additionally, a lower starting salary may be acceptable if the salary adjustment, normally made after the first annual review, is made after six months (Hall & Goodale, 1986).

Two techniques for dealing with feelings of inequity experienced by current employees have been presented (Hall & Goodale, 1986). First, a one-time adjustment can be made to the salaries of employees who are not in high-demand disciplines. A second alternative would be to set up several different salary structures from one job evaluation. The different structures would depend upon the market conditions of the various disciplines. Therefore, there is more of an accepted range of salaries for the same position or level.

External Factors and Economic Conditions

A major problem concerning external and economic factors on the reward system is the lack of documentation about the relationship between these concepts. Much of the work done in the mid-1960s through the late 1970s focused on psychological approaches to understanding monetary compensation and ignored the relationship between monetary compensation and external factors (Cummings, 1984). Milkovich (1988) concurred with this finding when he suggested that there was insufficient research on the effects of environmental differences on compensation strategies.

Economic conditions of late have also caused problems with reward systems. First, the types of monetary compensation provided must be reexamined each year to verify that the benefits are in line with the employees' efforts. This is extremely important during times of increased inflation where the consumer buying power is declining. A merit raise that was a substantial increase one year may barely cover the increase in the cost of living if inflation is high. The cost of living may differ substantially from one area to another, which makes it difficult to develop a reward system that does not either adversely affect or provide unusual benefits to transferred employees. Further, taxes and commutation costs must be examined before adjusting relocated individuals' salaries (Walker, 1980).

Unionization, another external factor that may influence a reward system, has a substantial research base that has recently begun to be integrated into models of strategic human resources management (Milkovich, 1988). However, the environmental jolts a union can inflict upon a firm may trigger varying responses concerning compensation adjustments. A systematic evaluation of whether organizations faced with similar jolts will adopt similar patterns of response is still needed (Milkovich, 1988).

A final external factor that has been shown to influence the compensation policies of an organization is the growth history of an organization (Cummings, 1984). Specifically, problems in reward systems can occur when multi-unit companies, whose products are at various growth stages, attempt to develop a reward system congruent with the growth needs of the organization. Balancing the compensation needs of each unit based on its specific growth stage can be a complex endeavor.

Legal Issues

Legislative pressures can influence monetary compensation policies in a variety of ways. Because legislative changes occur continuously and are frequently unpredictable, constant examination of the influence of legislative changes on compensation policies must be performed. Some of the legislative changes allow organizations some room to interpret the changes, while others are mandatory changes that must be implemented.

One example of a mandatory change that leaves no room for interpretation is the minimum wage law. If the legally required minimum wage is increased, then that wage must be paid. Changes in tax regulations, although just as strictly followed as minimum wage laws, offer more of a chance to interpret how the changes will influence a firm's compensation policies. When tax changes occur, the most frequently influenced compensation policies involve executive compensation (Walker, 1980). As tax laws change, shifts in the attractiveness of the compensation package occur. Innovations that take advantage of the current tax situation are necessary.

The range of employers covered by legislative changes varies as does the degree of change required of the reward system to comply with the new legislation. For example, federal legislation requiring maternity leaves to be considered paid disability only affected a portion of the work force. Similarly,

court decisions concerning violations of the Age Discrimination in Employment Act would also only influence a portion of the work force. Because
different segments of the work force are affected by different legislative changes, problems can occur. Specifically, if legislation mandates a wage increase for
only one segment of the work force, inequities may arise.

Providing the Wrong Form of Rewards

Some companies have used inappropriate forms of compensation, thus
rendering the reward system virtually useless. Spratt and Steele (1985)
reported that one organization used an incentive-stock-option program as a
retention device. However, because of past and projected stock performance,
the investment necessary to provide any sizable return was much larger than
the income of the stock-program recipients would allow. Also, if the fair market
value of the stock dropped below the option price before it was exercised, the
benefits would be nullified. Further, employees who feel they have little impact
on the performance of corporate stock may not view a stock option program
as an attractive benefit or as monetary compensation.

Similar problems can arise with pay raises or monetary bonuses. If the
raise or bonus is not substantial enough to be deemed a reward, the bonus or
raise may only reinforce the perceived disparity between value received by the
organization (i.e., the individual's contribution for which the reward was
offered) and the value received by the employee. When funds are low,
monetary compensation may be an inappropriate form of reward.

Up to this point, this chapter has focused specifically on aspects of the
reward system. As previously mentioned, the major focus of this chapter is to
examine ways in which the various components of the reward system can be
strategically managed. Now that the basic elements of the reward system have
been discussed, the focus can now be turned to how to strategically manage
this system.

IMPORTANCE OF LINKING
THE REWARD SYSTEM AND STRATEGY

Basically, two reasons have been delineated in the literature that under-
score the importance of linking the firm's reward system to its strategic business
plans. The first reason is so that corporate performance and effectiveness will
increase. Linking reward systems and strategy has been suggested as one way
for U.S. companies to more effectively compete with overseas manufacturers.
The second reason is that by linking the reward system and business strategy,
managers may be forced to think more long-term. If rewards are linked to
long-term success, then behaviors consistent with this policy will begin to
emerge, thus increasing the emphasis placed on long-term operations. Both of
these reasons are discussed on the next page.

Increase Competitiveness and Effectiveness

The U.S. industry's competitive decline has been attributed, by some, to the short-term strategic orientation of U.S. managers. This orientation has been fostered by the reward systems offered by U.S. companies (Tomasko, 1982). By changing the short-term focus of the reward systems of U.S. companies, these firms may also be able to change the strategic foci of their managers.

Balkin and Gomez-Mejia (1987) suggested that the challenge of competing with the Japanese in a global market, as well as the frequently changing world of high technology can only be faced by increasing the emphasis placed on human resources management. By viewing human resources management practices as a way to gain a competitive advantage, innovations in practices are sure to follow. The reward system may be the best place to start.

Long-Term Emphasis by Managers

The second, and more frequently mentioned reason for linking the reward system to the strategy of the organization, is to increase the emphasis placed on long-term objectives. Stonich (1981) suggested that the most important aspect of an effective strategy implementation is future orientation on the part of managers. Structuring the company's reward system around this notion can increase the long-term perspective of the managers.

Evidence of the importance of a long-term view was reported by Meyer (1983). She suggested that having stability in their executive groups and having executives who held long-term strategic views explained why some firms outperformed their rivals. Both of these characteristics can be created and enforced through a well-planned reward system, as suggested in the previous section.

A well-designed reward system should be developed from the business strategy (Green & Roberts, 1983). However, government regulations, specifically tax regulations, may pose design problems (Walker, 1980). Essential to the system is a mechanism to measure long-term performance (Hoskisson, Hitt, Turk, & Tyler, 1989). A reward system, based on performance measurement, tied to long-term success will create a mechanism that will get U.S. managers thinking more long-term (Stonich, 1984).

SUCCESS STORIES

Several anecdotal accounts of companies' successful linking of their reward systems to their business strategy, and the benefits earned from doing so, have been reported. Although the problems faced by the companies were similar (i.e., lack of emphasis on the future), how each company chose to deal with the problem differed. This reinforces the idea presented earlier that no one reward system will work for every company.

The first story was reported by Stonich (1981). The company he named King was attempting to reorient itself to the future, but was almost defeated because the reward system emphasized a short-term focus. Managers who accepted the new long-term perspective would have been penalized by the current reward system, thus leading to a lack of commitment to the new strategy. To solve their problem, a new reward system was developed. First, each of the strategic business units was categorized as high, medium, or low growth. Then, new ways to measure performance were developed for each type of growth pattern. The new performance standards were based on behaviors that would help develop a longer-term perspective. The end result was a management team that placed much more emphasis on the future.

A second company faced a similar problem, how to encourage key managers to stop ignoring long-term strategies (Tomasko, 1982). The problem was traced to the reward system, so changes were made to correct the problem. Specifically, how the bonus pay-out was determined was modified. The new formula included varying mixes of annual figures and strategic milestones. For instance, the CEO and division vice-presidents received a bonus based on short-term results while executives who played coordinating roles for the divisions received bonuses based on longer-term results. Also, a carefully selected group of managers in the functional areas received bonuses based entirely on strategic results. These managers' performances were judged by measuring the progress each had made toward the two or three strategic objectives agreed upon at the beginning of the year.

Finally, a third company, faced with a decline in performance due to foreign markets and an eroding market share, also found key employees were joining start-up companies (Spratt & Steele, 1985). This company also needed to change its current strategy and become an entrepreneurial organization. In order to solve its problems and change its strategy, the company decided to create a new reward system. The system consisted of two parts. The first part emphasized product development and short-term objectives. The second part focused on introducing the product to the market and the sales of the product. This part was more long-term, having a three- to five-year time frame. In order to motivate employees even more, there was no maximum reward. This allowed a perception of equity between the possible return of the new products to the company and to the employees.

RESEARCH ON THE REWARD
SYSTEM-STRATEGY LINKAGE

Although various anecdotal accounts of linking reward systems to strategy have been reported, little research has been performed to suggest ways in which specific strategies can be linked to the various components. Only two corporate strategies have been examined in the literature: organization life cycle and diversification (Hoskisson, Hitt, Turk, & Tyler, 1989). However, neither of these strategies has been examined directly, only proxy measures have been used (Milkovich, 1988).

Organization Life Cycles

The original application of organization life cycles to reward systems focused on executive compensation. However, this has been expanded to include the monetary compensation of all employees (Milkovich, 1988). Different types of rewards have been recommended at each stage of the organization's life cycle. When the organization is in the first phase, monetary compensation should include a low base salary with high incentives and low benefits. As the firm enters the mature stage, rewards should be changed to emphasize internal equity, a high base salary with low incentives, and high benefits (Milkovich, 1988). These rewards were suggested as a way to focus on the unique needs of each stage in the organization's life cycle.

One of the few empirical examinations of the influence of organization life cycle on reward systems was performed by Balkin and Gomez-Mejia (1984). These authors examined the hypothesis that high-technology firms in the growth stage were more likely to follow incentive-based monetary compensation strategies than firms in the mature stage. The results supported an outcome opposite to what was predicted. Mature, not high-growth, firms were more likely to adopt incentives than firms in the growth stage.

Anderson and Zeithaml (1984) categorized two thousand manufacturing firms into growth, mature, or declining stages while examining monetary compensation policies. Results indicated that firm competitiveness with respect to pay increased as each new life cycle stage was entered. This aggressive compensation posture adversely affected mature firms' return on investments, but increased growing firms' market share.

Criticisms of organization life cycles in the literature on reward systems have also been reported. First, confusion over which type of life cycle should be used exists. That is, should product life cycle, company life cycle, or market life cycle be used. If product life cycle is selected, other problems can arise. Typically, an organization has more than one product, and these products may be in different phases. If this is the case, classification of the organization into one phase may be difficult (Milkovich, 1988). Finally, more than one reward system may be appropriate for a given cycle (Milkovich & Newman, 1987). As previously mentioned, one reward system will not work for all companies, so too, one reward system will not work for every life cycle phase.

Diversification

Diversification has been used as a way to classify organizations based upon whether they exhibit single, dominant, related, or unrelated product-diversification strategies (Milkovich, 1988). The more diversified, the greater the need for mechanisms to control the separate, diversified business units. One mechanism that has been examined is the reward system.

Pitts (1974), as previously mentioned, classified companies as diversified through internal growth (IGDs) or diversified through acquisition growth (AGDs). Six companies were placed in the IGD category while five were placed in the AGD category. When examining how pay-increase determination differed between these two types of diversified companies, he found that four of the AGDs had pay increases determined strictly on division results. The IGDs used some combination of corporate, group, and division results in determining pay increases. Similarly, four of the AGDs calculate bonuses on a quantitative formula based on financial performance, while the other firms allowed some discretion in determining bonuses. Napier and Smith (1987) found similar results where they compared firms of different diversification levels.

In a more recent study, Kerr (1985) examined the reward system of 20 firms. The firms were categorized according to their compensation strategies. This resulted in the identification of three strategies; (1) hierarchy-based, (2) performance-based, and (3) mixed. In hierarchy-based firms "evaluations were based on the perceptions and judgments of superiors, and the distribution of rewards based on position in the hierarchy" (Kerr, 1985: 167). Individual bonuses were based on the manager's position in the hierarchy and the performance of the corporation. Performance-based systems "stressed precise definition and measurement of performance and a close link between performance and rewards" (Kerr, 1985: 167). The performance of the manager's unit was the only criteria cited in determining bonuses. In mixed system firms, both performance-based and hierarchy-based criteria were used, which resulted in the use of both subjective and objective measures. The compensation strategy chosen was not related to the growth strategy of the firm; but a growth through diversification, merger or joint venture was found to accelerate the development of a compensation strategy.

SUMMARY AND CONCLUSIONS

Although much is known about reward systems and various forms of monetary compensation, much more must still be learned. The link between compensation and business strategies has only been examined by a few and in a limited fashion (Muczyk, 1988). However, before more research of this nature is performed, there are more fundamental questions that should be answered.

More research is needed to determine more accurate descriptions of the content of strategies related to reward systems and how they are formulated. Research techniques used in strategy-formulation studies may be applicable to this type of research. The outcomes of such research may answer questions raised concerning the critical dimensions of monetary compensation and the extent to which these dimensions change for each group of employees (Milkovich, 1988).

Once the critical dimensions of reward systems have been determined, specific types of rewards that support these dimensions should be delineated.

The list of rewards generated should include new and innovative ideas as well as the tried and true forms utilized by virtually every organization.

Innovative ways of examining reward systems should also be encouraged. By examining an old concept with a new perspective, much can be learned. A recent example of an innovative attempt at examining executive compensation in relation to corporate strategy was introduced by Hoskisson et al. (1989). These authors proposed to explain the relationship, or lack thereof, between executive compensation and performance through the use of agency theory. Hopefully, this type of research will motivate others to think creatively about compensation research.

It is also important to examine reward systems in relation to human resources strategies. Two studies have found that reward systems are influenced by an organization's human resources strategies (de Bejar & Milkovich, 1986; Wils & Dyer, 1984). These studies found that reward systems were not always considered important to an organization. Instead, their importance varied with the business strategies an organization pursued.

These findings in conjunction with a suggestion by Tomasko (1982) that preliminary studies suggested that executive monetary compensation itself should not be overly relied upon to induce strategic results, may suggest that compensation may not be the answer to America's organizational problems, as previously thought. Reward systems need further investigation before it can be determined just how useful they may be in helping organizations become productive, effective, and long-term oriented.

The main focus of the present chapter was to examine ways in which reward systems have been linked to an organization's business strategy. To do so, research concerning monetary compensation in general was reviewed, followed by an examination of how reward systems have been examined in relation to an organization's business strategy.

It is important to note that very few studies have empirically examined the link between strategy and reward systems. However, there has been much written about this relationship. Most of this literature is anecdotal in nature, simply reviewing success stories of different firms. From all of this literature, an overarching theory of compensation and strategy has yet to be developed. Perhaps this can be attributed to the recurring suggestion that one reward system will not be successful in all companies.

Just as organizations select a competitive business strategy to fit the needs of the organization, so should reward systems be selected. Perhaps by treating reward systems as a business strategy and not continuing to try to *link* it to business strategies, progress will be made.

STRATEGIC HUMAN
RESOURCES DEVELOPMENT

*Discoveries and inventions are not terminals; they are
fresh starting points from which one can climb to new
knowledge.*[1]

Several major changes have been suggested as a way for U.S. firms to
remain competitive (Haas, 1987; Skinner, 1986). First, managers need to be
more concerned with extending the time horizon for strategic planning (Haas,
1987). Short-term increases need to be de-emphasized if they interfere with
long-term gains. Similarly, managers need to spend more time planning what
their human resources needs will be three to five years from now instead of
being concerned only with maintaining a full staff on a day-by-day basis.
According to Sonnenfeld (1985), to be successful in maintaining or regaining
the competitive advantage, U.S. companies must concentrate on developing
the human infrastructure in the organization. Relating employee development to the competitive strategy of the firm has come to be viewed as an
effective way to bring about these changes in managerial attitudes. Combined
with other developmental programs, which have an impact on the success of
the firm's strategy, these efforts are referred to as strategic human resources
development.

Strategic human resources development has been defined as "the identification of needed skills and active management of employee learning for the
long-range future in relation to explicit corporate and business strategies"
(Hall, 1984, p. 159). Later, Hall and Goodale (1986) extended the concept to
include intermediate-range planning. Organizational career management
(OCM) has been described as activities and opportunities sponsored by the
organization in an attempt to ensure that they will meet or exceed the future
human resources requirements of the organization (Stumpf & Hanrahan,
1984). Although the titles differ, the concepts are similar because they require
that managers plan for the future now.

This chapter argues that the criticisms made concerning the lack of
emphasis placed on long-term strategic business planning also can be made
about long-term human resources development. Integration of these two areas
may become even more essential as managers learn to strategically plan for the
future. By integrating these areas now, techniques used to plan for the future

---

[1] Dr. Willis R. Whitney, cited in *Professional Management in General Electric* (Book
Three), (New York: General Electric, 1954) p. 4.

131

can be applied to both areas instead of only reinventing what the other has already learned.

Strategic human resources development encompasses a wide variety of activities that an organization can sponsor to ensure a strong human infrastructure.

DEVELOPMENT ACTIVITIES

From the list of 13 possible activities that may be appropriate for an organization to offer its employees (Stumpf & Hanrahan, 1984), a modified version of five activities relating directly to the development of employees was selected for discussion. These include (1) career planning, (2) training activities, (3) targeted development, (4) assessment centers, and (5) mentoring. Obviously, cost-benefit analysis and the firm's strategy will dictate the programs the firm selects.

Although these activities all relate to the development of employees, they also differ. One major difference is the time that is needed to implement them. Thus, each activity can be positioned on a time line, as is depicted in Figure 9-1.

As can be seen in Figure 9-1, training activities are on the short-term end of the time line, because these activities can be implemented in a relatively short period of time. The next item on the time line is assessment centers. Although the time needed to develop an assessment center can be quite long, the actual assessment-center procedure does not take very long, perhaps a week. In the middle of the time line is targeted development. Specifically, needs isolated in the assessment center are targeted through various training and development activities in order to keep options open to individuals as they progress through their careers. Mentoring is the next item on the time line. This activity was placed near the long-range end of the time line because benefits to the employee from the mentoring relationship may take some time to emerge. Further, the relationship between the two individuals will take some time to develop. Finally, career planning was placed at the extreme long-term side on the time line. Career planning is an ongoing process that should occur throughout the career of an employee. Although there are specific activities that generally occur in a typical career-planning procedure, they occur over the

FIGURE 9-1. A time line of developmental activities.

life of the employee's career. Some research has been conducted in each of these areas, and the following sections review the findings.

Training Activities

Training has been defined as a planned effort by an organization to facilitate employees' learning job-related skills and obtaining knowledge that will help to improve their performance and further the organization's goals (Hall & Goodale, 1986; Wexley & Latham, 1981). Training focuses on immediate needs of employees and is stimulated by an organization's desire to improve its effectiveness (Alpander, 1982). However, for training to be effective and increase an employee's productivity, the work environment the trainee returns to must be supportive of the new behaviors learned (Odiorne, 1984).

Virtually every employee in the United States receives some type of training during his or her career (Alpander, 1982). Hall and Goodale (1986) identified four specific times when training an employee is necessary. The first situation when training is needed is when the base rate, or the percentage of employees who are qualified to adequately perform the job, is low. When base rates are low, successfully recruiting employees who can immediately begin producing is difficult, even when extensive recruiting and selection techniques are utilized. To overcome this problem, companies are forced to hire the best available candidates and then immediately begin training them.

A second situation that calls for the immediate training of employees occurs when selection procedures are unsuccessful or when selection errors are costly. When selection errors occur, organizations are faced with employees who are not qualified to perform the jobs for which they were hired. Faced with this problem, organizations can choose to dismiss unqualified employees or to train them. When the costs of dismissing the current employee and hiring a replacement exceed those associated with properly training the current employee, organizations will choose to train. When selection errors are costly, such as for airplane pilots, the best applicants are hired and immediately placed in training programs that may last for many months. These training programs focus on eliminating as many of the costly outcomes as possible.

Training is also required when the job functions and performance standards for a job change. This type of situation is occurring more frequently because technological advances have had major impacts on most industries. As new functions are added to a job, employees must be thoroughly trained to perform them. Also, as jobs become more automated, performance standards may increase training in a way to make employees aware of these new standards through training.

Finally, training may be necessary when the output of employees performing the same job is highly variable. If one or two employees continually outperform all other employees, it may be necessary to determine what the outstanding performers know that the other employees do not. When these skills or knowledge are determined, the other employees should be made aware of them. This transfer of information is especially important for firms with strategies tied to low production costs. In addition, firms that are able to effectively transfer knowledge across employees should have a competitive advantage.

Often, each of these situations may require different methods of training. For example, when the base rate is low, and individuals are being hired for a specific job, on-the-job training (OJT) may be an appropriate technique to utilize. However, when the costs are high, OJT may need to be replaced with simulations, such as for pilots.

Many different training techniques have been mentioned in the literature. Stumpf and Hanrahan (1984) suggested that off-site training activities might include courses, workshops, and classes and that these activities could be handled by an internal training staff, by sending employees to external training programs, or by hiring an external group to provide in-house training for employees.

Training Problems.   Sonnenfeld (1985, p. 300) identified five troubles that currently plague training in organizations. One of these troubles he named the "confusing kaleidescope of suppliers." Under this section he reviewed the drawbacks to each type of trainer available.

First, he examined problems that can arise when internal trainers are used. The most obvious problem was the overwhelming emphasis placed on behavioral concepts such as interpersonal behavior, team work, group dynamics, motivation, leadership, and organizational development. He suggested that the emphasis placed on these types of activities resulted because of differences in the trainers' backgrounds and the consultants outside the organization with whom they choose to communicate.

Sonnenfeld (1985) also examined problems that arise when commercial vendors are used. Specifically, he mentioned that the services available are highly skewed toward professional and technical job-specific training and toward managers at all levels in the organization. After reviewing these figures, he questioned the priorities of commercial vendors. Are the people who actually need the training in an organization going to receive it if a commercial vendor is used?

Finally, problems that can arise by sending employees out for training were addressed. According to Sonnenfeld (1985), colleges and universities are the largest providers of off-site training programs. Residence-based programs offer distinct advantages such as lack of instructor condescension, a stimulating atmosphere, and relevant course material. However, several drawbacks also occur. The most serious for the organization is the increased exposure participants have with other companies. Two possible results from this exposure can occur: (1) increased turnover because of an increase in networking allowed by the training program and/or (2) the loss of trade "secrets" through open discussions during the training program. Although steps have been taken by training program directors to alleviate these problems, they still persist.

Phases of the Training Process.   Whichever method is selected, the training process is normally the same. According to Hall and Goodale (1986), the training process consists of three basic phases: (1) preparation for training, (2) implementation of training, and (3) evaluation of training. The phases form a cyclical process in that the output from the final phase, evaluation of training, becomes input to the first phase, preparation for training, in the next cycle.

The first phase, preparation for training, consists of two parts, analyzing training needs and designing the training. When analyzing training needs, three separate analyses must be performed: (1) organizational analysis, (2) job analysis, and (3) person analysis (McGehee & Thayer, 1961). Organizational analysis is necessary because training should be designed to further the goals of the organization. Through an organizational analysis, these goals become apparent. Further, an organizational analysis provides an opportunity to examine the quality of the human resources available in the organization and the degree to which these resources facilitate and encourage the achievement of the organization's goals. In this sense, training can support both the intended and emergent components of the firm's strategy because it is directed toward the underlying goals of the organization.

Job analysis provides a clearer understanding of what each job in the organization entails and how each job interrelates to other jobs in the organization. Once what is to be achieved on the job is determined, the knowledge, skills, and abilities needed by a job incumbent can be determined. Training is warranted when employees do not possess these skills.

Finally, person analysis should be performed. This will determine an employee's performance and identify the knowledge and skills necessary to reach that level of performance. Once this benchmark is established, training aimed at increasing the current performance can be delineated.

With the information gleaned from the analysis phase, the type of training program needed can be designed. When designing training programs, what is to be taught and how it will be taught must be examined. By creating training objectives and determining the content, what is to be taught becomes apparent. Further, the methods needed to present the new content may become more obvious as objectives become clearer.

In the second phase, implementation of training, the actual training is performed. Just how this is accomplished depends upon the method of training selected. For example, if self-study was deemed the most appropriate method, trainees could be issued materials that they are expected to have completed by a specific date. This type of arrangement allows the trainees to work and learn at their own pace.

The final phase involves the evaluation of the training process. The evaluation process is essential for several reasons. First, the evaluation process provides the feedback necessary to determine the effectiveness of the training. It can also help determine the extent to which the training programs are supporting the strategy of the organization. This information is useful in designing the next training program so that deficiencies identified during the evaluation of the current program can be eliminated.

Whatever type of training procedures are implemented, the total time the employee is actually involved in the learning process is normally very short. The short-term nature of the training process has not diminished the number of companies who utilize it. The next activity on the time line, assessment centers, normally requires more time of the participants than a simple training class.

Assessment Centers

An assessment center is a standardized program consisting of a series of exercises, performed either by an individual or a group, administered over a period of a few days (Stumpf & Hanrahan, 1984). The goal of an assessment center is to simulate critical work situations so that trained assessors can observe individuals exhibiting behaviors that are related to managerial success (Moses, 1977). The outcome from an assessment center may be used to determine who gets promoted or selected for more specific development programs (Stumpf & Hanrahan, 1984).

Although the specific procedures used in an assessment center may vary, the primary benefit remains the same: the ability to evaluate the work skills of select employees, and to use the information gathered to further employee development (Stumpf & Hanrahan, 1984). An added benefit is the ability of the assessment center to recognize long-term potential in an individual, thus minimizing unsuitable career appointments (Odiorne, 1984). This can be especially important for large diversified corporations because it is important for them to match the talents of managers to the needs of various business units. Assessment centers' results are also valuable when making decisions concerning long-term succession prospects (Walker, 1980).

Assessment centers have also been found to be good selection tools for jobs involving contact with people, such as management positions (Dunnette & Borman, 1979). Assessment centers seemed to have face validity, and the feedback was both accurate and useful. This is probably the reason that Boehm (1982) found that participants react positively toward them. However, participants did indicate that the behavior exhibited during the assessment center was atypical of their behavior in general (Dodd, 1977).

Unforeseen problems can also occur with the use of assessment centers. Candidates for assessment centers are normally identified by their current supervisors as having "potential" (Odiorne, 1984). However, Linkow (1985) suggested that managers follow both formal and informal policies. The formal policies may require that managers survey their current employees for the best possible candidates for the assessment centers. These individuals should have already indicated "potential." The informal policies managers follow are based on intuition, negotiation, and compromise. Actions based on these policies are often political in nature, and may not be in the organization's best interests. Due to this, special efforts may be required to ensure that the appropriate candidates are selected to participate in the assessment center.

The identification of training needs of participants is one of the outcomes of an assessment center. Targeted development, the next activity on the time line, can be used to overcome the identified deficiencies.

Targeted Development

The purpose of targeted development is to enhance current strengths and to improve skill development, with an eye toward future uses of the skills. In contrast to training, which tends to be aimed more at improving current performance, targeted development has a more futuristic nature.

Targeted development may arise from the results of an assessment-center program, or because of an update to a succession plan (Stumpf & Hanrahan, 1984). In either case, the emphasis is on preparing an individual for future effectiveness (Hall & Goodale, 1986). Targeted development helps both the organization and the individual to cope effectively with change (Alpander, 1982).

According to Hall (1984), long-term outcomes of targeted development include adaptability and identity. Adaptability is the extent to which the person is prepared to meet future career demands. Identity is a measure of how well the employee sees the parts of his or her career fitting together. When an organization-sponsored activity enhances either the adaptability or the identity of an employee, development has occurred.

There are numerous specific activities that can be considered developmental. For instance, Hall (1984) identified at least 15 different activities that organizations can use to develop their employees. Some of these include socialization, counselling, coaching, job assignments, feedback, and self-assessment. The specific activities selected depend upon the goals the organization has for its development program.

Different strategies should be followed depending on the goals of the development program. Specific strategies for achieving these goals were outlined by Wexley and Latham (1981). These include: (1) cognitive strategies that are aimed at altering thoughts and ideas, (2) behavioral strategies that attempt to directly change behaviors, and (3) environmental strategies that are directed at changing the immediate work environment of the individual. Each of these strategies can be matched to specific activities, which in turn can be matched to specific organizational goals.

The activities depicted on the long-term end of the time line in Figure 9-1 are more individualized. Training can be performed in large groups and at all levels. Assessment centers have a smaller number of participants than most training programs and are normally reserved for high-potential candidates. Next, targeted development specializes even further by focusing on specific needs of an individual. Mentoring, the fourth activity depicted on the time line in Figure 9-1, is even more specialized than targeted development.

Mentoring

Mentoring has been defined as a relationship between a junior and senior colleague, which is viewed by the junior colleague as having a positive contribution to his or her development (Kram, 1984). A junior colleague would consider a relationship as contributing positively to his or her development if it provided either career advancement activities or personal support, or both (Kram, 1983).

There is some evidence that indicates that mentor relationships evolve through predictable stages (Hunt & Michael, 1983; Kram, 1983; Missirian, 1982; Phillips, 1977; Phillips-Jones, 1982). Bretz and Dreher (1988) summarized this evolution as a four-stage process. Stage one is the beginning of the relationship. Either party can initiate the relationship, or it can be a mutual attraction. Once the parties have met, a mutually strong attraction evolves. The junior member sees the senior member as a respected and competent individual from whom much can be learned. The senior member views the junior member as an outlet for the knowledge and values collected through the years. The duration of this phase is usually six months to a year. Following this phase is stage two, the developmental stage.

During stage two, which lasts between two and five years, the junior member is given opportunities to make decisions that build his or her confidence. Also, during this stage the greatest amount of sponsoring occurs. By allowing the junior member to work on challenging projects that provide exposure and visibility, future contacts can be made that would not have been available without the mentor relationship.

As the relationship moves into the third stage, a separation normally occurs. The separation may arise due to a geographical transfer, or because one or the other member may withdraw from the situation. The senior member may withdraw if he or she feels his or her assistance is no longer necessary, while the junior member may withdraw because the need for the support and security of the senior member is no longer needed.

After an indefinite period of separation, the final stage, redefinition, begins. Any hard feelings created through the separation further diminish the original relationship, and the two become redefined as peers.

The benefits of having a mentor can be seen by tracing the training of several well-known chief executives (Odiorne, 1984). For instance, Ernest Breech, who was trained by Alfred Sloan at General Motors, went from General Motors to Ford where he developed such talents as Henry Ford II, Robert McNamara, and Tex Thorton. Thorton, who moved to Litton Industries, trained Roy Ash of Dictaphone, Harry Gray of United Technology, Fred Sullivan of Walter Kidde, and many others. This pattern suggests "the best route to the top is to perform extremely well and find a competent, nurturing boss" (Odiorne, 1984, p. 135).

Career Planning

Career planning is depicted as the most long-term development activity on the time line (See Figure 9-1). Career-planning activities serve to coach and guide employees through self-assessment and goal setting (Stumpf & Hanrahan, 1984). The primary goal of career planning is to increase employees' awareness of themselves and their career goals (Wexley & Latham, 1981). This is achieved by providing information and opportunities to employees.

Specific activities that provide information to employees are varied. Walker and Gutteridge (1979) surveyed 225 members of the American Management Association in an attempt to determine what activities organizations provided for employees' career planning. The results indicated that career counselling by human resource staff or supervisors was the most common form of career planning offered by companies.

The activities that were reported as the most frequently discontinued included psychological testing and assessment, aptitude and interest testing, and feedback. Reasons given for discontinuing their use included: (1) the impact of EEO, (2) testing programs that were not validated, and (3) increasing costs.

Stumpf and Hanrahan (1984) presented a list of career-planning activities for which the individual, the organization, or both were responsible. The individual must provide self-assessment and set career objectives and goals. The organization must provide skill-assessment exercises as well as information concerning organizational practices, policies, and opportunities. Both the individual and the organization are jointly responsible for preliminary career and life planning, sharing relevant information, developing a career-development plan, and routine reevaluation of the plan.

Walker (1980) listed several reasons why a company would want to implement a career-planning program. First, career planning can reduce turnover. Providing an employee with an opportunity to preview his or her future at the present company, may result in his or her being less anxious to leave. Second, career planning may improve performance. Also, career planning has been found to specifically help individuals whose career expectations are too low. By providing these employees with career-planning opportunities, both the organization and the individual will benefit.

STRATEGIC BUSINESS PLANNING

As outlined in Chapter Five, strategic business planning is the process of setting organizational objectives and determining action plans that will achieve these objectives (Walker, 1980). Three elements are vital to a successful strategic plan: (1) a corporate mission and strategy, (2) a corporate structure, and (3) human resources (Tichy, Devanna, & Fomburn, 1982). In order to survive and prosper, organizations must have a well-developed and well-maintained business strategy. Thus, it is useful to see planning in terms that relate to organizational, managerial, and strategic activities (Hall & Goodale, 1986). Figure 9-2 depicts these planning activities in terms of their appropriate time frame.

As can be seen in Figure 9-2, operational planning is at the short-term end of the continuum. Operational planning includes planning for everyday activities. This type of planning would involve making sure that the product or service is available to customers.

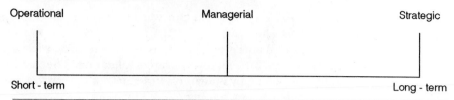

FIGURE 9-2. Types of organizational planning.

Managerial planning is positioned in the middle of the continuum. Managerial planning involves controlling the major resources of the organization, such as capital, information, and employees. The focus is on internal policies, practices, and systems.

At the long-term end of the continuum is strategic planning. Strategic planning is done by examining the organization's internal and external environment. Plans made at this stage are for the organization as a whole, and therefore must be broad.

Although the types of planning are presented as separate, they need to be integrated into an overall business plan. Too much emphasis on any one type of planning will not best serve the needs of the organization. Recent criticisms of U.S. business have often focused on the lack of integrated strategic planning. These criticisms are revived and compared to criticisms of human resources development in organizations.

Criticisms

The lack of strategic business planning was indicated as the primary concern of one thousand chief executive officers who were recently surveyed (Winer, 1983). Wissema, Brand, and Van Der Pol (1981) listed several specific reasons for the nonexistence of strategic planning. First, many companies view strategic business planning as a compulsory chore, culminating in reams of paper being used to produce a document that few read. Second, the results of strategic planning are often too abstract to be useful to the organization. Third, strategic business planning is often not integrated with everyday operational planning, causing a duplication of efforts. Finally, strategic business plans are often not followed up in the functional departments once they have been determined.

Each of these arguments also can be applied to employee development in organizations. Employee-development programs also tend to generate a considerable amount of paper. The paper can consist of assessment results, organizational policies, procedures, and opportunities, or individual goals and objectives. The amount of paper generated can be overwhelming and therefore likely to be discarded or ignored.

Second, the career-development plans that an individual creates may be too abstract to be of use. If the plan developed cannot be easily implemented or specific steps to take cannot be created, the plan may be useless.

If career-development procedures are not linked to the organization's strategic business plan or long-range forecasts, development efforts may be wasted or inappropriately used. For example, if a manager is provided with targeted development in a particular area, the effort may be wasted if the business plan indicates the area will be phased out in two years.

Finally, career-development activities are not followed up in the future. Transfer of training is one of the most difficult outcomes to achieve. Without a formal check-up procedure, the amount of knowledge transferred back to the job may be minimal.

Because the problems faced by strategic planners and employee-development staff are similar, the strides that have recently been taken by strategic planners, in an attempt to better plan for the future of the organization, may be applicable to developers of human resources. By sharing this type of information, reinvention of the wheel may be avoided. One specific way this information can be shared is through linking the strategic business plan to human resources development.

LINKING STRATEGIC BUSINESS PLANNING AND HUMAN RESOURCES DEVELOPMENT

Reasons for linking strategic business planning and human resources development are numerous. However, the most important and often-mentioned reason is that business performance is highly dependent upon the behavior, aspirations, and dedication of the work force (Caldwell, 1984). If the behavior, aspirations, and dedication of the work force can be developed and directed toward supporting the overall business plan, positive performance outcomes are likely.

Various procedures that delineate how these two processes can be linked have been reported (Harvey, 1983a; Sweet, 1981; Winer, 1983; Wissema et al., 1981). Although each procedure attempts to achieve the same outcome, how these results are achieved differs.

Harvey (1983a) suggested that if human resources development is to be integrated into the overall business plans, then it is up to the HRM staff. Because the human resources development effort cannot fulfill its maximum potential without a clear and direct link to the strategic business plan, the burden rests with the HRM staff to provide integration into the strategic plan.

Three specific suggestions were given to facilitate this integration (Harvey, 1983a). First, the HRM staff needs to formulate human resources development plans. Even if the original plan is not developed so that it can be integrated with the strategic business plan, at least the strategic planners will recognize that the HRM staff can create a plan.

Finally, the HRM staff should ask planning questions. Because the majority of the information required to create a strategically-linked human resources development plan must come from the corporate planners, communication between these departments is vital. By showing an interest in strategic planning through continual questioning, the human resources development staff eventually may be included in corporate planning.

An eight-step multi-strategic plan was suggested by Winer (1983), as a way to link business planning with human resources development. The first two steps include listing and prioritizing all current objectives. The prioritizing is done by utilizing a hierarchical model. Next, any strengths, weaknesses, opportunities, or threats are listed. With these in mind, step four allows a readjustment in the prioritization of the objectives. Step five focuses on finding ways to capitalize on the strengths and opportunities and defend against the weaknesses and threats. Strategies are then linked to the objectives followed by selecting the most feasible and useful ones. Finally, the strategies are monitored to ensure the outcomes expected. If unexpected results occur, contingency plans can be activated or the entire plan can be reevaluated.

A more specific link between corporate business strategy and human resources development was suggested by Wissema et al. (1981). Their plan revolves around dynamic function and dynamic manager profiles. A dynamic function profile describes the present and intermediate future (3 to 5 years) functions of the organization, while a dynamic manager profile describes the present performance and the career outlook for a manager. A comparison of these two profiles results in a "management gap" (Wissema et al., 1981, p. 366). The gap is the shortage or surplus of the company's management potential. Once these gaps are found, corrective actions can be taken. These actions may take the form of management-development programs, recruitment, transfers, or training programs.

A thorough four-step process that parallels the tactical activities of the organization was developed by Sweet (1981) to integrate human resources development into the strategic business plan. The first step is a human resources forecast. This is an attempt to project the quantity and quality of the managerial work force that will be required to implement the strategic business plans and objectives.

The second step, which is somewhat removed from the strategic plan, is the development of a human resources inventory. The question "What have we got now?" is answered with respect to the current and potential management talent. In order for the pool of managerial talent to grow, sound career-development and appraisal systems must be utilized.

Once managerial resources supply and demand have been determined, a matching process takes place. This step is vital to ensure there will be no future imbalances. Two possible imbalances are predicted. First, "career blocks" could occur, which exist when, during a particular year, more managers are ready for promotion than opportunities are available. The reverse situation, "resource gaps," occurs when the opportunities for advancement outnumber the qualified applicants.

The final step, human resources development alternatives, arises because the first three steps were performed. By following the procedure outline, human resources development can be looked upon as a way to plan for the future instead of a crisis-intervention technique. By heading off future problems before they occur, human resources development can become a positive and valuable process in an organization.

The four techniques reviewed are by no means the only alternatives available to an organization interested in linking its strategic business plan to its human resources development. However, these plans did offer a variety of techniques. One thing they all have in common are potential benefits that can be reaped through a careful integration.

Benefits of Linking Planning with Development Efforts

The "bottom line" is still an extremely important factor in organizations today. Ways to improve the bottom line are always being examined. Linking the strategic business plan to human resources development may be one avenue toward this end.

One benefit that may arise because of steps taken to link the strategic business plan to human resources development is reduced costs. According to Friedman and LeVino (1984), when organizations do not take management development seriously, it may be a costly mistake. Repercussions from ignoring management development consist of high replacement costs because the company is forced to recruit from outside. In essence, this means the firm is paying for another company's development programs. This practice of raiding companies with good development programs was once common in the banking and brokerage businesses. Further, lack of an integrated management-development program leads to a loss of motivation and increased instability in the managerial ranks.

Another cost reduction that can occur when companies link their strategic business plan to human resources development was mentioned by Abelson, Ferris, and Urban (1988). Human resources development programs are extremely costly. When development programs are initiated with no clear connection to the needs of the company, time and money are wasted. However, if every development activity performed was clearly linked to the organization's goals, each program would be beneficial for both the individual and the company.

Similarly, Abelson et al. (1988) suggested that by linking the strategic business plan to human resources development, employees are more aware of what their future with the company will be like. Common are the stories of a young manager being introduced to a top manager at a social function. The top manager informs the young manager that the company has "big" plans for her. However, she never reveals the nature of these plans. Sharing these plans with young managers may increase dedication to the company, reducing turnover and costs.

Another important reason for explaining future plans to young managers is so they understand why they are being trained (Sonnenfeld, 1985). By showing the importance of the training and development being offered the individual, the opportunity may become a productive and useful exercise, instead of a waste for both the organization and the individual. Showing the importance of the training and development offered an individual can only be accomplished when there is a clear link between the company's business plan and its human resources development.

Another benefit that may arise because of a clear link between the company's business plan and human resources development is the opportunity for the human resources development effort to fulfill its maximum potential (Harvey, 1983a). By integrating human resources development planning into strategic planning, all activities sponsored by the human resources development effort become more legitimate. Both the company and the employees realize that being involved in a human resources development program means a better future for both the company and the worker.

The benefits afforded a company that integrates its strategic planning and human resources development are numerous. But is it feasible and worthwhile to actually link these two units? The following section presents examples of various companies that have linked strategic planning with human resources development and indicates the success they have achieved.

Success Stories

Three large organizations, IBM, General Electric, and Ford, have all developed a managerial-development program directly linked to the corporate mission. Each of these programs is discussed.

IBM. Thomas J. Watson, Sr. established a policy that provided total job security. Instead of laying off employees, they were trained or retrained. This is a formidable task considering the rapid changes that occur in the electronics industry. Of specific interest here is management development at IBM.

The importance of IBM's commitment to development can be seen in the management-development programs provided. IBM attempts to bring new managers in the United States to the company's management-development center in Armonk, New York, within 30 days of their appointment (Sonnenfeld & Ingols, 1986). IBM links its management-education programs to succession planning. By recognizing and developing high-potential personnel today, IBM will have its needed managers of tomorrow.

General Electric (GE). A program entitled Executive Management Staff (EMS) was developed by GE as a way to develop top-echelon managers for the whole organization (Friedman & LeVino, 1984). The EMS program is intended to locate top performers and provide them with experience that will enhance their growth.

The program evolved in the 1960s because Fred Borch, president and chief executive officer at the time, was about to restructure the company and felt there were not enough qualified managers to run the new divisions. The purpose of EMS was to locate and "bring along" high-potential employees. This was done by sending talent scouts out to search for candidates. Currently, the talent scouts hold the title of Executive Management Consultants and are responsible for working with executives in charge of sectors of the business to locate and develop top managers for GE.

EMS was started for two reasons. First, the task of developing general managers was not being done as well as needed to meet the company's growth objectives. Second, too much emphasis was placed on the hourly worker, and not enough on the managerial staff. When EMS was initiated, the development of hourly staff was delegated to another division so that EMS could focus solely on developing managers.

Ford. In recent years, Ford has recognized the importance of training and development as a way to provide flexibility of the work force so that it can respond to external market conditions (Caldwell, 1984). Not only do the line workers need to be continually trained, but managers also need to be prepared to meet the competitive challenges.

When market conditions are poor, training and development are the first to be cut. However, Ford has recognized that training and development cannot be treated as an expendable fringe benefit. Ford has instead decided to treat these activities as critical elements of meeting the organization's goals and building a stronger future. By focusing on training and development of employees, Ford can provide the knowledge needed for employees to be productive for the company, and the knowledge necessary for employees to build a successful and long-term career.

SUMMARY AND CONCLUSIONS

The correspondence, over time, between the training and development and strategic business planning processes was discussed in this chapter. The problems inherent in both practices were reviewed and similarities were noted. Next, ways to link these two processes, which have been identified in the literature, were examined. Benefits that can occur because of a strong linkage between strategic business planning and human resources development were then presented. Finally, organizations that have been successful in linking these two ideas were discussed.

Although strategic planning is difficult to perform, in order for organizations to be successful, it must be done. Further, in order to succeed in business, an organization must have a well-trained staff that can react to any situation. By focusing on these two goals in unison, an organization can prosper and survive.

STRATEGIC
INDUSTRIAL RELATIONS

*"The puzzling fact about the American labor movement is,
after all, its limited objective . . . The American trade
unionist wants, first, an equal voice with the employer in
fixing wages and, second, a big enough control over the
productive processes to protect job, health, and organization. Yet he does not appear to wish to saddle himself and
fellow wage earners with the trouble of running industry
without the employer." (Perlman, 1922, p. 279).*

If Perlman's (1922) comment is viewed in contemporary light, one could
argue that trade unionists want involvement in the strategic-management
process: "to protect job, health, *and* organization." This chapter examines
recent discussions of the role of industrial relations in that process, completing
the chapters dealing with traditional human resources functional areas and
their relationships to strategy.

The industrial-relations function encompasses activities associated with
the relationship between organized labor and management in unionized
firms. These activities include, for example, the procedures for establishing the
legitimacy of a union (certification), negotiation of a contract through collective bargaining outlining working conditions, and determining how to deal
with problems in the workplace (e.g., rules of discipline).

In some ways, industrial relations is similar to the other HRM functions,
yet there are also marked differences. Like other human resources areas,
industrial relations comprises a set of processes and procedures that govern
how a firm deals with employees in achieving certain employment-related
tasks. Similar to selection and compensation guidelines, for example, many
industrial-relations processes stem from legal requirements (e.g., Taft-Hartley
Act, Wagner Act).

The industrial-relations function diverges from other HRM areas, however, in several ways. First, by definition, the industrial-relations function
implies a unionized setting with two parties involved, organized labor and
management. Industrial relations makes formal the employee-representation
activities that are typically assumed to be part of the human resources
department's responsibility. Where a human resources department oversees
relationships with all employees, a union typically represents a more limited

group. Thus, the industrial-relations function defines and guides the behavior of management and labor, and their relationship, which can frequently be adversarial. Industrial relations further differs from traditional HRM functions in the way the labor-management relationship is defined: it is determined by a negotiated, written contract. While other human resources activities are often informal (e.g., decisions regarding promotion, selection) or not explicit (e.g., pay increases), such aspects of the employee-employer relationship are clearly specified in a unionized setting.

The emphasis of this chapter is on the current environment facing firms and unions and the role that industrial relations and unions can play in the formulation and implementation of corporate strategy. This follows the pattern of discussion in earlier chapters about other HRM areas. In addition, this chapter discusses strategic management from the union perspective; specifically, the chapter reviews research suggesting that unions are increasingly using strategic planning as a means to gain greater control over their own futures.

From a firm's perspective, incorporating industrial-relations issues into the strategic-management process has both benefits and drawbacks. In formulating strategy, unions could provide necessary input from a clearly defined group of employees (Lawler & Mohrman, 1987). Because labor is often a critical cost component for businesses, management may seek input regarding how the firm and the union can work together to increase efficiency without damaging the labor-management relationship. In addition, implementation may be smoother in a positive labor-management relationship where a union can provide a structure and format to transfer information to employees about a firm's strategy and direction. Finally, union leaders and representatives who have had business training should be able to understand business plans and transfer that knowledge to rank and file workers. Having union leaders convey strategic goals (on their own or in conjunction with management) may lend credibility and legitimacy to the plan.

Union involvement in firm strategy formulation and implementation may generate drawbacks, however. If union leaders and members have difficulty understanding or accepting a strategy, top management may face a major time commitment to clarify and gain employee acceptance of the strategic direction and process of implementation. Second, even with acceptance from union members and use of the union structure to transfer information, the structure may nevertheless be quite bureaucratic and cumbersome, slowing the implementation process.

Involvement in the strategic-management process holds benefits and risks for unions as well. Threats from environmental and organizational changes have led to a reduction in relative union influence in many countries. Particularly as firms emphasize cost efficiency, unions (and all internal staff areas, such as human resources) find themselves increasingly forced to justify their necessity. For staff areas, this means showing a contribution to firm performance. Unions must show members and firms that they can wield influence in achieving both union and organization goals. As a result, some unions are learning about and applying strategic management to their own situations. At a minimum, many unions are learning enough about corporate strategy formulation and implementation to forge a role for themselves in the process. In addition to helping unions achieve their own goals (Stratton & Brown, 1988), knowledge about strategic management makes the process less formidable when unions encounter it in firms. A negative aspect of formal involvement in corporate strategy formulation and implementation is, of course, the fear that unions will be seen as a "tool" of management and lose their position as a voice for employees. Several labor-relations scholars have voiced such a concern (Barbash, 1986; Fossum, 1987; McKersie, 1985), while others (e.g., Lewin, 1987) predict a continued advocacy role for unions.

Chapter Ten comprises four sections. The chapter's first section is a brief review of industrial-relations research history, drawing on Lewin and Feuille (1983), Kochan, Katz, and McKersie (1986), and Fossum (1987). The discussion places industrial relations, and research on it, in an historical and topical context. The next section examines the environmental context affecting unions and industrial relations in recent years. The third section of the chapter focuses on how firms can incorporate unions and industrial relations into the strategy formulation and implementation processes. A final section briefly assesses strategic management from the union's perspective.

The problem of limited research evidence, familiar in the earlier chapter discussions of strategic human resources management functions, is especially frustrating for the strategic industrial-relations literature. While industrial relations has attracted researchers from several disciplines and perspectives, only very recently have any addressed strategy issues. This chapter makes some speculations, therefore, about how firms *could* incorporate industrial relations into the strategic-management process, rather than providing only research evidence that has tested whether firms have done so.

INDUSTRIAL RELATIONS RESEARCH: AN OVERVIEW

Industrial-relations history and research is, in a sense, much richer than other HRM areas. The field has a long history and has been the domain of researchers from many disciplines, including law, economics, psychology, and sociology.

The industrial-relations system in the U.S. was relatively well established by the early 1900s. Kochan et al. (1986) have argued that the American industrial-relations system, based upon a New Deal model providing labor-relations stability and satisfying economic needs of management and labor, dominated the U.S. scene until the 1970s. The system, which seemed able to withstand economic and other attacks into the 1960s, was shaken dramatically in the 1970s by a series of unforeseen, or perhaps unacknowledged factors. Since the mid-1960s, a nonunion industrial-relations system has developed as a result of external environmental changes as well as increased management opposition toward unions. Kochan et al. (1986) have predicted continuing union-nonunion competition in the U.S.

Economic and Noneconomic Issues

In the early 1980s, Lewin and Feuille (1983) reviewed behavioral literature in the industrial-relations field, which they divided into research that
focused on economic issues and that which addressed noneconomic issues.
The economic research (e.g, Parsley, 1980) focused on issues such as the
impact of unions on the wages that employers pay workers. As Lewin and
Fueille noted, in economic research, the unions themselves have not been
studied but rather the focus has been on their effect on firms' economic issues.
In essence, unions have been seen almost as "black boxes," when researchers
compare unionized and nonunionized firms.

Noneconomic research, on the other hand, has focused more on behavioral aspects of the parties involved in industrial relations. Specifically,
Lewin and Feuille (1983) classified the research into four major clusters of
topics: (1) unions and union members (i.e., joining patterns, structure), (2) the
way firms structure their union-related functions, (3) the bargaining process,
and (4) outcomes related to bargaining (e.g., Anderson, Busman, & O'Reilley,
1982; Kochan, 1981; Kochan & Freedman, 1979; Walton & McKersie, 1965).
Union-member research has examined attitudes of employees toward joining
unions and their commitment to unions. Other research has investigated union
structure and the industrial-relations-function structure in unionized firms.
Behavioral research on the bargaining process has focused on the dynamics of
the process and models of conflict resolution. Finally, the research on outcomes
has taken a broad view in assessing political, legal, economic, and organizational factors contributing to bargaining outcomes. The research has also evaluated
union roles in affecting changes in management policy.

Research Topic Categories

More recently, Fossum (1987) examined industrial-relations research
since the early 1900s and classified it by topic categories. He has suggested that
research in the years before the 1930s followed an institutional perspective and
focused on rules of interaction between labor and management (Commons,
1934). During the 1930s, the emphasis was on the employment relationship
(Heneman, 1969). Dunlop's (1958) "web of rules" framework and industrial-
relations systems dominated research discussion and efforts in the late 1950s,
complemented by several descriptive comparative studies (e.g., Kerr, Harbison,
Dunlop, & Myers, 1960) in the 1960s. In the late 1960s and into the 1970s,
research seemed to stagnate (Strauss & Feuille, 1978), but since the mid-1970s
has gone through a "revival." Lewin and Feuille (1983), like other scholars,
have focused on such topics as union-representation elections (Getman,
Goldberg, & Herman, 1976), the individual union member or potential member (White, 1982), and the effects of unions on productivity, profit, or the
economy in general (Kochan et al., 1986).

In classifying recent research streams, Fossum (1987) noted that researchers have examined industrial relations issues at four levels: societal,
industrial/national union, firm/local union, and individual. The societal-level
research has investigated patterns of union membership, labor force employ-

ment, and (de)certification patterns (Dickens & Leonard, 1985; Freeman & Medoff, 1984; Heneman & Sandver, 1981). The national- or industry-level research has focused on legislative initiatives that affect the employment relationship (Saltzman, 1985), as related to unions in the private and public sectors, and patterns of union membership in various industries (Block, 1980). The context of the labor-management relationship, union elections, and more recently, how firms attempt to eliminate or avoid unions (e.g., use of labor consultants) has been the focus of the firm-level and local-union-level research (Kochan, McKersie, & Chalykoff, 1986; Lawler, 1984). In particular, Kochan, McKersie, and Cappelli (1984) have noted that different levels of management may pursue inconsistent policies or goals in their union relations. While shop-floor managers may seek more harmonious relationships, corporate-level management may pursue union avoidance. Finally, some researchers have focused their efforts on understanding issues at the individual level, such as the characteristics of union members or potential union members as a way to predict individuals' willingness to vote in union elections, or the outcome of the vote itself (White, 1982; Zalesny, 1985).

Fossum (1987) summarized changes since the late 1970s by noting the tremendous shifts in employer attitudes and approaches toward unions and speculated about the impact of these changes on union behavior. For example, employers have adapted to environmental changes by initiating lower wages, staffing with fewer permanent employees, and locating new facilities in areas less amenable to organizing efforts. Although such attitudes and actions have forced unions to focus on increasing employment security and would be expected to encourage greater labor-management schism, the environment may in fact encourage unions and employers to work together. With an increasing emphasis on the service sector and a resulting focus on human capital rather than equipment, both employers and unions should recognize a need for more cooperation and investment in humans to gain future output. In fact, Fossum (1987) has suggested that the American labor-relations scene is moving from a period of union contract patterns, with cost differences externalized (passed on) to customers, to a period where employers are externalizing cost differences to employees. As a result, unions may be forced to learn more about business and costs, bringing them into the strategic-management process, almost by default.

ENVIRONMENTAL FORCES AFFECTING INDUSTRIAL RELATIONS

Several environmental factors have affected the role of unions and the nature of union-management relationships in recent years (Kochan, 1985). Among others, Barbash (1986), Fossum (1987), Farber (1985), and Freeman (1985) have identified numerous factors that have contributed to the relative decline in union power: recent economic recessions, foreign competition, market instabilities, structural changes in the economy, firms' attempts to remain (or become) nonunion, and a new political order initiated by the

Reagan administration, made clear with the PATCO strike in 1981. In addition, as mentioned above, sectoral shifts (i.e., a growing service sector) and demographics of the work force, such as more women and minorities in the labor force, have challenged unions' ability to organize new members and have forced unions to consider different economic issues like child care (Barkin, 1985; Farber, 1985). Furthermore, there may be "diminishing returns" in union organizing: the workers who are relatively easy to organize are probably already in a union; it may be increasingly difficult to organize remaining nonunion workers (Farber, 1985).

Shifts in the extent of union influence have occurred outside the U.S. as well. Elsewhere in the industrialized world, political and economic environments have fostered a general decline in the importance of unions' influence in business and social welfare during the 1980s. For instance, in Great Britain, Prime Minister Thatcher has continually pushed to reduce union rights; on the Continent, the Belgian government imposed wage restraints despite major union resistance. Finally, Canadian firms have begun moving toward more conciliatory ties with unions, as a backlash to the severe economic disruption from union strife in the 1970s (Atkinson, 1986).

Barkin (1985) suggested one other, perhaps more subtle, environmental force that has further contributed to the relative decline in union influence: public interest about labor-management issues. In general, the American public's concern about employment and union issues waned in the 1980s. Up to the early 1980s, concern for employee safety, discrimination, pay practices, and unfair treatment of union members were topics of popular interest, reflected in movies (e.g., *Norma Rae*, about the attempt to organize a textile mill; *Silkwood*, about a worker's attempt to report dangerous management practices) and nationwide boycotts of certain firms (e.g., J.P. Stevens) because of their perceived unfair employment practices. The current "hot" topics in the public's interest, however, deal with issues such as nuclear war, acquired immune deficiency syndrome (AIDS), child abuse, and the homeless. As a result, Barkin (1985) has voiced concern that the labor movement and unions will further wither from lack of popular interest and support.

In such an environment, unions are clearly in a vulnerable position, leading them to seek ways to remain viable. One such way is to be seen as a contributor to firm performance by becoming a part of the strategic-management process. Although the drive for increasing involvement of unions in strategy planning and implementing may be expected to come more from unions, it also makes sense for firms to incorporate industrial relations into the process as discussed in the next section.

INDUSTRIAL RELATIONS AND STRATEGY FORMULATION AND IMPLEMENTATION

As mentioned earlier, the focus of this book has been on how HRM and industrial-relations processes and activities come into play in the formulation and implementation aspects of strategic management. The viewpoint throughout the book has been primarily that of corporate top management and the human resources department in determining how HRM and industrial relations can play a role in making and carrying out corporate-level and business-level strategies.

The industrial-relations function, however, is clearly different from other HRM areas. Two discrete parties are involved, one of which operates inside a firm but with a distinct voice coming from outside the firm. It is important then to consider the conditions under which industrial relations should be involved in strategy formulation and implementation. There are at least two aspects to consider: (1) the range of topics that are appropriate to include in discussion of industrial relations in strategy and (2) the participants who should be involved in strategy formulation and implementation.

As representatives of a key resource, union leaders presumably would wish to give input on organization actions that could affect employees. Strategic decisions to engage in new product development, divest or shut down businesses that are less profitable, or establish new facilities that may be detrimental to existing ones are issues which clearly can benefit or harm current employees. Such moves might lead unions to seek the chance to provide input to both strategy formulation and implementation.

On the other hand, there are forces inhibiting union involvement in strategic management. By formal involvement in strategy decision-making and implementation, unions may appear to forfeit their presumed advocacy role for employees. Thus, the implications of union involvement in making and carrying out strategy, including a change in image and possible loss of leverage, may discourage unions from seeking full involvement.

As mentioned earlier, from a firm's perspective, gaining early union input and support on strategic decisions, whether beneficial or harmful, could smooth the strategic-management process. As flexibility and swift response to environmental change become an increasingly important competitive advantage, firms would presumably seek a cooperative open relationship with unions. Cooperation might insure faster response to changes in policy on human resources and industrial relations. On the other hand, union involvement in strategic decision making may not always be feasible. There are frequently some decisions that management would prefer are *only* discussed within senior-management levels. Moreover, for some strategic decisions, such as mergers and acquisitions, management is legally prohibited from discussing details until they are approved by governmental and stakeholder groups. In such situations, high union involvement vanishes.

Thus, an important issue for both management and unions to consider is what topics, if any, should be included in union input to strategy formulation and implementation. A related issue is the likely implication of the decision to limit or expose the full strategic-management process to unions. Such issues could also lead nonunion firms to address similar concerns: how much, if any, employee involvement in strategic management is beneficial for the firm and the employees?

Should management decide to pursue union involvement in forming and implementing strategy, a second area to consider is who to involve in the process. In the U.S., a firm could feasibly have several unions operating within its facilities. Thus, it is probable that management and unions would negotiate over which specific groups are to participate in strategic management. In addition to the issue of how to determine *which* unions to involve in strategy formulation and implementation, firms and unions must determine which *level* of union representative to involve. The union level most affected by specific firm actions will typically be the local union. Thus, it would be the logical group to involve in the process. The local union, however, would not typically endorse practices markedly different from the national-level union, which may occur if the local union becomes intimately involved in strategic management in a specific firm.

As a result of such practical questions on which unions and union levels to involve as well as concerns about the extent of their involvement in strategy formulation and implementation, firms may pursue a more conservative and traditional approach. Firms typically should and do consider industrial-relations issues in strategic management but do not require input from union constituencies. This approach, which also follows the pattern suggested for other HRM functions, allows firms to be alert to emerging strategies, through the issues unions bring to the bargaining table, but keeps control over final strategic decisions within the firm.

INCORPORATING INDUSTRIAL RELATIONS INTO CORPORATE STRATEGY FORMULATION

Kochan, McKersie, and Katz (1985) have offered a comprehensive framework placing industrial relations in a broader environment and strategic-management context. Like many strategic HRM models (e.g., Napier, 1988), theirs suggests that external forces (e.g., technology, economic conditions) influence firm-level activities (e.g., strategic actions, industrial-relations policies), and in turn, affect outcomes (for the firm, union, employees, society). The link between external environmental factors and firm-level variables is moderated by business strategies, firm history and structure, and values of firm managers. By suggesting that business strategies precede firm-level industrial-relations and HRM policies, Kochan et al. (1985) have positioned their model to be more implementation- than formulation-oriented. In other words, the business strategies exist before industrial-relations and HRM policies and activities are developed. Hence, industrial relations becomes a method to implement strategy.

Elsewhere, however, Kochan, McKersie, and Capelli (1984) raised the issue of the union's input and influence on industrial-relations strategy. They and other industrial-relations researchers (e.g., Lewin, 1987), have argued that strategy implies control over events: Lewin (1987) has argued, for instance, that there is no "strategy" unless a firm (or union) has control over the events in its environment. Unless an organization can control events, it is only reacting to environmental forces and not taking strategic action. Likewise, Kochan et al. (1985, p. 21) have stated, "strategic decisions can only occur where . . . environmental constraints do not severely curtail the parties' [labor and management] choice of alternatives," resulting in an emphasis on the "process of forming strategy, rather than the actual content or outcomes associated with strategies."

Other researchers, however, have suggested that firms (or unions) may not have full control over events and that, in fact, "reacting" may be a default strategy (e.g., Miles & Snow, 1978). In such a situation, a firm may seek a strategy of being a better "reactor" than its competitors. In these cases, industrial relations may contribute to strategy formulation through helping management determine potential problems and how to react most appropriately.

Several researchers have suggested other reasons for and ways to incorporate industrial relations into strategy formulation. Lawler and Mohrman (1987), for example, have made the case that management must learn to view unions as a potential source of competitive advantage. Rather than ignoring union input in formulating, or implementing strategy and losing ideas and potential commitment from a major stakeholder, Lawler and Mohrman (1987) proposed that managers and unions more creatively use their relationships and traditional means of interaction (i.e., collective bargaining), to achieve such goals as in a jointly developed new organizational culture. An example of a situation where management, in this case Japanese, worked with existing employees (who were unionized) to create a new culture was the General Motors-Toyota joint venture in Fremont, California. Prior to the joint venture, the New United Manufacturing Motor plant (NUMMI) had a reputation for poor labor relations. With GM employees remaining on-site working at the plant after the joint venture, Toyota created a new culture stressing more worker involvement, efficiency, and quality (Holusha, 1988).

Unions may come into the strategy-formulation process in other ways as well. Kovack and Millspaugh (1987) have suggested that, as unions bring new issues to the negotiating table (e.g., what to do about impacts from plant closings, child care), such concerns could initiate the development of intended, or unintended, strategies. For example, repercussions from potential plant closings (e.g., severance payments, lost reputation) may lead a firm to consider diversifying into new business areas that take advantage of existing employee skills. Managers may also find that incorporating union input into planning becomes a way to facilitate subsequent union give-backs and concessions (Kirkpatrick, 1986).

Further, Block, Kleiner, Roomkin, and Salsburg (1987) have suggested that union activity can affect corporate strategy in a very public way. When United Airlines pilots sought ownership of Allegis's UAL division in 1987, they were essentially exhibiting disapproval of the Allegis strategy of further diversification. The move placed United up for acquisition, forced the Allegis chairman to resign, and initiated an unintended redirection in strategy (i.e., refocusing) for the firm.

A final example of the possible way unions could influence corporate strategy is, at present, more speculative. An April 20, 1988 Supreme Court decision broadening union rights to conduct secondary boycotts may have more immediate impacts on firms' industrial-relations policies, but could ultimately influence strategy (*Business Week*, 1988). Several unions (e.g., United Paperworkers International, unions at Eastern Airlines) have begun secondary boycotts of the financial institutions that lend to the unions' main targets. For example, the Paperworkers began boycotts against two lenders (that also have directors in common with the target firm) to International Paper Company, by distributing leaflets and handbills.

While the initial results from secondary boycotts are likely to focus more on direct labor issues (e.g., increased wages, working conditions), they could eventually influence corporate strategy. For example, a severe secondary boycott against an airline might, at the extreme, lead management to sell off some of its airline units, which would constitute a major shift in strategy.

Thus, industrial-relations involvement in the strategy-formulation process may contribute to the creation of intended or unintended corporate strategies. Furthermore, it could also help managers anticipate and avoid potential implementation problems. For example, a firm considering a cost-reduction strategy may bring union leaders into the discussion to gain insight on likely employee reactions and ways to adjust the strategy to be more acceptable and give it a greater chance of succeeding.

Even when management has support of the union leaders, reactions of rank and file may generate unintended strategies, however. For example, a firm considering diversification into areas requiring new skills may seek union input in assessing that strategy option. Managers may be able to convince union leaders of the soundness of the strategy, and indeed try to "sell" other employees by stressing their leaders' acceptance of the plan. If the rank and file, however, perceive the agreement as leaders' relinquishing their advocacy roles in favor of following management's lead, the intended strategy may be doomed. An unintended strategy may be the final outcome, such as diversification into areas requiring knowledge or skills similar to those already possessed in the work force.

In developing overall strategy, therefore, managers must carefully gauge how to consider industrial-relations issues or, further, use input from and apparent desire by unions for cooperation (Mosier, 1986). Finally, Kanter (1986) warned managers to be alert to union reactions and not underestimate union leaders' ability to read management sincerity (or lack thereof) in asking for involvement in planning.

INCORPORATING INDUSTRIAL RELATIONS INTO CORPORATE STRATEGY IMPLEMENTATION

One of the few empirical studies relating corporate strategy and in-dustrial-relations practices was by Christiansen (1983). By examining strategy types and labor-relations patterns among successful and unsuccessful firms, she found a relationship between strategy (cost reduction vs. differentiating) and labor-relations practices. Cost-reduction firms tended to have large industrial-relations staffs, while differentiated firms had small, central labor-relations staffs that advised the plant industrial-relations staffs, which were much larger. The differentiated strategy, which demanded more flexibility so that a firm could anticipate and react quickly in the marketplace, was reflected in industrial-relations programs that pushed the labor-relations functions to the plant level.

Lawler and Mohrman (1987) suggested other ways that unions can assist in implementation of strategy. As representatives of the work force to top management, union leaders could provide insights into ways to facilitate a strategic direction. For example, a strategy of cost reduction or diversification may require new approaches to job design or incorporating technology into the system. Unions that have a cooperative relationship with management could assist in job redesign or developing reward systems to encourage strategy acceptance (e.g., gain sharing).

One of the outcomes typically anticipated from successful strategy-implementation and industrial-relations programs is good firm performance. A collection of recent research papers (Kleiner et al., 1987) examined the relationship between labor-management practices and firm performance, and found disappointing results in many instances. Employee-participation programs, for example, have tended to generate employee satisfaction but little return on performance. Becker and Olson (1987) have suggested that the equity market looks unfavorably toward unions or union-related events: the market value of a firm, reflected in stock price, falls when something occurs to increase the chance of unionism in that firm. Further, Davidson, Worrell, and Garrison (1988) found that the market reacts negatively when a unionized firm begins a strike, positively (but not significantly) to the conclusion of a strike, and not at all when a firm takes action to avoid a strike.

Finally, as Freeman and Medoff (1984, p. 190) have summarized:

> Beneficial to organized workers, almost always; beneficial to the economy
> in many ways; but harmful to the bottom line of company balance sheets:
> this is the paradox of American trade unionism. . . .

Such findings may lead firms to alter industrial-relations policies and practices in a way to enhance likely future firm performance. Because of the types of environmental threats discussed earlier, some unions have been more favorable toward becoming part of strategy implementation in firms (Barbash, 1986). As economic and stockholder pressures lead firms to seek greater efficiencies, companies may seek to cut labor costs, initiate methods to make monetary compensation more of a variable cost (e.g., through merit pay, profit sharing, stock ownership), reduce health-care costs, or use two-tier wage systems. Unlike the situation of the 1960s, some current union leaders appear more likely to discuss and work with managers in implementing strategy through industrial-relations policy.

Even so, managers view unions as a competitive advantage (rather than liability) only in certain circumstances, such as when external forces are extremely threatening (McKersie, 1985). For instance, when Chrysler's survival was at stake, Douglas Fraser (President, United Auto Workers) assumed a position on the Chrysler board of directors, partly as a concession to the union and external stakeholders. His involvement helped the board view the union as part of the solution, rather than the cause, of the firm's problems. Only such dire conditions, however, would have led to the idea of placing a union member on the board.

Firms may be wiser to consider unions as possible contributors to competitive advantage during all sorts of economic conditions. Some nonunion firms already view their unionized competitors with trepidation when those competitors have cooperative labor-management relations. One representative of a nonunion high-technology firm commented on General Motors' ability to marshal employees companywide to initiate changes in operation or direction: "For all our good [human-resources] practices . . . we have no way of engaging a cross-section of the organization in the design of a new product in the way that General Motors [can] . . . because of their collective relationship [with their unions] and ability to mobilize the work force" (McKersie, 1985). Although some researchers have argued that industrial relations can help in the successful implementation of firm direction, Lewin (1987) has discounted that, saying that industrial relations is not a "strategic-choice" variable because management's actions are the result of reacting to external changes, rather than concerted decision to choose certain practices. In his view, management develops an approach to industrial relations as a way to seek solutions to current labor-management problems, not as a result of conscious decision to implement strategy. He has argued that if industrial relations was a "strategic-choice" variable, researchers would be able to predict industrial-relations policy and structure within firms. According to Lewin (1987), because of the clear dualism in approaches to labor relations (both cooperative and adversary relationships, by firms within the same industries), existing research has not yet shown industrial relations to play a clear role in strategic management.

Lewin's argument has raised an important issue: industrial-relations (and other) researchers claiming a role for HRM aspects in strategy implementation need to consider a broader range of variables in explaining strategic action or choices. In other words, Lewin (1987) has argued that other factors may lead firms to choose their industrial-relations practices, factors such as external conditions. It may be that the current research is too unsophisticated to sort out the extent to which external factors versus other variables (e.g., strategy) affect industrial relations.

There are, however, anecdotal examples that may suggest a link between strategy and industrial relations, even if it is not always successful in the long run. In 1977, the Japanese television manufacturer Sanyo diversified into the U.S. and purchased a failing plant in Forrest City, Arkansas (Beazley, 1988). Sanyo made technological, capital, and management investments, rehired many laid-off employees, and worked with the union to increase the plant's product quality and overall performance. Sanyo began operations by seeking consensus management, working with the union and a committee of American and Japanese workers. The early attitude of the Japanese appeared to be to design a union relationship that would help foster growth and performance. Unfortunately, poor communications (few Japanese spoke English) and cultural misunderstandings led to a declining relationship and ultimately a tough stance by Sanyo and strikes by the American workers. In this area, the industrial-relations practices that were supposed to implement a strategy of high-quality U.S. production have not been successful thus far in implementing Sanyo's long-term goals.

More recently, firms responding to changes in external competitive pressures are using union contract negotiations as a way to carry out goals of maintaining or reducing expenses (Karr, 1988). Lewin (1987) would argue this approach is not "strategic" because firms are reacting as opposed to controlling their environment. Nevertheless, others such as Miles and Snow (1978) and Porter (1985) might argue that cost control and leadership is a strategic choice and any method of doing so is a way to implement such a strategy.

STRATEGY FORMULATION AND IMPLEMENTATION BY UNIONS

The last section of the chapter takes the perspective of unions, a second key party in the labor-management relationship. There is increasing evidence that unions are learning about and applying strategic-management skills to their own situations, especially since their environments have changed so dramatically. Cohen-Rosenthal and Burton (1986) have suggested that unions are pursuing a form of "strategic planning," by identifying future goals, working on joint planning efforts with management, and conducting training sessions for members to help implement union goals. Stratton and Brown (1988) examined 114 responses from a survey of all national and international unions in the U.S. and found that while a majority of unions (65 percent) use no formal planning, those that did reaped benefits. Stratton and Brown (1988) classified unions into three groups: unions that were proactive and pursued a growth strategy, unions that were reactive and pursued a defensive approach to dealing with their environments, and unions that tried to modify their environments through steps to "change the game." Planner unions that sought a "growth" strategy tended to have success in increasing membership. The unions that tried to "change the game" also felt they achieved success using such practices as initiating more cooperative relationships with management, using corporate campaigns (e.g., pressuring members of boards of directors to resign from anti-union firms), and seeking to change public policy.

Other research has suggested that unions may in the future increasingly seek to control their destinies more through cooperative arrangements with firms (Lawler & Mohrman, 1987; McKersie, 1985). While business managers, in particular, view this trend positively, McKersie (1985) has exhibited concern that such a strategy may backfire in the long run. Greater participation by union leaders in management issues may make labor law obsolete: there would result no need for "mandated and non-mandated subjects" for discussion, since unions will participate in a wider range of decisions. As a trade-off for the involvement, McKersie (1985) has predicted more concession bargaining by unions, coupled with contingency compensation and gain sharing. Such arrangements, while favorable in positive economic times, could generate severe repercussions from the lack of pay in downturns.

Barbash (1986) has predicted that labor-management relations will follow a middle ground, and suggested a different kind of strategy for unions to pursue. While fearful that a shift from the traditional American labor-relations system will lead to a "protective void" for employees, providing them with no advocating voice, Barbash (1986) has argued that there will still be a need for legislative protection, in areas such as employment at will. Thus, in formulating strategy, unions may consider focusing their resources on likely necessary future changes in the legislation.

Finally, some researchers have refuted the predictions of inevitable cooperative relationships between labor and management. Lewin (1987), for example, has predicted a range of relationships, from the very traditional adversarial to more cooperation. He based his conclusion on the inability of current research in strategic industrial relations to explain why a dualism (cooperation and adversary) of union-management relationships exists in similar clusters of firms, such as within the airlines industry.

Union-implementation activities follow from the directions that unions pursue to adapt to environmental and organizational changes. Schuster (1984) and Kanter (1986) discussed four tactics that unions have used to implement more cooperative approaches: gain sharing (e.g., increasing employee involvement, Scanlon plans), labor-management committees, quality circles, and local common-interest forums (to increasing union involvement in implementing new technology). In a different vein, Wheeler (1989) suggested four approaches unions use to dealing with corporate mergers and acquisitions: collective bargaining, lawsuits, pursuing corporate ownership, and seeking new legislation.

It is yet unclear what long-term impact strategic planning by unions may have on their performance or relationship with firms. They may well face comparable impact from human resource issues in setting their own intended and unintended strategies. For example, if child-care issues begin to dominate the bargaining slate, and if unions are amenable to working for those issues and indeed gain ground, that may generate new avenues for increasing membership (e.g., single parents, minorities). Likewise, if education benefits for members and dependents become a major priority, ethnic groups such as Asian refugees might join.

SUMMARY AND CONCLUSIONS

The focus of Chapter Ten has been on the possible ways industrial relations may play a role in creating and implementing corporate strategy.

While skeptics will remain, other researchers and managers have suggested that there can be a link between strategy and industrial relations.

In addition, the chapter reviewed recent evidence that unions are beginning to use strategic-management processes. Such knowledge may help both management and unions better understand each others' goals and positions in negotiations. It should also encourage firms to view unions as partners in business, while respecting their positions as representatives of employees.

ENTREPRENEURIAL LINKS

The search for the source of dynamic entrepreneurial performance has much in common with hunting the Heffalump. The Heffalump is a rather large and very important animal.[1] He has been hunted by many individuals using various ingenious trapping devices, but no one so far has succeeded in capturing him. All who claim to have caught sight of him report that he is enormous, but they disagree on his particularities. Not having explored his current habitat with sufficient care, some hunters have used as bait their own favorite dishes and have then tried to persuade people that what they caught was a Heffalump. However, very few are convinced, and the search goes on (Kilby, 1971, p.1).

In a recent popular-press book, Pinchot (1985) uses the subtitle "Why you don't have to leave the corporation to become an entrepreneur." This subtitle captured the generally accepted notion that entrepreneurial behavior is more difficult in large corporations (e.g., Kanter, 1985; Peterson, 1981). Peterson (1981) believed the value of entrepreneurship relates to an organization's tendency toward "ossification," which occurs as organizations increase in size and acts to stifle innovative behavior. Kanter (1985) believed entrepreneurship decreased because the requirements for administrative success are related to control, and this becomes more important in organizations as they grow. This focus on administrative control makes it less likely that the organization will have mechanisms that encourage the freedom and flexibility in behavior that are associated with entrepreneurial success. The role that HRM can play in developing and sustaining entrepreneurial and innovative behavior at the firm level is examined in this chapter. First, the nature of entrepreneurship and entrepreneurial behavior is examined. This lays the theoretical groundwork needed to appreciate why organizations should adjust to capture these benefits. The means by which corporations can engage in entrepreneurial behavior are then examined. This is done in a manner that is consistent with the strategic process outlined in Chapters Three and Four. Next, the role that HRM can play in facilitating entrepreneurial behavior, especially with respect to its ability to affect the culture of the organization, is examined. Finally, the

---

[1] See A.A. Milne, *Winnie-The-Pooh* (London: 1926), Ch. 5.

relationship between entrepreneurial behavior, HRM, and strategy is discussed, and a model outlining the relationship between these actors is presented.

ENTREPRENEURS AND ENTREPRENEURIAL BEHAVIOR

The term entrepreneur is often subsumed by the concept of entrepreneurial behavior. As pointed out in the introductory quotation to this chapter, it is generally agreed that entrepreneurship is important. What is less clear is exactly why this is so and how that importance is manifested. An examination of the historical descriptions of the entrepreneur shows a range from risk-taker to rogue. This may have occurred because the definition process is essentially aiming at a moving target. The entrepreneurial process is dynamic in nature and entrepreneurs continually find new ways to operate; the currently accepted descriptions will always be somewhat outdated. However, this evolution of definition should help convince firms that entrepreneurial behavior cannot be institutionalized through controls, because the exact nature of the behavior cannot be anticipated.

Firms populated with more entrepreneurs, holding size constant, should be more capable of entrepreneurial behavior. Thus, the first step for the firm is to attract and retain entrepreneurs. While the presence of entrepreneurs is not a sufficient condition for ongoing corporate innovation, it appears to be a necessary one. Beyond this, characteristics associated with the organization's design and the control mechanisms it uses may also be important in explaining why some firms are more capable of exhibiting entrepreneurial behavior than others. To effect a change from an administrative to an entrepreneurial mode, HRM tools may be among the most appropriate and powerful. Before discussing the specific nature of the HRM impact, some discussion of what the literature says about the "entrepreneur" and "entrepreneurial behavior" is warranted.

Entrepreneurs

The popular-press notion of an entrepreneur as the business founder, who operates in isolation while running against the tide of public opinion, is too restrictive for a corporate application. This "heroic" notion of the entrepreneur is better suited for magazines such as *Venture* or *INC.* The image of Steven Jobs starting Apple Computer, or of William Gates starting Microsoft, appeals to the imagination, but it represents a very limited notion of the entrepreneur. While there are many corporations that may envy the success of these visible individuals, developing a pattern of ongoing innovative and entrepreneurial behavior is more important. Unless the entrepreneurial behavior becomes part of the cultural baggage of the organization, the firm will find that it is just engaged in a delaying action with respect to the process of ossification (Peterson, 1981). A historical look at the entrepreneur is useful in providing some basis for categorizing how entrepreneurs bring value to the organization. The extent of this value is important because there are also costs associated with permitting entrepreneurship, because much of this behavior occurs outside of the organization's control system, which was designed to minimize costs.

The term entrepreneur has its lexicographic roots in France. It was originally used to refer to contractors engaged in the draining of bogs (Montchretien, 1615), but the meaning was later extended to all contractors (Isambert, 1829). This notion of the entrepreneur being associated with unusual manufacturing or construction activity is reflected in early dictionary references, such as the *Dictionnaire Universal de Commerce* (Savary des Bruslons, 1723).

In Britain, the word "undertaker" was a synonym, until it gradually took on its more morbid, present meaning. Here again, entrepreneurs were seen as those who engaged in activities that were out of the ordinary. In some cases adjectives were used to indicate whether the entrepreneur was considered honorable (Beverly, 1705). More recently, Vesper (1980) also felt the need to distinguish between entrepreneurship and fraud. This distinction is necessary because the term was used to describe those accused of official corruption (Moryson, 1617) as well as for those providing valuable service to the Queen (Payne, 1589). Thus, while entrepreneurs have exhibited high ethical variance, perceptions seem to be more uniform with respect to the rewards that were seen flowing to them.

It is difficult to get, from historical references, the complete sense of their contemporaries' perceptions of these early entrepreneurs. However, it seems obvious that the term entrepreneur evolved because the existing vocabulary was inadequate. As commerce developed, certain new activities became possible. These activities called upon certain skills and abilities that were not possessed by all individuals involved in commerce, and a separate term was needed to define them. Thus, the term entrepreneur emerged as a way of referring to individuals capable of these unique, and apparently desired, activities.

The specific behavioral characteristics that were exhibited by the entrepreneur were gradually reflected in the academic literature. Cantillon (1755) suggested entrepreneurs were better able to cope with uncertainty. Belidor (1729) believed entrepreneurs were better collectors, or interpreters, of information. Others (e.g., Baudeau, 1771; Turgot, 1766) believed risk-bearing was what distinguished the entrepreneur from the ordinary business person. J. B. Say (1844), who was both a business person and theoretician, presented the notion of an entrepreneur as an individual who was best able to combine the factors of production in the manufacture of a product. Say believed entrepreneurial profit was the appropriate compensation for individuals with this talent. What Say did not do was elaborate on the details of this insight or the conditions under which entrepreneurs best operate.

Thanks largely to Adam Smith (1776), the entrepreneur disappeared from the scene for the next century. What Smith did was replace the entrepreneur with the capitalist, and it was not until more recent times that the entrepreneur was reincorporated into the theoretical literature. Recently, Baumol (1968) urged a reconsideration of the entrepreneur in economic analysis, and this renewed interest has also been reflected in the business community. This recent interest in reintroducing the entrepreneur into the dominant theoretical frameworks revolves around the concept of entrepreneurial behavior, rather than on developing definitions about the entrepreneur. While some may be inclined to view the entrepreneur as a sort of "miracle worker," that is not reflected in the academic literature (e.g., Casson, 1982). Entrepreneurs are a necessary component in a innovative firm, but they are not meant to replace or substitute for other factors associated with the operation of a sound and efficient business. The entrepreneur is best seen as a provider of supplemental benefits through entrepreneurial behavior, which leads to entrepreneurial profit.

Entrepreneurial Behavior

From a corporate perspective, it is natural to be interested in entrepreneurial behavior and the profit it generates. This is because entrepreneurial behavior may facilitate the ability of firms to sustain above-average levels of profit, which do not converge to the industry average (Jacobsen, 1988). Much like the emergent concept of strategy (See Chapter Four), entrepreneurial behavior can also be related to the market-adjustment process. Figure 11-1 outlines a standard equilibrium position where supply and demand intersect. As discussed in Chapter Three, this intersection defines both the purchase price (P^*) and the quantity demanded (Q^*). However, as is well know by individuals purchasing an automobile or contracting to have a house painted, the price that should be charged is seldom known with certainty. What individuals tend to discuss is if they got a good deal. From a theoretical perspective, this disparity occurs because each individual has a different notion about just what is the appropriate price. This also occurs when individuals take jobs, because they are trying to guess what is the maximum salary that can be demanded. This uncertainty reflects the uncertainty that suppliers also have when making production decisions.

There are two prominent views about how entrepreneurship can extract extraordinary profits during the market-adjustment process. In the first case, Schumpeter (1934) believed that the innovations of entrepreneurs caused disequilibrium. He believed entrepreneurs did this by introducing new products, or making major innovations with respect to existing products, which disrupted the present state of market equilibrium. This disruption accounted for economic growth.

In Figure 11-2 a simplified version of the process is depicted. The demand curve is shown as shifting out from D_1 to D_2. This is the kind of shift that might be expected when a new and innovative version of a product is introduced. Although there is a price increase from P^* to P_2, customers' demand is reflected in the increased quantity that suppliers are willing to produce, in this example the difference between Q^* and Q_2. This example represents a long-

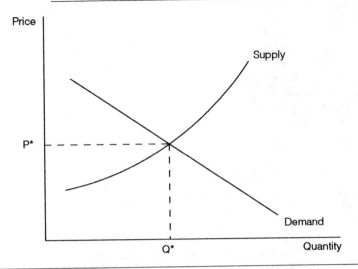

FIGURE 11-1. Standard calculation of price and quantity, without any consideration of entrepreneurial behavior.

term situation, but the end result is higher demand for a better product. Obviously, the early entrants are able to exploit the situation by charging more than P_2 because supplies are limited during the initial periods. After competitors have copied the innovation the situation adjusts to a price, in this case P_2, which reflects normal profits for the industry or product. During this period between the initial introduction and the adjustment by competitors, the initial entrant earns entrepreneurial profit.

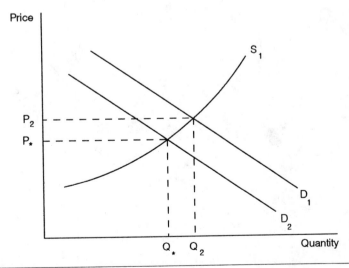

FIGURE 11-2. A market adjustment reflecting an outward shift of the demand curve, caused by a product innovation.

This type of market adjustment would be typical for a new product that is recognized as vastly superior and, because of its limited initial supply, commands a high price. The older version, being supplied by noninnovating firms, would be less in demand and characterized by overcapacity. A recent example of this occurred when compact disks were introduced. Compact disks commanded high prices, initially, because of the limited supply. However, facilities capable of producing standard records found that there was much less demand for their services. Gradually, there has been a downward price adjustment, but the compact disk still reflects a price that is higher than that charged for 331/3 rpm records, and the quantity being sold greatly exceeds initial forecasts.

A second view of the market-adjustment process, as it relates to entrepreneurial behavior, has been refined by Kirzner (1973, 1979, 1985). Kirzner suggested that the essential nature of markets is confused because information is fragmented and different individuals are likely to always have different perceptions about prices (Hayek, 1937). Figure 11-3, which is a variation of Figure 4-2, depicts the market-adjustment process as described by Kirzner.

In this case, a series of supply and demand curves are seen that are representative of the perceptions of different people. What this essentially means is that the perceptions of different individuals can be exploited. This occurs because the price perception of individual A is higher than the perception of individual X. Now, if individual C comes along and buys from X at the lower price (P_X), she can then sell to A at the higher price (P_A). The entrepreneurial profit is her reward for having the insight to notice that this discrepancy between A's and X's perceptions of price could be exploited. In

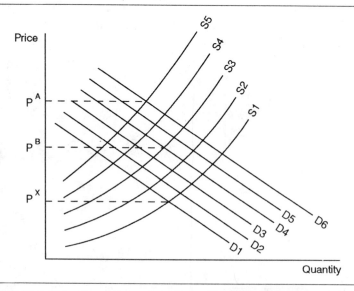

FIGURE 11-3. Price/quantity perceptions of various market participants, with respect to a single product, component, or service.

this case individual C not only had a more accurate perception of where price and quantity should be, but also had insights about others' perceptions.

A classic example of this type of market adjustment occurred in the case of the brewers' dried grain industry. For years, beer brewers dumped the residuals from brewing in the public sewer system. In the 1950s many municipalities prohibited this. To the brewers this residual grain was garbage, with a negative value since they had to pay to have it hauled away. An "entrepreneur" who was hauling the "garbage" quickly discovered that the grain could be dried, bagged, and sold to farmers as pig feed. To the pig farmers, the grain was considered a high-quality food and commanded a premium price because of its high-protein value. In this case, the entrepreneur exploited the different perceptions of value between the beer producers and pig farmers. This is, of course, an extreme case because she was able to get the brewer's to pay to get rid of a product that the farmers were willing to buy at a premium. This would be an example of Kirzner's entrepreneur, because she accumulated large quantities of entrepreneurial profit, before the brewers discovered their garbage-grain had a market value. They then stopped paying to have it hauled away and began selling the hauling rights. Obviously, the key issue is what was it about the entrepreneurial firm that allowed the idea to be developed and facilitated the allocation of capital to the new venture.

Corporate Entrepreneurship

As one moves away from theoretical notions of entrepreneurship to an actual organization setting, the issue becomes more complex. One way to have an entrepreneurial firm appears to be being blessed with a strong founding entrepreneur who is capable of maintaining the innovative spirit. Edward Land and Thomas Edison were classic examples of the this type of CEO-entrepreneur. Since it is unlikely that established firms can reinvent themselves, this path to innovation is beyond the reach of most firms. Acquiring these upper-tail-of-the-distribution entrepreneurs is a supply-side problem and, in any case, even they must be eventually replaced.

The second path to corporate entrepreneurship is through culture or vision. A much-cited, classic example of this type of organization is the 3M Company. 3M has a culture that stresses innovation, and has a series of corporate stories that support this notion. Stories about individuals disobeying company directives to abandon development efforts, which eventually led to the invention of new products, are the lifeblood of the 3M hero. 3M now allows managers to spend 15 percent of their time pursuing independent ideas (Price, 1986). This second path, which attempts to create an entrepreneurial culture, seems to offer the most fruitful ground for making a firm more receptive to entrepreneurial behavior and for using HRM to facilitate this process

While the definition of corporate entrepreneurship has been cast rather broadly in this book, narrower views are common. For instance, in a meeting between business executives and academics, entrepreneurship was cast in terms of internal corporate venturing. Then venturing was "defined as those activities required to achieve growth through the establishment of new businesses which differ significantly from the ongoing enterprise in technology, markets or financial characteristics" (Block, 1983, p.382). By casting entrepreneurship in this manner, many of the "arbitrage-like" activities emphasized in this chapter can be eliminated. Morris and Paul (1987, p.248) supported an expanded notion of corporate entrepreneurship and defined it more broadly as "the organization's willingness to encourage creativity, flexibility, and to support risk."

No matter which definition is used or how a firm accommodates entrepreneurial behavior, what is really important is to identify why some organizations are successful and others are not. In this way, policies and procedures can be identified that allow HRM to be an effective tool in making the organization more entrepreneurial. Reasons cited for a lack of firm-level entrepreneurial behavior include: (1) a lack of entrepreneurial talent within the firm (Block & Ruff, 1986), (2) a lack of top-management commitment (Block & Ruff, 1986), (3) incentive systems that induce the fear of failure (Sathe, 1985; Block & Ornati, 1987), (4) too much emphasis on control through the administrative function (Kanter, 1985) and, (5) a lack of autonomy (Sykes, 1986). At a more unified level, Price (1986, p.709) pointed out that nonentrepreneurial firms have failed to recognize that "old styles of hierarchical management, analysis and control no longer foster the independent thinking, risk-taking and innovation required for survival in today's competitive environment." This anti-entrepreneurial mind-set still exists and one manager, in the Block (1983, p. 385) study, reported "you can't have entrepreneurs in the company, they're too undisciplined."

Research has also begun to identify things firms can do to be more entrepreneurial. Kanter (1985) believed that the entrepreneurial mode of operation needs the same consideration as the administrative components. She stated that "an entrepreneurial corporation . . . emphasizes . . . flexibility and broadly-skilled sets of employees in flexible units that can be grouped or regrouped as changing circumstances require" (Kanter, 1985, p.48). Thus, entrepreneurial firms seem more capable of balancing the control needs of the firm with the flexibility needs of the entrepreneur.

A corporate culture that is supportive is also seen as necessary. In a study of AT&T after it had been broken up, Cohen, Graham, and Shils (1985) found the establishment of a new culture to be extremely important. They found that everyone favored a more entrepreneurial environment, but that the behavior needed to achieve this new culture was not the only critical factor. After the entrepreneurial transformation began, they identified (Cohen et al., 1985, p.634) several factors that facilitated this process. These included (1) the identification and support of "insurgency groups" as role models for other managers, (2) staff training so that those in control and facilitating positions are more supportive of entrepreneurial needs, (3) more organizational-level support, and (4) that those in charge of these new ventures "are successful in managing profitable operations *and* they prevail politically."

In examining four extremely large corporations, Sathe (1985, p.645) found that successful "companies motivated entrepreneurial behavior by offering status and advancement as rewards, and by insuring these managers against the low success rates and risks of failure that entrepreneurial activities entail." Sathe (1985) found that a strong entrepreneurial culture was absolutely necessary to sustain innovative activity. The important issue is how the HRM function can be used to help facilitate the corporate transformation needed to sustain an entrepreneurial environment.

HRM'S ROLE IN CORPORATE ENTREPRENEURSHIP

The entrepreneurial component appears to be closely tied to both the prevailing culture of the organization and the way individuals are selected, trained, and rewarded. This indicates that these major areas of HRM responsibility are closely tied to any effective transformation effort. George and MacMillan (1984) saw this linkage as occurring over a range of entrepreneurial activities. Activities ranged from the enhancement of existing products to inventions that replace existing products or develop entirely new markets. HRM practices act to facilitate the development of practices that foster this entrepreneurial activity (Schuler & Martocchio, 1987).

Staffing

While the psychological profile for entrepreneurs is not different than for successful executives, both exhibit certain characteristics that distinguish them from the general pool of managerial applicants (Brockhaus & Horwitz, 1986). These include: (1) high need for achievement (McClelland, 1961), (2) an internal locus of control (Rotter, 1966), and (3) the propensity to take a moderate amount of risk (Brockhaus, 1980; Kogan & Wallach, 1964). Thus, at the selection stage there is some information that can be used to facilitate choosing of the type of individuals capable of being assimilated into an entrepreneurial mode of operation.

As part of its "gatekeeping" function, the HRM group plays an important role in the recruitment of this talent. It is the first contact for most managerial applicants and is best positioned to convey the culture of the firm to applicants. The preparation of printed material designed to attract new managerial talent is also likely to be controlled by this group. Thus, by insuring that both the initial contacts and published material relating to recruitment portray the management style in a particular way, they may be more likely to attract the appropriate managers. Psychological profiles may also be useful as a way to insure that individuals more suited to an administrative mode are not recruited into units seeking to move toward an entrepreneurial model.

In addition to their own selection activities the HRM group is likely to be seen as the group with the most expertise in this area. Since functional managers and senior executives involved in recruiting above the entry level are likely to be less in touch with, and less inclined to use standardized recruiting techniques, it is important to maintain an HRM input for mid-range and top-level executive positions. This requires the same type of HRM input for executive recruiting at higher levels as has been argued for HRM in general. If HRM is seen as having no selection role for higher-level positions, it is likely that entry-level managers capable of entrepreneurial behavior will find themselves working for supervisors as likely to stifle as encourage an entrepreneurial mode of operation.

Training and Development

Training and development is probably the most crucial stage for firms desiring to increase the amount of innovative or entrepreneurial behavior, because it is not generally possible to repopulate the organization with a new set of managers. Thus, while selection is geared toward providing a new set of entrepreneurially inclined managers on the supply side, some entrepreneurial pressure needs to be applied on the demand side. Here again, the HRM function would appear to be the optimal choice. Because of their expertise, and their position in the organization, the HRM group may be capable of designing training and development efforts that extend across the entire organization.

Since the organization has two sets of managers, those well-entrenched and comfortable in the administrative mode and those inclined toward entrepreneurial behavior, dual programs are necessary. Those managers inclined toward, and comfortable in, the administrative mode need to be made aware of the entrepreneurial needs of the organization. They also need to be made aware of the type of behavior they as supervisors should engage in, or avoid, if an entrepreneurial culture is to flourish. Efforts, such as behavioral simulations, may be useful in increasing awareness among this set of managers.

While the encouragement of entrepreneurially inclined managers appears to be simpler, it must be remembered that these individuals have adjusted their behavior to suit organizational requirements. These individuals may not wish to consciously admit that they have become "organizational creatures." Training here has to be focused on convincing these managers both that there is, and should be, a better way of managing. To be encouraged to become more entrepreneurial they have to be convinced that there are going to be new procedures for adopting and evaluating entrepreneurial endeavors in the organization. On a second level, some functional training may also be needed. The popular notion of an entrepreneur starting new business ventures "willy nilly" has to be replaced with an entrepreneurial option that is compatible with the administrative realities of the organization. As the organization relaxes it controls, functional-level expertise will become more important because the firm will have to produce additional efficiencies to help feed entrepreneurial ideas.

Reward Systems

One of the best ways to convince both administrative and entrepreneurially inclined managers of the change in organizational behavior is through the reward system. It is important for HRM to be involved in this adjustment because the reward system serves both the administrative and the entrepreneurial needs of the organization. For instance, the notion that entrepreneurs may value higher wages appears less than valid, but this may be important to other managers. The HRM group is most likely to be able to develop a series of rewards that are appropriate to the entrepreneur-manager but do not upset the status quo.

A second characteristic of the reward system relates to the monetary compensation of those who facilitate and encourage, because they also help make the system work. This involves both the senior-level executives and the work force in general. To truly achieve the entrepreneurial effect, the compensation scheme must ensure that all share in the entrepreneurial benefits. This might include some type of bonus or retirement plan that is specifically tied to the performance of entrepreneurial ventures. This would invoke support from all employees and could also be used to encourage a proactive role by senior executives.

Industrial Relations

For a firm to be entrepreneurial, employee support is necessary. The organizational dynamics associated with numerous new product/market choices can have negative effects on the existing work force. If collective-bargaining agreements are constructed in a manner that inhibits organizational flexibility, this will have a negative impact on the ability to successfully operate in the entrepreneurial mode. However, it would be naive for the firm to expect that employees are willing to bear all of the down side costs so that the firm can earn these entrepreneurial profits.

One way for the firm to ensure employee cooperation and support, for entrepreneurial decisions, is to transfer some of the benefits to them. A mechanism could be developed to calculate profits that could not have been earned without employee cooperation, or this could be done by negotiating a more general profit-sharing plan into the contract. Severance payments could also be used to signal the firm's commitment to the concept of permanent employment. By having liberal severance payments incorporated into the collective-bargaining agreement, the firm may be able to reduce employees' fears with respect to layoffs.

While largesse is being suggested in some areas, the prescription is not offered to "to give away the store." For this reason, it is probably better if contractual adjustments come later in the entrepreneurial-transformation process. The entrepreneurial mode of operations needs strong management support, open communication with employees, and probably a few success stories. A few successful programs that can be clearly delineated from past operating practices are an excellent way to communicate management's seriousness about institutionalizing new operating modes. Tangible evidence of this type helps ensure that new contractual arrangements receive the desired interpretation by employees.

In addition to removing employee resistance, some attention should be directed toward developing enthusiastic employee cooperation. In many cases, especially with respect to process innovations, employees at all levels are equally likely to be the source for the ideas that eventually lead to entrepreneurial returns. Some mechanism, beyond trivial devices such as suggestions boxes, needs to be found so that these ideas are communicated upward. In this respect the industrial-relations effort has to also be directed toward including all employees in the cultural transformation that is providing the underlying support for the entrepreneurial mode of operation. This relates back to the training and development efforts of the HRM group.

CULTURE

If there is one area where the research appears clear it is the need to establish and maintain an entrepreneurial culture within the organization. While the culture research is highly varied, it appears that something is needed beyond the highly visible support of top management. If the culture of the organization is viewed as some set of underlying values that employees "buy into," then it makes the behavior they are likely to exhibit more predictable. Since it is impossible for the organization to monitor all decision-making, the establishment of a corporate culture that emphasizes certain values is one way to ensure that market opportunities are likely to be exploited.

No function, other than accounting, crosses all the functional and staff areas of a firm as extensively as does HRM. In addition, HRM has an impact on employees regardless of their level in the organization. The standardization of selection, training, and rewards across all levels and functional areas, and a consistent industrial-relations posture, helps ensure the desired change in organizational culture. In addition, the HRM group may be best positioned to monitor this change. This may be done through observational or survey methods (e.g., Covin & Slevin, 1986), which can be used to help top management gauge the extent of any corporate culture changes. By monitoring these changes the organization will be better able to gauge the extent to which the pace at which entrepreneurial behavior can be expected to supplement the firm's strategy.

HRM, STRATEGY, AND
CORPORATE ENTREPRENEURSHIP

Much like SHRP, the value of the interface between strategy and entrepreneurship is the driving force behind extending HRM into this area. The original model of strategy as both incremental and deliberate action relates directly to the entrepreneurial function. While some entrepreneurial behavior will flow from the deliberate-planning process of the firm, much of it will be incremental-type action.

HRM's role in facilitating both spontaneous behavior and action tied to formalized plans is supportive of the notion of strategy as both deliberate and emergent action, which developed in this research. A slight recasting of the model used to describe the strategic process (Figure 4-3) is illustrated in Figure 11-4 and shows how this is accomplished.

The entrepreneurial culture is depicted as having a direct relationship to the percentage of the realized strategy that reflects entrepreneurial behavior. This entrepreneurial component should have both deliberate and emergent elements. However, it is the direct link from HRM to the entrepreneurial culture that determines the absolute size of the entrepreneurial component. The active participation of the HRM group in this process, designed to develop an entrepreneurial mode of operation, ensures participation and support throughout the organization. While top management may be able to muscle innovation programs or products through the organizational bureaucracy, this cannot be an effective mechanism to achieve widespread innovative behavior. The various HRM tools can moderate the natural tendencies of the bureaucracy to help ensure that the desired entrepreneurial culture provides the right set of supporting tools.

SUMMARY AND CONCLUSIONS

The use of entrepreneurial behavior as a source of competitive advantage is available to all firms. However, to capture these benefits, an appreciation of

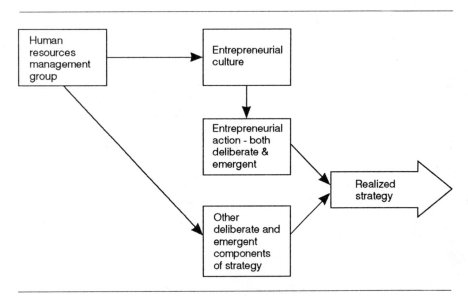

FIGURE 11-4. HRM's role in developing an entrepreneurial culture that is reflected in the firm's realized strategy.

both the historical position of the entrepreneur and the mechanism by which entrepreneurial behavior brings value to the firm is needed. Both topics are discussed so that concepts developed later can be logically related to them.

Historical notions of individual entrepreneurial behavior are applied to corporations. This is directly tied to the concept of the corporate culture, which is required if the firm is to be capable of supporting entrepreneurial behavior. The HRM group plays a key role in developing the organizational culture needed to support more entrepreneurial behavior through (1) the selection of entrepreneurs, (2) the training and development functions, (3) the development and administration of appropriate reward systems, and (4) consistent industrial-relations policies. A mode that relates HRM to entrepreneurial components, in both deliberate and emergent strategy, is presented. This relationship is a key link in producing entrepreneurial action, which supports the general strategy of the firm and enriches the realized strategy that ultimately defines the firm's competitive advantage.

INTERNATIONAL HUMAN RESOURCES MANAGEMENT

"We are caught in an inescapable network of mutuality, tied in a single garment of destiny. Whatever affects one directly, affects all indirectly."
Martin Luther King, Jr.
Letter from Birmingham Jail, 1963

Throughout the book, it has been argued that HRM is linked to strategy formulation and implementation. As the discussion broadens to include international variables, the "network of mutuality," as King suggests above, is even more important. Human resources expertise is increasingly viewed as a contributor to international competitive advantage (Porter, 1985; Napier, Taylor, & Slater, 1988; Schuler & MacMillan, 1984), and thus understanding its role in improving performance of firms operating globally is critical.

For this chapter, the term "international HRM" (IHRM) refers to human resources practices in firms that have operations outside their home countries (Figure 12-1). From the U.S. perspective, other aspects of HRM research that have international links include literature dealing with HRM issues in a comparative context (two or more countries) or single-country context (outside the U.S.), and that dealing with managing a multicultural work force. Comparative HRM refers to research that discusses similarities and differences between HRM and related practices in two or more countries (e.g, Gerpott & Domsch, 1985; Morgan & Bottrall, 1988). Single-country studies focus on descriptions of HRM activities typically in countries outside the U.S (e.g., Nonaka, 1988). A relatively new subset of HRM for U.S. managers, a subset that has received little research attention, is the managing of a multicultural work force (Ondrack, 1987). This involves determining what practices to use in a

---

- Research on HRM practices in multinational firms.
- Research comparing HRM practices in two or more countries.
- From the U.S. perspective, research on HRM practices in a country outside the U.S.
- Research on managing a multicultural work force.
- Research on strategic HRM issues in multinational firms.

FIGURE 12-1. Categories of IHRM Research in the Literature.

firm that has employees whose backgrounds are culturally different. Finally, recent research in strategic management has increasingly focused on IHRM issues (e.g., Lorange, 1986; Pucik & Katz, 1986).

IMPORTANCE OF INTERNATIONAL HRM

Several researchers (Dowling, 1986; Newman, Bhatt, & Gutteridge, 1978; Schollhamer, 1975; Tung, 1984b, 1987) have stressed the importance of recognizing differences between HRM in international and domestic settings. The importance was further emphasized in the success of a conference held in Singapore in 1987, on the topic of International Personnel and Human Resources Management (Ferris, Rowland, & Nedd, 1989).

Too often, researchers and managers assume that what works in one country applies elsewhere. Unfortunately, there is much evidence that when organizations select executives for international assignments, they often wrongly rely on the managers' past domestic performance. "Good managerial performance" in a domestic setting seldom translates into similar "good performance" in the international arena.

International HRM can also be a contributor to an organization's intended- and unintended-strategic components, discussed in Chapter Four. As a facilitator of a centralized global strategy, or of a strategy stressing local autonomy and a decentralized structure, IHRM practices can increase or decrease the autonomy and ultimately the ability of overseas managers to perform their jobs. Control systems, performance-evaluation practices, and compensation policies can facilitate the flexibility of a subsidiary, and of headquarters, to maintain competitive advantage.

Other reasons to examine human resources issues in an international context are unrelated to the role of multinational corporations (MNCs). Two trends are forcing the U.S.-based firms to gain familiarity with international issues of HRM. First, with the more than 300 acquisitions annually of U.S. firms by foreign-owned companies in the latter half of the 1980s, U.S. managers must deal with owners who are foreign. Thus, it will be more important to understand other cultures and HRM policies from different countries.

Second, an influx of foreign-born employees means that, in certain parts of the U.S., a multicultural work force may become more the rule than the exception. In 1987, in the state of Florida, for instance, there was a call for a vote (which was never taken) on what its "official language" should be: English or Spanish. Other countries, such as West Germany and Switzerland, have long dealt with this issue as "guest workers" have flooded their job markets. The phenomenon is only recently gaining attention in the U.S. as immigrants from Eastern Asia, India, and Central and South America increasingly work for firms that may do no "international business." In California, by the year 2000, Hispanics are projected to outnumber Caucasians and become the majority ethnic group in California. Such factors force firms to manage employees whose backgrounds, cultures, and expectations regarding work and performance may be very different from the "typical" U.S. worker.

This chapter focuses on reviewing research and ways to integrate IHRM into the unified strategic human resources model described in Chapter Four. The chapter begins with an examination of recent research on HRM issues within an international context. Next, it discusses studies that emphasize a more strategic HRM focus. Throughout, the chapter discussion considers the role of IHRM in the unified model, as a potential contributor to the unintended and intended aspects of strategy.

RESEARCH ON INTERNATIONAL HUMAN RESOURCES MANAGEMENT

The research on HRM in an international context has followed at least four general streams. First, the research has addressed functional issues and practices in international firms. This research includes: the types of practices multinational firms use or should use in making transfer decisions, such as (1) whether to use host- or parent-country nationals in staffing a subsidiary, (2) which criteria are most important in selecting expatriates, (3) whether to send women overseas, (4) developing training programs, and (5) designing evaluation and compensation programs.

A second research direction, stemming mainly from work done in industrial relations, focuses on macro-theory development, as discussed in Chapters Two and Ten. In general, industrial-relations research in the 1960s-1970s sought to identify and examine macro-level variables, (e.g., institutions, legal processes) that supported arguments of convergence or divergence (countries' systems becoming more similar or different).

Third, research on international HRM and international industrial relations has included single-country and comparative studies. The single-country studies, many of which were conducted on industrial-relations systems in the 1950s and done mostly by Americans and Europeans, investigated and described systems in specific countries, with no comparison to other countries. Comparative studies described similarities and differences on certain issues such as performance appraisal or collective bargaining in two or more countries.

A final, more recent, stream has focused on how HRM fits into the international strategic-management process. This research has tended to be conceptual, and often focuses primarily on strategic or other issues such as control systems, information systems, taxonomies of cooperative ventures rather than on HRM components.

FUNCTIONAL ISSUES

The research on functional HRM issues developed out of very practical problems. MNCs made, and still make, serious HRM mistakes, especially in the area of staffing. As a result, researchers began examining how to improve selection decisions. The research has tended to be normative, with more empirical and theoretical research coming only recently. The general conclusion from the research is that MNCs should consider criteria other than just technical and managerial competence in selecting expatriates. Unfortunately, it appears that practicing managers do not typically follow that advice (Tung, 1987).

The functional areas receiving most of the research attention have included staffing, training, and to a lesser extent, compensation. There has been relatively little research on planning, recruitment, career management, or benefits.

International Staffing

By far, the bulk of research on international human resources management has been in the area of staffing. The source, especially among practitioners, appears to stem from the costs of making poor staffing decisions.

There are at least two types of repercussions from staffing errors: (1) the financial and emotional costs of an executive's early return from an overseas assignment, and (2) the possible "invisible" damage to local relations. Most research suggests that U.S. firms, more so than Western European and Japanese firms, have been plagued with a high proportion of expatriates who return to their parent companies before completing overseas assignments (Dowling, 1986, 1987; Tung, 1982, 1984a).[1] Most U.S. MNCs (nearly 70 percent of all) must recall 10-20 percent of their worldwide expatriates early; the recall rate is less than 5 percent for most Japanese and West European MNCs doing business in the same countries (Tung, 1984a). In addition to likely insufficient preparation for overseas assignments, American firms may exacerbate the problem through relatively little assistance given expatriates during their transfer period or upon return to the U.S. (Harvey, 1989).

With overseas transfers costing about three times an executive's salary (Lanier, 1979), early return translates into an expensive replacement process as well as the cost of finding the returning executive a position stateside. In addition, the returning manager may face retribution for not completing an assignment, possibly resulting in the manager leaving the firm.

Beyond the financial and emotional costs of early return, there can be long-term "invisible" repercussions from faulty staffing decisions. For example, misplaced executives may damage relationships with constituencies overseas (e.g., officials in the host government, local staff members, or customers) (Dowling, 1986). Such repercussions may be difficult to identify and assess, given local culture and customs, and may mean years of painstaking effort to repair relationships. Such problems are unfortunately common and frequently go unrecognized, as MNCs typically underestimate the significance of using formal selection approaches (Alpander, 1973; Miller, 1973; Tung, 1987), or requiring certain characteristics, beyond technical and managerial com-

---

[1] In a more recent study, Dowling and Welch (1988), challenged these figures, finding that the failure rates in four firms doing business in Australia were substantially lower.

petence, in expatriate managers (e.g., ability to develop good interpersonal relations) (Mendenhall & Oddou, 1986).

The main topics in international staffing research have focused on nationality of subsidiary managers, selection criteria for managers, and, more recently, on models or systematic approaches to use in the staffing process.

Nationality. The issue of nationality in making staffing decisions focuses on whether to use primarily (1) parent-country nationals (PCN) (i.e., expatriates), (2) host-country nationals (HCN), or (3) third-country nationals (TCN) in staffing a subsidiary. The nationality question centers on: (1) human resources concerns, including the cost of placement, availability of personnel, chance for development and promotion opportunities for various groups, (2) strategic concerns related to the firm's flexibility in making strategic shifts, and (3) on maintaining a global perspective versus meeting local needs. The research reflects both the human resources and the more strategic orientations.

Human resources arguments for using parent-country nationals, an "ethnocentric approach", has been the presumably greater ability of the PCNs to coordinate subsidiary-parent relations and to transfer know-how from the parent to the subsidiary (Dowling, 1986; Edstrom & Galbraith, 1977; Kumar & Steinmann, 1986). Staffing with HCNs, a "polycentric approach," has several advantages: (1) a continuity of management within the host country, (2) no language barrier in the host country, (3) the possibility of a lower profile in the host country, (4) enhancement of subsidiary staff morale and career opportunities for HCNs, and (5) lower cost from using local people (Dowling, 1986; Kuin, 1972; Zeira, 1975). A "geocentric approach" involves sending the "best person" to a job, regardless of nationality. This method requires lead time to develop a cadre of managers but has the advantage of flexibility. A final approach responds more to specific regional or country needs and moves toward a more strategic perspective. For example, in a country requiring a major marketing adaptation, a MNC may use a polycentric approach, because HCNs presumably have the local knowledge and expertise to respond more quickly. In a country where production and technical knowledge are more critical, an ethnocentric approach is likely to be more appropriate since PCNs can transfer such expertise more quickly than it could be developed at the HCN level (Edstrom & Galbraith, 1977).

The literature taking a more strategic perspective on nationality of subsidiary managers has emphasized the need for a MNC to have a global strategy, with the flexibility to shift resources among units, allowing the firm to meet and surpass global competitors more quickly. A global strategy demanding that staffing decisions be centralized at headquarters means trade-offs for the MNC. First, there is less flexibility in adapting to local markets. Second, when a firm pursues a global strategy, it frequently emphasizes the organizational culture worldwide, trying to supersede local culture. This may lead to conflicts between country culture and corporate culture. In most cases, the strength of local culture overpowers corporate culture (Laurent, 1986), thwarting, or at least inhibiting, consistency in IHRM within a firm.

Recent research has moved away from an "either-or" orientation in nationality decisions, and has tended to put such questions in a more strategic context. In an effort to capture the range of possible headquarters-subsidiary relationships, researchers are suggesting more "variety" (Doz, & Prahalad, 1986) in approaches to staffing and other IHRM activities (Boyacigiller, 1987; Kobrin, 1988). In certain subsidiaries, for example, an ethnocentric approach may be appropriate; in others, a geocentric approach may work better. Rather than adhering to a particular policy, researchers are urging MNCs to consider global strategy as well as local conditions in determining appropriate staffing approaches.

There may be other reasons for maintaining a flexible staffing policy. Kobrin (1988) has argued that there is a danger when firms staff subsidiaries with locals and TCNs to the near exclusion of parent-country expatriates. If this becomes more common, he predicted that managers' ability to identify with the firm worldwide will decrease. In a 1986 survey of IHR managers, Dowling (1988) found that these managers see one of the major issues MNCs face as encouraging managers to think globally. Thus, if Kobrin's (1988) concern is legitimate, an unintended strategy of reduced expatriate transfer may be a firm that becomes less flexible, with managers who are less global in their outlook. This may ultimately lead a firm to decrease its international involvement.

Criteria.   Beyond the issue of nationality, a second focus in the international-staffing literature has been on identifying appropriate criteria for selecting expatriates. Again, the drive behind such research seems to be to quell the typical problems from staffing mistakes (e.g., expatriate dissatisfaction and culture shock) (Harris, 1979; Rahim, 1983; Tung, 1987).

Research has revealed several remedies to overcome or prevent these typical problems. Miller (1973) found that multinationals often transferred "overqualified" managers for overseas posts. The rationale was that selecting overqualified managers helped reduce two kinds of risk. First, since the job was below the talents of the manager selected, that person was more likely to perform better in the short run. Second, the decision was a hedge against damage to the selector's career from choosing the "wrong" manager for transfer.

This practice of selecting overqualified managers offers an interesting example of how such an action could lead to unintended strategic change. Selecting such managers could have the result of demotivating transferred managers, who report to colleagues that the transfer was beneath their talents and a step back in a career path, thus making international assignments less attractive. Such actions might lead a firm to withdraw from international markets, if it failed to convince good managers to transfer, or it could begin a staffing policy of using host- or third-country nationals, if the firm intended to remain active internationally.

Conversely, such a selection process may cause top management to view the transfer of these managers as a sign that the area of international business demanded greater expertise and qualifications. If this led to more resources being committed to international business, it might give a signal to other managers that it made good sense to gain international experience.

A basic assumption behind the literature on international staffing stems from whether firms should pursue a compensatory or non-compensatory approach in selection. A compensatory approach, more common in MNCs, favors managers who perform very well in a few areas, usually technical. A non-compensatory approach requires that managers have minimal-level competence in several dimensions. Newman et al. (1978) have argued that a compensatory approach overemphasizes certain dimensions to the detriment of others, leading firms to choose managers with skills appropriate for domestic situations but highly inappropriate for foreign assignments. The research on selection criteria for expatriate managers has focused on two elements: (1) technical/managerial qualifications, and (2) personal qualifications. Technical expertise and managerial competence have long been the primary selection criteria (Baker & Ivancevich, 1971; Dowling, 1986), almost to the exclusion of other criteria. Typically used to assess technical and managerial competence are factors such as managerial skills, in-depth familiarity with the parent firm, and expertise regarding the domestic market (Dowling, 1986; Zeira & Harari, 1979). The assumption, repeatedly shown to be invalid (Mendenhall & Oddou, 1986; Tung, 1981, 1982, 1987), is that good domestic performance translates into good overseas performance. Part of the reason these criteria continue to be used may be that others are hard to measure and are not traditionally used, even in domestic selection decisions.

Some of the personal criteria are difficult to validate or have not been substantiated elsewhere (Heenan, 1970; Heller, 1980; Howard, 1974; Stoner, Aram, & Rubin, 1972). For example, Howard (1974) argued that an expatriate manager should have "an unblemished moral character" but offered no guidance on how to measure such a criterion or how important it is relative to others. Heller (1980) proposed such criteria as cultural empathy, adaptability, language capability, leadership ability, motivation, maturity, and having an adaptive family. Stoner et al. (1972) stressed the need for very clear expectations on the part of the expatriate, strong competence technically, and an enthusiastic spouse as contributors to success of the manager overseas. Newman et al. (1978) suggested that managers should have an ability to generate interpersonal trust, a cosmopolitan locus of control, and an acceptance of several value systems. Again, these are hard to measure and not readily used, even domestically.

In a more comprehensive approach, Mendenhall and Oddou (1986) argued that, in addition to individual-level criteria, there are certain factors, beyond the control of individual or company, that affect expatriate success. As predictors of success, they proposed three individual-level "orientations": (1) self-orientation, such as knowledge of self and ability to adapt; (2) others-orientation or relationship skills; and (3) perceptual orientation, namely, a tolerance for ambiguity.

A final factor, beyond the individual's or MNC's control, is "toughness of culture," which is the degree of similarity between cultures in the expatriate's home and the host country. Mendenhall and Oddou (1986) concluded that, regardless of a manager's strength of orientation, some cultures will simply be more difficult for a manager to adjust to and thus increase the chance of failure. Miller (1975) suggested a similar idea when he found that regional location affected managers' success. U.S. managers, for example, adapt better to Europe and Australia than to Japan or the Middle East countries.

Finally, some early research by Heenan (1970) still seems valid almost 20 years later. He reported that ability to adapt to a new culture was a critical factor affecting success and that this could be enhanced several ways. The parent company should unfetter local decision-making, giving the on-site manager greater autonomy, improve development opportunities for managers in overseas posts, and provide better parent-company support.

More Systematic Approaches to Selection.   Since the late 1970s, several researchers have suggested models or more systematic means for selecting expatriates. Tung (1981) proposed factors for choosing either parent- or host-country nationals for subsidiary management. Her model favored HCNs, for example, when there was potential difficulty of understanding the local culture, availability of strong candidates locally, a large amount of manager-host-government interaction, and the anticipation of a long relationship between the parent company and host country.

Newman et al. (1978), in a model to predict tenure on an overseas assignment, suggested that the environment (external and organizational) affects the agreement or "correspondence" between individual factors (ability and needs) and job factors (the requirements and reinforcements). They concluded that the greater the agreement or correspondence, the higher an individual manager's performance and satisfaction with the assignment are likely to be and, ultimately, she or he would be more likely to complete the assignment.

More recently, in reviewing her empirical research since the early 1980s, Tung (1987) noted that Western European and Japanese firms were consistently more successful than U.S. firms in their international staffing. She identified several reasons for their success: (1) long-term orientation that is reflected in longer overseas assignments for expatriates and longer performance-evaluation periods, (2) better training before, during, and on return from an assignment, (3) more support for expatriates while they were overseas, and (4) stronger candidates, not only in their technical/managerial qualifications but also in their personal skills. In addition, firms from Western Europe typically have more of an international orientation, a longer history of overseas activities, and managers with multiple-language capabilities. Japanese firms use more systematic, formal selection processes and the families of Japanese managers play a very different role from U.S. families. There is sometimes an implicit assumption that U.S. firms should follow practices similar to their Japanese and European counterparts to enhance staffing patterns. Unfortunately, there is little research to confirm or deny the validity of such practices for North American firms. In fact, there is some evidence (Ishida, 1986) that such transfer of policies is extremely difficult.

Training and Development

Although staffing has received most of the attention in the international human resources literature, some research has focused on training and development. Much of the literature on training, however, seems almost "evangelical": researchers and managers agree on the importance of pre-assignment training, but it rarely seems to happen in the manner and depth called for.

The arguments for cross-cultural training are widely acknowledged (Copeland, 1985; Dowling, 1986). One of the reasons the United States is losing its leadership position in worldwide markets is partly because of a general lack of knowledge about conducting international business. MNCs often commit avoidable "blunders" because of insufficient research before plunging into foreign business markets. Finally, as mentioned earlier, the influx of foreigners to the U.S. (e.g., managers, workers, customers) demands greater knowledge of other cultures.

Western European and Japanese firms consistently provide more and better training for their international business managers than do U.S. firms (Dowling, 1986; Tung, 1984a). Unfortunately, even when U.S. firms seek training, there is little research to guide them in what type of training is most effective, the conditions under which various programs should be used, and what contributes to expatriate retention and success overseas (Rahim, 1983; Zeira, 1975).

Researchers have suggested that if firms do train, the programs should recognize the influence of both external-environmental factors, (e.g., culture, location), and internal-organizational influences (e.g., relationships between headquarters and subsidiary offices) (Dowling, 1986). The specifics of an acceptable training program might include such elements as a pre-transfer visit to the overseas post, basic language training, area study, country-specific information, and family counseling before transfer (Lanier, 1979; Tung, 1981). Firms have a variety of training methods to choose from. Few can afford in-house cross-cultural training staffs, and thus some use consulting firms which range from providing training to full relocation advice. Others, particularly European firms, use foreign subsidiaries as training grounds, for technical as well as cross-cultural managerial experience (Zeira & Pazy, 1985). Earley (1987) suggested that firms use both documentary and interpersonal methods to prepare managers for intercultural assignments.

To avoid the problem of the expatriate losing touch with headquarters, and falling into a situation of "out of sight, out of mind," some firms use a "home-country mentor" program. During a period in which it sent several managers abroad, an electronics firm in Seattle, Washington, assigned a manager in the home office to maintain contact with and be responsible for an expatriate manager. The duties included keeping the manager informed of parent-company activities, changes, and general information. Also, when the expatriate was due to return, the mentor was responsible for finding a position for the manager, thus easing "reentry" problems.

Like the staffing process, training and development can play a role in unintended changes in strategy, as well as enhancing intended strategy. For example, a firm's HRM staff may take the initiative to provide thorough training to expatriates and their families in preparation for overseas assignments. Training families as well as managers may reduce the chance of problems from dissatisfaction or disappointment and may allow the manager to become productive more quickly. In the long run, the firm may change strategy to emphasize international business more strongly.

Training can also enhance an existing strategy. If a MNC pursues a global strategy requiring consistency across units, training of host-country and third-country on-site nationals might enhance the strategy by helping these employees to understand the overall firm and its direction, and how they fit into the global strategy.

Compensation

Dowling's (1986) review of the literature on compensation of international executives and survey of international HR managers (Dowling, 1989) identified several important issues, such as parent-and-host country national equity and dealing with currency effects and benefits. Much of the literature has been written by practicing managers and consultants, however, with limited scholarly research (Pucik, 1984a, 1984b; Toyne & Kuhne, 1983).

One of the main issues faced by MNCs is that of equity among parent-, host-, and, if appropriate, third-country nationals. In many MNCs, there is a policy of keeping the parent-country national "whole." This means that, when a PCN lives outside her home country, the person should live in a manner approximating her normal home-country standard. As a result, a PCN typically receives compensation that exceeds her or his domestic equivalent pay, because of special allowances for living overseas, (e.g., housing, childrens' schooling, home leave, and "hardship" pay for certain areas). The PCN pay also usually exceeds the equivalent host country nationals' pay. Such a policy can generate discrepancy between PCN and HCN compensation, which can contribute to conflicts between the parent and subsidiary.

In this arena, HRM could play a potentially major role in affecting unintended strategy. For example, to reduce conflict among parent- and host-country nationals, the HRM staff might initiate a policy of paying all subsidiary employees at the local level. In this case, such an action could have severe repercussions on global strategy. If parent-country nationals refuse to transfer, as a result, the firm might have to reduce its international efforts or shift to a policy of relying on host- or third-country nationals. Unless such a shift was accompanied by clear training, the strategy might develop into one emphasizing local responsiveness, thus decreasing the MNC's flexibility in responding to competitors pursuing a more global strategy.

Another compensation issue is the matching of staffing and compensation policies. If, for example, a firm has an ethnocentric staffing policy, its compensation policy should be one of keeping the PCN whole. If, however, the staffing policy follows a geocentric approach, (i.e., staffing a position with the "best person," often a TCN, regardless of nationality), there may be no clear "home" for the TCN and as a result, no policy of keeping that person "whole." These types of issues are complex and there is little research to date. Finally, much of the practitioner-international-compensation literature has focused on the practical aspects of managing compensation and benefits (Pinney, 1982), such as tax plans and dealing with current-rate impacts of international compensation.

MACRO THEORIES IN INDUSTRIAL RELATIONS

During much of the 1960s, industrial-relations researchers conducted large multicountry studies, from which developed several overview theories and frameworks (e.g., Dunlop, 1958). These theories were based on broad examinations of macro-level issues including institutions, relationships among parties, and value systems of managers.

These studies raised the issue of whether comparative industrial-relations and management systems were "converging" or "diverging." The conclusion was that the determining factor influencing the perception of convergence was the level of variables studied. Researchers studying macro-level issues, such as institutions and legal systems, subscribed to a convergence theory: systems in different countries were becoming more similar (Kerr, Dunlop, Harbison, & Myers, 1960). Others, studying specific firms, micro-level and individual-level variables and even earlier "convergence" proponents, argued that factors such as cultural differences, assumptions underlying personnel practices, and philosophy toward employees remain very dissimilar across countries. The area of international industrial relations has languished since the mid-1960s. The link between industrial relations and strategy has been particularly weak, as discussed in Chapter Ten.

SINGLE-COUNTRY AND COMPARATIVE STUDIES

A next stream of literature placing HRM in an international context concentrates on examining HRM practices in particular countries, such as Japan (Bartlett & Yoshihara, 1988; Ouchi, 1981; Pucik, 1984 a), and in the case of comparative studies, assessing the similarities and differences. Traditionally, research in IHRM and comparative industrial relations has started with the U.S. model and discussed how American practices could apply overseas (Peterson, 1986). Other research has examined what exists in other countries, most commonly Japan in recent years, and how these policies could be used elsewhere (Ishida, 1986). Finally, while the emphasis on linking strategy to HRM has developed primarily in the U.S., there is growing evidence of such research developing in other countries (e.g., Sparrow, Hendry, & Pettigrew, 1987).

Managers are increasingly observing practices in other countries to anticipate future challenges in their own. For instance, Kaminski and Paiz (1984) suggested that blue-chip Japanese firms can anticipate the likely future role of women in the work force, by watching U.S. firms and "second tier" Japanese firms, many of which have employed women for several years. In the early 1980s, for instance, the president of the joint venture Fuji-Xerox noted that blue-chip Japanese firms tended to avoid hiring educated Japanese women. Women seeking professional positions found acceptance, however, in "second tier" firms, joint ventures, or foreign companies operating in Japan. Fuji-Xerox, as a joint venture, did not hold the status for male graduates from the top universities and thus, the company hired women graduates from those schools instead. This manager's assessment was that he was hiring top-notch employees, while his competition was ignoring an important resource.

Another perspective in this stream of research has suggested that managers should understand and, where appropriate, incorporate approaches from different cultures into their views (Adler & Jelinek, 1986; Hofstede, 1984). For example, American firms might look to other countries for ideas about career management of professionals. Gerpott and Domsch (1985) suggested that hiring only U.S. professionals can lead to some negative outcomes (e.g., vertical polarization within a firm, lack of adequate technical training of managers, and overemphasis on breakthrough technologies). They suggested that American firms should learn about professionalism in other cultures.

There are also many examples of how developing or newly industrialized countries learn from the U.S. or other developed countries. Latham and Napier (1989) found that firms in Hong Kong and Singapore have taken much of the current management knowledge in the U.S. and applied it to their particular situations. Indeed, Singapore subsidiaries that are owned by American, British, or Japanese firms have become adept at selecting those practices that "fit" the Singapore culture and rejecting those that would not work. For instance, in a Japanese-owned firm, the Singapore personnel manager stressed that he has adapted the strict Japanese tardiness policies to be somewhat more forgiving for the Singapore setting. His reason was that because the labor force is so tight in Singapore, he would rather try to keep his existing employees than punish and fire them because of minor tardiness infractions (Napier & Latham, 1987).

HR INVOLVEMENT IN STRATEGIC PLANNING

Recent literature in the U.S. has focused increasingly on links between international HRM management and strategic issues. The limited empirical research has examined the actions by HRM in formulating and implementing intended strategy (e.g., Kobrin, 1988; Ondrack, 1985). In these studies, the researchers have examined HRM as a player in the formal design of strategy (formulation), as well as its role as an enhancer of strategy, concentrating on the implementation role that HRM plays.

Miller, Beechler, Bhatt, and Nath (1986) examined the role of the HRM staff and executives in strategic planning of multinational firms. The study assessed whether and how the HRM department and staff were involved in planning at the corporate and strategic-business-unit (SBU) levels. The study concluded that human resources involvement at the corporate level tended to be informal, limited in scope, and heavily dependent upon the competence and personal characteristics of the senior HRM executive. The HRM executive thus played a major role separate from the department or functional area. Staffing was the main area in which the HRM executive was involved in strategy formulation; other traditional HRM areas (e.g., compensation and evaluation of manager performance) were viewed as general top-management concerns and not primarily related to human resources. At the SBU level, the human resources department staff was much more involved in strategic planning; its role was more established and the emphasis was on how the human resources staff could help implement a strategy (Miller et al., 1986).

Napier and Smith (1987) and Napier (1986) examined links between diversification strategy and performance criteria and compensation components of corporate managers in large U.S. and Japanese firms. The studies tested Galbraith and Nathanson's (1978) expectations that, as firms diversify, the types of criteria and compensation systems they use become more objective and incentive-based. Except for predictions about the importance of bonuses for managers, the empirical studies did not strongly support the model. Instead, they suggested that high and low diversifiers had patterns of performance criteria more similar to each other than they did to mid-range diversifiers (i.e., related firms). The studies call for much more empirical research in all areas of strategic human resources management, especially in IHRM, where there is almost no work.

New Organizational Arrangements

Other research in the strategic international HRM area has tended to focus on aspects other than HRM in particular. The studies are broad in their emphases: much of the work focuses more on describing the various organizational frameworks in multinational settings and identifies HRM policy issues important in those settings. The international settings extend beyond the multinational and its subsidiaries, which was the focus for early research. Rather, the new international organizational arrangements include, for instance, cooperative ventures such as joint ventures and temporary project-based arrangements (e.g., Pucik, 1988), or mergers and acquisitions that blend firms from different countries (Napier, Schweiger, & Csiszar, 1989).

Lorange (1986) classified four types of cooperative ventures: (1) project-based, (2) licensing, (3) ventures with permanent complementary roles, and (4) joint ownership. A particular type of venture emerges as a function of strategic importance of the venture to the parent companies and the extent to which the parents seek control over the resources allocated to the venture. For each of the four types, Lorange suggested there will be several HRM policy issues: (1) assignment of executives, (2) evaluation and promotion of managers, (3) the type of control systems used, (4) loyalty of managers, to the venture or to their respective parents, and (5) expected time for managers to spend on strategic versus operational issues.

The issue of manager loyalty has emerged in several studies (e.g., Edstrom & Galbraith, 1977; Galbraith & Kazanjian, 1986; Pucik & Katz, 1986). Edstrom and Lorange (1984) discussed the problems of determining HRM activities (e.g., staffing, training, transfers) when MNCs face differences between their country and globally oriented goals. In addition, HRM activities will contribute to corporate and unit strategy in different stages. Staffing, for example, is crucial for initiating and formulating strategy, whereas transfer policies are more important for anticipating strategic shifts.

Doz and Prahalad (1986) addressed the global versus local balance issue in terms of MNC control systems. Like others, they recognized the difficulties of managers being sensitive to local conditions and loyal to the corporation. They argued for "strategic control variety," which involves adapting control systems to fit three dimensions in MNCs. Those dimensions are (1) the type of business (ranging from purely local markets to global focus), (2) the type of subsidiary (from operating as an export platform to operating as a local manufacturer), and (3) the ownership of the venture (ranging from a fully owned subsidiary to a collaborative agreement between two or more MNCs). Depending on the type of venture, there will be differences in HRM activities and expectations for managers to have local versus global perspectives.

Pucik and Katz (1986) also discussed the importance of fitting HRM practices to MNCs and their subsidiaries, where information and control systems differ. Because headquarters must transfer different types of information, both technical and social, control systems must likewise vary. As a result, balancing bureaucratic (Baliga & Jaeger, 1984) and cultural (Ouchi, 1977) control systems becomes critical, and Pucik and Katz (1986) discussed the type of HRM activities that fit both types of control systems. For example, in situations where technical information is transferred and the control system is more bureaucratic, the organization will have clear rules about how promotion decisions are made and will use formal training programs for managers. In MNCs transferring more social information and using a cultural control system, planned transfers will be used to promote socialization of managers within the firm.

Shenkar and Zeira (1987) have decried the lack of research attention given to HRM issues in international joint ventures (IJVs), and proposed a model to identify various HRM problems in such joint ventures. They suggested that characteristics of each parent (e.g., composition of the work force, source of employees), system characteristics of the firm (e.g., strategy and differentiation), and structural characteristics of the firm (e.g., size) affect the number and types of employee groups for the IJV, and the managerial and personnel processes to use with employees.

A final avenue puts strategic IHRM in a macro context. Napier et al. (1988) used Porter's (1985) value-chain model to argue that a MNC can have HRM competence that supports primary value-chain activities (e.g., marketing and sales, inbound logistics). The HRM competence contributes to the firm's overall competitive advantage. Thus, in assessing an intended strategic decision to diversify, MNC management may consider whether the IHRM competence can be transferred to subsidiaries. If it can transfer expertise and competence, this should help the firm maintain its competitive advantage and develop its global strategy more quickly.

SUMMARY AND CONCLUSIONS

The chapter has reviewed recent research on human resources management issues in an international and strategic context. The research has been uneven in the topics covered (much on staffing, little on career management, benefits, etc.), more descriptive than analytical, and largely conceptual or normative. The empirical research has tended to be based on surveys (Miller et al., 1986; Napier, 1986; Tung, 1982, 1984b), interviews (Latham & Napier, 1989), case studies (Sparrow et al., 1987), or anecdotes (Ouchi, 1981).

There is a great need for rigorous, systematic research in international HRM in general, and particularly in the area of how it relates to strategy. It appears IHRM could affect unintended strategy but, empirically this issue has not been explored at all.

PLANNING FOR AND MANAGING MERGERS AND ACQUISITIONS[1]

Alien they seemed to be:
No mortal eye could see
The intimate welding of their later history.

Or sign that they were bent
By paths coincident
On being anon twin halves of one august event,

Till the Spinner of the Years
Said "Now!" And each one hears,
And consummation comes, and jars two hemispheres.
—Thomas Hardy, (1978) "The Convergence of the
Twain."

During the 1980s, the United States business community encountered a fourth merger "wave" rivaling the last major cycle in the 1960s. Each year since 1983 has generated over twenty-five hundred mergers and acquisitions in the U.S.; by 1986, American firms were involved in over four thousand. Mergers are important, not only because there are so many, but because so often they fail, wreaking trouble for many people directly and indirectly involved. As a result, planning for and managing mergers, especially as they affect human resources issues, is critical in SHRM.

Mergers and acquisitions (M&As) represent part of a strategic approach used by many firms to achieve various objectives. There are many other strategic actions firms take to accomplish goals. Much literature in recent years, for example, has discussed "restructuring" or dealing with reducing or rearranging the organizational work force. Such change in organizations can stem from turnover (Martin & Bartol, 1985; Mowday, 1984), layoffs (Greenlaugh, Lawrence, & Sutton, 1988; Howard, 1988; Reed & Brockner, 1986) and retirement (Rosen & Jerdee, 1986). Mergers and acquisitions represent a common cause for such shifts and, given the overwhelming attention to them during the 1980s and into the 1990s, their impact on HRM form the basis for this chapter.

---

[1] Portions of this chapter also appeared in *Journal of Management Studies*, 1989, *26* (3), 271–289.

Mergers can be used to expand into new markets, gain technical expertise or knowledge, or allocate excess capital. The motive or purpose of a merger, in turn, may influence the extent to which the two firms are integrated after the merger and the types of human resources practices that result in each firm. The need to plan well in advance, and have a systematic procedure or set of policies for mergers and acquisitions, particularly the HRM issues, affects the structure of the resulting HR function.

FRAMEWORK FOR UNDERSTANDING M&As

This chapter discusses links among the motives for mergers and acquisitions, degree of integration between merging firms, and human resources practices. In addition, the chapter suggests ways to manage the human resources issues raised by mergers and acquisitions.

Although the terms "merger" and "acquisition" are frequently used interchangeably, they are different activities. A "merger" usually refers to two organizations of relatively similar size joining forces to form a "new," presumably stronger, firm. In an acquisition, one firm, usually larger, purchases another, usually smaller. Nonetheless, even when the activity is clearly an acquisition (e.g., Bank of America's purchase of Seattle First National Bank) it is often referred to in the press and internally as a "merger."

Current M&As Contrasted with 1960s

The current wave of M&As, and research on them, differs from that of the 1960s in several ways. First, where the 1960s mergers emphasized diversification, resulting in many conglomerate, unrelated mergers, current mergers include more related-business purchases (*Business Week*, 1984b). Second, present merger-and-acquisition activity includes industries relatively unaffected by mergers 20 years ago (e.g., financial services) (Bradley & Korn, 1982; Rhoades, 1983). Finally, there seems to more interest in the human resources aspects affected by mergers (Ivancevich, Schweiger, & Power, 1987; Jemison & Sitkin, 1986).

Although knowledge about the human resources impacts of mergers has been limited, recent literature addresses mergers' effects on a wide range of management issues, such as culture (Bowditch & Buono, 1987; Buono, Bowditch, & Lewis, 1985), structure (Mirvis, 1985), human resources policies (Profusek & Leavitt, 1984), and employee reactions (Graves, 1975; Napier & Stratton, 1987; Wishard, 1985). Such knowledge about the impact of mergers and acquisitions on human resources issues is important for several reasons. Mergers affect numerous constituency groups, such as shareholders, consumers, and employees (Marks, 1982; Rhoades, 1983). Also, because M&As continue to be poorly understood and managed, especially regarding human resources issues, they frequently end in divestiture or do not meet performance expectations. Indeed, between 1980 and 1985, an estimated one-third of mergers and acquisitions ended in divestiture (*Business Week*, 1985). Much of the academic and managerial literature mentions issues related to human resources as contributors to merger failures (Buono & Bowditch, 1989; Marks, 1982; Sinetar, 1981).

Understanding human resources issues in current M&As is important for other reasons as well. First, much of the available information on human resources impacts is dated (Kitching, 1967; Leighton & Tod, 1969; Mace & Montgomery, 1962; Stewart, Wingate, & Smith, 1983). Second, although the topic is increasingly studied by researchers, much of the information on mergers and their impact is anecdotal, unrelated to theory, and thus cannot be broadly applied. In addition, there is criticism (Paine & Power, 1984) of generally accepted approaches to planning for and implementing mergers and acquisitions (Drucker, 1982). Finally, while the finance literature provides some theoretical direction on the motives or causes for mergers (Jensen & Ruback, 1983), there is little in the way of conceptual frameworks or theory explaining M&As as they affect human resources issues. There is a need, therefore, for more systematic investigations and better understanding of the impact of mergers.

This chapter offers a framework for understanding the impact that mergers may have on human resources practices and how managers can anticipate and deal with those impacts. The chapter has three parts: (1) a brief review of what is known from research on M&As; (2) a model relating motives, degree of merger integration, and human resources practices; and (3) suggestions for managers on planning for and managing mergers and acquisitions.

REVIEW OF THE LITERATURE ON MERGERS AND ACQUISITIONS

In the research and business press, there are four major aspects of discussion of mergers: (1) motives or reasons for mergers; (2) planning mergers (e.g., finding a candidate, negotiating); (3) implementing mergers; and (4) assessing the outcomes of mergers. Each of these is discussed briefly below.

Motives for Mergers and Acquisitions

Our knowledge about motives or causes for mergers comes primarily from research in finance, economics, and business policy. There are two generally accepted categories of motives for mergers: (1) financial or value-maximizing motives, and (2) managerial or non-value-maximizing motives (Halpern, 1983; Mueller, 1977). Value-maximizing motives suggest that the major reason for a merger or acquisition is to create value for the shareholder through increased profits or some other means designed to increase share price or dividends (Bradley & Korn, 1984; Davidson, 1981). Non-value-maximizing motives assume there are reasons for mergers other than creating value for the shareholder, such as management's desire to increase sales, prestige, or monetary compensation (Allen, Oliver, & Schwallie, 1981; Davidson, 1981; Mace & Montgomery, 1962; Rhoades, 1983).

Value-maximizing motives include increasing synergy through economies of scale or scope, applying knowledge and skills from one organization to another, and controlling a target firm's management and board to affect future performance (Halpern, 1983; Jensen & Ruback, 1983; Salter & Weinhold, 1979). Non-value-maximizing reasons include increasing sales or asset growth (Halpern, 1983), increasing management's prestige or power (Rhoades, 1983), and using mergers as a way to decrease uncertainty in the firm's external environment (Pfeffer, 1972).

As with any area of research, there are questions and gaps in our knowledge about motives for mergers. First, although Mueller (1980) concluded that there are many motives for mergers, rather than one clear or dominant approach, the orientation of research in the finance and policy literature continues to focus on economically-based reasons for mergers (Hirsch, 1987). The literature concentrates less on managerial motives. For instance, Barrett (1973) suggested that purchasing a troubled firm, rather than liquidating it, may be a way to avoid higher unemployment. Rhoades (1983) argued that managers merge firms in an effort to increase their own power. Jemison and Sitkin (1986) suggested that managers' decisions to merge may have emotional aspects. Even though the literature acknowledges the other motives, there is little information about the conditions under which managers pursue acquisitions for non-financial reasons.

Second, partly because we do not know much about the motives leading managers to acquire firms, we also do not know just how those acquisitions may affect the subsequent structure or characteristics of the merged firms in the implementation stage. For instance, does an acquisition for reasons of increasing the exchange of knowledge and skills imply that the two firms remain relatively independent, do they join ranks, or does one firm dominate? The impact of the motives in terms of the subsequent relations of the firms is unclear.

Finally, related to the preceding problem with research, the literature on motives is not linked to changes in policy or practice within the firms. For instance, the research does not address whether or how mergers undertaken to achieve economies of scale affect careers, reporting relations, or compensation policies of both firms. Although researchers have suggested these are important topics to consider (Jensen & Ruback, 1983), the questions are not formally addressed. Likewise, it is unclear whether mergers carried out for different motives are related to outcomes such as employee reactions. In summary, knowledge about motives has been developed in isolation. Finance researchers have argued that there are a variety of reasons for mergers and acquisitions but neglect the question of what impact those reasons have on the merger's implementation and how it affects human resources aspects. Some of those researchers have acknowledged that the human resources impacts are among the most interesting and important (Jensen & Ruback, 1983), yet the focus seems to have been least on these issues.

Planning a Merger or Acquisition

There are two broad topic areas discussed in the literature on planning for a merger: (1) seeking and evaluating an acquisition candidate (Jensen,

1982), or from the opposite perspective, positioning a firm as an attractive candidate (O'Conor, 1985), and (2) organizing and carrying out the legal, financial, and related technical issues considered during the negotiation (Hayes, 1979).

Seeking a candidate for acquisition is usually considered as part of the strategic process (Ebeling & Dooney, 1983). However, Jemison and Sitkin (1986) suggested that, although managers like to think mergers are part of a rational, strategic decision, emotional factors sometimes override the rational thinking.

The literature on positioning a firm for buyout often has been authored by managers who have gone through the process (O'Conor, 1985), and provided suggestions on "how to" control the purchase of one's firm. Interestingly, Hayes (1979) found that many top managers involved in their firms' sale would not sell if they had it to do again. Literature on the negotiation of mergers exists from the perspective of the firms (Hayes, 1979) as well as the arbitrager and investment bankers involved (or formerly involved!) (Boesky, 1985).

As with the motives literature, there is little discussion in the planning literature on human resources aspects. DeNoble (1984) and Boland (1970) found that human resources issues were not among top-management priorities during planning for a merger or acquisition. Marks (1982) suggested that the only human resources issues discussed in the planning phase related to the strengths and weaknesses of specific top executives. Because human resources issues are so important during the subsequent implementation phase, it is surprising that there is so little emphasis on such topics in the planning stage. For example, if a manager could identify crucial human resources aspects that are likely to contribute to subsequent success or failure of a merger, such information could be incorporated into the planning process. This area will likely become viable in the future as some researchers (e.g., Hawkins, 1987) develop approaches to using human resources data in the selection of merger/acquisition candidates.

Merger Implementation

Most of the literature dealing with human resources issues and mergers falls under the category of merger implementation. Major topics include the importance of formal internal communications about a merger (Brockhaus, 1975; Graves, 1981; Ivancevich et al., 1987; Napier, Simmons, & Stratton, 1989; Schweiger & DeNisi, 1987; Sinetar, 1981), changes in organizational structure (Gill & Foulder, 1978; Mirvis, 1985; Stewart et al., 1963), and problems of merging different human resources policies (Gill & Foulder, 1978; Leighton & Tod, 1969).

There are general findings about communication which include the following (Bastien, 1987; Napier & Stratton, 1987):

- Employees often draw on numerous information sources, including informal modes, such as rumor mills, the grapevine, and sources outside the two firms (e.g., newspaper accounts), as well as formal communication from within the organizations.

- Communication is usually perceived to be in short supply; there never seems to be "enough" and employees often feel they are not getting the full story.

- There may be a need to provide different types of communication and use different methods for various groups within each organization. For example, staff employees and middle managers in the target firm may be most affected by mergers and need greater attention or information about changes than non-management or line employees.

Literature on organization-structure changes usually focuses on the differences in the ways the two firms manage basic operations and the general levels of decision-making and authority felt by members of each firm. This type of reaction seems to vary as a function of the degree to which the two firms are integrated after the merger or acquisition. The degree of integration is discussed later in the chapter.

Very often, in mergers where the two firms are very integrated, there is an actual or perceived change in status that is most often felt by target firm members. In one merger, a bank manager in the acquired bank graphically illustrated this change in status (Napier & Stratton, 1987, page 16):

After the merger, I was in a meeting with operations managers and officers. It was a humbling experience. Not only did most of the people in that meeting used to work for me, most of their bosses did too. Now I was just an officer with no management authority.

Finally, there seem to be some general findings based on merging human resources policies. First, it appears that the first policies to be changed, if there are changes, are those that are tangible and visible to employees (e.g., the reward system) (Steele & Osborne, 1983). Employees can quickly spot discrepancies across firms in such areas, and thus managers must deal with possible inequities and differences between the programs, even if it is just to acknowledge the differences and announce that no changes will occur (Brockhaus, 1975). Another possible reason why these areas change first may be that, once the policy decision has been made to change the programs, technical experts can implement the changes. Other human resources areas, such as succession planning or management transfers, can be more sensitive and demand greater top-management input. As a result, such changes may come later.

Despite the widespread interest and more than 20 years of research and writing on mergers, current knowledge about how to deal with the human resources issues of mergers is limited in several ways. First, there is little description of actual (versus normative) changes in human resources practices and structure in both firms. Frequently, the literature has relied upon anecdotal reports (Brockhaus, 1975), very general case studies (Stewart et al., 1963), or information about what happened in only one of the two firms (Mirvis, 1985). Part of the problem is that "each merger is unique," and it is difficult to develop consistent information about what happens across all mergers.

A second problem is the lack of discussion on how the degree of integration of the two firms after the merger influences human resources practices. For example, in acquisitions, where the target firm is left to operate fairly independently, how do the human resources practices change (if at all), compared with cases where the two firms mesh various systems, such as data processing and marketing? How are those decisions made? If there is to be integration of the two firms, which practices change and in what ways? Finally, with regard to integration, more recent research (Napier, Schweiger, & Csiszar, 1989) has raised the issue of whether there are certain areas and functions that will be more "merged" than others within a transaction. Namely, there is no need for mergers and acquisitions to be thought of as an "all or no" integration approach.

A third area where there is a lack of information is what happens, or should happen, to human resources practices during the various stages of the merger. A merger can be a lengthy process; it is not uncommon for a year to pass from initial discussions to the final consummation. Few specifics exist on what actions should occur before the announcement to merge, during the period when government agencies review the merger, and after the effective date of the merger (Buono et al., 1985; Graves, 1975).

Outcomes of Mergers and Acquisitions

The financial-outcome literature is generally negative about the results of mergers and acquisitions. Although a merger or acquisition may benefit shareholders of the acquired or target firm (Jensen, 1984), the results for the acquiring firm are less encouraging (*Business Week*, 1985). In his examination of mergers in Western European countries and the U.S., Mueller (1977, 1980) found no net gain to acquiring firms. Similarly, Lubatkin's (1983) review of the literature found little evidence of the expected benefits of efficiency presumed to result from a merger, although recent research has raised questions regarding the measurement process to assess gains (Lubatkin, 1987; Lubatkin & Shrieves, 1986). Finally, Louis's (1982) assessment of ten mergers also revealed mixed results. He estimated that earnings per share would have gone up for five firms had they not undergone mergers, and gone down for the other five.

A second way to assess mergers focuses on the reactions, behaviors, and actions by parties involved in the transaction, especially employees. Research on attitudes, usually from the perspective of the acquired firm, has examined how managers and employees react to the announcement of an intent to merge (Costello, Kubis, & Schaffer, 1963), and to the official completion of the merger (Blake & Mouton, 1985; Buono et al., 1985; Ivancevich et al., 1987; Marks & Mirvis, 1985; Wishard, 1985). Typically, reactions include feelings of fear, "being sold out," loss of autonomy, anxiety, stress, and low morale. The general findings suggest that (1) well-planned, effectively communicated mergers generate higher satisfaction and less anxiety (Shirley, 1977; Marks, 1982), and (2) people with generally good attitudes about their jobs and organizations are more likely to view a merger positively than people with poor attitudes (Costello et al., 1963).

The literature also suggests that employee performance will "sag" (Perry, 1962) during a merger. One estimate is that as much as two hours of productive work time are lost per employee per day for the duration of the merger process (Wishard, 1985)! Much of the loss stems from an increasing amount of time spent gossiping about the merger (Cabrera, 1982; Napier & Stratton, 1987). People create their own reality and respond to it even if it is not accurate. This means there is good reason to keep employees informed and communication channels open.

There are several areas where more information is needed regarding merger outcomes. First, as mentioned earlier, it is critical to know more about what happens in a single merger over time. So far, much knowledge has been based on assessing effects of a merger after a relatively short time period (e.g., three to six months). It may take several years for the full impact of a merger to be felt (Drucker, 1982; Louis, 1982), so there is a need for sustained examination of a merger or groups of mergers over time. Data collection should include changes in financial performance of the firms involved, as well as measures of reactions of typical employees, customers, and investors. A more detailed examination could also include not only attitudes and employee behaviors (e.g., turnover, performance, absenteeism), but also various behaviors, which may be difficult to attribute directly to the merger process (as opposed to other possibilities). Finally, the degree of integration (ranging from none or little to complete integration of the firms with each other) may influence performance of firms over time.

Summary of Research on Mergers and Acquisitions

Despite the lack of definitive knowledge on human resources issues in mergers, there seem to be some general conclusions for human resources scholars, students, and managers. First, there are no set "rules" about how best to implement a merger or about what makes a merger or acquisition "successful" (Paine & Power, 1984). This is particularly true for issues related to human resources. Implementation approaches seem to vary widely.

Second, existing research frequently has examined human resources issues from only one firm's perspective, often that of the target or acquired firm (Mirvis, 1985). Some researchers are beginning to provide information about a given merger or mergers from the perspective of both firms. Buono et al. (1985) considered both perspectives but focused on employee reactions and changes in culture. Napier and Stratton (1987) considered both perspectives in assessing changes in human resources practices, structural changes, and employee reactions, as well as methods of communicating about the merger.

Finally, research has progressed substantially since the 1960s (Kitching, 1967; Mace & Montgomery, 1962). Besides the increased interest in human resources issues and primarily prescriptive research (i.e., what a merger "should" be like), there is a growing body of descriptive research as well as increasingly rigorous quasi-experimental and longitudinal research designs (Brockhaus, 1975; Buono et al., 1985; Cabrera, 1982; Napier, Simmons, & Stratton, 1989; Schweiger & DeNisi, 1987; Sinetar, 1981). Once observation and description can be made of what actually goes on in mergers, researchers will be in a better position to provide prescriptions for coping with mergers. But at present, prescriptions seem premature, at best, given the current state of knowledge.

While no one approach to implementation seems appropriate for all mergers, some issues seem critical regardless of the type of merger. These include attention to (1) the human resources policies and practices (Barrett, 1973; Cabrera, 1982; DeNoble, 1984), (2) the process of communicating information about the merger and related changes (Bastien, 1987; Brockhaus, 1975; Ivancevich et al., 1987; Leighton & Tod, 1969; Shirley, 1977), and (3) the design or structure of the merged organization (Marks, 1982; DeNoble, 1984).

CONCEPTUAL FRAMEWORKS FOR PLANNING FOR AND COPING WITH MERGERS AND ACQUISITIONS

A goal of this book has been to integrate knowledge from several disciplines to help scholars, students, and managers understand strategic human resources management. To integrate different disciplines, it is often useful to have models that illustrate how the various aspects of strategy and human resources may link together.

This chapter briefly discusses several existing merger-and-acquisition typologies, most of which do not explicitly address the nature of how HR issues are affected by a merger.

A frequently used way to classify mergers is by motive. Several researchers have discussed the financial and non-financial reasons for mergers (Halpern, 1983; Jemison & Sitkin, 1986; Jensen & Ruback, 1983). Pritchett (1985) described five types of mergers: cooperation, rescue, collaborative, contested, and raid. Similarly, Schweiger and Ivancevich (1987) used four types of mergers: merger, planned divestiture, friendly acquisition, and hostile takeover. Each type of merger is linked to likely outcome impacts on HR issues.

Finally, moving beyond basic classifications, Tyler and Ferris (1987) and Tyler (1988) have argued that mergers must be considered in overall corporate strategy formulation. In discussing three generic corporate strategies (i.e., vertical integration, related, and unrelated diversification), they have proposed that corporate strategy will influence the type of merger (i.e., vertical, horizontal, concentric, marketing, concentric technology, or conglomerate) a firm pursues. In this, the role of the human resources department can and should vary in the strategy-formulation/merger selection process. The range of involvement for the department can be very active (i.e., part of the strategy-formulation process) to very passive (i.e., carrying out record-keeping activities).

A FRAMEWORK LINKING MOTIVE, DEGREE OF INTEGRATION, HUMAN RESOURCES PRACTICES, AND OUTCOMES

Napier (1989) has developed a model incorporating several key variables: (1) motive or reason for the merger (financial, non-financial), (2) merger type (i.e., extension, collaborative, redesign) based upon degree of integration, (3) human resources policies (e.g., selection, pay, transfers), and (4) merger outcomes. Essentially, the model suggests that motives and degree of integration are related and that they in turn are linked to the types of human resources practices most affected in a merger. The model also suggests that managers should consider the motive and expected degree of integration between two firms in planning for and implementing human resources changes resulting from a merger. In addition, the discussion raises the issue of how HR staff can play a role in the intended—and unintended—strategy association with a merger.

Motive and Merger Types

The motives for mergers (financial, non-financial) may relate to the degree of integration (i.e., type of merger) and subsequent relationships of two firms after the merger. The relationships between the two firms could vary

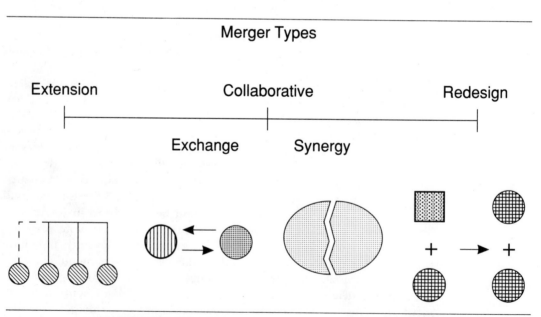

FIGURE 13-1. Merger types.

from very loose (extension), to very tight (redesign), to cooperative (collaborative) (Figure 13-1). The extension relationship is distant, in which the acquired firm becomes part of a holding company, and essentially operates independently. A redesign relationship suggests a high degree of integration (i.e., one firm or unit dominates and "redesigns" the other). A collaborative relationship implies two firms working toward building a better organization as a merged firm. A more detailed discussion will better define the nature of each type of relationship.

Extension Mergers.   In extension mergers, one firm typically merges with or acquires another for any of several non-value-maximizing motives. The motives usually relate to increasing firm growth: (1) as a managerial pursuit to enhance power or prestige; (2) as a way to diversify to avoid risk; or (3) as a way to take advantage of a "good buy." Acquisitions for managerial pursuit include those to reduce risk (Mueller, 1977), increase sales or assets (Halpern, 1983), or control a larger empire (Rhoades, 1983).

Diversifying is achieved by increasing the business-unit portfolio of the firm (Mueller, 1977), and decreasing dependence upon some part of the environment (i.e., reducing uncertainty) (Mueller, 1977; Pfeffer, 1972). Finally, growth may be "purchased" when there are mismatches in the value of a firm (i.e., the actual vs. perceived price) (Mueller, 1977), or when a firm is worth more than its current selling price ("underpriced") and the buyer expects it to grow (Halpern, 1983).

Often, a merger or acquisition is in an area outside the buyer's primary business competency. In such a case, then, the usual policy for dealing with the new acquisition is one of "hands off." There is little integration and the new acquisition is treated as an "extension" of the existing firm. Because many acquisitions are of high-performing firms, this policy is one that firms often follow: let the acquisition continue doing what it had been doing well before the purchase. In this case, there is likely to be little change in the human resources policy or structure of either firm. IBM's purchase of Rolm Corporate was initially an extension merger. Many such mergers change, however, during the course of their negotiation and implementation, and the degree of integration may increase.

In other situations, the target firm may be in poor financial shape, but the acquirer anticipates growth and better future performance. Bank of America's (B of A) purchase of Seattle First National Bank (Seafirst) represents this type of extension merger. In this case, Seafirst was rescued from financial disaster stemming from bad oil loans. Since the managers responsible for Seafirst's problems had been replaced six months prior to the merger, and its problems seemed to focus mainly on its energy portfolio, B of A did not make significant changes inside Seafirst. Rather, the expectation (later borne out) was that the acquired bank would recover, given financial support and reasonable time.

The human resources area can play a major role in enhancing and facilitating the extension merger strategy. For example, if the HRM staff agrees to maintain separate policies and practices, they may also coordinate to keep the firms "separate" in other ways (e.g., no official exchange of newsletters, no official transfer of employees). On the other hand, the HRM groups could initiate or encourage the firms moving to a different (unintended) strategy. The HRM groups may begin exchanging information on policies and learn there are areas where each could gain from incorporating aspects of the other's practices. If this happens, the firms may begin moving toward a collaborative merger, which may or may not have been the initial intention of top management.

Collaborative Mergers and Acquisitions. In collaborative mergers, two firms join (1) if the combination will benefit both firms in terms of operation output (production, marketing, or pricing) or financial gains, or (2) if one of the two firms will benefit in either output (e.g., exchanging skills) or financial gains. The first type of collaboration is a "synergy" merger and the latter is an "exchange" acquisition or merger. The mergers stem primarily from value-maximizing motives.

Synergy combinations generate benefits from both product output and financial gains. Product-output advantages to both firms include creating a critical mass of resources to outperform the competition (Salter & Weinhold, 1979), coordinating prices (Jensen & Ruback, 1983), reducing competition through horizontal acquisition and integrating production through vertical acquisition (Pfeffer, 1972), as well as creating economies of scale and scope (Halpern, 1983). Financial gains for both firms develop through (1) decreasing expected bankruptcy costs, (2) increasing debt capacity and cash flow, (3) creating "P/E magic" (when one firm buys another that has a lower price/earnings (P/E) ratio than itself, the P/E ratio of the combined firms is often higher than the acquirer's was prior to purchase), (4) gaining tax exemptions from corporate reorganization, (5) redeploying excess capital, and (6) reducing agency costs by bringing related assets under common ownership (Halpern, 1983; Jensen & Ruback, 1983; Mueller, 1977).

Exchange mergers benefit the surviving firm when skills of one partner are applied to the other (Salter & Weinhold, 1979). These benefits can be in either product output or financial gains. Very often, exchange mergers are those in which an acquirer seeks some specific skills that can be transplanted from the acquired firm back to the acquirer as a way to create financial value.

Collaborative mergers are likely to generate changes in both organizations in terms of structure and human resources policies. The changes may be organizationwide (synergy mergers), or focus on specific areas. The Norfolk & Western-Southern Railway merger represents an example of synergy collaborative merger. The new firm attempted to create synergy by (1) combining names (changed to Norfolk Southern), (2) locating its headquarters in a neutral city (Norfolk, Va.), (3) balancing the membership of the board of directors with representatives from each company, and (4) cross training key managers. The resultant synergy forced changes in human resources practices (e.g., transfers), and in the structure of each organization.

The acquisition of Electronic Data Systems (EDS) by General Motors could be classified as an exchange merger. The goal was to bring EDS's skills into an area (data processing) of General Motors (GM) that needed upgrading. The merger resulted in radical changes in policies, structure, and culture in that GM division, but did not affect other areas as much. As seen, of course, sometimes the "redesigner" gets carried away (and resulted in this case in Ross Perot leaving GM's board)! As with extension mergers, HRM groups in the two firms may enhance the intended collaboration, or may lead a firm toward another, unintended approach. Enhancing exchange or synergy collaborative mergers can be done through such actions as exchanges of knowledge on HR issues and transfers of people or policies. If, however, the exchange of people or knowledge generates undesirable friction (e.g., major compensation inequities, overwhelming culture clash), the firms may be pushed toward other, unintended strategies. Overwhelming culture clash as a result of trying to mesh firms may encourage either a distancing (i.e., extension) approach, or, a forceful redesign, in which one of the cultures clearly dominates.

Redesign Mergers and Acquisitions. Redesign mergers are characterized by a condition where integration of one firm into another is common and the policies and practices of one firm (usually the target) change dramatically. A typical motive (financial) in redesign mergers is to improve performance of the target organization (i.e., gain control of the board and/or management) (Halpern, 1983). In such a case, changes in the acquired firm are likely to be much greater than those in extension or collaborative mergers. These changes can be in the direction of becoming more like the buyer ("molding"), or of altering the target's policies and structure from its original form ("reshaping") to something else, unlike the acquirer.

Empirical evidence suggests that redesign mergers can also occur even when the acquired firm is performing well. An example is retailer Best Company's acquisition of Jafco, a discount retail house in the Pacific Northwest. Best Company purchased Jafco and treated it essentially as an extension for two years, before redesigning it to fit Best's structure and policies. Finally, the HRM groups can once again play a role in implementing the redesign strategy or in formulating a different approach. Providing clear, timely, and accurate information to both firms regarding the redesign should enhance its success. Early recognition of gains to both firms from another approach, such as collaboration, could shift the direction from being a clear-cut redesign.

Human Resources Practices and Outcomes

The existing literature suggests that mergers may lead to changes in one or both firms in the major policy areas (e.g., human resources planning, selection, development, compensation, performance appraisal and employee relations) (Bradley & Korn, 1982), and ultimately, to outcomes of the merger.

The model presented here suggests that motive and degree of integration will influence the type and extent of change in human resources practices in each firm. For example, the extent of human resources changes shortly after the merger is expected to vary from very low in each firm, in extension mergers, to medium to high in the target firm in redesign mergers. A financially motivated redesign acquisition could greatly affect performance appraisal in the target firm because of the likelihood that performance expectations will change.

Top managers frequently leave merged firms within three years after a merger (*Wall Street Journal*, 1985). Even so, the present framework suggests that the degree of integration following a merger may influence the turnover of those top mangers. In particular, managers may be more likely to leave sooner in redesign and collaborative mergers. For example, because of anticipated changes in human resources practices affecting performance expectations in the "redesigned" firm, there is a high chance that many managers in the firm will leave, voluntarily or not (Brockhaus, 1975). Top managers may also be likely to leave in collaborative mergers because of a perception of lack of control following a merger. Whereas in an extension merger, the two organizations should remain essentially independent, in redesign and collaborative mergers there is greater integration and likelihood that one (usually the acquired) or both firms will undergo alterations in management, policies, and direction. For top managers, this often requires relinquishing long-held control. In addition, mergers have weakened managers' sense of commitment to a firm. The result has been a "free agent manager," looking after himself and his own career, rather than having any loyalty to a firm (Hirsch, 1987).

Such changes may mean the acquiring firm will need to develop an approach for retaining key managers, provide outplacement for the terminated managers, and restructure human resources planning in the acquirer to incorporate remaining target managers.

Given a merger where major change in human resources policies is likely (i.e., redesign and collaborative mergers), the areas most likely to change first will likely be compensation and benefits policies (Steele & Osborne, 1983). As discussed earlier, such areas are likely to change first because they are tangible, affect all employees (as opposed to certain groups like executives), and are more technical in nature, allowing specialists to examine them and make recommendations.

Because these policies are more visible, they are likely to lead to cross-firm comparison among employees, further suggesting the need for consistency of policies (Marks, 1982). For instance, in a retail firm acquisition, the compensation practices and wage levels for salespeople in the target firm were better than those in the acquiring firm. As salespeople in the acquiring firm learned about the discrepancies, there were morale problems and uncertainty about what the firm would do to resolve the perceived inequities. The final decision was to increase wage levels to match those in the target firm. This was, of course, very costly in terms of money and lost morale and productivity in the acquiring firm during the uncertain period.

Merger outcomes may also be affected by motive and degree of integration of the two firms. We might expect the performance of extension acquisitions to improve sooner than that of collaborative and redesign mergers. If an extension acquisition has been performing relatively well before the merger, its performance should actually improve because of the increased resources available from the acquiring firm. For instance, when Bank of America purchased Seattle First National Bank in 1982, Seafirst's officers felt they gained by having the full network of Bank of America's domestic overseas branches and facilities available to them.

In collaborative and redesign mergers, performance of the combined firm may not improve or increase dramatically within the first year for several reasons. First, there may be major losses of managers (voluntary as well as forced resignations), which could slow the process of integrating the firms. In addition, there may be overt or subtle lack of employee support for the merger. Finally, in combinations where the cultures of the firms must merge (through meshing or exchanging talents, or shaping and molding the acquired firm), there will be more time and effort required for the combination to be successful in terms of performance (Buono et al., 1985; Marks & Mirvis, 1985; Napier & Stratton, 1987).

Finally, the extent of reaction outcomes by employees in both firms is likely to vary in mergers where there are different degrees of integration. For both firms, reactions are likely to be strongest in collaborative mergers. In this case, both acquiring and target firms will probably undergo some change in human resources policies, forcing employees to adapt to changes. For acquired firms, the redesign mergers are likely to generate the most change, since one of the merged firms will be reshaped or molded dramatically. Moving from one set or practices or culture to another often leads to strong negative reactions by target employees (Buono et al., 1985).

In addition to the extent of reaction expected in firms that are more or less integrated, the length of time needed for employees to assimilate the merger changes can vary, and often be extremely lengthy. For redesign and collaborative mergers, the general consensus seems to be to make most changes within the first year following the merger's consummation. Some researchers suggest making changes immediately after the merger is official (Searby, 1969) so the process of recovery can begin right away. Others suggest a phases approach (Barrett, 1973), with the first three to six months used to retire or replace managers no longer compatible with the merged firm's goals and the six-nine-month period for converting human resources policies. Even when changes in operational and human resources practices, are made immediately, however, the residual reactions of employees can extend for more than 18 months following the initial announcement about the impending merger (Napier & Stratton, 1987).

MERGERS AND ACQUISITIONS AS PART OF THE STRATEGIC MANAGEMENT PROCESS

This chapter has focused on applying the knowledge gained from research linking human resources issues with mergers and acquisitions. As mentioned earlier, there are few consistent "rules" on how to manage mergers. Even so, there seem to be some important issues that consistently arise in assessing and managing mergers.

The Importance of Considering Human Resources Issues as Part of the Strategic-Management Process

Mergers and acquisitions typically represent major strategic decisions within firms. Such decisions suggest two key points related to HRM. First, given the strategic motive or reason behind a merger or acquisition, it is important to consider what such a decision means with regard to possible impacts on HRM issues. Not all acquisitions are for the purpose of gaining economies; some may be solely to allow the buyer to "strip" off key assets before reselling the firm. In such a case, attention to human resources is unlikely to be a major priority. Thus, it is important for researchers and managers to understand the extent to which a strategic reason for an acquisition relates to HRM actions.

A second point in mergers and acquisitions is that when HR issues are likely to be important, they should be considered as early as possible. Very often, human resources concerns are raised only after a merger has been completed, even though managers often acknowledge that a major reason for merger failures is the "people problems" that emerge "after the deal is done." Human resources concerns should be raised and planned for early in merger discussions. Such concerns would include not only those that could cost the acquiring firm money (e.g., unresolved lawsuits, union contracts, pensions), but also those that will help or hinder the smooth transition after the merger (e.g., employee reactions, potential culture clashes). In addition, early involvement may lead to recognition of unintended but perhaps more appropriate strategies.

It is critical, as argued throughout this book, for human resources and line managers to consider human resources concerns as part of the strategy-formulation process, not just as an important aspect of implementation. Human resources managers must gain credibility and be involved in strategy-making on a consistent, regular basis, not just when a merger possibility arises.

Realistic Expectations

Even the best planned and executed mergers generate confusion, distraction and upheaval for employees and managers, often in both firms. In addition, although the acquiring firm may have carried out the merger in what it considers to be a humane, fair, and open manner, it is very probable that the target employees especially will feel anxious, and show it through performance declines. If managers *and* employees in both firms can be told to expect upheaval for several months following a merger, they may be able to handle it better (Schweiger & DeNisi, 1987). There are numerous management books, articles, and consultants available to help managers and employees understand what they will face in a merger (Schweiger et al., 1987).

Open Communication

Managers will often not have much information about a merger or, for legal reasons, be unable to give out as much information as they wish. Even so, some managers report that communicating the same information in different ways is often an important part of quelling employee anxiety. During mergers, employees may hear even more selectively than under normal conditions, and thus need to hear information from their managers several times before believing it. The very posture of being open as well as the actual information that is communicated will establish a climate of greater trust and potentially realize few counterproductive implications or consequences.

SUMMARY AND CONCLUSION

Mergers and acquisitions have been a fact of life for business in the 1980s and are likely to continue into the 1990s. Research on mergers is increasing and beginning to provide some guidance to managers on how to cope with the effects of major organizational changes. Managers should realize that mergers occur for various reasons and that those reasons may affect the extent to which the firms mesh or integrate. The type of merger (i.e., extension, collaborative, redesign) may then affect the degree of human resources practice changes and the outcomes of the merger.

CHAPTER	CONCLUSIONS AND PLANNING
14	FOR THE FUTURE

CONCLUSIONS AND PLANNING FOR THE FUTURE

Climb High
Climb Far
Your Goal the Sky
Your Aim the Star.[1]

THE FUTURE-STRATEGY AND HRM

What is apparent from the existing research is that a single, all-encompassing, theory of SHRM has not emerged. However, relevant midrange theories, in both strategy and HRM, have been developed. More importantly, the common threads that link these theories have begun to be identified. These between-discipline linkages constitute the essence of SHRM, as it exists today. Hopefully this represents its primitive state of knowledge development, which will serve as the base for a future body of research. That future paradigm is one of the subjects of discussion in this conclusions chapter.

While this volume has attempted to be comprehensive, in terms of the existing literature, the pace of research in both the strategy and HRM areas has made that impossible. The major research streams of strategy and HRM have been included, but the full extent to which these are related is not completely known. In addition, some emerging areas, although not an all-inclusive set, were selected because they appear to have the potential to have a major impact. Areas such as entrepreneurship, mergers and acquisitions, and international business fall into this category. These areas tend to reflect the current state of research and are not as theoretically developed as areas such as compensation or planning. Controversy has not been avoided, as demonstrated by the debate about the existence of strategic industrial relations, but there is little doubt that industrial relations can have a major strategic impact. Focusing research on emerging and controversial areas will add to the main body of research that defines SHRM. This is another challenge for the future.

Implementation also needs additional theoretical development. In many cases, the implementation issue has skirted the political realities that govern much of the behavior within most organizations. The relationship between organizational politics, standard HRM practices, and the evolution of firms

---

[1] From the Hopkins Memorial Steps, Williams College, Williamstown, MA. Cited in Safire & Safire, (1982: 15).

toward a SHRM approach has certain political ramifications and consequences. Thus, this chapter sets an agenda for further research by exploring both content and implementation issues.

Content Extensions

As HRM and strategy continue to evolve as research fields, it is important that the linkages be maintained. This is because academic fields tend to become increasingly fixed as they develop, and theoretical extensions become more incremental. Incremental approaches to the development of a paradigm result in ever smaller contributions. Further, it is common for such research to be excluded from the journals, since it does not conform to existing frames of reference. Research that is seen as being cross-disciplinary may be shut out of both fields, rather than being seen and valued as a linking mechanism. The continuing development of a stream of research directed toward SHRM may be one way to ensure that these desired results continue to flow.

For this to occur, strategy and HRM research must continue to be coupled around areas of evolving interests. This continual evolution will force researchers trying to deal with the common linkages to stay in a dynamic mode. On the HRM side, staffing must continue to be viewed in a strategic context. Performance evaluation and rewards must be related to the major strategic thrusts of the firm. Industrial relations must be considered in an expanded light that relates to strategic value rather than to some negotiating outcome.

On the strategy side the linkages are even more complex because finance, marketing, and economics are providing contributions that accelerate the pace of research. In entrepreneurship, internal corporate venturing is being developed as a stream of research, with little attention being paid to the role of HRM in this evolving context. Problems associated with entrepreneurial growth are still being treated as though all that is required is a structural adaptation. The growing importance of international markets and the evolving international ownership of United States firms makes international business an important area. The increasing pace of mergers and acquisitions has created conditions that are optimal for both empirical and theoretical research. Yet, little work has been done to integrate these various research foci.

A final concern for the future relates to the the narrowing of research method, which seems to characterize so many business disciplines. The research area of SHRM contains a variety of research questions. In some cases the inclusion of SHRM represents an incremental addition to a well-established existing stream of research. In these cases, empirical validation through statistical inference is appropriate. In other cases, where the nature of the SHRM impact has yet to be uncovered, a clinical approach is appropriate. Thus, the full spectrum of scientific methods is appropriate depending on which bite of the apple the researcher takes. This variety of available methods means that method-capability should exclude few researchers and may increase the population of researchers in this area, which should accelerate the completion of the research agenda.

Strategy-Implementation Extensions

Initially, there was little need to encourage researchers to examine the strategy-HRM link. Despite its early stage of development most of the basic areas of interest, at least, have been uncovered. This volume has suggested a expanded agenda for SHRM but has carefully skirted directly addressing the area of organizational politics. The relationship among HRM, strategy, and organizational politics deserves to be part of the ongoing research agenda. Initial efforts to address this issue suggest that staffing, performance evaluation, and reward systems are affected by organizational power (e.g., Ferris, Russ, & Fandt, in press). The ability of these areas to facilitate strategy implementation is affected by organizational politics and power considerations. This political agenda also emerges in the basic functional duties, such as staffing, performance evaluations, and the administration of reward systems.

The employment interview provides the initial opportunity for political behavior. During the interview the discussion is directed toward the political agenda of either party, although most probably toward that of the interviewer. The extent to which these private political agendas may be supportive of the general thrust of the entire organization is unknown, as are ways to ensure that this initial posturing is directed toward the long-term needs of the firm.

Politics is replayed in the performance-evaluation process, only this time between the subordinate and the supervisor. At this point supervisors can use the performance-evaluation process to enhance their own political agenda (Longenecker, Sims & Gioia, 1987). Other research has shown that subordinates can also manipulate this process (e.g., Wood & Mitchell, 1981). While the optimal strategy-implementation needs of the organization may require that behavior be directed toward areas for which objective evaluation is difficult, the ongoing political agenda of both subordinate and supervisor may direct their behavior in another direction. The impact that this ongoing political behavior has on the strategy-implementation issue needs to be addressed, to determine the extent to which this distorts the use of the evaluation process as a useful tool to achieve strategic aims.

Finally, the impact of organizational politics on the reward system needs more attention. Much of the SHRM literature has suggested that these systems be adjusted to support behavior that will support the implementation of the chosen strategy. However, organizational politics tend to distort the established reward systems, in terms of both salary and promotions (Dreher, Dougherty, & Whitely, 1988). Since the strategy of the firm is unlikely to coincide with the personal agendas of all the employees, these political sidegames can be expected to have a significant impact on the strategy-implementation effort. To the extent that private political agendas encourage ingratiatory behavior, HRM policies will have to be directed toward minimizing these distortions.

While research on the political agendas is just emerging, it highlights the nature of SHRM. The dynamic nature of organizations, as well as their surrounding environments, ensures that additional factors will be identified that are relevant to strategy implementation. It also requires that research efforts directed toward problems identification, at early stages, be ongoing if HRM is to be an effective tool in strategy implementation.

On a broader front, Walker (1989) suggested that HRM must respond to a broader set of considerations if it is to continue to make an enhanced contribution in the future. Walker (1989, p. 55) pointed out that line managers "will increasingly expect HR to think and act as they themselves think and act." This amounts to a considerable organizational evolution because line managers will assume that HRM professionals can be entrusted with many line-type decisions. It also suggests that organizations will begin to expect a more organizationally-focused, rather than professionally-specialized, perspective from HRM managers. However, the fast pace of research in the HRM area is pushing professionals to become more specialized. This will require a HRM department with professionals capable of defining HRM priorities in terms of their organization's competitive position and strategy, as well as those with highly specialized bases of knowledge. This may mean that new career tracks for HRM professionals, and new organizational forms for HRM departments, will have to be developed (Walker, 1989).

SUMMARY AND CONCLUSIONS

At the end of a scholarly monograph it is customary for the authors to offer some set of profound comments. Such thoughts are not warranted here because this volume, on a rather broad front, has attempted to capture the state of existing research. It has also attempted to develop, extend, and link theory. By combining breadth of coverage with a strong theoretical focus, it is hoped that it will serve as a springboard toward further interest and research in this area. Hopefully, that will occur in both the applied and academic areas.

While SHRM has served to link fields that had previously been comfortable in their isolation, it should also serve as a link between practicing managers and academics. Academic research that is not directed toward real problems is unlikely to be highly energized. It is through the inputs and collaboration of practicing managers that real problems are brought to the attention of academics. The size and relevance of this problem inventory determine whether SHRM will continue to be a viable area of research or fade into the academic attic.

The imagination and dreams of researchers and practicing managers will also be relevant to the future of SHRM. Perhaps the advice given to Biff, Willy Loman's son, in *Death of a Salesman* captures this best. "A salesman has got to dream, boy. It comes with the territory" (Miller, 1949, p. 138).

SUGGESTED READINGS

BOOKS

Alpander, G. G. (1982). *Human resources management planning.* New York: AMACOM.

Beer, M., Spector, B., Lawrence, P. R., Mills, D. Q., & Walton, R. E. (1985). *Human resource management: A general manager's perspective.* New York: Free Press.

Beer, M., Spector, B., Lawrence, P. R., Mills, D. Q., & Walton, R. E. (1984). *Managing human assets.* New York: Free Press.

Fombrun, C. J., Tichy, N. M., & Devanna, M. A. (1984). *Strategic human resource management.* New York: Wiley.

Foulkes, F. K. (1980). *Strategic human resources management: A guide for effective practice.* Englewood Cliffs, NJ: Prentice-Hall.

Foulkes, F. K. (1980). *Personnel policies in large nonunion companies.* Englewood Cliffs, NJ: Prentice-Hall.

Galbraith, J. R., & Nathanson, D. A. (1978). *Strategy implementation: The role of structure and process.* St. Paul, MN: West.

Keller, G. (1983). *Academic strategy.* Baltimore: Johns Hopkins University Press.

Luce, S. R. (1983). *Retrenchment and beyond: The acid test of human resource management.* Ontario, Canada: The Conference Board of Canada.

Odiorne, G. S. (1984). *Strategic management of human resources: A portfolio approach.* San Francisco: Jossey-Bass.

Tichy, N. M. (1983). *Managing strategic change.* New York: Wiley.

Walker, J. W. (1980). *Human resource planning.* New York: McGraw-Hill.

Walton, R. E. & Lawrence, P. R. (Eds.) (1985). *HRM trends & challenges.* Boston: Harvard Business School Press.

ARTICLES
Overview of Strategy and Human Resources Management

Andrews, J. A. (1986). Is there a crisis in the personnel department's identity? *Personnel Journal,* 65, 86–93.

Angle, H. L., Manz, C. C., & Van de Ven, A. H. (1985). Integrating human resource management and corporate strategy: A preview of the 3M story. *Human Resource Management, 24,* 51–68.

Baird, L., & Meshoulam, I. (1984). The HRS matrix: Managing the human resource function strategically. *Human Resource Planning, 7,* 1–30.

Baird, L., & Meshoulam, I. (1984). Strategic human resource management: Implications for training human resource professionals. *Training and Development Journal, 37*(January), 76–78.

Baird, L., & Meshoulam, I. (1988). Managing two fits of strategic human resource management. *Academy of Management Review, 13,* 116–128.

Beer, M., & Spector, B. (1984). *Transformations in human resource management.* Cambridge, MA: (Unpublished paper), Harvard Graduate School of Business Administration.

Beer, M., Spector, B., Lawrence, P. R., Mills, D. Q., & Walton, R. E. (1985). Managing human assets, Part 1: A general manager's perspective. *Personnel Administrator, 30,* 60–69.

Beer, M., Spector, B., Lawrence, P. R., Mills, D. Q., & Walton, R. E. (1985). Managing human assets, Part 2: Unifying human resource management. *Personnel Administrator, 30,* 78–85.

Bloom, N. L. (1988). HRMS planning pays off. *Personnel Journal, 67,* 64–70.

Butler, J. E., Ferris, G. R., & Smith Cook, D. (1988). Exploring some critical dimensions of strategic human resources management. In R. S. Schuler, S. A. Youngblood, & V. Huber (Eds.), *Readings in personnel and human resource management* (3rd ed.) (pp. 3–13). St. Paul, MN: West.

Butler, J. E. (1988). Human resource management as a driving force in business strategy. *Journal of General Management, 13*(4), 88–102.

DeBejar, G., & Milkovich, G. T. (1986). *Human resource strategy at the business level: Theoretical model and empirical verification.* Paper presented at the Academy of Management, 46th annual national meeting. Chicago.

Deutsch, A. (1982). How employee retention strategies can aid productivity. *The Journal of Business Strategy, 2,* 106–109.

Devanna, M. A., Fombrun, C. J., & Tichy, N. M. (1981). Human resources management: A strategic perspective. *Organizational Dynamics, 9,* 51–64.

Devanna, M. A., Fombrun, C. J., & Tichy, N. M. (1984). A framework for strategic human resource management. In C. J. Fombrun, N. M. Tichy, & M. A. Devanna (Eds.), *Strategic human resource management* (pp. 33–51). New York: Wiley.

Dyer, L. (1983). Bringing human resources into the strategy formulation process. *Human Resource Management, 22,* 257–272.

Dyer, L. (1984). Linking human resource and business strategies. *Human Resource Planning, 7,* 78–84.

Dyer, L. (1984). Studying human resource strategy: An approach and an agenda. *Industrial Relations, 23,* 156–169.

Ferris, G. R., & Curtin, D. (1985). Shaping strategy: Tie personnel functions to company goals. *Management World, 14,* 32–38.

Finney, M. I., (1987). Strategic planning: Hedging future shock. *Personnel Administrator, 32,* 72–80.

Finney, M. I. (1988). A game of skill or chance. *Personnel Administrator, 33,* 38–43.

Fitz-enz, J. (1986). How to market the HR department. *Personnel, 63,* 16–24.

Fitz-enz, J. (1986). HR Inc. *Personnel Journal, 65,* 34–41.

Fombrun, C., & Tichy, N. (1984). Strategic planning and human resource management: At rainbow's end. In R. B. Lamb (Ed.), *Competitive strategic management* (pp. 319–322). Englewood Cliffs, NJ: Prentice-Hall.

Fombrun, C. J., & Devanna, M. A. (1984). *Designing the integrated planning and human resource systems.* Paper presented at the Academy of Management, 44th annual national meeting, Boston.

Fombrun, C. J., Devanna, M. A., & Tichy, N. M. (1984). The human resource management audit. In C. J. Fombrun, N. M. Tichy, & M. A. Devanna (Eds.), *Strategic human resource management* (pp. 235–248). New York: Wiley.

Fossum, J. R., & Parker, D. F. (1983). Building state-of-the-art human resource strategies. *Human Resource Management, 22,* 97–110.

Friedman, S. D., Tichy, N. M., & Ulrich, D. O. (1984). Strategic human resource management at Honeywell, Inc. In C. J. Fombrun, N. M. Tichy, & M. A. Devanna (Eds.), *Strategic human resource management* (pp. 249–270). New York: Wiley.

Frohman, M. A. (1984). Human resource management and the bottom line: Evidence of the connection. *Human Resource Management, 23,* 315–334.

Golden, K. A., & Ramanujam, V. (1985). Between a dream and a nightmare: On the integration of the human resource management and strategic business planning process. *Human Resource Management, 24,* 429–454.

Golden, K. A., & Salipante, P. F. (1986). *An integrative scheme for human resource strategy and information.* Paper presented at the Academy of Management, 46th annual national meeting, Chicago.

Gomez-Mejia, L. R. (1987). *The role of human resources strategy in export performance: A longitudinal study.* Paper presented at the Academy of Management, 47th annual national meeting, New Orleans.

Gordon, G. G. (1987). Getting in step. *Personnel Administrator, 32,* 44–48, 134.

Gosselin, A. (1987). *The relationship between HRM practices and strategic thinking and behavior of top management: An exploratory study.* Paper presented aat the Academy of Management, 47th annual national meeting, New Orleans.

Gosselin, A., & Paine, F. J. (1983). *Beyond the proposition for a strategic human resource management.* Paper presented at the third annual conference of the Strategic Management Society, Paris.

Gould, R. (1984). Gaining competitive edge through human resource strategies. *Human Resource Planning, 7,* 31–38.

Halcrow, A. (1987). Preretirement planning: Making the golden years rosy. *Personnel Journal, 66,* 91–101.

Henn, W. R. (1985). What the strategist asks from human resources. *Human Resource Planning, 8,* 193–200.

Hodgetts, J. L., Lawrence, P. R., & Schlesinger, L. A. (1985). Tiner Trucking company: From control to commitment. *Human Resource Management, 24,* 25–50.

Kanter, R. M. (1983). Frontiers for strategic human resource planning and management. *Human Resource Management, 22,* 9–22.

Koys, D. J., Briggs, S., & Ross, S. C. (1987). *Organizational effectiveness and evaluating the human resource function.* Paper presented at the Academy of Management, 47th annual national meeting, New Orleans.

Lorange, P., & Murphy, D. (1984). Strategy and human resources: Concepts and practice. *Human Resource Management, 22,* 111–135.

Lundberg, C. C. (1985). Toward a conceptual model of human resource strategy: Lessons from the Reynolds Corporation. *Human Resource Management, 24,* 91–112.

Lyles, M. A., & Watson, K. M. (1982). Strategy implementation: The interface with human resources. *Proceedings of the National Academy of Management Meeting*, New York, 56–58.

Magnus, M. (1987). Personnel policies in partnership with profit. *Personnel Journal, 66*, 102–109.

McCabe, D. M. (1981). Strategy and tactics: Military analogies for human resources managers. *Personnel Journal, 60*, 958.

McDonough, E. F., III. (1986). How much power does HR have, and what can it do to win more? *Personnel Journal, 63*, 18–25.

Meshoulam, I., & Baird, L. (1987). Proactive human resource management. *Human Resource Management, 26*, 483–502.

Miles, R. E., & Snow, C. C. (1984). Designing strategic human resources systems. *Organizational Dynamics, 12*, 36–52.

Miller, E. L., Beechler, S., Bhatt, B., & Nath, R. (1986). The relationship between the global strategic planning process and the human resource management function. *Human Resource Planning, 9*, 9–23.

Mirvis, P. H. (1985). Formulating and implementing human resource strategy: A model of how to do it, two examples of how it's done. *Human Resource Management, 24*, 385–412.

Misa, K. F., & Stein, T. (1983). Strategic HRM and the bottom line. *Personnel Administrator, 28*, 27–30.

Napier, N. K. (1988). Strategy, human resources management, and organizational outcomes: Coming out from between the cracks. In G. R. Ferris & K. M. Rowland (Eds.), *Human resources management: Perspectives and issues.* (pp. 16–22). Boston: Allyn and Bacon.

Nkomo, S. M. (1980). Stage three in personnel administration: Strategic human resources management. *Personnel, 57*, 69–77.

Odiorne, G. S. (1981). Developing a human resource strategy. *Personnel Journal*, (July), 545–586.

Odiorne, G. S. (1986). The crystal ball of HR strategy. *Personnel Administrator, 31*, 103–106.

Oppenheim, L., Kydd, C. T., Carini, G. R., & Starr, J. (1986). *Linking human resource management with corporate strategic direction: A comparative study.* Paper presented at the Academy of Management, 46th annual national meeting, Chicago.

Schein, V. E. (1983). Strategic management and the politics of power. *Personnel Administrator, 28,* 55–58.

Schlesinger, L. A. (1984). *Linking human resource management and business strategy.* Paper presented at the Harvard Business School Human Resource Management Futures Conference, May 9–11.

Schlesinger, L. A. (1983). The normative underpinnings of human resource strategy. *Human Resource Management, 22,* 83–96.

Schuler, R. S. & Jackson, S. E. (1987). Linking competitive strategies with human resource management practices. *Academy of Management Executive, 1,* 207–219.

Schuler, R. S. (1986). Fostering and facilitating entrepreneurship in organizations: Implications for organization structure and human resource management practices. *Human Resource Management, 25,* 607–629.

Schuler, R. S. (1988). Human resource management choices and organizational strategy. In R. S. Schuler, S. A. Youngblood, & V. Huber (Eds.), *Readings in personnel and human resource management* (3rd ed.) (pp. 24–39). St. Paul, MN: West.

Schuler, R. S., & MacMillan, I. C. (1984). Gaining competitive advantage through human resource management practices. *Human Resource Management , 23,* 241–256.

Schuler, R. S., Galante, S. P. & Jackson, S. E. (1987). Matching effective HR practices with competitive strategy. *Personnel , 64,* 18–27.

Smith, E. C. (1982). Strategic business planning and human resources: Part I. *Personnel Journal,* (August), 606–610.

Snell, S. A., & Wright, P. M. (1987). *The relationship of strategy and administrative uncertainty to characteristics of human resource management practices: Theoretical management and empirical test.* Paper presented at the Academy of Management, 47th annual national meeting, New Orleans.

Tichy, N. M. (1983). Managing organizational transformations. *Human Resource Management, 22,* 45–60.

Tichy, N. M., Fombrun, C., & Devanna, M. A. (1982). Strategic human resource management. *Sloan Management Review, 23,* 47–61.

Tsui, A. S. (1984). Personnel department effectiveness: A tripartite approach. *Industrial Relations, 22,* 184–197.

Ulrich, D., Geller, A., & DeSouza, G. (1984). A strategy, structure, human resource database: OASIS. *Human Resource Management, 23,* 77–90.

Ulrich, D. O., Clack, B. A., & Dillon, L. (1985). Blue Cross of California: Human resources in a changing world. *Human Resource Management, 24,* 69–80.

Wils, T. (1984). *Business strategy and human resource strategy.* Unpublished doctoral dissertation, Cornell University.

Wils, T., & Dyer, L. (1984). *Relating business strategy to human resource strategy: Some preliminary evidence.* Paper presented at the Academy of Management, 44th annual national meeting, Boston.

Wissema, J. G., Van der Pol, H. W., & Messer, H. M. (1980). Strategic management archetypes. *Strategic Management Journal, 1,* 37–47.

Wright, P. M. (1986). *Human resource strategies: A reconceptualization.* Paper presented at the Academy of Management , 46th annual national meeting, Chicago

Strategic Human Resources Planning

Alpander, G. G., & Botter, C. H. (1981). An integrated model of strategic human resource planning and development. *Human Resource Planning, 4,* 189–208.

Baird, L., Meshoulam, I., & Degive, G. (1983). Meshing human resources planning with strategic business planning. *Personnel, 60,* 14–25.

Burack, E. H., (1985). Linking corporate business and human resource planning: Strategic issues and concerns. *Human Resource Planning, 8,* 133–145.

Clarke, W. E. (1984). Human resources planning: The need for strategic skills. *Journal of Business Strategy, 5,* 101–102.

Desanto, J. F. (1983). Work force planning and corporate strategy. *Personnel Administrator, 28,* 33–38.

Dyer, L. (1985). Strategic human resource management and planning. In K. M. Rowland & G. R. Ferris (Eds.), *Research in personnel and human resources management* (Vol. 3, pp. 1–30). Greenwich, CT: JAI Press.

Galosy, J. R. (1983). Meshing human resources planning with strategic business planning. *Personnel, 30,* 26–35.

Gatewood, R. D., & Gatewood, E. J. (1983). The use of expert data in human resource planning: Guidelines from strategic planning. *Human Resource Planning, 6,* 83–94.

Hooper, J. A., Catalanello, R. F., & Murray, P. L. (1987). Shoring up the weakest link. *Personnel Administrator, 32,* 49–55 & 134.

James, R. M. (1980). Effective planning strategies. *Human Resource Planning, 3*, 1–10.

Kelleher, E. J., & Cotter, K. L. (1982). An integrative model for human resource planning and strategic planning. *Human Resource Planning, 5*, 15–27.

Nkomo, S. M. (1986). The theory and practice of HR planning: The gap still remains. *Personnel Administrator, 31*, 71–84.

Nkomo, S. M. (1987). Human resource planning and organization performance: An exploratory analysis. *Strategic Management Journal, 8*, 387–392.

Oppenheim, L. S., Hyman, S. D., & Kydd, C. T. (1985). *Strategic management for organizational effectiveness: The effect of human resource planning or retention and related issues.* (Vols. 1, 2, and 3). Philadelphia: Wharton Applied Research Center, The Wharton School, University of Pennsylvania.

Shurplin, A. D. (1985). Human resource planning: Low-cost strategies to improve workers' job security. *Journal of Business Strategy, 5*, 90–93.

Sibson, R. E. (1983). Strategic personnel planning. *Personnel Administrator, 28*, 39–42.

Smith, C. S., & Ferris, G. R. (in press). Human resources strategy and planning in higher education. *Human Resource Planning.*

Walker, J. W. (1978). Linking human resource planning and strategic planning. *Human Resource Planning, 1*, 1–18.

Walker, J. W. (1986). Moving closer to the top. *Personnel Administrator, 31*, 52–57 & 117.

Strategic Staffing and Management Succession

Allen, P., Panian, S., & Lotz, R. (1979). Managerial succession and organizational performance: A recalcitrant problem revisited. *Administrative Science Quarterly, 24*, 167–180.

Bartunek, J. M., & Louis, M. R. (1988). The design of work environments to stretch managers' capacities for complex thinking. *Human Resource Planning, 11*, 13–22.

Borucki, C. C., & Lafley, A. F. (1984). Strategic staffing at Chase Manhattan Bank. In C. J. Fombrun, N. M. Tichy, & M. A. Devanna (Eds.), *Strategic human resource management* (pp. 69–86). New York: Wiley.

Bowman, E. H. (1986). Concerns of the CEO. *Human Resource Management, 25*, 267–285.

Brady, G. F., Fulmer, R. M., & Helmich, D. L. (1982). Planning executive succession. The effect of recruitment source and organizational problems on anticipated tenure. *Strategic Management Journal, 3*, 169–175.

Brittain, J., & Freeman, J. H. (1980). Organizational proliferation and density dependent selection: Organizational evolution in the semiconductor industry. In J. Kimberly & R. Miles (Eds.), *The organizational life cycle* (pp. 291–341). San Francisco: Jossey-Bass.

Brown, M. C. (1982). Administrative succession and organizational performance: The succession effect. *Administrative Science Quarterly, 27*, 1–16.

Carroll, G. R. (1984). Dynamics of publisher succession in newspaper organizations. *Administrative Science Quarterly, 29*, 93–113.

Channon, D. (1979). Leadership and corporate performance in the service industries. *Journal of Management Studies, 16*, 185–201.

Child, J. (1974). Managerial and organizational factors associated with company performance. *Journal of Management Studies, 11*, 13–27.

Cowherd, D. M. (1986). On executive succession: A conversation with Lester B. Korn. *Human Resource Management, 25*, 335–347.

Dalton, D. R., & Kesner, I. F. (1983). Inside/outside succession and organizational size: The pragmatics of executive replacement. *Academy of Management Journal, 26*, 736–742.

Daum, S. M. (1968). Entrepreneurial succession. *Administrative Science Quarterly, 13*, 401–416.

DeLuca, J. D. (1988). Strategic career management in non-growing, volatile business environments. *Human Resource Management, 11*, 49–62.

Eitzen, D. S., & Yetman, N. R. (1972). Managerial change, longevity and organizational effectiveness. *Administrative Science Quarterly, 17*, 110–116.

Friedman, S. D. (1986). Succession systems in large corporations: Characteristics and correlates of performance. *Human Resource Management, 25*, 191–214.

Friedman, S. D., & Singh, H. (1986). *Why he left: An explanation for the succession effect.* Paper presented at the Academy of Management, 46th annual national meeting, Chicago.

Gamson, W. A., & Scotch, N. A. (1964). Scapegoating in baseball. *American Journal of Sociology, 70*, 69–72.

Gerstein, M., & Reisman, H. (1983). Strategic selection: Matching executives to business conditions. *Sloan Management Review, 24*(Winter), 33–49.

Goldman, M., & Fraas, M. (1965). The effects of leader selection on group performance. *Sociometry, 28,* 82–88.

Gordon, G. E., & Rosen, N. (1981). Critical factors in leadership succession. *Organization Behavior and Human Performance, 27,* 227–254.

Grimm, C. M., & Smith, K. G. (1986). *The organization as a reflection of its top managers.* Paper presented at the Academy of Management, 46th annual national meeting, Chicago.

Grusky, O. (1960). Administrative succession in formal organizations. *Social Forces, 39,* 105–115.

Grusky, O. (1961). Corporate size, bureaucratization, and managerial succession. *American Journal of Sociology, 67,* 261–269.

Grusky, O. (1963). Managerial succession and organizational effectiveness. *American Journal of Sociology, 69,* 21–31.

Grusky, O. (1969). Succession with an ally. *Administrative Science Quarterly, 14,* 155–170.

Guest, R. (1962). Managerial succession in complex organizations. *American Journal of Sociology, 68,* 47–56.

Gupta, A. K., & Govindarajan, V. (1984). Business unit strategy, managerial characteristics, and business unit effectiveness at strategy implementation. *Academy of Management Journal, 27,* 25–41.

Gupta, A. K. (1984). Contingency linkages between strategy and general manager characteristics: A conceptual examination. *Academy of Management Review, 9,* 399–412.

Gupta, A. K. (1986). Matching managers to strategies: Point and counterpoint. *Human Resource Management, 25,* 215–234.

Hall, D. T. (1986). Dilemmas in linking succession planning to individual executive learning. *Human Resource Management, 25,* 267–185.

Hambrick, D. C., & Mason, P. A. (1984). Upper echelons: The organization as a reflection of its top managers. *Academy of Management Review, 9,* 193–206.

Hambrick, D. C., & Mason, P. A. (1982). The organization as a reflection of its top managers. *Proceedings of the 42nd Annual Meeting of the Academy of Management.* New York, pp. 12–16.

Helmich, D. (1977). Executive succession in the corporate organization: A current integration. *Academy of Management Review, 2,* 252–266.

Helmich, D. (1974). Organizational growth and succession patterns. *Academy of Management Journal, 17*, 771–775.

Helmich, D. L., & Brown, W. B. (1972). Successor type and organizational change in the corporate enterprise. *Administrative Science Quarterly, 17*, 371–381.

Helmich, D. L. (1978). Leader flows and organizational process. *Academy of Management Journal, 21*, 463–478.

Helmich, D. L. (1980). Board size variation and rates of succession in the corporate presidency. *Journal of Business Research, 8*, 51–63.

Kazanjian, R. K., & Drazin, R. (1984). Implementing manufacturing innovations: Critical choices of structure and staffing roles. *Human Resource Management, 25*, 385–403.

Kerr, J. (1982). Assigning managers on the basis of the life cycle. *Journal of Business Strategy, 2*, 58–65.

Kriesberg, L. (1962). Careers, organization size, and succession. *American Journal of Sociology, 68*, 355–359.

Leontiades, M. (1982). Choosing the right manager to fit the strategy. *Journal of Business Strategy, 3*, 58–69.

Lieberson, S., & O'Conner, J. F. (1972). Leadership and organizational performance: A study of large corporations. *American Sociological Review, 37*, 117–130.

Lundberg, C. C. (1986). The dynamic organizational contexts of executive succession: Considerations and challenges. *Human Resource Management, 25*, 287–304.

Mahler, W. R. (1981). Management succession planning: New approaches for the 80s. *Human Resource Planning, 4*, 221–228.

Matching managers to a company's life cycle. *Business Week*, February 23, 1981, p. 30.

Miller, E. (1984). Strategic staffing. In C. J. Fombrun, N. M. Tichy, & M. A. Devanna (Eds.), *Strategic human resource management* (pp. 57–68). New York: Wiley.

Miller, D., Kets de Vries, M. R. R., & Roulouse, J. M. (1982). Top executive locus of control and its relationship to strategy-making, structure, and environment. *Academy of Management Journal, 25*, 237–253.

Olian, J. D., & Rynes, S. L. (1984). Organizational staffing: Integrating practice with strategy. *Industrial Relations, 23*, 170–183.

Osborn, R. N., Jauch, L. R., Martin, T. N., & Glueck, W. F. (1981). The event of CEO succession, performance, and environmental conditions. *Academy of Management Journal, 24,* 183–191.

Perrucci, R., & Mannweiler, R. A. (1968). Organization size, complexity, and administrative succession in higher education. *Sociological Quarterly, 9,* 343–355.

Pfeffer, J., & Leblebici, H. (1973). Executive recruitment and the development of interfirm organizations. *Administrative Science Quarterly, 18,* 449–461.

Pfeffer, J., & Salancik, G. R. (1977). Organizational context and the characteristics and tenure of hospital administrators. *Academy of Management Journal, 20,* 74–88.

Pinfield, L. T., & Morishima, M. (1989). *Relating human resource flow to corporate performance, the external labor market and staffing policy.* Working Paper. Burnaby, B. C., Canada: Simon Fraser University.

Sahl, R. J. (1987). Succession planning - A blue print for your company's future. *Personnel Administrator, 32,* 101–106.

Salancik, G. R., & Pfeffer, J. (1977). Constraints on administrative discretion: The limited influence of mayors on city budgets. *Urban Affairs Quarterly, 12,* 475–498.

Salancik, G. R., & Pfeffer, J. (1980). Effects of ownership and performance on executive tenure in U.S. Corporations. *Academy of Management Journal, 23,* 653–664.

Salancik, G. R., Staw, B. M., & Pondy, L. (1980). Administrative turnover as a response to unmanaged organizational interdependence. *Academy of Management Journal, 23,* 422–437.

Song, J. H. (1982). Diversification strategies and the experience of top executives of large firms. *Strategic Management Journal, 3,* 377–380.

Sonnenfeld, J. A. (1986). Heroes in collision: Chief executive retirement and the parade of future leaders. *Human Resource Management, 25,* 305–333.

Stumpf, S. A. (1988). Choosing career management practices to support your business strategy. *Human Resource Planning, 11,* 33–48.

Stybel, L. J. (1982). Linking strategic planning and management manpower planning. *California Management Review, 25,* 48–56.

Szilagyi, A. D., & Schweiger, D. M. (1984). Matching managers to strategies: A review and suggested framework. *Academy of Management Review, 9,* 626–637.

Trow, D. B. (1961). Executive succession in small companies. *Administrative Science Quarterly, 6,* 182–239.

Vicere, A. A. (1987). Break the mold: Strategies for leadership. *Personnel Journal, 66,* 66–73.

Virany, B., & Tushman, M. L. (1986). *Executive succession: The changing characteristics of top management teams.* Paper presented at the Academy of Management, 46th annual national meeting, Chicago.

Wanted: A manager to fit each strategy. *Business Week,* February 25, 1980, pp. 166–173.

Weiner, N., & Mahoney, T. (1981). A model of corporate performance as a function of environmental, organizational, and leadership influences. *Academy of Management Journal, 24,* 453–470.

Welsh, M. A., & Dehler, G. E. (1986). *The political context and consequences of administrative succession.* Paper presented at the Academy of Management, 46th annual national meeting, Chicago.

Strategic Performance Evaluation and Reward Systems

Balkin, D. (1987). *Compensation strategy in emerging and rapidly growing industries* Paper presented at the Academy of Management, 47th annual national meeting, New Orleans.

Balkin, D. (1988). Compensation strategy for firms in emerging and rapidly growing industries. *Human Resource Planning, 11,* 207–214.

Balkin, D., & Gomez-Mejia, L. R. (1984). Determinants of R and D compensation strategies in high tech industry. *Personnel Psychology, 37,* 635–650.

Balkin, D., & Gomez-Mejia, L. R. (1987). Toward a contingency theory of compensation strategy. *Strategic Management Journal, 8,* 169–182.

Beatty, R. W. (1989). Competitive human resource advantage through the strategic management of performance. *Human Resource Planning, 12(3),* 179–194.

Beatty, R. W., & Schneier, C. E. (1988). Strategic performance appraisal issues. In R. S. Schuler, S. A. Youngblood, & V. L. Huber (Eds.), *Readings in personnel and human resource management* (3rd ed.) (pp. 256–266). St. Paul: West.

Bernardin, H. J. (1989). Increasing the accuracy of performance measurement: A proposed solution to erroneous attributions. *Human Resource Planning, 12(3),* 239–250.

Brindisi, L. J. (1984). Paying for strategic performance: A new executive compensation imperative. In R. B. Lamb (Ed.), *Competitive strategic management* (pp. 333–343). Englewood Cliffs, NJ: Prentice-Hall.

Carroll, S. J. (1988). Handling the need for consistency and the need for contingency in the management of compensation. *Human Resource Planning, 11,* 191–196.

Crystal, G. S., & Hurwich, M. R. (1986). The case for divisional long-term incentives. *California Management Review, 29,* 60–74.

Cummings, L. L. (1984). Compensation, culture, and motivation: A systems perspective. *Organizational Dynamics, 12,* 33–44.

Devanna, M. A. (1984). The executive appraisal. In C. J. Fombrun, N. M. Tichy, & M. A. Devanna (Eds.), *Strategic human resource management* (pp. 101–110). New York: Wiley.

Ellig, B. R. (1983). Pay policies while downsizing the organization: A systematic approach. *Personnel, 60,* 26–35.

Fombrun, C. J., & Laud, R. L. (1983). Strategic issues in performance appraisal: Theory and practice. *Personnel, 60,* 23–31.

Friedman, S. D., & Levino, T. P. (1984). Strategic appraisal and development at General Electric Company. In C. J. Fombrun, N. M. Tichy, & M. A. Devanna (Eds.), *Strategic human resource management* (pp. 183–202). New York: Wiley.

Gomez-Mejia, L. R., & Welbourne, T. M. (1988). Compensation strategy: An overview and future steps. *Human Resource Planning, 11,* 173–190.

Gomez-Mejia, L. R., Tosi, H., & Hinken, T. (1987). Managerial control, performance, and executive compensation. *Academy of Management Journal, 30,* 51–70.

Govincharajan, V., & Gupta, A. K. (1982). *Business unit strategy, reward systems, and business unit performance.* Paper presented at the Academy of Management, 42nd annual national meeting, New York.

Greene, R. J., & Roberts, R. G. (1983). Strategic integration of compensation and benefits. *Personnel Administrator, 28,* 79–82.

Haigh, T. (1989). Organizational performance and the strategic allocation of indirect compensation. *Human Resource Planning, 12(3),* 221–228.

Hoskisson, R. E., Hitt, M. A., Turk, T., & Tyler, B. (1989). Balancing corporate strategy and executive compensation: Agency theory and corporate governance. In G. R. Ferris & K. M. Rowland (Eds.), *Research in personnel and human resources management* (Vol.7). Greenwich, CT: JAI Press.

Hufnagel, E. M. (1987). Developing strategic compensation plans. *Human Resource Management, 26,* 93–108.

Kaye, B., & McKee, K. (1986). New compensation strategies for new career patterns. *Personnel Administrator, 31*, 61–68.

Kerr, J., & Bettis, R. A. (1987). Boards of directors, top management compensation, and shareholder returns. *Academy of Management Journal, 30*, 645–664.

Kerr, J. L. (1985). Diversification strategies and managerial rewards. *Academy of Management Journal, 28*, 155–179.

Kerr, J. L. (1988). Strategic control through performance appraisal and rewards. *Human Resource Planning, 11*, 215–224.

Kerr, J. L., & Slocum, J. W. (1987). Managing corporate culture through reward systems. *Academy of Management Executive, 1*, 99–108.

Kerr, J. L., & Snow, C. C. (1982). *A conceptual model of the reward system design process.* Paper presented at the Academy of Management, 42nd annual national meeting, New York.

Kosnik, R. D., & Bettenhausen, K. L. (1988). *The motivational impact of executive compensation systems in problems of corporate control.* Paper presented at the Academy of Management, 48th annual national meeting, Anaheim.

Latham, G. P. (1984). The appraisal system as a strategic control. In C. J. Fombrun, N. M. Tichy, & M. A. Devanna (Eds.), *Strategic human resource management* (pp. 87–100). New York: Wiley.

Laud, R. L. (1984). Performance appraisal practices in the Fortune 1300. In C. J. Fombrun, N. M. Tichy, & M. A. Devanna (Eds.), *Strategic human resource management* (pp. 111–126). New York: Wiley.

Lawler, E. E., III. (1982). *The strategic design of reward systems* (Technical Report G 82-11 [30]); ONR Contract N-00014-81-K-0048.

Lawler, E. E., III. (1984). The strategic design of reward systems. In C. J. Fombrun, N. M. Tichy, & M. A. Devanna (Eds.), *Strategic human resource management* (pp. 127–148). New York: Wiley

Lewellyn, W., & Huntsman, B. (1970). Managerial pay and corporate performance. *American Economic Review, 60*, 710–720.

McCune, J. T. (1989). Aligning executive total compensation with business strategy. *Human Resource Planning, 12(3)*, 195–204.

McGill, A. R. (1984). Applying rewards and compensation theory to the real world of business: A case study of General Motors Corporation. In C. J. Fombrun, N. M. Tichy, &

M. A. Devanna (Eds.), *Strategic human resource management* (pp. 149–158). New York: Wiley.

Meyer, P. (1983). Executive compensation must promote long-term commitment. *Personnel Administrator, 28*, 37–42.

Migliore, R. H. (1982). Linking strategy, performance, and pay. *The Journal of Business Strategy, 3,* 90–94.

Milkovich, G. T. (1988). A strategic perspective on compensation management. In G. R. Ferris & K. M. Rowland (Eds.), *Research in personnel and human resources management* (Vol. 6, pp. 263–288). Greenwich, CT: JAI Press.

Muczyk, J. P. (1988). The strategic role of compensation. *Human Resource Planning, 11,* 197–206.

Murthy, K. R., & Salter, M. S. (1975). Should CEO pay be linked to results? *Harvard Business Review* (May-June), 66–73.

Napier, N. K., & Smith, M. (1987). Product diversification, performance criteria, and compensation at the corporate manager level. *Strategic Management Journal, 8,* 195–201.

Newman, J. M. (1988). Compensation strategy in declining industries. *Human Resource Planning, 11,* 197–206.

Pitts, R. A. (1974). Incentive compensation and organization design. *Personnel Journal, 53,* 338–348.

Rajagopolan, N., & Prescott, J. E. (1988). *Economic, behavioral, and strategic determinants of top management compensation.* Paper presented at the Academy of Management, 48th annual national meeting, Anaheim.

Salschieder, J. (1981). Devising pay strategies for diversified companies, *Compensation Review,* 5–24.

Salter, M. S. (1973). Tailor incentive compensation to strategy. *Harvard Business Review,* (July-August), 81–88.

Schneier, C. E. (1989). Implementing performance management and recognition and rewards (PMRR) systems at the strategic level: A line management-driven effort. *Human Resource Planning, 12(3),* 205–220.

Spratt, M. F., & Steele, B., (1985). Rewarding key contributors. *Compensation and Benefits Review, 17,* 24–37.

Stonich, P. J. (1981). Using rewards in implementing strategy. *Strategic Management Journal, 2,* 345–352.

Stonich, P. J. (1984). The performance measurement and reward system: Critical to strategic management. *Organizational Dynamics, 12,* 45–57.

Strata, R., & Maidique, M. A. (1980). Bonus system for balanced strategy. *Harvard Business Review, 58,* 15–24.

Terborg, J. R., & Ungson, G. R. (1983). *Strategic policy and management compensation: A longitudinal study of bonus pay and unit performance.* Paper presented at the Academy of Management, 43rd annual national meeting, Dallas.

Todd, J. (1981). Management control systems: A key link between strategy, structure, and employee performance. In M. Jelinek, J. Litterer, & R. Miles (Eds.), *Organization by design* (pp. 474–487). Plano, TX: Business Publications, Inc.

Tomasko, R. M. (1982). Focusing company reward systems to help achieve business objectives. *Management Review, 71,* 8–18.

Von Glinow, M. A. (1985). Reward strategies for attracting, evaluating, and retraining professionals. *Human Resource Management, 24,* 191–206.

Strategic Human Resources Development and Careers

Abelson, M. A., Ferris, G. R., & Urban, T. F. (1988). Human resource development and employee mobility. In R. S. Schuler S. A. Youngblood, & V. Huber (Eds.), *Readings in personnel and human resource management* (3rd ed.) (pp. 320–329). St. Paul, MN: West.

Caldwell, P. (1984). Cultivating human potential at Ford. *The Journal of Business Strategy, 4,* 74–77.

Conroy, W. G. (1980). Human resource development: The private sector's role in public policy. *Sloan Management Review, 22,* 63–70.

De Luca, J. R. (1988). Strategic career management in non-growing, volatile business environments. *Human Resource Planning, 11,* 49–62.

Fandt, P. M. (1988). Linking business strategy and career management: An integrative framework. In G. R. Ferris & K. M. Rowland (Eds.), *Human resources management: Perspectives and issues* (pp. 56–63). Boston: Allyn and Bacon.

Hall, D. T. (1984). Human resource development and organizational effectiveness. In C. J. Fombrun, N. M. Tichy, & M. A. Devanna (Eds.), *Strategic human resource management* (pp. 159–182). New York: Wiley.

Hall, D. T. (1985). Project work as an antidote to career plateauing in a declining engineering organization. *Human Resource Management, 24*, 271–292.

Harvey, L. J. (1983). Effective planning for human resource development. *Personnel Administrator, 28*, 45–52, 112.

Jackson, T., & Vitberg, A. (1987). Career development, part 1: Careers and entrepreneurship. *Personnel, 64*, 12–17.

Jackson, T., & Vitberg, A. (1987). Career development, part 2: Challenges for the organization. *Personnel, 64*, 68–72.

Jackson, T., & Vitberg, A. (1987). Career development, part 3: Challenges for the individuals. *Personnel, 64*, 54–57.

Linkow, P., (1985). HRD at the roots of corporate strategy. *Training and Development Journal, 39*(May), 85–87.

London, M. (1988). Organizational support for employees' career motivation: A guide to human resource strategies in changing business conditions. *Human Resource Planning, 11*, 23–32.

Slocum, J. W., Cron, W. L., Hansen, R. W., & Rawlings, S. (1985), Business strategy and the management of plateaued employees. *Academy of Management Journal, 28*, 133–154.

Sparrow, P. R., & Pettigrew, A. M. (1987). Britains's training problems: The search for a strategic human resources management approach. *Human Resource Management, 26*, 109–127.

Stumpf, S. A. & Hanrahan, N. M. (1984). Designing organizational career management practices to fit strategic management objectives. In R. S. Schuler & S. A. Youngblood (Eds.), *Readings in personnel and human resource management* (2nd ed., pp. 326–348). St. Paul, MN: West.

Stumpf, S. A. (1988). Choosing career management practices to support your business strategy. *Human Resource Planning, 11*, 33–48.

Sweet, J. (1981). How manpower development can support your strategic plan. *The Journal of Business Strategy, 2*, 77–81.

Viner, L. (1983). Applying strategic planning in human resource development. *Training and Development Journal* (November), 81–84.

Wissema, J. G., Brand, A. F., & Van Der Pol, H. W. (1981). The incorporation of management development in strategic management. *Strategic Management Journal*, *2*, 361–377.

Strategic Labor Relations

Christiansen, E. T. (1983). Strategy, structure, and labor relations performance. *Human Resource Management*, *22*, 155–168.

Christiansen, E. T. (1987). Challenges in the management of diversified companies: The changing face of corporate labor relations. *Human Resource Management*, *26*, 363–383.

Fossum, J. A. (1984). Strategic issues in labor relations. In C. J. Fombrun, N. M. Tichy, & M. A. Devanna (Eds.), *Strategic human resource management* (pp. 343–360). New York: Wiley.

Goodman, J. P., & Sanberg, W. R. (1981). A contingency approach to labor relations strategies. *Academy of Management Review*, *6*, 145–154.

Kochan, T. A., McKersie, R. B., & Cappelli, P. (1984). Strategic choice and industrial relations theory. *Industrial Relations*, *23*, 16–39.

Lewin, D. (1987). Industrial relations as a strategic variable. In M. M. Kleiner, R. N. Block, M. Roomkin, & S. W. Salsbug (Eds.), *Human resources and the performance of the firm* (pp. 1–43). Madison, WI: Industrial Relations Research Association.

Miller, P. (1987). Strategic industrial relations and human resource management - distinction, definition and recognition. *Journal of Management Studies*, *24*, 347–361.

Mills, D. Q. (1983). When employees make concessions. *Harvard Business Review*, *61*, 103–113,

Schuler, R. S. (1986). *Strategic human resource management and industrial relations.* Unpublished manuscript, Graduate School of Business, New York University.

Schuster, M. (1984). Cooperation and change in union settings: Problems and opportunities. *Human Resource Management*, *23*, 145–160.

Sisson, K., & Sullivan, T. (1987). [editorial] Management strategy and industrial relations. *Journal of Management Studies*, *24*, 427–432.

Stratton, K., & Brown, R. B. (1989). Strategic planning in U.S. labor unions. In B. D. Dennis (Ed.), *Proceedings of the Forty-First Annual Meeting.* Madison, WI: Industrial Relations Research Association.

Stratton, K., & Reshef, Y. (1989). Private sector unions and strategic planning: A research agenda. Working paper, Edmonton, Alberta, Canada: University of Alberta.

Wheeler, H. N. (1989). Trade unions and takeovers: Labor's response to mergers and acquisitions. *Human Resource Planning, 12,* 167–177.

Strategic Human Resources Management and Organizational Exit

Abelson, M. A., Ferris, G. R., & Urban, T. F. (1988). Human resource development and employee mobility. In R. S. Schuler, S. A. Youngblood, & V. Huber (Eds.), *Readings in personnel and human resource management* (3rd ed.) (pp. 320–329). St. Paul, MN: West.

Barton, E. J. (1986). *Layoffs and effective management.* Paper presented at the Academy of Management, 46th annual national meeting, Chicago.

Bishchoff, C. F. (1986). *Management of the survivors of workforce reductions.* Paper presented at the Academy of Management, 46th annual national meeting, Chicago.

Howard, C. G. (1988). Strategic guidelines for terminating employees. *Personnel Administration, 33,* 106–109.

Ladhams, A. (1986). *Observations on the effect of layoffs at Polaroid corporation.* Paper presented at the Academy of Management, 46th annual national meeting, Chicago.

Martin, D. C., & Bartol, K. M. (1985). Managing turnover strategically. *Personnel Administrator, 30,* 63–73.

Mowday, R. T. (1984). Strategies for adapting to high rates of employee turnover. *Human Resource Management, 23,* 365–380.

Reed, T. F., & Brockner, J. (1986). *Factors moderating the impact of layoffs on survivors: A field study.* Paper presented at the Academy of Management, 46th annual national meeting, Chicago.

Rosen, B., & Jerdee, T. H. (1986). Retirement policies for the 21st century. *Human Resource Management, 25,* 405–420.

Rufe, J. H. (1986). *The impact of significant workforce downsizing on those who remain.* Paper presented at the Academy of Management, 46th annual national meeting, Chicago.

Watts, P. (1987). Preretirement planning: Making the golden years rosy. *Personnel, 64,* 32–39.

Strategic Human Resources Management Under Conditions of Growth, Diversification, Innovation, or Merger and Acquisition

Barrett, M. L. (1973). *The human implications of mergers and takeovers.* London: Institute of Personnel Management.

Bastien, D. T. (1987). Common patterns of behavior and communication in corporate mergers and acquisition. *Human Resource Management, 26,* 17–33.

Bennett, A. (1986). After the merger, more CEOs left in uneasy spot: Looking for work. *Wall Street Journal,* (August 27), p. 16.

Berney, E. J. (1986). *An intergroup perspective to understanding organizational practices contributing to acquisition failure.* Paper presented at the Academy of Management, 46th annual national meeting, Chicago.

Blake, R., & Mouton, J. (1985). How to achieve integration on the human side of the merger. *Organizational Dynamics, 13,* 41–56.

Boland, J. R. (1970). Merger planning: How much weight do personnel factors carry? *Personnel, 47,* 8–13.

Bradley, J. W., & Korn, D. H. (1979). Acquisitions and mergers: A shifting route to corporate growth. *Management Review* (March), 46–51.

Buono, A. F., & Bowditch, J. L. (1989). *The human side of mergers and acquisitions.* San Francisco: Jossey Bass.

Clarkson, W. M. E., & Mirvis, P. H. (1986). *Coping with a conglomerate acquisition.* Paper presented at the Academy of Management, 46th annual national meeting, Chicago.

Conway, M. A. (1986). Mergers and acquisitions, 3: Ten pitfalls of joint ventures. *Personnel, 63*(9), 50–51.

Crandall, R. E. (1987). Company life cycles: The effects of growth on structure and personnel. *Personnel, 64,* 28–36.

Fulmer, R. M. (1986). Mergers and acquisitions, 2: Role of management development. *Personnel, 63*(9), 37–49.

Galbraith, J. R. (1984). Human resource policies for the innovating organization. In C. J. Fombrun, N. M. Tichy, & M. A. Devanna (Eds.), *Strategic human resource management* (pp. 319–342). New York: Wiley.

Galbraith, J. R. (1984). Designing the innovation organization. In R. B. Lamb (Ed.), *Competitive strategic management* (pp. 297–318). Englewood Cliffs, NJ: Prentice-Hall.

Gridley, J. D. (1986). Mergers and acquisitions, 1: Premerger human resources planning. *Personnel, 63*(9), 28–36.

Hayes, R. H. (1979). The human side of acquisitions. *Management Review, 68,* 41–46.

Ivancevich, J. M., & Stewart, K. A. (1989). Appraising management talent in acquired organizations: A four tiered recommendation. *Human Resource Planning, 12,* 141–154.

Kotter, J., & Sathe, V. (1978). Problems of human resource management in rapidly growing companies. *California Management Review, 21,* 29–36.

Leana, C. R., & Feldman, D. C. (1989). When mergers force layoffs: Some lessons about managing the human resource problems. *Human Resource Planning, 12,* 123–140.

Levin, D. P. (1984). Fearing takeover of Gulf Oil, employees showing myriad symptoms of stress. *Wall Street Journal* (February 28), p. 35.

Levinson, H. (1970). A psychologist diagnoses merger failures. *Harvard Business Review, 48,* 138–147.

Marks, M. L. (1982). Merging human resources: A review of current research. *Mergers & Acquisitions, 17,* 38–44.

Marks, M. L., & Cutcliffe, J. (1986). *Debunking merger mythology: interventions to facilitate post-merger integration.* Paper presented at the Academy of Management, 46th annual national meeting, Chicago.

Marks, M. L. & Mirvis, P. H. (1986). The merger syndrome. *Psychology Today, 20,* 36–42.

Marks, M. L. & Mirvis, P. H. (1985). Merger syndrome: Stress and uncertainty. *Mergers & Acquisitions, 20,* 50–55.

Mirvis, P. H., & Marks, M. L. (1985). Merger syndrome: Management by crisis. *Mergers & Acquisitions, 20,* 70–76.

McMillan, J. D., & Reisinger, G. (1983). Takeover protection for executives: The "golden parachute." *Compensation Review, 15,* 34–43.

Merrell, D. W. (1985). Playing hardball on a mergers and acquisitions team. *Personnel, 62*(10), 22–27.

Miller, J. R. (1984). Revitalization: The most difficult of all strategies. *Human Resource Management, 23,* 293–314.

Napier, N. K. (1987). *Links between mergers and acquisitions and human resources management: A review and directions for researchers and managers.* Paper presented at the Western Academy of Management, Hollywood, CA.

Napier, N. K. (1989). Mergers and acquisitions, human resource issues and outcomes: A review and suggested typology. *Journal of Management Studies, 26,* 271–289.

Napier, N. K., Schweiger, D. M., & Csiszar, E. (1989). *A model for implementing international mergers and acquisitions.* Strategic Management Society Conference on the Wave of Mergers, Acquisitions, and Alliances, Paris.

Napier, N. K., Simmons, G., & Stratton, K. (1989). Communications during a merger: Experience of two banks. *Human Resource Planning, 12,* 105–122..

Nienstedt, P. R. (1989). Effectively downsizing management structures. *Human Resource Planning, 12,* 155–165.

Rentsch, J. R. (1986). *Expectations for mergers and acquisitions.* Paper presented at the Academy of Management, 46th annual national meeting, Chicago.

Robino, D., & De Meuse, K. (1985). Corporate mergers and acquisitions: Their impact on HRM. *Personnel Administrator* (November), 33–44.

Schweiger, D. L., & Ivancevich, J. M. (1985). Human resources: The forgotten factor in mergers and acquisitions. *Personnel Administrator, 30,* 47–61.

Schweiger, D. M., Ivancevich, J. M., & Power, F. R. (1987). Executive actions for managing human resources before and after acquisition. *Academy of Management Executive, 1,* 127–138.

Schweiger, D. M., & Weber, Y. (1989). Strategies for managing human resources during mergers and acquisitions: An empirical investigation. *Human Resource Planning, 12,* 69–86.

Shirley, R. C. (1977). The human side of merger planning. *Long Range Planning, 10,* 35–39.

Siehl, C. J., Ledford, G. E., & Siehl, J. (1986). *Strategies for managing post-merger integration.* Paper presented at the Academy of Management, 46th annual national meeting, Chicago.

Sinetar, M. (1981). Mergers, morale, and productivity. *Personnel Journal, 60,* 863–867.

Silverman, R., & Fay, P. (1986). *Managing cultural differences in mergers and acquisitions: Role of the human resource function.* Paper presented at the Academy of Management, 46th annual national meeting, Chicago.

Swain, R. W. (1985). Mergers - The personnel squeeze. *Personnel Journal* (April), 34–40.

Ulrich, D., Cody, T., LaFasto, F., & Rucci, T. (1989). Human resources at Baxter Healthcare Corporation: A strategic partner role. *Human Resource Planning, 12,* 87–103.

Strategic Human Resources Management
Under Conditions of Decline and Downsizing

Ferris, G. R., Schellenberg, D. A., & Zammuto, R. F. (1984). Human resource management strategies in declining industries. *Human Resource Management, 22,* 381–394.

Gilmore, T. N., & Hirschborn, L. (1984). Managing human resources in a declining context. In C. J. Fombrun, N. M. Tichy, & M. A. Devanna (Eds.), *Strategic human resource management* (pp. 297–318). New York: Wiley.

Greenhalgh, L. (1983). Managing the job insecurity. *Human Resource Management, 22,* 431–444.

Greenhalgh, L., Lawrence, A. T., & Sutton, R. I. (1986). *The determinants of workforce reduction strategies in declining organizations: A framework for analysis.* Paper presented at the Academy of Management, 46th annual national meeting, Chicago.

Greenhalgh, L., Lawrence, A. T., & Sutton, R. I. (1988). Determinants of work force reduction strategies in declining organizations. *Academy of Management Review, 13,* 241–254.

Mohrman, S. A., & Mohrman, A. M. (1983). Employee involvement in declining organizations. *Human Resource Management, 22,* 445–465.

Moore, P. (1985). The problems and prospects of cutback management. *Personnel Administrator, 30,* 91–96.

Perry, L. T. (1984). Key human resource strategies in an organization downturn. *Human Resource Management, 23,* 61–76.

Price, R. H., & D'Aunno, T. (1983). Managing work force reduction. *Human Resource Management, 22,* 413–430.

Ropp, K. (1987). Downsizing strategies. *Personnel Administrator, 32,* 61–64.

Silverthorne, C. P. (1987). Planning for a smaller organization: A guide for HR managers. *Personnel, 64,* 60–66.

Smith Cook, D., & Ferris, G. R. (1986). Strategic human resource management and firm effectiveness in industries experiencing decline. *Human Resource Management, 25,* 441–458.

Sharplin, A. D., & Wall, J. L. (1985). Serving HRM purposes through Chapter 11? *Personnel Administrator, 30*(2,) 103–111.

International Strategic Human Resources Management

Adler, N. J., & Jelinek, M. (1986). Is "organization culture" culture bound? *Human Resource Management, 25,* 73–90.

Baker, J. C., & Ivancevich, J. M. (1971). The assignment of American executives abroad: Systematic, haphazard, or chaotic? *California Management Review, 13,* 39–44.

Blue, J. L., & Haynes, U. (1977). Preparation for the overseas assignment. *Business Horizons, 20,* 61–67.

Brooks, B. J. (1985). Long-term incentives for the foreign-based executive. *Compensation and Benefits Review, 17,* 46–53.

Copeland, L. (1985). Cross-cultural training: The competitive edge. *Training, 22,* 49–53.

Derr, C. B. (1986). *Managing high-potential employees in European firms.* Paper presented at the Academy of Management, 46th annual national meeting, Chicago.

Desatnick, R. L., & Bennett, M. L. (1978). *Human resource management in the multinational company.* New York: Nichols.

Doz, Y., & Prahalad, C. K. (1986). Controlled variety: A challenge for human resource management in the MNC. *Human Resource Management, 25,* 55–71.

Edstrom, A., & Galbraith, J. (1977). Alternative policies for international transfer of managers. *Management International Review, 17,* 11–22.

Edstrom, A., & Galbraith, J. (1977). Transfer of managers as a coordination and control strategy in multinational organizations. *Administrative Science Quarterly, 22,* 248–263.

English, D. (1986). *Labor negotiations strategies in a Japanese company.* Paper presented at the Academy of Management, 46th annual national meeting, Chicago.

Evans, P. A. L. (1984). *Conceptions of human resource management: A comparative assessment.* Working paper INSEAD, Fountainebleau, France.

Evans, P. A. L. (1984). On the importance of a generalist conception of human resource management: A cross-national look. *Human Resource Management, 23,* 347–364.

Evans, P. A. L. (1986). The strategic outcomes of human resource management. *Human Resource Management, 25,* 149–167.

Ferris, G. R., Rowland, K. M., & Nedd, A. N. B. (Eds.) (1989). *International human resources management, Supplement Volume 1, Research in personnel and human resources management.* Greenwich, CT: JAI Press.

Fombrun, C. J. (1986). *International growth strategy and human resource management: An exploratory analysis.* Paper presented at the Academy of Management, 46th annual national meeting, Chicago.

Gajek, M., & Sabo, M. M. (1986). The bottom line: What HR managers need to know about the new expatriate regulations. *Personnel Administrator, 31,* 87–92.

Galbraith, J. R., & Kazanjian, R. K. (1986). Organizing to implement strategies of diversity and globalization: The role of matrix designs. *Human Resource Management, 25,* 37–54.

Gerpott, T. J., & Domsch, M. (1985). The concept of professionalism and the management of salaried technical professionals: A cross-national perspective. *Human Resource Management, 24,* 207–226.

Gomez-Mejia, L. R. (1988). The role of human resources strategy in export performance: A longitudinal study. *Strategic Management Journal, 9,* 493–506.

Hanada, M. (1986). *Organizational commitment of Japanese workers: Impact of its changes on human resources management practices.* Paper presented at the Academy of Management, 46th Annual National Meeting, Chicago.

Hays, R. D. (1974). Expatriate selection: Insuring success and avoiding failure. *Journal of International Business Studies, 5,* 25–37.

Heenan, D. A., & Perlmutter, H. V. (1978). *Multinational organization development.* Reading, MA: Addison-Wesley.

Heller, J. E. (1980). Criteria for selecting an international manager. *Personnel, 57,* 47–55.

Hixon, A. L. (1986). Why corporations make haphazard overseas staffing decisions. *Personnel Administrator, 31,* 91–94.

Hofstede, G. (1983). The cultural relatively of organizational practices and theories. *Journal of International Business Studies, 14,* 75–89.

Ishida, H. (1986). Transferability of Japanese human resource management abroad. *Human Resource Management, 25,* 103–120.

Jaeger, A. M. (1986). Organization development and national culture: Where's the fit? *Academy of Management Review, 11,* 178–190.

Jenner, S. R. (1986). *Perceived similarity, identification with organizational objectives and values, and commitment of U.S. managers in Japanese subsidiaries.* Paper presented at the Academy of Management, 46th annual national meeting, Chicago.

Kaminski, M., M., & Paiz, J. (1984). Japanese women in management: Where are they? *Human Resource Management, 23,* 277–292.

Kendall, C. W. (1981). Repatriation: An ending and a beginning. *Business Horizons, 24,* 21–25.

Kumar, B. N., & Steinman, H. (1986). *Management conflicts between expatriate and local executives in German and Japanese firms.* Paper presented at the Academy of Management, 46th annual national meeting, Chicago.

Latham, G. P., & Napier, N. K. (1989). Chinese human resource management practices in Hong Kong and Singapore. In. G. R. Ferris, K. M. Rowland, & A. Nedd (Eds.), *International human resources management* (pp. 173–199). Greenwich, CT: JAI Press.

Laurent, A. (1986). The cross-cultural puzzle of international human resource management. *Human Resource Management, 25,* 91–102.

Lorange, P. (1986). Human resource management in multinational cooperative ventures. *Human Resource Management, 25,* 133–148.

Mendenhall, M. & Oddou, G. (1985). The dimensions of expatriate acculturation: A review. *Academy of Management Review, 10,* 39–47.

Miller, E. L. (1986). *Comparative management research on human resource management: Implications for strategy formulation.* Paper presented at the Academy of Management, 46th annual national meeting, Chicago.

Mroczkowski, T. (1983). *Japanese and European systems of industrial relations—which model is more applicable for the U.S.?* Paper presented at the American International Business Conference.

Murray, F. T., & Murray, A. H. (1986). Global managers for global businesses. *Sloan Management Review, 27,* 75–80.

Napier, N. K. (1986). Diversification strategy, performance criteria, and compensation for top managers in U.S. and Japan. *Proceedings of the Academy of Management* (pp. 97–101), 46th annual national meeting, Chicago.

Newman, J., Bhatt, B. & Gutteridge, T. (1978). Determinants of expatriate effectiveness: A theoretical and empirical vacuum. *Academy of Management Review, 4,* 655–661.

Ondrack, D. A. (1985). International transfers of managers in North American and European MNEs. *Journal of International Business Studies, 16,* 1–19.

Pazy, A., & Zeira, Y. (1983). Training parent country professionals in host country organizations. *Academy of Management Review, 8,* 262–272.

Pinney, D. L. (1982). Structuring an expatriate tax reimbursement program. *Personnel Administrator, 27,* 19–25.

Pucik, V. (1984). The international management of human resources. In. C. J. Fombrun, N. M. Tichy, & M. A. Devanna (Eds.), *Strategic human resource management,* (pp. 403–419). New York: Wiley.

Pucik, V. (1984). White-collar human resource management in large Japanese manufacturing firms. *Human Resource Management, 23,* 252–276.

Pucik, V., & Katz, J. H. (1986). Information, control, and human resource management in multinational firms. *Human Resource Management, 25,* 121–132.

Pulatie, D. (1985). Comment on how do you ensure success of managers going abroad? *Training and Development Journal, 39,* 22–23.

Raffael, C. (1982). How to pick expatriates. *Management Today, 85*(April), 59–62.

Rahim, A. (1983). A model for developing key expatriate executives. *Personnel Journal, 62,* 312–317.

Schermerhorn, J. R., Bussom, R. S., Elasid, H. & Wilson, H. K. (1982). *Interorganizational contingencies affecting management training activities in developing countries.* Paper presented at the Academy of International Business.

Shenkar, O., & Zeira, Y. (1987). Human resource management in international joint ventures: Directors for research. *Academy of Management Review, 12,* 546–557.

Stern, J. H. (1986). *Sony's approach to human resource management in the United States.* Paper presented at the Academy of Management, 46th annual national meeting, Chicago.

Teague, B. W. (1972). *Compensating key personnel overseas.* New York: The Conference Board.

Torbiorn, I. (1982). *Living abroad: Personal adjustment and personnel policy in the overseas setting.* New York: Wiley.

Toyne, B., & Kuhne, B. J. (1983). The management of the international executive compensation and benefits process. *Journal of International Business Studies, 14,* 37–50.

Tung, R. L. (1984). Strategic management of human resources in the multinational enterprise. *Human Resource Management, 23,* 129–144.

Tung, R. L. (1981). Selection and training of personnel for overseas assignments. *Columbia Journal of World Business, 16,* 68–78.

Tung, R. L. (1982). Selection and training procedures of U.S., European, and Japanese multinationals. *California Management Review, 25,* 57–71.

Zeira, Y. (1976). Management development in ethnocentric multinational corporations. *California Management Review, 18,* 34–42.

Zeira, Y., & Banai, M. (1984). Present and desired methods of selecting expatriate managers for international assignments. *Personnel Review, 13,* 29–35.

Zeira, Y., & Pazy, A. (1985). Crossing national borders to get trained. *Training and Development Journal, 29,* 53–57.

Context, Culture, and Strategy

Adler, N. J., & Jewlinek, M. (1986). Is "organizational culture" culture bound? *Human Resource Management, 25,* 73–90.

Davis, S. M. (1983). Corporate culture and human resource management: Two keys to implementing strategy. *Human Resource Planning, 6,* 159–168.

Dimick, D. E., & Murray, V. V. (1978). Correlates of substantive policy decisions in organizations: The case of human resource management. *Academy of Management Journal, 21,* 611–623.

Fombrun, C. J. (1984). The external context of human resource management. In C. J. Fumbrun, N. M. Tichy, & M. A. Devanna (Eds.), *Strategic human resource management* (pp. 3–18). New York: Wiley.

Fombrun, C. J. (1984). Corporate culture and competitive strategy. In C. J. Fombrun, N. M. Tichy, & M. A. Devanna (Eds.), *Strategic human resource management* (pp. 203–216). New York: Wiley.

Fombrun, C. J. (1983). Corporate culture, environment, and strategy. *Human Resource Management, 22,* 139–152.

Fombrun, C. J. (1982). Environmental trends create new pressures on human resources. *Journal of Business Strategy, 3,* 61–69.

Harris, S. (1984). Hewlett-Packard: Shaping the corporate culture. In C. J. Fombrun, N. M. Tichy, & M. A. Devanna (Eds.), *Strategic human resource management* (pp. 217–234). New York: Wiley.

La Belle, C. M. (1983). *Human resources strategic decisions as responses to environmental challenges.* Unpublished master's thesis, Cornell University.

Murray, V. V., & Dimick, D. E. (1978). Contextual influences on personnel policies and programs: An exploratory model. *Academy of Management Review , 3*, 750–761.

Posner, B. Z., Kouzes, J. M. & Schmidt, W. H. (1985). Shared values make a difference: An empirical test of corporate culture. *Human Resource Management, 24*, 293–310.

Schwartz, H., & Davis, S. M. (1981). Matching corporate culture and business strategy. *Organizational Dynamics, 9*, 30–48.

Snell, S. A. (1988). *The relationship of organizational context to human resource management: An empirical test of management control theory.* Paper presented a the Academy of Management, 48th annual national meeting, Anaheim.

Solberg, S. (1985). Changing culture through ceremony: An example from GM. *Human Resource Management, 24*, 329–340.

Tichy, N. M., Fombrun, C. J., & Devanna, M. A. (1984). The organizational context of strategic human resource management. In C. J. Fombrun, N. M. Tichy, & M. A. Devanna (Eds.), *Strategic human resource management* (pp. 19–32). New York: Wiley.

Ulrich, W. L. (1984). HRM and culture: History, ritual, and myth. *Human Resource Management, 23*, 117–128.

Wilkins, A. L. (1984). The creation of company cultures: The role of stories and human resource systems. *Human Resource Management, 23*, 41–60.

BIBLIOGRAPHY

———(1981). Matching managers to a company's life cycle. *Business Week*, February 23, p. 30.

———(1984). Why Gulf lost its fight for life. *Business Week*, March, 19, pp. 76–81.

———(1984). How the new merger boom will benefit the economy. *Business Week*, 21 March, pp. 122–126.

———(1984). New formula to restore glow. *Business Week*, July 2, 15 & 4, p. 7.

———(1985). After the merger. *The Wall Street Journal*, 21 October, p. 25.

———(1985). Do mergers really work? *Business Week*, 3 June, pp. 88–100.

———(1987). Competitiveness survey: HBR readers respond. *Harvard Business Review, 65*(5), 8–12.

———(1988). The secondary boycott gets a second wind. *Business Week*, 27 June, p. 82.

Abelson. M. A., Ferris, G. R., & Urban, T. F. (1988). Human resource development and employee mobility. In R. S. Schuler, S. A. Youngblood & V. L. Huber (Eds.), *Readings in personnel and human resource management* (3rd Ed., pp. 320–329). St. Paul, MN: West.

Abernathy, W. J. (1978). *The productivity dilemma*. Baltimore: The John Hopkins University Press.

Adams, W. R., & Shea, M. B. (1986). Structuring the organization after a merger. *The Bankers Magazine, 169*(1), pp. 40–44.

Adler, N. J. (1983). Cross-cultural management research: The ostrich and the trend. *Academy of Management Review, 8*, 226–232.

Adler, N. J. (1983). A typology of management studies involving culture. *Journal of International Business Studies, 14*(2), 29–47.

Adler, N. J. (1984). Women do not want international careers and other myths about international management. *Organizational Dynamics, 13*(2), 66–79.

Adler, N. J., & Jelinek, M. (1986). Is "organization culture" culture bound? *Human Resource Management, 25*, 73–90.

Aesop, (1973). *Aesop's Fables.* New York: Arenel Books.

Albro, W. L. (1922). Personnel administration today. *Management Engineering, 3*(1), 17–22.

Allen, M. G., Oliver, A. R., & Schwallie, E. H. (1981). The key to successful acquisitions. *Journal of Business Strategy, 2*(2), 14–24.

Allen, M. P., Panian, S. K., & Lotz, R. E. (1979). Managerial succession and organizational performance: A recalcitrant problem revisited. *Administrative Science Quarterly, 24,* 167–180.

Alexander, L. D., O'Neill, H., Snyder, N., & Townsend, J. (1984). *How academy members teach the business policy course.* Paper Presented at the National Academy of Management meeting, Boston.

Almaney, A. (1974). Intercultural communication and the mnc executive. *Columbia Journal of World Business, 9* (4), 23–28.

Alpander, G. G. (1973). Foreign MBA: Potential managers for American international corporations. *Journal of International Business Studies, 4*(1), 1–13.

Alpander, G. G. (1982). *Human resources management planning.* New York: American Management Association

Alpander, G. G., & Bottler, C. H. (1981). An integrated model of strategic human resource planning and development. *Human Resource Planning, 4,* 189–208.

Anderson, J. C., Busman, G. & O'Reilly, C. A. (1982). The decertification process: Evidence from California. *Industrial Relations, 21* (2), 178–195.

Anderson, J. C., Milkovich, G. T., & Tusi, A. (1981). A model of intraorganizational mobility. *Academy of Management Review, 6,* 529–538.

Anderson, C. R., & Zeithaml, C. P. (1984). Stage of the product life cycle, business strategy, and business performance. *Academy of Management Journal, 27,* 5–14.

Andrews, K. R. (1980). *The concept of corporate strategy.* Homewood, IL: Irwin.

Ansoff, H. I. (1965). *Corporate strategy.* New York: McGraw-Hill.

Ansoff, H. I. (1979). *Strategic management.* New York: Wiley.

Apcar, L. M. (1985). Odetics in Anaheim thinks fun lovers make better workers. *Wall Street Journal,* December 4, pp. 1, 17.

Aquilar, F. J. (1967). *Scanning the business environment.* New York: Macmillan.

Arthur D. Little, Inc. (1984) Managing for strategic performance. In R. B. Lamb (Ed.), *Advances in applied business strategy* (Vol. 1, pp. 77–112). Greenwich, CT: JAI Press.

Astley, W. G. (1984). Toward an appreciation of collective strategy. *Academy of Management Review, 9,* 526–535.

Astley, W. G. (1985). Administrative science as socially constructed truth. *Administrative Science Quarterly, 30,* 497–513.

Astley, W. G., & Van de Ven, A. H. (1983). Central perspectives and debates in organization theory. *Administrative Science Quarterly, 28,* 245–273.

Atkinson, K. (1986). State of the unions. *Personnel Administration, 31* (9), 54–59.

Baird, L., & Meshoulam, I. (1984) Strategic human resource management: Implications for training human resource professionals. *Training and Development Journal, 38*(1), 76–78.

Baird, L., & Meshoulam, I. (1988). Managing two fits of strategic human resource management. *Academy of Management Review, 13,* 116–128.

Baird, L., Meshoulam, I., & DeGive, G. (1983). Meshing human resources planning with strategic business planning: A model approach. *Personnel, 60*(5), 14–25.

Baker, J. C., & Ivancevich, J. M. (1971). The assignment of American executives abroad: Systematic, haphazard or chaotic? *California Management Review, 13*(3), 39–44.

Baker, H. K., Miller, T. O., & Ramsperger, B. J. (1981). An inside look at corporate merger and acquisition. *M.S.U. Business Topics, 29*(1), 49–57.

Baliga, B. R., & Jaeger, A. M. (1984). Multinational corporations: Control systems and delegation issues. *Journal of International Business Studies, 15*(2), 25–40.

Balkin, D. B. (1988). Compensation strategy for firms in emerging and rapidly growing industries. *Human Resource Planning, 11,* 207–214.

Balkin, D. B., & Gomez-Mejia, L. R. (1984). Determinants of R & D compensation strategies in the high tech industry. *Personnel Psychology, 37,* 635–650.

Balkin, D. B., & Gomez-Mejia, L. R. (1987). Toward a contingency theory of compensation strategy. *Strategic Management Journal, 8,* 169–182.

Balkin, D. B., & Gomez-Mejia, L. R. (1988). Entrepreneurial compensation. In R. S. Schuler, S. A. Youngblood, & V. L. Huber (Eds.), *Readings in personnel and human resources management* (3rd ed., pp. 291–296). St. Paul, MN: West.

Barbash, J. (1986). The new industrial relations. *Labor Law Journal-IRRA Spring Meeting Proceedings, 37* (August), 528–533.

Barkin, S. (1985). An agenda for the revision of the American industrial relations system. *Labor Law Journal, 36,* 857–860.

Baron, J. N., Davis-Blake, A., & Bielby, W. T. (1986). The structure of opportunity: How promotion ladders vary within and among organizations. *Administrative Science Quarterly, 31,* 248–273.

Baron, J. N., Dobbin, F., & Jennings, P. D. (1986). War and peace: The evolution of modern personnel administration in U.S. industry. *American Journal of Sociology, 92,* 350–383.

Baron, J. N., Jennings, P. D., & Dobbin, F. (1988). Mission control: The development of personnel systems in U.S. industry. *American Sociological Review, 53,* 497–514.

Baron, J. N., & Bielby, W. T. (1986). The proliferation of job titles in organizations. *Administrative Science Quarterly, 31,* 561–586.

Barrett, P. F. (1973). *The human implications of mergers and takeovers.* London: Institute of Personnel Management.

Bartlett, C., & Ghoshal, S. (1986). Tap your subsidiaries for global reach. *Harvard Business Review, 64*(6), 87–94.

Bartlett, C. A., & Yoshihara, H. (1988). New challenges for Japanese multinationals: Is organization adaptation their Achilles heel? *Human Resource Management, 27,* 19–44.

Bartunek, J. M. (1984). Changing interpretive schemes and organizational restructuring: The example of a religious order. *Administrative Science Quarterly, 29,* 355–372.

Bastien, D. T. (1987). Common patterns of behavior and communication in corporate mergers and acquisitions. *Human Resource Management, 26,* 17–33.

Baudeau, N. (1771). *Premiere introduction a la philosophie economique; ou anlayse de etate policies.* Paris: Chez Didot.

Baumol, W. J. (1968). Entrepreneurship and economic history. *American Economic Review, 58,* 64–71.

Baysinger, B. D., & Mobley, W. H. (1983). Employee turnover: Individual and organizational analysis. In K. M. Rowland & G. R. Ferris (Eds.), *Research in personnel and human resources management* (Vol. 1, pp. 269–319). Greenwich, CT: JAI Press.

Baysinger, R. A. (1985). *Organizational control: The link between strategy, structure, technology, and individual performance.* College Station, TX: Working Paper, Texas A & M University.

Beatty, R. W., & Schneier, E. E. (1988). Strategic performance appraisal issues. In R. S. Schuler, S. A. Youngblood, & V. L. Huber (Eds.), *Readings in personnel and human resource management* (3rd ed., pp. 256–266). St. Paul MN: West.

Beatty, R. P., & Zajac, E. J. (1987). CEO change and firm performance in large corporations: Succession effects and manager effects. *Strategic Management Journal, 8,* 305–317.

Beazley, J. E. (1988). In spite of mystique, Japanese plants in U.S. find problems abound. *The Wall Street Journal,* 22 June, pp. 1, 10.

Becker, B. E., & Olson, C. A. (1987). Labor relations and firm performance. In M. M. Kleiner, R. N. Block, M. Roomkin, & S. W. Salsburg (Eds.), *Human resources and the performance of the firm* (pp. 43–87). Madison, WI: Industrial Relations Research Association.

Beehr, T. A., Taber, T. D., & Walsh, J. T. (1980). Perceived mobility channels: Criteria for intra-organizational job mobility. *Organizational Behavior and Human Performance, 26,* 250–264.

Beer, M., & Spector, B. (1984). *Transformation in human resource management,* May 9–11, Boston: Summary of remarks for Harvard Business School's Human Resource Management Futures conference.

Beer, M., Spector, B., Lawrence, P. R., Mills, D. Q., & Walton, R. E. (1984). *Managing human assets.* New York: The Free Press.

Belidor, B. F.de (1729). *La science des ingenieurs das la conduite des travaux de civile.* Paris: C. A. Jambert.

Bennett, R. A. (1987). Pan Am's disappearing act. *The New York Times,* January 18, pp. F1, F8.

Bennis, W. G., & Slater, P. L. (1964). *The temporary society.* New York: Harper & Row.

Berlew, D. E., & Hall, D. T. (1966). The socialization of managers: Effects of expectation on performance. *Administrative Science Quarterly, 11,* 207–223.

Bernardin, H. J., & Beatty, R. W. (1984). *Performance appraisal: Assessing human behavior at work.* Boston: Kent.

Bernardin, H. J., & Buckley, M. R. (1981). Strategies in rater training. *Academy of Management Review, 6,* 205–212.

Beverly, R. (1705). *The history of the present state of Virginia.* London: Printed for R. Parker.

Biggadike, E. R. (1981). The contributions of marketing to strategic management. *Academy of Management Review, 6,* 621–632.

Bills, D. B. (1987). Costs, commitment, and rewards: Factor influencing the design and implementation of internal labor markets. *Administrative Science Quarterly, 32,* 202–221.

Blake, R. R. & Mouton, J. S. (1985). How to achieve integration on the human side of the merger. *Organizational Dynamics, 13*(3), 41–56.

Block, R. N. (1980). Union organizing and the allocation of union resources. *Industrial and Labor Relations Review, 33,* 110–130.

Block, R. N., Kleiner, M. M., Roomkin, M., & Salsburg, S. W. (1987). Industrial relations and the performance of the firm: An overview. In M. M. Kleiner, R. N. Block, M. Roomkin, & S. W. Salsburg (Eds.), *Human resources and the performance of the firm* (pp. 319–343). Madison, WI: Industrial Relations Research Association.

Block, Z. (1983). Some major issues in internal corporate venturing. In J. A. Hornaday, J. A. Timmons, & K. H. Vesper (Eds.) *Frontiers of entrepreneurial research* (pp. 382–389). Wellesley, MA: Center for Entrepreneurial Studies, Babson College.

Block, Z., & Ornati, O. A. (1987). Compensating corporate venture managers. *Journal of Business Venturing, 2,* 41–51.

Block, Z., & Ruff, G. (1986). Corporate venturing in Sweden: A survey of practices, attitudes, obstacles and performance. In R. Ronstadt, J. A. Hornaday, R. Peterson, & K. H. Vesper (Eds.), *Frontiers of entrepreneurial research* (pp. 701–707). Wellesley, MA: Center for Entrepreneurial Studies, Babson College.

Boehm, V. R. (1982). Assessment centers and management development. In K. M. Rowland & G. R. Ferris (Eds.), *Personnel management* (pp. 327–362). Boston: Allyn and Bacon.

Boesky, I. F. (1985). *Merger mania.* New York: Holt, Reinhart, & Winston.

Bohm-Bawerk, E. von (1884) *Kapital und kapitalzins.* Innsbruck, Austria: Wagner.

Boland, R. J. (1970). Merger planning: How much weight do personnel factors carry? *Personnel, 47*(2), 8–13.

Borucki, C. C., & Lafley, A. F. (1984) Strategic staffing at Chase Manhattan Bank. In C. J. Fombrun, N. M. Tichy, M. A. Devanna (Eds.), *Strategic human resource management* (pp. 69–86). New York: Wiley.

Bourgeois, L. J. (1978). *Strategy making, environment and economic performance* (Doctoral dissertation, University of Washington, 1978). *Dissertation Abstracts International, 39*(2), 970A.

Bowditch, J. L., & Bruno, A. F. (1987). *Great expectations: When the hopes for a better life following a merger turn sour.* Paper presented at the National Academy of Management meeting, New Orleans.

Bower, J. L. (1983). Managing for efficiency, managing for equity. *Harvard Business Review, 61*(4), 83–90.

Bowman, E. H. (1986). Concerns of the ceo. *Human Resource Management, 25,* 267–285.

Boyacigiller, N. (1987). *The role of expatriates in the management of interdependence, complexity and risk in multinational corporations.* Paper presented at the Academy of International Business meeting, Chicago.

Brady, G. F., Fulmer, R. M., & Helmich, D. L. (1982). Planning executive succession. The effects of recruitment source and organizational problems in anticipated tenure. *Strategic Management Journal, 3,* 169–175.

Bradley, J. W., & Korn, D. H. (1982). The changing role of acquisitions. *Journal of Business Strategy, 2*(4), 30–42.

Bretz, R. D., & Dreher, G. F. (1988). Sponsored versus contest mobility: The role of mentoring in managerial careers. In R. S. Schuler, S. A. Youngblood, & V. L. Huber (Eds.), *Readings in personnel and human resource management* (3rd ed., pp. 311–319). St. Paul, MN: West.

Brinelow, P. (1981). Courting disaster. *Barrons,* July 27, *61,* 7.

Brockhaus, W. L. (1975). A model for success in mergers and acquisitions. *SAM Advanced Management Journal, 40*(1), 40–49.

Brockhaus, R. H. Sr. (1980). Risk taking propensity of entrepreneurs. *Academy of Management Journal, 23,* 509–520.

Brockhaus, R. H. Sr., & Horwitz, P. S. (1986). The psychology of the entrepreneur. In D. L. Sexton & R. W. Smilor (Eds.), *The art and science of entrepreneurship* (pp. 25–48). Cambridge, MA: Ballinger.

Brockner, J. (1988). The effects of work layoffs on survivors: Research, theory, and practice. In B. M. Shawno, & L. L. Cummings (Eds.), *Research in organizational behavior* (Vol. 10, pp. 213–255). Greenwich, CT: JAI Press.

Brooks, B. J. (1988). Long-term incentives for the foreign-based executive. *Compensation and Benefits Review, 17*(3), 46–53.

Brown, M. C. (1982). Administrative succession and organizational performance: The succession effect. *Administrative Science Quarterly, 27,* 1–16.

Bruton, G. D. (1988). *Organizational structure following a merger or acquisition: A program for study.* Paper Presented at the Southwest Academy of Management meeting, San Antonio, TX.

Buono, A. F., Bowditch, J. L., & Lewis, J. W. (1985). When cultures collide: The anatomy of a merger. *Human Relations, 38,* 477–500.

Burack, E. H. (1985). Linking corporate business and human resource planning: Strategic issues and concerns. *Human Resource Planning,* 8, 133–145.

Burack, E. H. (1988). A strategic planning and operational agenda for human resouces. *Human Resource Planning, 11,* 63–68.

Burgleman, R. A., & Sayles, L. R. (1986). Inside corporate innovation. New York: The Free Press.

Butler, J. E., Dutton, J. M., & Kabaliswaran, R. (1986). *The role of invisible colleges in the generation and diffusion of knowledge.* Paper Presented at the Annual Academy of Management meeting, Chicago.

Butler, J. E., Ferris, G. R., & Smith, D. A. (1988). Exploring some critical dimensions of strategic human resources management. In R. S. Schuler, S. A. Youngblood, & V. L. Huber (Eds.), *Readings in personnel and human resource management* (3rd ed., pp. 3–13). St. Paul MN: West.

Cabrera, J. C. (1982). Takeovers. . . . The risks of the game and how to get around them. *Management Review 71*(11), 17–21.

Caldwell, P. (1984). Cultivating human potential at Ford. *The Journal of Business Strategy, 4*(4), 74–77.

Cantillon, R. (1755). *Essai sur la nature de commerce en general.* London: Fletcher Gyles.

Capon, N., Farley, J. V., & Hulbert, J. (1980). International diffusion of corporate and strategic business practices. *Columbia Journal of World business, 15* (Fall), 5–13.

Carroll, G. R. (1984). Dynamics of publisher succession in newspaper organizations. *Administrative Science Quarterly, 29,* 93–113.

Carroll, S. J., & Schneier, C. E. (1982). *Performance appraisal and review systems.* Glenview, IL: Scott, Foresman.

Casson, M. (1982). *The entrepreneur*. Totowa, NJ: Barnes & Noble.

Chaganti, R., & Sambharya, R. (1987). Strategic orientation and characteristics of upper management. *Strategic Management Journal, 8*, 393–401.

Chakravarthy, B. S., & Lorange, P. (1984). Managing strategic adaptation: Options in administrative systems design. *Interfaces, 14*(1), 34–46.

Chandler, A. D. Jr. (1962). *Strategy and structure: Chapters in the history of the American industrial enterprise*. Cambridge, MA: The M. I. T. Press.

Chandler, A. D. Jr. (1977). *The visible hand: The managerial revolution in American business*. Cambridge, MA: The Belkap Press of Harvard University Press.

Channon, D. (1979). Leadership and corporate performance in service industries. *Journal of Management Studies, 16*, 185–201.

Child, J., & Kieser, A. (1981). Development of organizations over time. In P. C. Nystrom & W. H. Starbuck (Eds.), *Handbook of organizational design* (Vol. 1, pp. 28–64). New York: Oxford University Press.

Christiansen, E. T. (1983). Strategy, structure and labor relations performance. *Human Resource Management, 22*, 155–168.

Chung, K. H., Lubatkin, M., Rogers, R. C., & Owers, J. E. (1987). Do insiders make better CEO's than outsiders? *Academy of Management Executive, 1*, 325–331.

Clark, J. B. (1907). *Essentials of economic theory*. New York: Macmillan.

Clausewitz, K. von (1832). *Hinterlassene werke des generals Carl von Clausewitz über Krieg und Kriegfahrung*. Berline: F. Dummler.

Clausewitz, C. von (1976). *On war*. Princeton, NJ: Princeton University Press.

Cohen, D. J., Graham, R. J., & Shils, E. B. (1985). La Brea tar pits revisited: Corporate entrepreneurs and the AT&T dinosaur. In J. A. Hornaday, E. B. Shils, J. A. Timmons, & K. H. Vesper (Eds.), *Frontiers in entrepreneurship research*, (pp. 636–658). Wellesley, MA: Center for Entrepreneurial Studies, Babson College.

Cohen, Y., & Pfeffer, J. (1986). Organizational hiring standards. *Administrative Science Quarterly, 31*, 1–24.

Cohen-Rosenthal, E., & Burton, C. (1986). Union-management cooperation. *Training and Development Journal, 40* (5), 96–98.

Commons, J. R. (1934). *Institutional economics: Its place in the political economy.* New York: Macmillan.

Conway, M. A. (1987). Manage expatriate expenses for capital returns. *Personnel Journal, 66(7)*, 66–70.

Copeland, L. (1985). Cross-cultural training: The competitive edge. *Training, 22,* 49–53.

Costello, T. W., Kubis, J. F., & Shaffer, C. L. (1963). An analysis toward a planning merger. *Administrative Science Quarterly, 8,* 235–249.

Covin, J. G., & Slevin, D. P. (1986). The development and testing of an organizational-level entrepreneurship scale. In R. Ronstadt, J. A. Hornaday, R. Peterson, & K. H. Vesper (Eds.), *Frontiers of entrepreneurship research,* (pp. 628–639). Wellesley, MA: Center for Entrepreneurial Studies, Babson College.

Cowherd, D. M. (1986). On executive succession: A conversation with Lester B. Korn. *Human Resource Management, 25,* 335–347.

Crane, D. (1972). *Invisible colleges.* Chicago: University of Chicago Press.

Crystal, G. S., & Hurwich, M. R. (1986). The case for divisional long-term incentives. *California Management Review, 29(1),* 60–74.

Cullum, L. (1988). The human side of management. *Harvard Business Review, 66(3),* 90–91.

Cummings, L. L. (1978). Toward organizational behavior. *Academy of Management Review, 3,* 90–98.

Cummings, L. L. (1984). Compensation, culture, and motivation: A systems perspective. *Organizational Dynamics, 12,* 33–44.

Dahl, H. L. Jr. (1988). Human resource cost and benefit analysis: New power for human resources approaches. *Human Resource Planning, 11,* 69–78.

Dalton, G. W., Thompson, P. H., & Price, R. L. (1977). The four stages of professional careers: A new look at performance by professionals. *Organizational Dynamics, 6(1),* 19–42.

Dalton, D. R., & Kesner, I. F. (1983). Inside/outside succession and organizational size: The pragmatics of executive replacement. *Academy of Management Journal, 26,* 736–742.

Dalton, D. R., & Kesner, I. F. (1985). Organizational performance as an antecedent of inside/outside chief executive succession: An empirical assessment. *Academy of Management Journal, 28,* 749–762.

Dalzell, R. F., Jr. (1987). *Enterprising elite.* Cambridge, MA: Harvard University Press.

Daum, J. W. (1975). Internal promotion - a psychological asset or debit? A study of the effects of leader origin. *Organizational Behavior and Human Performance, 13,* 404–413.

Davidson, K. M. (1981). Looking at the strategic impact of mergers. *Journal of Business Strategy, 2*(1), 13–22.

Davidson, W. N., Worrell, D. L., & Garrison, S.H. (1988). Effect of strike activity on firm value. *Academy of Management Journal, 32,* 387–394.

Deal, T. R., & Kennedy, A. A. (1982) *Corporate cultures.* Reading, MA: Addison-Wesley.

De Bejar, G., & Milkovich, G. T. (1986). *Human resource strategy at the business level. Study 2: Relationship between strategy and performance components.* Paper Presented at National Academy of Management Annual meeting, Chicago.

DeNoble, A. F. (1984). *Mergers and acquisitions: An analysis of the postmerger integration process.* Paper presented at the Strategic Management Conference, Philadelphia.

Desatnick, R. L., & Bennett, M. L. (1978). *Human resource management in the multinational company.* New York: Nichols.

Devanna, M. A. (1984). The executive appraisal. In C. J. Fombrun, N. M. Tichy, & M. A. Devanna (Eds.), *Strategic human resource management,* (pp. 101–109). New York: Wiley.

Devanna, M. A., Fombrun, C., & Tichy, N. (1981). Human resource management: A strategic perspective. *Organizational Dynamics, 9,* 51–64.

Devanna, M. A., Fombrun, C. J., & Tichy, N. M. (1984). A framework for strategic human resource management. In C. J. Fombrun, N. M. Tichy and M. A. Devanna (Eds.), *Strategic human resource management* (pp. 33–51). New York: Wiley.

Dickins, W. T., & Leonard, J. S. (1985). Accounting for the decline in union membership, 1950–1980. *Industrial and Labor Relations Review, 38,* 323–334.

Diffenbach, J. (1983). Corporate environmental analysis in large U.S. corporations. *Long Range Planning, 16*(3), 107–116.

Dodd, W. E. (1977). Attitudes toward assessment center programs, In J. L. Moses & W. C. Byham (Eds.), *Applying the assessment center method.* New York: Pergamon.

Dolan, E. G. (Ed.) (1976). *The foundations of modern Austrian economics.* Kansas City: Sheed & Ward.

Dowling, P. J. (1986). *International personnel/human resource management: An overview and synthesis.* Ithaca, NY: (working paper) Cornell University.

Dowling, P. J. (1987). The international human resource practitioner: A 1986 profile. Paper presented at the annual meeting of the Academy of Management, Chicago.

Dowling, P. J. (1988). International human resource management. In L. Dyer (Ed.) *Human resource management: Evolving roles and responsibilities* . Washington: American Society for Personnel Administration/ BNA Books.

Dowling, P. J. (1989). Hot issues overseas. *Personnel Administrator, 34* (1), 66–72.

Dowling, P. J., & Welch, D. E. (1988). *International human resource management in Australian companies.* Paper presented at the International Personnel and Human Resource Management Conference, Singapore. (Management Paper No. 13) Graduate School of Management, Monash University. Clayton, Victoria, Australia.

Doz, Y., & Prahalad, C. K. (1986). Controlled variety: A challenge for human resource management in the mnc. *Human Resource Management, 25,* 55–71.

Dreher, G. F., Dougherty, T. W., & Whitely, W. (1988). *Influence tactics and salary attainment: A study of sex-based salary differentials.* Paper presented at the annual meeting of the Academy of Management, Anaheim, CA.

Drucker, P. F. (1958) Business objectives and survival needs: Notes on a discipline of business enterprise. *The Journal of Business, 31,* 81–90.

Drucker, P. F. (1982). Why some mergers work and many more don't. *Forbes, 129*(2), 34–36.

Dunbar, R. L. M. (1981). Designs for organizational control. In P. C. Nystrom & W. H. Starbuck (Eds.), *Handbook of organizational design* (Vol. 2, pp. 85–115). New York: Oxford University Press.

Dunlop, J. T. (1958). *Industrial relations systems.* New York: Henry Holt.

Dunnette, M. D., & Borman, W. C. (1979). Personnel selection and classification systems. *Annual Review of Psychology, 30,* 477–525.

Dyer, L. (1980). *Personnel policy theory and research: The need and the reality.* Paper presented at the National Academy of Management meeting, Detroit.

Dyer, L. (1983). Bringing human resources into the strategy formulation process. *Human Resource Management, 22,* 257–271.

Dyer, L. (1984). Studying human resource strategy: An approach and an agenda. *Industrial Relations, 23,* 156–169.

Dyer, L. (1985). Strategic human resources management and planning. In K. M. Rowland & G. R. Ferris (Eds.), *Research in personnel and human resources management* (Vol. 3, pp. 1–30). Greenwich,CT: JAI Press.

Dyer, L. (Ed.) (1988). *Human resource management: Evolving roles and responsibilities.* Washington: American Society for Personnel Administration/BNA Books.

Dyer, L., & Schwab, D. P. (1982). Personnel/human resource management research. In T. A. Kochan, D. J. B. Mitchell, & L. Dyer (Eds.), *Industrial relations research in the 1970s: Review and appraisal,* (pp. 187–220). Madison, WI: Industrial Relations Research Association.

Earley, P. C. (1987). Intercultural training for managers: A comparison of documentary and interpersonal methods. *Academy of Management Journal, 30,* 685–698.

Ebeling, H. W. Jr., & Doonley, T. L., III (1983). A strategic approach to acquisitions. *Journal of Business Strategy, 3*(3), 44–54.

Edstrom, A., & Galbraith, J. (1977). Alternative policies for international transfer of managers. *Management International Review, 17*(2), 11–22.

Edstrom, A., & Galbraith, J. (1977). Transfer of managers as a coordination and control strategy in multinational organizations. *Administrative Science Quarterly, 22,* 248–263.

Edstrom, A., & Lorange, P. (1984). Matching strategy and human resources in multinational corporations. *Journal of International Business Studies, 15,* 125–137.

Edwards, L. (1978). Present shock and how to avoid it abroad. *Across the Board,* (February), pp. 36–43.

Eiger, A., Jacobs, J. M., Chung, D. B., & Selsor, J. L. (1988). The U.S. army's occupational specialty manpower decision support system. *Interfaces, 18*(1), 57–73.

Eilbirt, H. (1959). The development of personnel management in the United States. *Business History Review, 33,* 345–364.

Ellig, B. R. (1983). Pay policies while downsizing the organization: A systematic approach. *Personnel, 60*(3), 26–35.

Eitzen, D. S., & Yetman, N. R. (1972). Managerial change, longevity, and organizational effectiveness. *Administrative Science Quarterly, 17,* 110–116.

Evans, P. A. L. (1986). The strategic outcomes of human resource management. *Human Resource Management, 25,* 149–167.

Farber, H. S. (1985). The extent of unionization in the United States. In T. A. Kochan (Ed.), *Challenges and choices facing American labor* (pp. 15–44). Cambridge: The MIT Press.

Fayol, H. (1961). Administration industrille et generale; prevoyance, organization, commandement, coordination, controle. *Bulletin de la Societe de l'Industrie Minerale* (3^e livraison). For English edition see *General and industrial management.* London: Sir Isaac Pitman & Sons, Ltd. (1949).

Feldman, D. C. (1976). A contingency theory of socialization. *Administrative Science Quarterly, 21,* 433–452.

Feldman, D. C. (1984). The development and enforcement of group norms. *Academy of Management Review, 9,* 47–53.

Ferris, G. R., Buckley, M. R., Yee, A. T., & West, C. K. (1988). *Performance evaluation systems in high technology firms.* Paper presented at International Personnel and Human Resources Management Conference, Singapore.

Ferris, G. R., & Curtin, D. (1985). Shaping strategy: Tie personnel functions to company goals. *Management World, 14*(1), 32–38.

Ferris, G. R., Fedor, D. B., Chachere, J. G., & Pondy, L. R. (1989). Myths and politics in organizational contexts. TX *Groups & Organization Studies, 14,* 83–103.

Ferris, G. R., & Rowland, K. M. (Eds.) (1988). *Human resources management: Perspectives and issues.* Boston: Allyn & Bacon.

Ferris, G. R., Rowland, K. M., & Nedd, A. (1989) (Eds.). *International personnel and human resources management.* Greenwich, CT: JAI Press.

Ferris, G. R., Russ, G. S., & Fandt, P. M. (in press). Politics in organizations. In R. A. Giacalone & P. Rosenfeld (Eds.), *Impression management in organizations.* Hillsdale, NH: Erlbaum.

Ferris, G. R., Schellenberg, D. A., & Zammuto, R. F. (1984). Human resource management strategies in declining industries. *Human Resource Management, 23,* 381–394.

Fisher, C. D., & Shaw, J. B. (1987). *Does business strategy affect personnel management practices?* Paper presented at International Personnel and Human Resources Management Conference, Singapore.

Folger, R., & Greenberg, J. (1985). Procedural justice: An interpretive analysis of personnel systems. In K. M. Rowland & G. R. Ferris (Eds.), *Research in personnel and human resources management* (Vol. 3, pp. 141–183). Greenwich, CT: JAI Press.

Fombrun, C. J. (1983). Strategic management: Integrating the human resource systems into strategic planning. In R. B. Lamb (Ed.), *Advances in strategic management* (Vol. 2, pp. 191–210). Greenwich, CT: JAI Press.

Fombrun, C. J. (1984a). Corporate culture and competitive strategy. In C. J. Fombrun, N. M. Tichy, & M. A. Devanna (Eds.), *Strategic human resource management* (pp. 203–216). New York: Wiley.

Fombrun, C. J. (1984b). The external context of human resource management. In C. J. Fombrun, N. M. Tichy, & M. A. Devanna (Eds.), *Strategic human resource management*, (pp. 3–18). New York: Wiley.

Fombrun, C. J. (1984c). An interview with Reginald H. Jones and Frank Doyle. In C. J. Fombrun, N. M. Tichy, & M. A. Devanna (Eds.), *Strategic human resource management* (pp. 423–446). New York: Wiley.

Fombrun, C. J., & Laud, R. L. (1983). Strategic issues in performance appraisal: Theory and practice. *Personnel, 60*(6), 23–31.

Fombrun, C. J., & Tichy, N. M. (1984). Strategic planning and human resource management: At rainbow's end. In R. B. Lamb (Ed.) *Competitive strategic management* (pp. 319–332). Englewood Cliffs, NJ: Prentice-Hall.

Fombrun, C. J., Tichy, N. M., & Devanna, M. A. (1984). *Strategic human resource management.* New York: Wiley.

Forbes, J. B. (1987). Early intraorganizational mobility: Patterns and influences. *Academy of Management Journal, 30*, 110–125.

Foss, S. W. (1918). The calf path. In B. E. Stevenson (Ed.) *The home book of verse*, (pp. 1896–1898). New York: Henry Holt.

Fossum, J. A. (1987). Labor relations: Research and practice in transition. *Journal of Management, 13*, 281–299.

Freeman, R. B. (1985). Why are unions faring poorly in NLRB representation elections? In T. A. Kochan (Ed.), *Challenges and choices facing American labor* (pp. 45–64). Cambridge, MA.

Freeman, R. B., & Medoff, J. L. (1984). *What do unions do?* New York: Basic Books.

Freeman, R. E. (1984). *Strategic Management: A stakeholder approach.* Boston: Pitman.

French, W. L. (1986). *Human resources management.* Boston: Houghton Mifflin.

Friedman, S. D. (1986). Succession systems in large corporations: Characteristics and correlates of performance. *Human Resource Management, 25,* 191–213.

Friedman, S. D., & LeVino, T. P. (1984). Strategic appraisal and development at General Electric Company. In C. J. Fombrun, N. M. Tichy, & M. A. Devanna (Eds.), *Strategic human resource management,* (pp. 183–201). New York: Wiley.

Frohman, M. A. (1984). Human resource management and the bottom line: Evidence of the connection. *Human Resource Management, 23,* 315–334.

Fry, J. N., & Killings, J. P. (1986). *Strategic analysis and action.* Englewood Cliffs, NJ: Prentice-Hall.

Galbraith, J. R. (1973). *Designing complex organizations.* Reading, MA: Addison-Wesley.

Galbraith, J., & Edstrom, A. (1976). International transfer of managers: Some important policy considerations. *Columbia Journal of World Business, 11*(2), 100–112.

Galbraith, J. R., & Kazanjian, K. R. (1986). Organizing to implement strategies of diversity and globalization: The role of matrix designs. *Human Resource Management, 25,* 37–54.

Galbraith, J. R., & Nathanson, D. A. (1978). *Strategy implementation: The role of structure.* St. Paul MN: West.

Galosy, J. R. (1983). Meshing human resources planning with strategic business planning: One company's experience. *Personnel, 60,* 26–35.

Gamson, W. A. (1968). *Power and discontent.* New York: McGraw-Hill.

Gamson, W. A., & Scotch, N. A. (1964). Scapegoating in baseball. *American Journal of Sociology, 70,* 69–76.

Gardiner, G. L. (1925). *Practical foremanship.* New York: McGraw-Hill.

Gatewood, R. D., & Gatewood, E. J. (1983). The use of expert data in human resource planning: Guidelines from strategic planning. *Human Resource Planning, 6,* 83–94.

George, R., & MacMillan, I. C. (1984). *Corporate venturing/senior management responsibilities.* New York: (working paper) Center for Entrepreneurial Studies, New York University.

Gerber, L. G. (1988). Corporatism in comparative perspective: The impact of the first world war on American and British labor relations. *Business History Review, 62,* 93–127.

Gerpott, T. J., & Domsch, M. (1985). The concept of professionalism and the management of salaried technical professionals: A cross-national perspective. *Human Resource Management, 24,* 207–226.

Gerstein, M., & Reisman, H. (1983) Strategic selection: Matching executives to business conditions. *Sloan Management Review, 24*(2), 33–49.

Getman, J. G. , Goldberg, S. B., & Herman, J. B. (1976). *Union representation elections: Law and reality.* New York: Russell Sage Foundation.

Gibson, C. H. (1973). Volvo increases productivity through job enrichment. *California Management Review, 15*(4), 64–66.

Gilbreth, L. M. (1914). *Psychology of management.* Easton, MD: Hive.

Gill, J., & Foulder, I. (1978). Managing a merger: The acquisition and the aftermath. *Personnel Management, 10*(1), 14–17.

Gilmore, D. C., & Ferris, G. R. (1989). The politics of the employment interview. In R. W. Eder & G. R. Ferris (Eds.), *The employment interview: Theory, research, and practice,* (pp. 195–203). Newbury Park, CA: Sage.

Gilmore, F. F., & Brandenburg, R. G. (1962). Anatomy of corporate planning. Harvard Business Review, *40*(6), 61–69.

Golden, K. A., & Ramanujam, V. (1985). Between a dream and a nightmare: On the integration of human resource management and strategic business planning processes. *Human Resource Management, 24,* 429–452.

Gomez-Mejia, L. R., Tosi, H., & Hinkin, T. (1987). Managerial control, performance, and executive compensation. *Academy of Management Journal, 30,* 51–70.

Gomez-Mejia, L. R., & Welbourne, T. M. (1988). Compensation strategy: An overview and future steps. *Human Resource Planning, 11,* 173–190.

Goold, M., & Campbell, A. (1987). Many best ways to make strategy. *Harvard Business Review. 65*(6), 40–46.

Gordon, G. E., & Rosen, N. (1981). Critical factors in leadership succession. *Organizational Behavior and Human Performance, 27,* 227–254.

Gould, R. (1984). Gaining competitive edge through human resource strategies. *Human Resource Planning, 7,* 31–38.

Graves, D. (1981). Individual reactions to a merger of two small firms of brokers in the re-insurance industry: A total population survey. *Journal of Management Studies, 18*(1), 89–113.

Green, R. J., & Roberts, R. G. (1983). Strategic integration of compensation and benefits. *Personnel Administrator, 28*(5), 79–82.

Greenhalgh, L., Lawrence, A. T., & Sutton, R. I. (1988). Determinants of work force reduction strategies in declining organizations. *Academy of Management Review, 13,* 241–254.

Greenwood, R. G., & Wrege C. D. (1987). The Hawthorne studies. In D. A. Wren, & J. A. Pearce II (Eds.), *Papers dedicated to the development of modern management,* (pp. 24–35). The Academy of Management.

Grimaldi, A. (1986). Interpreting popular culture: The missing link between local labor and international management. *Columbia Journal of World Business, 21*(4), 67–72.

Grusky, O. (1960). Administrative succession in formal organizations. *Social Forces, 39,* 105–115.

Grusky, O. (1961). Corporate size, bureaucratization, and managerial succession. *The American Journal of Sociology, 67,* 261–269.

Grusky, O. (1963). Managerial succession and organizational effectiveness. *The American Journal of Sociology, 69,* 21–31.

Grusky, O. (1964). Reply (to Gamson and Scotch). *The American Journal of Sociology, 70,* 72–76.

Grusky, O. (1969). Succession with an ally. *Administrative Science Quarterly, 14,* 155–170.

Guest, R. H. (1962). Managerial succession in complex organizations. *The American Journal of Sociology, 68,* 47–54.

Gupta, A. K. (1986). Matching managers to strategies: Point and counterpoint. *Human Resource Management, 25,* 215–234.

Gupta, A. K., & Govindarajan, V. (1984). Business unit strategy, managerial characteristics, and business unit effectiveness at strategy implementation. *Academy of Management Journal, 27,* 25–41.

Guth, W. D. (Ed.). (1985). *Handbook of business strategy. 1985/1986 Yearbook.* Boston: Warren, Gorham and Lamont.

Guth, W. D., & MacMillan, I. C. (1986). Strategy implementation versus middle management self-interest. *Strategic Management Journal, 7,* 313–327.

Gutteridge, T. G. (1988). The hrpd profession: A vision of tomorrow. *Human Resource Planning,* *11,* 109–124.

Haas, E. A. (1987). Breakthrough manufacturing. *Harvard Business Review, 65*(2), 75–81.

Halaby, C. N. (1978). Bureaucratic promotion criteria. *Administrative Science Quarterly, 23,* 466–484.

Hall, D. T. (1983). Human resource management. In M. H. Bazerman, & R. J. Lewicki (Eds.), *Negotiating in organizations* (pp. 339–359). Beverly Hills, CA: Sage.

Hall, D. T. (1984). Human resource development and organizational effectiveness. In C. J. Fombrun, N. M. Tichy & M. A. Devanna (Eds.), *Strategic human resource management,* (pp. 159–181). New York: Wiley.

Hall, D. T., & Goodale, J. G. (1986). *Human resource management.* Glenview, IL: Scott, Foresman.

Halpern, P. (1983). Corporate acquisition: A theory of special cases? A review of event studies applied to acquisitions. *Journal of Finance, 38,* 297–317.

Hambrick, D. C. (1979). *Environmental scanning, organizational strategy, and executive roles: A study in three industries.* University Park, PA: (Unpublished Dissertation) The Pennsylvania State University.

Hambrick, D. C. (1982). Environmental scanning and organizational strategy. *Strategic Management Journal, 3,* 159–174.

Hambrick, D. C. (1983). Some tests of the effectiveness and functional attributes of Miles' and Snow's strategic types. *Academy of Management Journal, 26,* 5–26.

Hambrick, D. C., & Mason, P. A. (1982). The organization as a reflection of its top managers. *Proceedings of the Academy of Management* (pp. 12–16).

Hambrick, D. C., & Mason, P. A. (1984). Upper echelons: The organization as a reflection of its top managers. *Academy of Management Review, 9,* 193–206.

Hardy, T. (1978). The convergence of the twain. In J. Gibson (ed.), *The complete poems of Thomas Hardy* (pp. 306–307). New York: Macmillan.

Harrigan, K. R. (1980). *Strategy for declining businesses.* Lexington, MA: Heath.

Harrigan, K. R. (1985). Exit barriers and vertical integration. *Academy of Management Journal, 28,* 686–697.

Harris, P. R. (1979). The unhappy world of the expatriate. *International Management, 34*(7), 49–50.

Harris, P. R., & Moran, R. T. (1979). *Managing cultural differences.* Houston: Gulf.

Harris, S. (1984). Hewlett-Packard: Shaping the corporate culture. In C. J. Fombrun, N. M. Tichy, & M. A. Devanna (Eds.), *Strategic management of human resources,* (pp. 217–233). New York: Wiley.

Harvey, M. G. (1983a). Effective planning for human resource development. *Personnel Administrator, 28,* 45–52,112.

Harvey, M. G. (1983b). The multinational corporation's expatriate problem: An application of Murphy's law. *Business Horizons, 26*(1), 71–78.

Harvey, M. G. (1985). The executive family: An overlooked variable in international assignments. *Columbia Journal of World Business, 20*(1), 84–92.

Harvey, M. G. (1989). Repatriation of corporate executives: An empirical study. *Journal of International Business Studies, 20*(1), 131–144.

Hawkins, M. (1987). *Using human resources data for selecting merger/acquisition candidates.* Paper Presented at the Human Resource Planning Research symposium, Newport, RI.

Hay, R. D. (1974). Expatriate selection: Insuring success and avoiding failure. *Journal of International Business Studies, 5*(1), 25–37.

Hayek, F. A. (1937). Economics and knowledge. *Economica, 4*(new series), 33–54.

Hayek, F. A. (1945). The use of knowledge in society. *American Economic Review, 35,* 519–550.

Hayes, R. H. (1979). The human side of acquisitions. *Management Review, 60,* 41–46.

Hayes, R. H., & Abernathy, W. J. (1980). Managing our way to economic decline. *Harvard Business Review, 58*(4), 67–77.

Hedberg, B. P., Nystrom, P., & Starbuck, W. H. (1976). Camping on seesaws: Prescriptions for self-designing organizations. *Administrative Science Quarterly, 21*(1), 41–65.

Heenan, D. A. (1970). The corporate expatriate: Assignment to ambiguity. *Columbia Journal of World Business, 5*(3), 49–54.

Heenan, D. A., & Reynolds, C. (1975). RPO's: A step through global human resources management. *California Management Review, 18*(1), 5–9.

Heller, J. E. (1980). Criteria for selecting an international manager. *Personnel, 57*(3), 47–55.

Helmich, D. L. (1977). Executive succession in the corporate organization: A current integration. *Academy of Management Review, 2,* 252–266.

Helmich, D. L. (1978). Leader flows and organizational process. *Academy of Management Journal,* *21,* 463–478.

Helmich, D. L. (1980). Board size variation and rates of succession in corporate presidency. *Journal of Business Research, 8,* 51–63.

Helmich, D. L., & Brown, W. B. (1972). Successor type and organizational change in the corporate enterprise. *Administrative Science Quarterly, 17,* 371–381.

Heneman, H. G., Jr. (1969). Toward a general conceptual system of industrial relations: How do we get there? In G. Somers (Ed.), *Essays in industrial relations theory* (pp. 1–25). Ames, IA: Iowa State University Press.

Heneman, H. G., III (1980). Quo vadis pair. *Personnel/Human Resources Division Newsletter, 1,* 204.

Heneman, H. G., III, & Sandver, M. H. (1981). Union growth through the election process. *Industrial Relations, 20,* 109–116.

Henn, W. R. (1985). What the strategist asks from human resources. *Human Resource Planning, 8,* 193–200.

Herbert, T. T., & Deresky, H. (1987). Should general managers match their business strategies? *Organizational Dynamics, 15*(3), 40–51.

Hirsch, P. (1987). *Pack your own parachute.* Reading, MA: Addison-Wesley.

Hitt, M. A., Ireland, R. D., & Palia, K. A. (1982). Industrial firms' grand strategy and functional importance: Moderating effects of technology and uncertainty. *Academy of Management Journal, 25,* 265–298.

Hofer, C. W., & Schendel, D. (1978) *Strategy formulation: Analytical concepts.* St. Paul, MN: West.

Hoffman, W. H., Wyatt, L., & Gordon, C. C. (1986). Human resource planning: Shifting from concept to contempory practice. *Human Resource Planning, 9,* 97–105.

Hofstede, G. (1984). *Culture's consequences.* Beverly Hills, CA: Sage.

Holusha, J. (1986). Roger Smith's troubled second act. *The New York Times, 135*(46652), pp. F1, F22.

Holusha, J. (1988). Mixing cultures on the assembly line. *The New York Times, 137* (5 June), Section 3: pp. 1, 8.

Hooper, J. A., Catalanello, R. F., & Murray, P. L. (1987). Shoring up the weakest link. *Personnel Administrator, 32*(4), 49–55, 134.

Hoskisson, R. E., Hitt, M. A., & Hill, C. W. L. (1987). *Managerial controls, incentives and risk preferences in large multi-product firms.* Paper presented at Western Academy of Management meeting, Hollywood, CA.

Hoskisson, R. E., Hitt, M. A., Turk, T., & Tyler, B. (1989). Balancing corporate strategy and executive compensation: Agency theory and corporate governance. In G. R. Ferris & K. M. Rowland (Eds.), *Research in personnel and human resources management* (Vol. 7). Greenwich, CT: JAI Press.

Howard, C. G. (1974). Model for the design of a selection program for multinational executives. *Public Personnel Management, 3*(2), 138–145.

Howard, C. G. (1983). Is your manager suitable for overseas assignment? *The Personnel Administrator, 18,* 25–28.

Hoyt, D., & Lewis, J. (1980). Planning for a career in human resource management. *Personnel Administrator, 25*(10), 53–43 & 67–68.

Hrebiniak, L. G., & Joyce, W. F. (1984). *Implementing strategy.* New York: Macmillan.

Hunt, D. M., & Michael, C. (1983). Mentorship: A career training and development tool. *Academy of Management Review, 8,* 475–485.

Hunt, J. W., & Lees, S. (1987). Hidden extras: How people get overlooked in takeovers. *Personnel Management, 19*(7), 24–28.

Isambert, F. A. (1829). *Tableau des progres du droit public et du droit des gens, jusqu'au XIXC siecle.* Paris: Brissot-Trivars.

Ishida, H. (1986). Transferability of Japanese human resource management abroad. *Human Resource Management, 25,* 103–120.

Ivancevich, J. M., Schweiger, D. M., & Power, F. R. (1987). Strategies for managing human resources during mergers and acquisitions. *Human Resource Planning, 10,* 19–35.

Jacobson, R. (1988). The persistence of abnormal returns. *Strategic Management Journal, 9,* 415–430.

Jacoby, S. M. (1983). Industrial labor mobility in historical perspective. *Industrial Relations, 22,* 261–282.

Janger, A. R. (1977). *The personnel function: Changing objectives and organization,* (Conference Board Report No. 712). New York: The Conference Board.

Jemison, D. B. (1981a). The importance of an integrative approach to strategic management research. *Academy of Management Review, 6*, 601–608.

Jemison, D. B. (1981b). The contributions of administrative behavior to strategic management. *Academy of Management Review, 6*, 633–642.

Jemison, D. B. (1987). *Process constraints on strategic capability transfer during acquisition integration.* Stanford, CA: Research Paper Series No 914r, Stanford University.

Jemison, D. B., & Sitkin, S. B. (1986). Corporate acquisitions: A process perspective. *Academy of Management Review, 11*, 145–163.

Jensen, A. E. (1982). Seeking a candidate for merger or acquisition. *Business Horizons, 25*(3), 80–84.

Jensen, M. C. (1984). Takeovers: folklore and science. *Harvard Business Review, 62*(6), 109–121.

Jensen, M. C., & Ruback, R. S. (1983). The market for corporate control. *Journal of Financial Economics, 11*, 5–50.

Kadat, J. M., & Gaughan, R. J., Jr. (1987). Oversee expatriate returns to curtail taxes. *Personnel Journal, 66*(7), 71–76.

Kamien, M. I., & Schwartz, N. L. (1976). On the degree of rivalry for maximum innovative activity. *Quarterly Journal of Economics, 90*, 245–260.

Kaminski, M., & Paiz, J. (1984). Japanese women in management: Where are they? *Human Resource Management, 23*, 277–292.

Kanter, R. M. (1983). Frontiers for strategic human resource planning and management. *Human Resource Management, 22*, 9–22.

Kanter, R. M. (1985). Supporting innovation and venture development in established companies. *Journal of Business Venturing, 1*, 47–60.

Kanter, R. M. (1986). Unions and management re-invent roles. *Management Review, 75* (9), 13–14.

Karr, A. R. (1988). Labor unions' chance for gains in '88 hits a wall of resistance. *The Wall Street Journal,* 29 June, pp. 1, 17.

Katz, D., & Kahn, R. L. (1978). *The social psychology of organizations* (2nd ed.). New York: Wiley.

Katz, H. C., Kochan, T. A., & Weber, M. R. (1985). Assessing the effects of industrial relations systems and efforts to improve the quality of work life on organizational effectiveness. *Academy of Management Journal, 30*, 509–526.

Kendall, D. W. (1981). Repatriation: An ending and a beginning. *Business Horizons, 24*(6), 21–25.

Kerr, C., Dunlop, J. T., Harbison, F., & Myers, C.A. (1960). *Industrialism and industrial man.* Cambridge, MA: Harvard University Press.

Kerr, J. (1982). Assigning managers on the basis of the life cycle. *Journal of Business Strategy, 2*(4), 58–65.

Kerr, J. L. (1985). Diversification strategies and managerial rewards: An empirical study. *Academy of Management Journal, 28,* 155–179.

Kerr, J. L. (1988). Strategic control through performance appraisal and rewards. *Human Resouce Planning, 11,* 225–240.

Kerr, J., & Bettis, R. A. (1987). Boards of directors, top management, compensation and shareholder return. *Academy of Management Journal, 30,* 645–664.

Kerr, J., & Slocum, J. W. Jr. (1987). Managing corporate culture through reward systems. *Academy of Management Executive, 1,* 99–108.

Kerr, J. L., & Slocum, J. W. (1988). Linking reward systems and organizational cultures. In R. E. Schuler, S. A. Youngblood, & V. L. Huber (Eds.), *Readings in personnel and human resource management,* (pp. 297–307). St. Paul, MN: West.

Kerr, J. L., & Snow, C. C. (1982). *A conceptual model of the reward system design process.* Paper presented at the Academy of Management annual meeting, New York.

Keynes, J. M. (1936). *The general theory of employment.* New York: Harcourt Brace.

Kiefer, F. (1983). Salaries, benefits: Undergoing numerous changes. *Houston Post,* (October 10), p. 5.

Kilby, P. (1971). Hunting for the heffalump. In P. Kilby (Ed.), *Entrepreneurship and economic development* (pp. 1–40). New York: The Free Press.

King, M. L. (1963). Letter from Birmingham jail. In F. D. Burt & E. C. Want (Eds.), *Invention & design* (pp. 433–449). New York: Random House.

Kirkpatrick, D. (1986). What givebacks can get you. *Fortune, 114* (2), 60–61, 64, 68, 72.

Kirzner, I. M. (1973). *Competition and entrepreneurship,* Chicago: University of Chicago Press.

Kirzner, I. M. (1979). *Perception, opportunity, and profit.* Chicago: University of Chicago Press.

Kirzner, I. M. (1985). *Discovery and the capitalist process.* Chicago: University of Chicago Press.

Kitching, J. (1967). *Why do mergers miscarry?* Harvard Business Review, *45* (6), 84–101.

Kleiner, M. M., Block, R. N., & Salsburg, S. W. (Eds.) (1987). *Human resources and the performance of the firm.* Madison, WI: Industrial Relations Research Association.

Kobrin, S. (1988). Expatriate reduction and strategic control in American multinational companies. *Human Resource Management, 27,* 63–71.

Kochan, T. A. (1981). Collective bargaining and organizational behavior research. In B. M. Staw & L. L. Cummings (Eds.), *Research in organizational behavior,* (Vol. 2, pp. 129–176). Greenwich, CT: JAI Press.

Kochan, T. A. (Ed.) (1988). *Challenges and choices facing American labor.* Cambridge, MA: The M.I.T. Press.

Kochan, T. A., & Cappelli, P. (1984). The transformation of the industrial relations and personnel. In P. Osterman (Ed.), *Internal labor markets* (pp. 133–161). Cambridge, MA: The M.I.T. Press.

Kochan, T. A., & Freeman, A. (1979). *Managing labor relations.* Report no. 765. New York: The Conference Board.

Kochan, T. A., Katz, H. C., & McKersie, R. B. (1986). *The transformation of American industrial relations,* New York: Basic Books.

Kochan, T. A., McKersie, R. B., & Chalykoff, J. (1986). The effects of corporate strategy and workplace innovations on union representation. *Industrial and Labor Relations Review, 39,* 487–501.

Kochan, T. A., McKersie, R. B., & Cappelli, P. (1984). Strategic choice and industrial relations theory, *Industrial Relations, 23,* 16–39.

Kochan, T. A., McKersie, R. B., & Katz, H. C. (1985). U.S. industrial relations in transition: A summary report. *Proceedings,* Industrial Relations Research Association (pp. 261–276). Madison, WI: IRRA.

Kochan, T. A., Mitchell, D. J. B., & Dyer, L. (1982). Appraising a decade's research: An overview. In T. A. Kochan, D. J. B. Mitchell, & L. Dyer (Eds.), *Industrial relations in the 1970's: Review and appraisal* (pp. 355–374). Madison, WI: Industrial Relations Research Association.

Kogan, N., & Wallach, M. A. (1964). *Risk taking.* New york: Holt, Rinehart and Winston.

Kotter, J., & Sathe, V. (1978). Problems of human resource management in rapidly growing companies. *California Management Review, 21*(2), 29–36.

Kovach, K. A., & Millspaugh, P. E. (1987). Plant closings: Is the American industrial relations system failing? *Business Horizons, 30* (2), 44–49.

Kram, K. E. (1983). Phases of the mentor relationship. *Academy of Management Journal, 26,* 608–625.

Kram, K. E. (1984). *Mentoring at work.* Glenview, IL: Scott, Foresman.

Kriesberg, L. (1962). Careers, organization size, and succession. *The American Journal of Sociology, 68,* 355–359.

Kuin, P. (1972). The magic of multinational management. *Harvard Business Review, 50*(6), 89–97.

Kumar, B. N., & Steinmann, H. (1986). *Management conflict between expatriate and local executives in German and Japanese multinational corporations.* Paper Presented at the National Academy of Management meeting, Chicago.

Lamb, R. B. (Ed.) (1984). *Competitive strategic management.* Englewood Cliffs, NJ: Prentice-Hall.

Landy, F. J., & Vasey, J. (1984). Theory and logic in human resources research. In K. M. Rowland & G. R. Ferris (Eds.), *Research in personnel and human resources management* (Vol. 2, pp. 1–34). Greenwich, CT: JAI Press.

Lanier, A. R. (1979). Selecting and preparing personnel for overseas transfers. *Personnel Journal, 58,* 160–163.

Larsson, R. (1988). *Career disintegration in mergers and acquisitions.* Paper Presented at the Western Academy of Management meeting, Big Sky, MT.

Latham, G. P. (1984). The appraisal system as a strategic control. In C. J. Fombrun, N. M. Tichy, & M. A. Devanna (Eds.), *Strategic human resource management* (pp. 87–100). New York: Wiley.

Latham, G. P., & Napier, N. K. (1989). Chinese human resource management practices in Hong Kong and Singapore. In G. R. Ferris, K. M. Rowland, & A. Nedd (Eds.), *International human resources management, supplement volume1, research in personnel and human resource management* (pp. 173–199). Greenwich, CT: JAI Press.

Latham, G. P., & Wexley, K. N. (1981). *Increasing productivity through performance appraisal.* Reading, MA: Addison-Wesley.

Laud, R. L. (1984). Performance appraisal practices in the Fortune 1300. In C. J. Fombrun, N. M. Tichy, & M. A. Devanna (Eds.), *Strategic human resource management* (pp. 111–126). New York: Wiley.

Laurent, A. (1986). The cross-cultural puzzle of international human resource management. *Human Resource Management, 25,* 91–102.

Lawler, E. E., III (1973). *Motivation in work organizations.* Monterey, CA: Brooks/Cole.

Lawler, E. E. (1981a). The role of pay in organizations. In M. Jelinek, J. A. Literer, & R. E. Mills (Eds.), *Organizations by design: Theory and practice* (pp. 376–385). Plano, TX: Business Publications, Inc.

Lawler, E. E. (1981b). *Pay and organizational development.* Reading, MA: Addison-Wesley.

Lawler, E. E. (1982). *The design of effective reward systems.* Technical report, ONR N-00014-81-K-0048.

Lawler, E. E. (1982). *The strategic design of reward systems.* Los Angeles, CA: Working paper, University of Southern California, Technical Report (G-82-11(3)); ONR contract N-00014-81-K-0048.

Lawler, E. E., III (1983). *What ever happened to incentive pay.* Paper Presented at Workshop on Taylorism, Paris.

Lawler, E. E., III (1984). The strategic design of reward systems. In C. J. Fombrun, N. M. Tichy, & M. A. Devanna (Eds.), *Strategic human resource management* (pp. 127–147). New York: Wiley.

Lawler, E. E., & Mohrman, S. A. (1987). Unions and the new management. *Academy of Management Executive, 1,* 293–300.

Lawler, E. E., Mohrman, A. M., & Resnick, S. M. (1984). Performance appraisal revisited. *Organizational Dynamics, 13*(1), 20–35.

Lawler, J. J. (1984). The influence of management consultants on the outcome of union certification elections. *Industrial and Labor Relations Review, 38,* 38–51.

Lawrence, P. R. (1985a). The HRM futures colloquium: The managerial perspective. In R. E. Walton & P. R. Lawrence (Eds.), *HRM trends & challenges* (pp. 349–367). Boston: Harvard Business School Press.

Lawrence, P. R. (1985b). The history of human resource management in American industry. In R. E. Walton & P. R. Lawrence (Eds.), *HRM trends & challenges* (pp. 15–34). Boston: Harvard Business School Press.

Leap, T., & Oliva, T. A. (1983). General systems precursor theory as a supplement of Wren's framework for studying management history: The case of human resource/personnel management. *Human Relations, 36,* 627–640.

Learned, E. P., Christensen, R. C., Andrews, K. R., & Guth, W. D. (1965) *Business policy.* Homewood, IL: Irwin.

Lee, T. H., Fisher, J. C., & Yau, T. S. (1986) Is your r & d on track? *Harvard Business Review, 64*(1), 34–44.

Leighton, C. M., & Tod, G. R. (1969). After the acquisition: Continuing challenge. *Harvard Business Review, 47*(2), 90–102.

Lenz, R., & Lyles, M. (1981). Tackling the human problems in planning. *Long Range Planning, 14*(2), 72–77.

Leontiades, M. (1982). Choosing the right manager to fit the strategy. *Journal of Business Strategy, 3*(2), 58–69.

Levinson, H. (1970). A psychologist diagnoses merger failures. *Harvard Business Review, 48*(2), 138–147.

Lewellen, W., & Huntsman, B. (1970). Managerial pay and corporate performance. *The American Economic Review, 60,* 710–720.

Lewin, D. (1987). Industrial relations as a strategic variable. In M. M. Kleiner, R. N. Block, M. Roomkin, & S. W. Salsburg (Eds.), *Human resources and the performance of the firm* (pp. 1–43). Madison, WI: Industrial Relations Research Association.

Lewin, D., & Feuille, P. (1983). Behavioral research in industrial relations. *Industrial and Labor Relations Review, 36,* 341–360.

Lieberson, S., & O'Connor, J. F. (1972). Leadership and organizational performance: A study of large corporations. *American Sociology Review, 37,* 117–120.

Linkow, P. (1985). HRD at the root of corporate strategy. *Training and Development Journal,* (May), 85–87.

Longenecker, C. O., Gioia, D. A., & Sims, H. P. (1987). Behind the mask: the politics of employee appraisal. *The Academy of Management Executive, 1,* 183–194.

Lorange, P. (1986). Human resource management in multinational cooperative ventures. *Human Resource Management, 25,* 133–148.

Lorange, P. & Vancil, R. F. (Eds.) (1977). *Strategic planning systems.* Englewood Cliffs, NJ: Prentice-Hall.

Louis, A. M. (1982). The bottom line of 10 big mergers. *Fortune,* May 3, pp. 84–89.

Lubatkin, M. (1983). Mergers and the performance of the acquiring firm. *Academy of Management Review, 8,* 218–225.

Lubatkin, M. (1987). Merger strategies and stockholder value. *Strategic Management Journal, 8,* 39–53.

Lubatkin, M., & Shrieves, R. E. (1986). Towards reconciliation of market performance measures to strategic management research. *Academy of Management Review, 11,* 497–512.

Lundberg, C. (1986). The dynamic organizational contexts of executive succession: Considerations and challenges. *Human Resource Management, 25,* 287–303.

Lyles, M. A., & Lenz, R. T. (1982). Managing the planning process: A field study of the human side of planning. *Strategic Management Journal, 3,* 105–118.

Maccoby, M. (1976). *The gamesman.* New York: Bantam.

Maccoby, W. F., & Comte, T. E. (1986). The CEO succession dilemma: How boards function in turnover at the top. *Business Horizons, 29*(3), 17–32.

Mace, M. L., & Montgomery, G. G. (1962). *Management problems of corporate acquisitions.* Boston: Harvard University.

Mahan, A. T. (1890). *The influence of sea power upon history 1660–1783.* Boston: Little, Brown.

Mahler, W. R. (1981). Management succession planning: New approaches for the 80's. *Human Resource Planning, 4,* 221–227.

Mahoney, T. A., & Deckop, J. R. (1986). Evolution of concept and practice in personnel administration/human resource management (PA/HRM). *Journal of Management, 12,* 223–241.

Mann, T. (1933). *Joseph und seine bruder.* Berlin: S. Fischer Verlag.

Manzini, A. O. (1988). Integrating human resource planning and development: The unification of strategic, operational and human resource planning systems. *Human Resource Planning, 11,* 79–84.

Marks, M. L. (1982). Merging human resources: A review of current research. *mergers and Acquisitions, 17,* 38–44.

Marks, M. L., & Mirvis, P. (1985). Merger syndrome: Stress and uncertainty. *Mergers and Acquisitions, 20*(2), 50–55.

Markham, W. T., Harlan, S. L., & Hackett, E. J. (1987). Promotion opportunity in organizations: Causes and consequences. In K. M. Rowland & G. R. Ferris (Eds.), *Research in personnel and human resources management* (Vol. 5, pp. 223–287). Greenwich, CT: JAI Press.

Marshall, A. (1890). *Principles of economics.* London: Macmillan.

Martin, D. C., & Bartol, K. M. (1985). Managing turnover strategically. *Personnel Administrator, 30,* 63–73.

Mayo, E. (1933). *The human problems of an industrial civilization.* New York: Viking.

McCain, B. E., O'Reilly, C., & Pfeffer, J. (1983). The effects of departmental demography on turnover: The case of a university. *Academy of Management Journal, 26,* 626–641.

McCarthy, D. J., Spital, F. C., & Lauenstein, M. C. (1987). Managing growth at high-technology companies: A view from the top. *Academy of Management Executive, 1,* 313–323.

McClelland, D. C. (1961). *The achieving society.* Princeton, NJ: D. VanNostrand.

McGehee, W., & Thayer, P. W. (1961). *Training in business and industry.* New York: Wiley.

McEnrue, M. P. (1988). Length of experience and the performance of managers in the establishment phase of their careers. *Academy of Management Journal, 31,* 175–185.

McGill, A. R. (1984). Applying rewards and compensation theory to the real world of business: A case study of General Motors Corporation. In C. J. Fombrun, N. M. Tichy, & M. A. Devanna (Eds.), *Strategic management of human resources,* (pp. 149–158). New York: Wiley.

McKersie, R. B. (1985). New dimensions in industrial relations. *Labor Law Journal, 36* (8), 645–648.

Mendenhall, M., & Oddou, G. (1985). The dimensions of expatriate acculturation: A review. *Academy of Management Review, 10,* 39–47.

Mendenhall, M., & Oddou, G. (1986). Acculturation profiles of expatriate managers: Implications for cross-cultural training programs. *Columbia Journal of World Business, 21*(4), 73–80.

Mercer, W. M. (1984). Employee attitudes toward compensation change and corporate values. *Career Development Bulletin, 4,* 5.

Metcalfe, L. (1981). Designing precarious partnerships. In P. C. Nystrom & W. H. Starbuck (Eds.), *Handbook of organizational design* (Vol. 1, 503–530). New York: Oxford University Press.

Metz, E. J. (1984). The missing "H" in strategic planning. *Managerial Planning. 32*(6), 19–23, 29.

Meyer, P. (1983). Executive compensation must promote long-term commitment. *Personnel Administrator, 28*(5), 37–42.

Migliore, R. H. (1982). Linking strategy, performance, and pay. *The Journal of Business Strategy, 3*(1), 90–94.

Milne, A. A. (1926). *Winnie-the-pooh.* London: Metheun & Co., Ltd.

Miles, R. E., & Snow, C. C. (1978). *Organizational strategy, structure and process.* New York: McGraw-Hill.

Milkovich, G. T. (1984). Introduction: Personnel strategy and evaluation. *Industrial Relations, 23,* 151–155.

Milkovich, G. T. (1988). A strategic perspective on compensation management. In G. R. Ferris & K. M. Rowland (Eds.), *Research in personnel and human resources management* (Vol. 6, pp. 263–288). Greenwich, CT: JAI Press.

Milkovich, G., & Newman, J. (1987). *Compensation.* Plano, TX: Business Publications, Inc.

Miller, A. (1949). *Death of a salesman: Certain private conversations in two acts and a requiem.* New York: Viking.

Miller, D., & Friesen, P. H. (1984). *Organizations: a quantum view.* Englewood Cliffs, NJ: Prentice-Hall.

Miller, D., Kets de Vries, M. F. R., & Toulouse, J. M. (1982). Top executive locus of control and its relationship to strategy-making, structure and environment. *Academy of Management Journal, 25,* 237–253.

Miller, E. L. (1972). The overseas assignment: How managers determine who is to be selected. *Michigan Business Review,* (May), 12–19.

Miller, E. L. (1973). The international selection decision: A study of some dimensions of managerial behavior in the selection decision process. *Academy of Management Journal, 16,* 239–253.

Miller, E. L. (1975). The job satisfaction of expatriate American managers: A function of regional location and previous international work experience. *Journal of International Business Studies, 6*(2), 65–73.

Miller, E. (1984). Strategic staffing. In C. J. Fombrun, N. M. Tichy, & M. A. Devanna (Eds.), *Strategic human resource management* (pp. 57–68). New York: Wiley.

Miller, E. L., Beechler, S., Bhatt, B., & Nath, R. (1986). The relationship between the global strategic planning process and the human resource management function. *Human Resource Planning, 9*(1), 9–23.

Miller, J. R. (1984). Revitalization: The most difficult of all strategies. *Human Resource Management, 23,* 293–313.

Mills, D. Q. (1985). Planning with people in mind. *Harvard Business Review, 63*(4), 97–105.

Mills, D. Q., & Balbaky. M. L. (1985). Planning for morale and culture. In R. E. Walton & P. R. Lawrence (Eds.), *HRM trends and challenges* (pp. 255–283). Boston: Harvard Business School Press.

Mintzberg, H. (1978). Patterns in strategy formulation. *Management Science, 24,* 934–948.

Mintzberg, H. (1987). Crafting strategy. *Harvard Business Review, 65*(4), 66–75.

Mintzberg, H., & McHugh, A. (1985). Strategy formation in an adhocracy. *Administrative Science Quarterly, 30,* 160–197.

Mintzberg, H., & Waters, J. A. (1982). Tracking strategy in an entrepreneurial firm. *Academy of Management Journal, 25,* 465–499.

Mintzberg, H., & Waters, J. A. (1984). Researching the formation of strategies: The history of Canadian lady, 1936–1976. In R. B. Lamb (Ed.), *Competitive strategic management* (pp. 62–93). Englewood Cliffs, NJ: Prentice-Hall.

Mintzberg, H., & Waters, J. A. (1985). Of strategies, deliberate and emergent. *Strategic Management Journal, 6,* 257–272.

Mirvis, P. H. (1985). Negotiations after the sale: The roots and ramifications of conflict in an acquisition. *Journal of Occupational Behavior, 6,* 65–84.

Misa, K. F., & Stein, T. (1983). Strategic HRM and the bottom line. *Personnel Administrator, 28,* 27–30.

Misel, L. (1986). The structural determinants of union bargaining power. *Industrial and Labor Relations, 40,* 90–104.

Mises, L. von (1949). *Human action: A treatise on economics.* New Haven, CT: Yale University Press.

Missirian, A. K. (1982). *The corporate connection.* Englewood Cliffs, NJ: Prentice-Hall.

Mobley, W. H. (1982). *Employee turnover: Causes, consequences, and control.* Reading, MA: Addison-Wesley.

Moffett, M. (1985). Fundamentalist Christians strive to apply beliefs to the work place. *The Wall Street Journal*, December 4, p. 33.

Montchretien, A. de (1615). *Traicte de l'economie politique*. Rouen: Jean Osmot.

Morgan, P. V., & Bottrall, P. J. (1988). Trends in international human resource management. *HRM: Resource Planning, 9*, 9–23.

Morgenstern, O. K. (1976). Perfect foresight and economic equilibrium. In A. Schotter (Ed.), *Selected economic writings of Oskar Morgenstern* (pp. 169–183). New York: New York University Press.

Morris, M. H., & Paul, G. W. (1987). The relationship between entrepreneurship and marketing in established firms. *Journal of Business Venturing, 2*, 247–259.

Moryson, F. (1617). *An itinary containing his ten yeares travel through the twelve dominions of Germany, Bohmerland, Switzerland, Netherland, Denmarke, Poland, Turkey, France, England, Scotland and Ireland*. London: John Beule.

Moses, J. L. (1977). The assessment center method. In J. L. Moses & W. C. Byham (Eds.), *Applying the assessment center method* (pp.3–12). Elmsford, NY: Pergamon.

Mowday, R. T. (1984). Strategies for adapting to high rates of employee turnover. *Human Resource Management, 23*, 365–380.

Mosier, K. C. (1986). Assuring the future. *Nation's Business, 74* (August), p. 4.

Mueller, D. C. (1980). The effects of conglomerate mergers. *Journal of Banking and Finances, 1 (4)*, 315–347.

Mueller, D. C. (1980). *The determinants and effects of mergers*. Cambridge, MA: Oelgeschlage, Gunn, & Hain.

Munsterberg, H. (1913). *Psychology and industrial efficiency*. Boston: Houghton Mifflin.

Murray, V. V., Jain, H. C., & Adams, R. J. (1976). A framework for the comparative analysis of personnel administration. *Academy of Management Review, 1*, 47–57.

Murthy, K. R., & Salter, M. S. (1975). Should CEO pay be linked to results? *Harvard Business Review, 53*(3), 66–72.

Napier, N. K. (1983). *Performance appraisal research: Where should we go?* Paper Presented at the National Academy of Management meeting, Dallas.

Napier, N. K. (1986). Firm diversification, performance and criteria and compensation for top managers in the U.S. and Japan: Two studies. *National Academy of Management Proceedings*, Chicago.

Napier, N. K. (1988). Strategy, human resources management, and organizational outcomes: Coming out from between the cracks. In G. R. Ferris & K. M. Rowland (Eds.), *Human resources management: Perspectives and issues* (pp. 16–22). Boston: Allyn and Bacon.

Napier, N. K. (1989). Mergers and acquisitions, human resource issues and outcomes: A review and suggested typology. *Journal of Management Studies, 21,* 271–289.

Napier, N. K., & Latham, G. P. (1986). Outcome expectancies of people who conduct performance appraisals. *Personnel Psychology, 39,* 827–837.

Napier, N. K., & Latham, G. P. (1987). *Enhancing intercultural communication in foreign subsidiaries in Hong Kong and Singapore.* Academy of International Business meetings, Chicago.

Napier, N. K., Schweiger, D. M., & Csiszar, E. (1989). *A model for implementing international mergers and acquisitions.* Strategic Management Society Conference on the Wave of Mergers, Acquisitions, and Alliances, Paris.

Napier, N. K., Simmons, G., & Stratton, K. (1989). Communications during a merger: Experience of two banks. *Human Resource Planning, 12,* 105–122.

Napier, N. K., & Smith, M. (1987). Product diversification, performance criteria and compensation at the corporate manager level. *Strategic Management Journal, 8,* 195–201.

Napier, N. K., & Stratton, K. (1987). *The impact of a merger on two banks.* Paper presented at Human Resource Planning Research Symposium, Newport, RI.

Napier, N. K., & Sullivan, J. J. (1983). *Demotion: Its conceptualization and implications for research.* Paper Presented at the Academy of Management Convention, Dallas, TX.

Napier, N. K., Taylor, M. S., & Slater, S. (1988). *Human resource competence as a source of competitive advantages in multinational companies: Issues affecting the transfer of human resource competence.* Boise, ID: (Working paper) Boise State University.

Negandhi, A. R. (1975). Comparative management and organization theory: A marriage needed. *Academy of Management Journal, 18,* 334–344.

Newman, J. (1988). Rewards in organizations. In R. A. Schuler, S. A. Youngblood, & V. L. Huber (Eds.), *Readings in personnel and human resource management* (pp. 267–274). St. Paul, MN: West.

Newman, J., Bhatt, B., & Gutterridge, T. (1978). Determinants of expatriate effectiveness: A theoretical and empirical vacuum. *Academy of Management Review, 3,* 655–661.

Niehaus, R. J. (1988). Models for human resource decisions. *Human Resource Planning, 11,* 95–108.

Nkomo, S. M. (1980). Stage three in personnel administration: Strategic human resource management. *Personnel, 57*(4), 69–77.

Nkomo, S. M. (1987). Human resource planning and organization performance: An exploratory analysis. *Strategic Management Journal, 8,* 387–392.

Nonaka, T. (1988). Self-renewal of the Japanese firm and the human resource strategy. *Human Resource Management, 27,* 45–62.

Norburn, D., & Birley, S. (1987). The top management team and corporate performance. *Strategic Management Journal, 9,* 225–237.

Odiorne, G. S. (1981). Developing a human resource strategy. *Personnel Journal, 60,* 534–536.

Odiorne, G. S. (1984). *Strategic management of human resources: A portfolio approach.* San Francisco: Jossey-Bass.

O'Conor, C. W. (1985). Packaging your business for sale. *Harvard Business Review, 63*(2), 52–58.

Olian, J. D., & Rynes, S. L. (1984). Organizational staffing: Integrating practices with strategy. *Industrial Relations, 23,* 170–183.

Ondrack, D. A. (1985). International transfers of managers in North American and European MNEs. *Journal of International Business Studies, 16*(3), 1–19.

Ondrack, D. A. (1987). *Internationalization of Canadian business: the impact on human resource management.* Toronto: Center for Organizational Effectiveness, University of Toronto.

O'Reilly, C. A., & Anderson, J. C. (1982). Personnel/human resource management in the United States: Some evidence of change. *Journal of Irish Business and American Research, 4,* 3–12.

Osborn, R. N., Jauch, L. R., Martin, T. N., & Glueck, W. F. (1981). The event of ceo succession, performance and environmental conditions. *Academy of Management Journal, 24,* 183–191.

O'Toole, J. (1985). Employee practices at the best managed companies. *California Management Review, 28*(1), 35–66.

Ouchi, W. G. (1977). The relationship between organizational structure and organizational control. *Administrative Science Quarterly, 22,* 95–113.

Ouchi, W. (1981). *Theory z: How American business can meet the Japanese challenge.* Reading, MA: Addison-Wesley.

Paine, F. T., & Power, D. J. (1984). Merger strategy: An examination of Drucker's five rules for successful acquisitions. *Strategic Management Journal, 5,* 99–110.

Papanastos, J., Hillman, L., & Cole, P. (1987). The human resource side of mergers. *Business: The Magazine of Managerial Thought and Action, 37*(3), pp. 3–11.

Papp, G. E., & Davis, H. J. (1984). American and Australian work reward preference patterns. *Asia Pacific Journal of Management, 2*(September), 62–64.

Parsley, C. J. (1980). Labor union effects on wage gains: A survey of recent literature. *Journal of Economic Literature, 58,* 1–31.

Pascal, R. T. (1978). Personnel practices and employee attitude: A study of Japanese and American managed firms in the United States. *Human Relations, 31,* 597–615.

Pascal, R., & Athos, A. (1981) *The art of Japanese management.* New York: Warner Books.

Payne, R. (1589). *A briefe description of Ireland: Made in this yeare, 1589.* London: T. Dawson.

Pazy, A., & Zeira, Y. (1983). Training parent-country professionals in host-country organizations. *Academy of Management Review, 8,* 262–272.

Pearce, J. L., Stevenson, W. B., & Perry, J. L. (1985). Managerial compensation based on organizational performance: A time series analysis of the effects of merit pay. *Academy of Management Journal, 28,* 261–278.

Perlman, S. (1922). *A history of trade unionism in the United States.* New York: Macmillan.

Perrow, C. (1972). *Complex organizations: A critical essay.* Chicago: Scott, Foresman.

Perry, J. (1962). What happens after the merger? *Management Review, 51*(7), 4–26.

Perry, L. T. (1984). Key human resource strategies in an organization downturn. *Human Resource Management, 23,* 61–75.

Perry, L. T. (1986). Merging successfully: Sending the "right" signals. *Sloan Management Review, 27*(3), 47–57.

Perucci, R., & Mannweiler, R. A. (1968). Organization size, complexity and administrative succession in higher education. *The Sociology Quarterly, 9,* 343–355.

Peters, J. W. (1988). Strategic staffing: A key link in business and human resource planning. *Human Resource Planning, 11,* 151–158.

Peters, T., & Austin, N. (1985). MBWA (Managing by walking around). *California Management Review, 28*(1), 9–34.

Peters, T. J., & Austin, N. K. (1985). *A passion for excellence.* New York: Random House.

Peters, T. J., & Waterman, R. H. (1982) *In search of excellence: Lessons from America's best-run companies.* New York: Harper & Row.

Peterson, R. A. (1981). Entrepreneurship and organization. In P. C. Nystrom & W. H. Starbuck (Eds.), *Handbook of organizational design,* (Vol. 1, pp. 65–83). New York: Oxford University Press.

Peterson, R. B. (1986). Research design issues in comparative industrial relations. Madison, WI: *Industrial Relations Research Association Proceedings,* 244–251.

Pfeffer, J. (1972). Merger as a response to organizational interdependence. *Administrative Science Quarterly, 17,* 382–394.

Pfeffer, J. (1977). Toward an examination of stratification in organizations. *Administrative Science Quarterly, 22,* 553–567.

Pfeffer, J. (1978). *Organizational design,* Arlington Heights, IL: AHM Publishing.

Pfeffer, J. (1981). Management as symbolic action: The creation and maintenance of organizational paradigms. In L. L. Cummings & B. M. Shaw (Eds.), *Research in organizational behavior* (pp. 1–52), Greenwich, CT: JAI Press.

Pfeffer, J. (1983). Organizational demography. In L. L. Cummings & B. M. Staw (Eds.), *Research in organizational behavior* (Vol. 5, pp. 299–357), Greenwich, CT: JAI Press.

Pfeffer, J., & Baron, J. N. (1988). Taking the workers back out: Recent trends in the structuring of employment. In B. M. Staw & L. L. Cummings (Eds.), *Research in organizational behavior* (Vol. 10, pp. 257–303). Greenwich, CT: JAI Press.

Pfeffer, J., & Cohen, Y. (1984). Determinants of internal labor markets in organizations. *Administrative Science Quarterly, 29,* 550–572.

Pfeffer, J., & Davis-Blake, A. (1987). The effect of the proportion of women on salaries: The case of college administrators. *Administrative Science Quarterly, 32,* 1–24.

Pfeffer, J., & Davis-Blake, A. (1987). Understanding organizational wage structures: A resource dependence approach. *Academy of Management Journal, 30,* 437–455.

Pfeffer, J., & Leblebici, H. (1973). Executive recruitment and the development of interfirm organizations. *Administrative Science Quarterly, 18,* 449–461.

Pfeffer, J., & Moore, W. L. (1980). Average tenure of academic department heads: The effects of paradigm, size, and departmental demography. *Administrative Science Quarterly, 25,* 387–406.

Pfeffer, J., & Ross, J. (1982). The effects of marriage and a working wife on occupational and wage attainment. *Administrative Science Quarterly, 27,* 66–80.

Pfeffer, J., & Salancik, G. R. (1977). Organizational context and the characteristics and tenure of hospital administrators. *Academy of Management Journal, 20,* 74–88.

Phillips, J. R., & Kennedy, A. A. (1980). *Shaping and managing shared values.* New York: (unpublished internal document) McKinsey.

Phillips, L. (1977). *Mentors and proteges: A study of the career development of women managers and executives in business and industry.* Dissertation Abstracts International, 38, 6414A.

Phillips-Jones, L. (1982). *Mentors and proteges.* New York: Arbor House.

Pinchot, G. (1985). *Intrapreneuring.* New York: Harper and Row.

Pinney, D. L. (1982). Structuring an expatriate tax reimbursement program. *Personnel Administrator, 27,* 19–23.

Pitts, R. A. (1974). Incentive compensation and organization design. *Personnel Journal, 53,* 338–348.

Podsakoff, P. M., Greene, C. N., & McFillen, J. M. (1988). Obstacles to the effective use of reward systems. In R. A. Schulder, S. A. Youngblood, & V. L. Huber (Eds.), *Readings in personnel and human resource management,* (3rd ed., pp. 275–290). St. Paul, MN: West.

Porter, M. E. (1980). *Competitive strategy: Techniques for analyzing industries and competitors.* New York: The Free Press.

Porter, M. E. (1981). The contributions of industrial organization to strategic management. *Academy of Management Review, 6,* 609–620.

Porter, M. E. (1985). *Competitive advantage.* New York: The Free Press.

Posner, B. Z., Kouzes, J. M., & Schmidt, W. H. (1985). Shared values make a difference. *Human Resource Management, 24,* 293–309.

Prahalad, C. K., & Bettis, R. A. (1986). The dominant logic: A new linkage between diversity and performance. *Strategic Management Journal, 7,* 485–501.

Price, C. (1986). An introduction to innovate: New venture creation in the health care industry. In R. Ronstadt, J. A. Hornaday, R. Peterson, & K. H. Vesper (Eds.), *Frontiers of entrepreneurship research* (pp. 708–721). Wellesley, MA: Center for Entrepreneurial Studies, Babson College.

Price, D. J. de S. (1963) *Little science, big science.* New York: Columbia University Press.

Pritchett, P. (1985). *After the merger: Managing the stock wars.* New York: Dow Jones/Irwin.

Profusek, R. A., & Leavitt, J. S. (1984). Dealing with employee benefit plans. *Mergers and Acquisitions, 18*(4), 44–51.

Pucik, V. (1984a). The international management of human resources. In C. J. Fombrun, N. M. Tichy, & M. A. Devanna (Eds.), *Strategic Human Resource Management* (pp. 403–419). New York: Wiley.

Pucik, V. (1984b). White collar human resource management in large Japanese manufacturing firms. *Human Resource Management, 23,* 257–276.

Pucik, V. (1988). Strategic alliances, organizational learning and competitive advantage: The hrm agenda. *Human Resource Management, 27,* 77–94.

Pucik, V., & Katz, J. H. (1986). Information, control, and human resource management in multinational firms. *Human Resource Management, 25,* 121–132.

Quinn, J. B. (1980). *Strategies for change: Logical incrementalism.* Homewood, IL: Dow-Jones/Irwin.

Quinn, J. B. (1985). Managing innovation: Controlled chaos. *Harvard Business Review, 63*(3), 73–84.

Rahim, A. (1983). A model for developing key expatriate executives. *Personnel Journal, 62,* 312–317.

Ramanujam, V., & Venkatraman, N. (1987). Planning and performance: A new look at an old question. *Business Horizons, 30*(3), 19–25.

Rayman, J., & Twinn, B. (1983). *Expatriate compensation & benefits: An employer's handbook.* London: Kogan Page.

Reed, T. F., & Brockner, J. (1986). *Factors moderating the impact of layoffs on survivors: A field study.* Paper presented at the Academy of Management, 46th annual national meeting, Chicago.

Reinganum, M. R. (1985). The effect of executive succession on stockholder wealth. *Administrative Science Quarterly, 30,* 46–60.

Rhoades, S. A. (1983). *Power, empire building, and mergers.* Lexington, MA: Lexington Books.

Richardson, G. B. (1960). *Information and investment.* New York: Oxford University Press.

Robertson, W. (1976). The directors woke up too late at Gulf. *Fortune, 96*(6), 121–125.

Robino, D., & DeMeuse, K. (1985). Corporate mergers and acquisitions: Their impact on HRM. *Personnel Administrator, 30*(11), 33–44.

Robins, J. A. (1987). Organizational economics: Notes on the use of transaction-cost theory in the study of organizations. *Administrative Science Quarterly, 32*, 68–86.

Robinson, R. B. Jr., & Pearce, J. A. III (1984). Evolving strategy in the venture capital industry: An empirical anlaysis. In J. A. Pearce III & R. B. Robinson Jr. (Eds.), *Academy of Management Proceedings* (pp. 69–73). Academy of Management.

Roethlisberger, F. J. (1977). *The elusive phenomena.* Cambridge, MA: Harvard University Press.

Rosen, B., & Jerdee, T. H. (1986). Retirement policies for the 21st century. *Human Resource Management, 25*, 405–420.

Rotter, J. B. (1966). Generalized expectations for internal versus external control of reinforcement. *Psychological Monographs: General and Applied, 80*(Whole No. 609). 1–28.

Rowland, K. M., & Ferris, G. R. (1982). Perspectives on personnel management. In K. M. Rowland & G. R. Ferris (Eds.), *Personnel management* (pp. 2–33). Boston: Allyn and Bacon.

Rumelt, R. P. (1974). *Strategy, structure, and economic performance.* Cambridge, MA: Harvard University Press.

Russ, G. S., & Bettenhausen, K. L. (1988). *Phantom threats and discovered threats: An evolutionary model of boundary spanning roles.* Paper presented at the Southwest Academy of Management meetings, San Antonio, TX.

Russell, J. S., Terborg, J. R., & Powers, M. L. (1985). Organizational performance and organizational level training and support. *Personnel Psychology, 38*, 849–863.

Safire, L., & Safire, W. (Eds.) (1982). *Good advice.* New York: Times Books.

Salancik, G. R., & Pfeffer, J. (1980). Effects of ownership and performance on executive tenure in U.S. corporations. *Academy of Management Journal, 23*, 653–664.

Salancik, G. R., Staw, B. M., & Pondy, L. R. (1980). Administrative turnover as a response to unmanaged organizational interdependece. *Academy of Management Journal,* *23*(4), 653–664.

Salschneider, J. (1981). Devising pay strategies for diversified companies. *Compensation Review,* *13*(2), 5–25.

Salter, M. S. (1973). Tailor incentive compensation to strategy. *Harvard Business Review, 51*(2), 94–102.

Salter, M. S., & Weinhold, W. A. (1979). *Diversification through acquisition—strategy for creating economic value.* New York: The Free Press.

Saltzman, G. M. (1985). Bargaining laws as a cause and consequence of the growth of teacher unionism. *Industrial and Labor Relations Review, 38,* 335–351.

Sathe, V. (1985). Managing an entrepreneurial dilemma: Nurturing entrepreneurship and control in large corporations. In J. A. Hornaday, E. B. Shils, J. A. Timmons, & K. H. Vesper (Eds.), *Frontiers of entrepreneurship* (pp. 636–657). Wellesley, MA: Center for Entrepreneurial Studies, Babson College.

Savary des Bruslons, J. (1723–1730). *Dictionnaire universal de commerce.* Paris: J. Estienne.

Say, J. B. (1844). *Cours complet d'economie politique de commerce.* Brusselles: Societe Typographique Belge, Ad. Wahlen and Compagnie.

Scheibar, P. (1986). Succession planning, 1: Senior management selection. *Personnel, 63*(11), 16–23.

Schendel, D. E., & Hofer, C. W. (1979). *Strategic management.* Boston: Little, Brown.

Schlesinger, L. A. (1983). The normative underpinnings of human resource strategy. *Human Resource Management, 22,* 83–96.

Schmitt, N., & Schneider, B. (1983). Current issues in personnel selection. In K. M. Rowland & G. R. Ferris (Eds.), *Research in personnel and human resources management* (Vol. 1, pp. 85–125). Greenwich, CT: JAI Press.

Schneira, T. C. (1971). *Army ants.* San Francisco: W. H. Freeman.

Schollhammer, H. (1975). Current research on international and comparative management issues. *Management International Review, 15*(2–3), 29–40.

Schuler, R. S. (1988). Human resource management choices and organizational strategy. In R. S. Schuler, S. A. Youngblood, & V. L. Huber (Eds.), *Readings in personnel and human resource management* (3rd ed., pp. 24–39). St. Paul MN: West.

Schuler, R. S., & Jackson, S. E. (1987). Linking competitive strategies with human resource management practices. *Academy of Management Executive, 1*, 207–219.

Schuler, R. S., & MacMillan, I.C. (1984). Gaining competitive advantage through human resource management practices. *Human Resource Management, 23*, 241–255.

Schuler, R. S., MacMillan, I. C., & Mantocchio, J. J. (1985). Key strategic question for human resource management. In W. D. Guth (Ed.), *Handbook of business strategy: 1985/1986 yearbook* (pp. 25.2–25.19). Boston: Warren, Gorham and Lamont.

Schuler, R. S., & Martocchio, J. J. (1987). *Human resource management practices that foster and facilitate entrepreneurship.* New York: (Working Paper) New York University.

Schumpeter, J. A. (1934) *The theory of economic development.* Cambridge, MA: Harvard University Press.

Schumpeter, J. A. (1942) *Capitalism, socialism and democracy.* London: Allen & Unwin.

Schuster, M. (1984). *Union-management cooperation: Structure process and impact.* Kalamazoo, MI: Upjohn Institute.

Schwartz, H., & Davis, S. M. (1981). Matching corporate culture and business strategy. *Organizational Dynamics*, Summer, 30–48.

Schweiger, D. M., & DeNisi, A. S. (1987). *The effect of a realistic merger preview on employees: A longitudinal field experiment.* Paper presented at the National Academy of Management meetings, New Orleans.

Schweiger, D. L., & Ivancevich, J. M. (1985). Human resources: The forgotten factor in mergers and acquisitions. *Personnel Administrator, 30* (11), 47–58.

Schweiger, D. M., & Ivancevich, J. M. (1987). *The effects of mergers and acquisitions on organizations and human resources: A contingency view.* Strategic Management Society Conference, Boston.

Schweiger, D. M., Ivancevich, J. M., & Power, F. R. (1987). Executive actions for managing human resources before and after acquisition. *Academy of Management Executive, 1*, 127–138.

Searby, F. W. (1969). Control post merger change. *Harvard Business Review, 47*(5), 4–12, 154–155.

Sethi, S. P., & Namiki, N. (1987). Top management compensation and corporate performance. *Journal of Business Strategy, 7*(4), 37–44.

Shackle, G. L. S. (1967). *The years of high theory.* Cambridge: Cambridge University Press.

Shenkar, O., & Zeira, Y. (1987). Human resources management in international joint ventures: Directions for research. *Academy of Management Review, 12,* 546–557.

Shirley, R. C. (1977). The human side of merger planning. *Long Range Planning, 10*(4), 35–39.

Shrivastava, P. (1986). Postmerger integration. *Journal of Business Strategy, 7*(1), 65–76.

Sibson, R. E. (1983). Strategic personnel planning. *Personnel Administrator, 28*(10), 39–42.

Siehl, C., Ledford, G., Silverman, R., & Fay, P. (1987). *Managing cultural differences in mergers and organizations: The role of the human resource function.* Los Angeles: Working paper G87-4 University of Southern California.

Simmonds, K. (1966). Multinations? Well, not quite. *Columbia Journal of World Business, 1*(4), 115–122.

Simon, H. A. (1976). *Administrative behavior.* New York: The Free Press.

Sinetar, M. (1981). Mergers, morale and productivity. *Personnel Journal, 60,* 863–867.

Skinner, W. (1969). Manufacturing—missing link in corporate strategy. *Harvard Business Review, 47*(3), 136–145.

Skinner, W. (1986). The productivity paradox. *Harvard Business Review, 64*(4), 55–59.

Smith, A. (1776). *An inquiry into the nature and causes of the wealth of nations.* London: W. Strahan and T. Cadell.

Smith Cook, D., & Ferris, G. R. (1986). Strategic human resouce management and firm effectiveness in industries experiencing decline. *Human Resource Management, 25,* 441–458.

Snell, S. A. (1988). *The relationship of organizational context to human resources management: An empirical test of management control theory.* Paper Presented at National Academy of Management meetings, Anaheim, CA.

Snow, C., & L.G. Hrebiniak (1980). Strategy, distinctive competence, and organizational performance. *Administrative Science Quarterly, 25,* 317–336.

Sonnenfeld, J. A. (1985). Education at work: Demystifying the magic of training. In R. E. Walton & P. R. Lawrence (Eds.), *HRM trends & challenges*, (pp. 285–317). Boston: Harvard Business School Press.

Sonnenfeld, J. A., & Ingols, C. A. (1986). Working knowledge: Charting a new course for training. *Organizational Dynamics, 15*(2), 63–79.

Sparrow, P., Hendry, C., & Pettigrew, A. (1987). Strategic change and human resource management in the United Kingdom. *The Industrial Organizational Psychologist, 24*, 64–68.

Spratt, M. F., & Steel, B. (1985). Rewarding key contributors. *Compensation and Benefits Review, 17*, 24–37.

Starbuck, W. H. (1965). Organizational growth and development. In J. March (Ed.), *Handbook of organizations* (pp. 451–533). Chicago: Rand McNally.

Starbuck, W. H., & Hedberg, B. L. T. (1977) Saving an organization from a stagnating environment. In H. B. Thorelli (Ed.) *Strategy + structure = performance* (pp. 249–258). Bloomington, IN: Indiana University Press.

Stata, R., & Maidique, M. A. (1980). Bonus system for balanced strategy. *Harvard Business Review, 58*(6), 156–163.

Stevenson, H. (1976). Defining corporate strengths and weaknesses. *Sloan Management Review, 17*(3), 51–68.

Steel, M. T., & Osborne, T. D. (1983). Consider the personnel side or risk souring a sweet merger. *ABA Banking Journal, 75*(2), 14–23.

Stewart, R., Wingate, P., & Smith, R. (1963). *The human effects of mergers: The impact on managers.* London: The Acton Society Trust.

Stieglitz, H. (1963). Effective performance overseas. *International Executive, 5*(2), 9–10.

Stigler, G. J. (1957). Perfect competition, historically contemplated. *Journal of Political Economy, 65*, 1–17.

Stoner, J. A. F., Aram, J. D., & Rubin, I. M. (1972). Factors associated with effective performance in overseas work assignments. *Personnel Psychology, 25*, 303–318.

Stonich, P. J. (1981). Using rewards in implementing strategy. *Strategic Management Journal, 2*, 345–352.

Stonich, P. J. (1984). The performance measurement and reward system: Critical to strategic management. *Organizational Dynamics, 12*(3), 45–57.

Stratton, K., & Brown, R. B. (1988). *Strategic planning in U.S. labor unions.* In B. D. Davis (Ed.) *Proceedings of the Forty First Annual Meeting.* Madison, WI: Industrial Relations Research Association.

Strauss, G. (1970). Organizational behavior and personnel relations. *Review of Industrial Relations Research, 1,* 145–206.

Strauss, G., & Feuille, P. (1978). IR research: A critical anlaysis. *Industrial Relations, 17,* 259–277.

Stumpf, S. A., Hanrahan, N. M. (1984). Designing organizational career management practices to fit strategic management objectives. In R. S. Schuler & S. A. Youngblood (Eds.), *Readings in personnel and human resource management,* (2nd ed., pp. 326–348). St. Paul MN: West.

Stumpf, S. A. (1988). Choosing career management practices to suppport your business strategy. *Human Resource Planning, 11,* 49–62.

Stybel, L. J. (1982). Linking strategi planning and management manpower planning. *California Management Review, 25,* 48–56.

Sun, E. (1973). On employment and curriculum on the international business program. *Journal of International Business Studies, 4*(2), 83–96.

Sutton, R. I., & Louis, M. R. (1987). How selecting and socializing newcomers influences insiders. *Human Resource Management, 26,* 347–361.

Sweet, J. (1981). How manpower development can support your strategic plan. *The Journal of Business Strategy, 2*(1), 77–81.

Sykes, H. B. (1986). The anatomy of a corporate venturing program: Factors influencing success. *Journal of Business Venturing, 1,* 275–293.

Szilagyi, A. D. & Schweiger, D. M. (1984). Matching managers to strategies: A review and suggested framework. *Academy of Management Review, 9,* 626–637.

Tannenbaum, A. S. (1968). *Control in organizations.* New York: McGraw-Hill.

Taylor, F. W. (1911). *Principles of scientific management.* New York: Norton.

Teague, B. W. (1976). Transplanting executives in foreign soil. *The Conference Board Record, 13,* 42–45.

Teague, F. A. (1970). International management selection and development. *California Management Review, 7*(3), 1–6.

Terborg, J. R., & Ungson, G. R. (1983) Strategic policy and management compensation. In K. H. Chung (Ed.), *Proceedings* (pp. 292–296). Dallas: Academy of Management.

Tichy, N. M. (1984). An interview with Edson W. Spencer and Foston A. Boyle. In C. J. Fombrun, N. M. Tichy, & M. A. Devanna (Eds.), *Strategic human resource management* (pp. 447–473). New York: Wiley.

Tichy, N. M., Devanna, M. A., & Fombrun, C. J. (1982). Strategic human resource management. *Sloan Management Review, 28,* 45–51.

Tichy, N. M., Fombrun, C. J., & Devanna, M. A. (1982). Strategic human resource management. *Sloan Management Review, 23,* 47–61.

Tichy, N. M., Fombrun, C. J., & Devanna, M. A. (1984). The organizational context of strategic human resource management. In C. J. Fombrun, N. M. Tichy, & M. A. Devanna (Eds.), *Strategic human resource management* (pp. 19–31). New York: Wiley.

Toffler, A. (1970). *Future shock.* New York: Bantam Books.

Tomasko, R. M. (1982). Focusing company reward systems to help achieve business objectives. *Management Review, 71,* 8–12.

Torbiorn, I. (1985). the structure of managerial roles in cross-cultural settings. *International Studies of Management and Organization, 15,* 52–74.

Toyne, B., & Kuhne, R. J. (1983). The management of the international executive compensation and benefit process. *Journal of International Business Studies, 14*(3), 37–50.

Tung, R. L. (1981). Selection and training of personnel for overseas assignments. *Columbia Journal of World Business, 16*(1), 68–78.

Tung, R. L. (1982). Selection and training procedures for U.S., European and Japanese multinationals. *California Management Review, 25*(1), 57–71.

Tung, R. L. (1984a). Human resource planning in Japanese multinationals: A model for U.S. firms? *Journal of International Business Studies, 15,* 139–150.

Tung, R. L. (1984b). Strategic management of human resources in the multinational enterprise. *Human Resource Management, 23,* 129–143.

Tung, R. L. (1987). Expatriate assignments: Enhancing sources and minimizing failure. *Academy of Management Executive, 1,* 117–126.

Turgot, A. R. J. (1776). Reflexions sur la formation et al distribution des richesses. In G. Schelle (Ed.), *Oeuvres de Turgot* (Vol.2). Paris: published anonymously.

Tyler, B. B. (1988). *Integrating human resources consideration in grand strategy formulation under conditions of merger and acquisition.* San Antonio, TX: Paper presented at Southwest Academy of Management Meetings.

Tyler, B. B., & Ferris, G. R. (1987). *Merger and acquisition: The competitive advantage of matching grand strategies, acquisition types, and human resource considerations during strategy formulation.* (Working paper) Texas A & M University, College Station, TX.

Ulrich, W. L. (1984). HRM and culture: History, ritual, and myth. *Human Resource Management, 23*(2), 117–128.

Van Cleve, R. R. (1982). Human resources administration: Curriculum for a profession. *Personnel Administrator, 27*(3), 61–67.

Vecsey, G. (1986). DeBusschere: The last shot. *The New York Times, 135*(Jan. 8), p. Y23.

Venkatraman, N., & Camillus, J. C. (1984). Exploring the concept of "fit" in strategic management. *Academy of Management Review, 9,* 513–525.

Vesper, K. H. (1980). *New venture strategies.* Englewood Cliffs, NJ: Prentice-Hall.

Viega, J. F. (1981). Do managers on the move get anywhere? *Harvard Business Review, 59*(2), 20–38.

Von Glinow, M. A. (1985). Reward strategies for attracting, evaluating, and retaining professionals. *Human Resource Management, 24,* 191–206.

Vroom, V. (1964). *Work and motivation.* New York: Wiley.

Walker, J. L., & Gutteridge, T. G. (1979). *Career planning practices: An AMA survey report.* New York: AMACOM.

Walker, J. W. (1978). Linking human resource planning and strategic planning. *Human Resource Planning, 1,* 1–18.

Walker, J. W. (1980). *Human resource planning.* New York: McGraw-Hill.

Walker, J. W. (1988). Managing human resoruces in flat, lean and flexible organizations: Trends for the 1990's. *Human Resource Planning, 11,* 125–132.

Walker, J. W. (1989). Human resource roles for the '90s. *Human resource planning, 12,* 55–61.

Wallace, M. J. Jr. (1983). Methodology, research practice, and progress in personnel and industrial relations. *Academy of Management Review, 8,* 6–13.

Walras, L. (1926). *Elements d'economie politique pure, ou theories de la richesse sociale.* Paris: R. Pichon and R-Durand-Auxium.

Walsh, J. P. (1988). Top management turnover following mergers and acquisitions. *Strategic Management Journal, 9,* 173–183.

Walter, G. A. (1987). *Key acquisition integration processes for four strategic orientations.* Hollywood, CA: Paper presented at the Western Academy of Management meeting.

Walton, R. E. (1975). Criteria for quality of working life. In L. E. Davis & A. B. Cherns (Eds.), *The quality of working life,* (pp. 88–104). New York: The Free Press.

Walton, R. E. (1985). Toward a strategy of eliciting employee commitment based on policies of mutuality. In R. E. Walton & P. R. Lawrence (Eds.), *HRM trends & challenges* (pp. 35–65). Boston: Harvard Business School Press.

Walton, R. E. & Lawrence, P. R. (Eds.) (1985) *HRM trends & challenges.* Boston: Harvard University Press.

Walton, R. E., & McKersie, R. B. (1965). *A behavioral theory of labor negotiations.* New York: McGraw Hill.

Wanous, J. P. (1979). *Organizational entry: Recruitment, selection and socialization of newcomers.* Reading, MA: Addison-Wesley.

Weber, Y., & K'obonyo, P. (1987). *A conceptual framework for staffing general managers for strategy implementation.* New Orleans: Paper Presented at National Academy of Management meeting.

Weiner, N., & Mahoney, T. A. (1981). A model of corporate performance as a function of environmental, organizational, and leadership influences. *Academy of Management Journal, 24,* 453–470.

Wells, K., & Hymowitz, C. (1984). Gulf's managers find merger into Chevron forces many changes. *The Wall Street Journal,* December, pp. 5, 110, 122.

Wexley, K. N., & Latham, G. P. (1981). *Developing and training human resources in organizations.* Glenview, IL: Scott, Foresman.

Wheeler, H. N. (1989). Trade unions and takeovers: Labor's response to mergers and acquisitions. *Human Resource Planning, 12,* 155–165.

Wheelwright, S. C. (1984). Strategy, management and strategic planning approaches. *Interfaces, 14*(1), 19–33.

White, M. D. (1982). The intra-unit wage structure and unions: A median voter model. *Industrial and Labor Relations Review, 35,* 565–577.

Wils, T., & Dyer, L. (1984). *Relating business strategy to human resource strategy: Some preliminary evidence.* Boston: Paper Presented at annual meeting of the Academy of Management.

Wils, T., Labelle, C., & Louarn, J. (1988). Human resource planning at Quebec-Telephone. *Human Resource Planning, 11,* 255–270.

Winer, L. (1983). Applying strategic planning in human resource development. *Training and Development Journal, 37*(November), 81–84.

Wishard, B. J. (1985). Merger — the human dimension. *The Magazine of Bank Administration, 61*(6), 74–79.

Wissema, J. G., Brand, A. F., & Van Der Pool, H. W. (1981). The incorporation of management development in strategic management. *Strategic Management Journal, 2,* 361–377.

Wood, R. E., & Mitchell, T. R. (1981). Manager behavior in a social context: The impact of impression management on attributions and disciplinary actions. *Organizational Behavior and Human Performance, 28,* 356–378.

Wright, P. M. (1986). *Human resource strategies: A reconceptualization.* Paper Presented at National Academy of Management meeting, Chicago.

Zalesny, M. D. (1985). Comparison of economic and noneconomic factors in predicting faculty voter preference in a union representation election. *Journal of Applied Psychology, 70,* 243–256.

Zammuto, R. F., & Connolly T. (1984a). Coping with disciplinary fragmentation. *Organizational Behavior Teaching Review, 9,* 30–37.

Zammuto, R. F., & Connolly, T. (1984b). *On the dubious health or of organizational research: Do we need a doctor or an undertaker?* Paper presented at the Western Academy of Management meeting, Vancouver, BC.

Zedeck, S., & Cascio, W. F. (1984). Psychological issues in personnel decisions. In M. R. Rosenzweig, & L. W. Porter (Eds.), *Annual review of psychology* (Vol. 35, pp. 461–519). Palo Alto, CA: Annual Reviews, Inc.

Zeira, Y. (1975). Overlooked personnel problems of multinational corporations. *Columbia Journal of World Business, 10*(2), 96–103.

Zeira, Y., & Banai, M. (1984). Present and desired methods of selecting expatriate managers for international assignments. *Personnel Review, 13*(3), 29–35.

Zeira, Y., & Harari, E. (1977). Genuine multinational staffing policy: Expectations and realties. *Academy of Management Journal, 20,* 327–333.

Zeira, Y., Harari, E. (1979). Host-country organizations and expatriate managers in Europe. *California Management Review, 21*(3), 40–50.

Zeira, Y., & Pazy, A. (1985). Crossing national borders to get trained. *Training and Development Journal, 39,* 53–57.

Zuboff, S. (1988). *In the age of the smart machine.* New York: Basic Books.

AUTHOR INDEX

Subject Index